FAITH
PHILOSOPHICAL ENQUIRIES

Series Editors:
Laurence Paul Hemming and Susan Frank Parsons

Inspired by the challenge to consider anew the relation of faith and reason that has been posed by the papal Encyclical Letter of 1998, *Fides et ratio*, this series is dedicated to paying generous heed to the questions that lie within its scope. The series comprises monographs by a wide range of international and ecumenical authors, edited collections, and translations of significant texts, with appeal both to an academic community and broadly to all those on whom the apologetic task impinges. The studies it encompasses are informed by desire for the mutual engagement of the disciplines of theology and philosophy in the problematic areas of current debate at the highest and most serious level of scholarship. These may serve to illuminate the foundations of faith in the contemporary cultural context and will thus constitute an ecumenical renewal of the work of philosophical theology. The series is promoted by the work of the Society of St. Catherine of Siena, in the spirit of its commitment to the renewal of the intellectual apostolate in the Catholic Church.

http://www.caterinati.org.uk/

PUBLISHED

Restoring Faith in Reason:
A new translation of the Encyclical Letter *Faith and Reason*
of Pope John Paul II together with a commentary and discussion

Laurence Paul Hemming and Susan Frank Parsons (editors)

Contemplating Aquinas:
On the Varieties of Interpretation

Fergus Kerr OP (editor)

The Politics of Human Frailty:
A Theological Defence of Political Liberalism

Christopher J. Insole

Postmodernity's Transcending:
Devaluing God

Laurence Paul Hemming

FORTHCOMING

Redeeming Truth:
Considering Faith and Reason

Susan Frank Parsons and Laurence Paul Hemming (editors)

Henri Cardinal de Lubac SJ

Corpus Mysticum

The Eucharist and the Church in the Middle Ages
historical survey

Translated by
Gemma Simmonds CJ
with Richard Price and Christopher Stephens

Edited by
Laurence Paul Hemming and Susan Frank Parsons

University of Notre Dame Press
Notre Dame, Indiana

First published in 2006 by SCM Press
9–17 St Albans Place, London N1 0NX

Published in the United States in 2007
by the University of Notre Dame Press
Notre Dame, Indiana 46556
www.undpress.nd.edu

Library of Congress Cataloging in-Publication Data

Lubac, Henri de, 1896–1991.
  [Corpus mysticum. English]
  Corpus mysticum : the Eucharist and the church in the Middle Ages : a historical
survey / Henri Cardinal de Lubac ; translated by Gemma Simmonds with Richard Price
and Christopher Stephens ; edited by Laurence Paul Hemming and Susan Frank Parsons.
    p. cm. — (Faith in reason)
  Includes bibliographical references.
  ISBN-13: 978-0-268-02593-9 (pbk. : alk. paper)
  ISBN-10: 0-268-02593-2 (pbk. : alk. paper)
  1. Lord's Supper—Catholic Church—History of doctrines—Middle Ages, 600–1500.
2. Jesus Christ—Mystical body—History of doctrines—Middle Ages, 600–1500.
3. Catholic Church—Doctrines—History. I. Hemming, Laurence Paul. II. Parsons,
Susan Frank. III. Title.
  BV823.L813 2007
  234'.1630902--dc22
                              2007006565

∞ *The paper in this book meets the guidelines for permanence and durability of
the Committee on Production Guidelines for Book Longevity of the
Council on Library Resources.*

Contents

Acknowledgements   vii

Abbreviations   viii

Editors' Preface   ix

Notes on the Translation   xix

CORPUS MYSTICUM

Preface to the First Edition   xxi

Preface to the Second Edition   xxiii

I   The Evolution of the Sense of *Corpus Mysticum*

Introduction   3

First Part

   1   The Eucharist as Mystical Body   13

   2   '*Mystery*'   37

   3   Memorial, Anticipation, Presence   55

   4   Sacramental Body and Ecclesial Body   75

   5   The Church as Mystical Body   101

Second Part

   6   '*Spiritual Flesh*'   123

   7   Interchangeable Expressions   143

   8   '*One Body*', '*One Flesh*'   168

   9   'Truth and Truth'   187

10   From Symbolism to Dialectic   221
Conclusion   248

II   Amalarius's *'Threefold Body'* and What Became of It

Introduction   265

  1   Amalarius's Text   268
  2   Evolution of the Doctrine   279
  3   Evolution of the Symbolism   292

Notes

Note A *'The Mystery of the Sacrament'*   305
Note B On the Eucharist as *'Antitype'*   314
Note C *'Mystical body'* in Bruno of Wurzburg?   321
Note D On the Interpretation of Jerome in Eph. 1   323
Note E *'Bodily'* and σωματικῶς   326
Note F An Illusion in the History of Theology   329
Note G An Explanation of Rupert   333

Acknowledgements

The Editors would like to express their gratitude to the number of people who have helped in various ways over the years to bring this project to completion. A debt of thanks is owed in the first instance to Graham Ward of the University of Manchester for his suggestion that a translation be undertaken and for his support in its early stages. Our confidence in pursuing this work was greatly encouraged by a small group comprising Graham Ward, and Fr. Richard Price and Sr. Gemma Simmonds CJ, both of Heythrop College, University of London, and the Editors, meeting on several occasions at the Margaret Beaufort Institute of Theology in Cambridge to consider both the scholarly and technical aspects of the task that lay ahead and to draw up a plan of work. We are grateful both to Sr. Simmonds for accepting the work of translation from the French, especially while simultaneously engaged in her doctoral researches at the University of Cambridge, and to Fr. Price for translation from Latin and Greek. Preparation of the numerous footnotes, with guidance to English translations of de Lubac's sources, was in large part completed by Christopher W. B. Stephens, of Christ Church Oxford. We are indebted to Gary Macy of the University of San Diego, California, Consultor to the translation, for his attention to the text and his advice at several crucial stages.

We also acknowledge with gratitude the initial approval given for this work by the Society of Jesus, to Fr. Peter Gallagher SJ at Heythrop, and those at the Centre Sèvres in Paris who assisted so kindly in negotiations with the publishing house, Flammarion (the inheritors of the *Aubier* imprint), for permission to publish an English translation of the French text. We have been greatly supported throughout this project by our UK publisher, SCM-Canterbury Press, and thank especially Jenny Willis, Barbara Laing and Christine Smith for their patience in what has proved to be a lengthy undertaking, with Chuck van Hof of Notre Dame University Press in the background.

Every effort has been made to keep this text as free from error and inconsistency as possible, and responsibility for its final form rests with the Editors.

Abbreviations

AAS – *Acta Apostolicae Sedis, Commentarium officiale*

DHGE – *Dictionnaire d'histoire et de géographie ecclésiastique* (A. Baudrillart, A. de Meyer, E. van Cauwenbergh, R. Aubert, eds., Paris 1912 –)

DTC – *Dictionnaire de théologie catholique* (E. Vacant, E. Mangenot, E. Amann, eds., 1903–50)

Mansi – *Sacrorum conciliorum nova et amplissima collectio* (J.-D. Mansi, ed., Paris 1899)

MGH – *Monumenta Germaniae Historica* (Deutsches Institut für Erforschung des Mittelalters)

PG – *Patrologia Graeca Cursus Completus* (J. P. Migne, ed., Paris 1857–66)

PL – *Patrologia Latina Cursus Completus* (J. P. Migne, ed., Paris 1844–64)

Texts in English translation:

ANF – *Ante-Nicene Fathers* (revised edition, A. Cleveland Coxe)

NPNF – *Nicene and Post-Nicene Fathers* (various editors)

For the convenience of those wishing to follow the original text alongside this translation, the nearest French pagination is indicated by the bracketed numbers at the inside margins of the running heads.

Editors' Preface

Long in the making, this translation is of a book that has had influence far beyond its readership – indeed that was our reason for persevering, so that those aware of this text and whose worshipping and scholarly lives had been influenced by it, but who had little or no French, could gain at first hand an understanding of what de Lubac had actually said. The version translated is the second edition, of 1949. The book was finished between 1938 and 1939, and did not appear until 1944 in the difficult wartime conditions of Vichy France. A critical edition in a series of de Lubac's entire French corpus is in preparation which will include a re-edition of the 1949 text, but we were unable to co-ordinate this translation to that edition, which at the time of publication has not yet appeared.

We had in mind two readerships. To a scholarly readership whom we envisaged might use this book alongside the original, we offer a handbook to the French text of 1949. A second, wider audience we envisaged to be those many – theologians, students of theology, educated laity, and interested readers of all kinds – who might welcome access to a book whose very complexity we believed had held back its appearance in English.

De Lubac's text in many ways reflects the confusions of the age in which it was written. His preparation and the editing of the book are often erratic and inconsistent: authors are given differing titles or descriptions across various points, the use of parentheses does not always reflect a clear purpose, and at times the referencing is confusing. We have not tried to edit by 'correcting' or 'improving' the text in preparing this translation, but rather have endeavoured to give the reader a feel for the rough-hewnness of the original. De Lubac himself said of *Corpus Mysticum* 'this book is a naïve book'[1] – it was only his

---

1 See H. Card. de Lubac, *Mémoire sur l'occasion de mes écrits* (Namur, Belgium: Culture et Verité, 1989), p. 28. 'Ce livre est un livre naïf.' (E. T. *At the Service of the Church: Henri de Lubac Reflects on the Circumstances That Occasioned His Writings* [San Francisco: Ignatius Press, Communio Books, 1993].)

second major work (after *Catholicism* of 1938)[2] – and he had fallen into its concerns almost by a series of accidents. He remarks how little formal training or background he had for the research he undertook, not least because the discipline was defined by scholarship that was almost entirely in German, a language de Lubac did not read or speak.

He notes, 'I was not encumbered by any of the categories and classical dichotomies into which I would necessarily have fallen if I had read the historians, who were nearly all German'[3] and so had to work out for himself how to read and interpret the sources. There is in this attitude something astonishing and at the same time utterly modern – that sources that arose from a disciplined (sometimes even febrile) tradition of self-interpretation in an age long past could simply fall open and announce their inner meaning to a reader unversed in, and unfamiliar with, the world in which they arose. Attending this is the unspoken suggestion by de Lubac that even had he been schooled in the leading (German) tradition of interpretation, he might not have gained better access to the sources: the tradition of interpretation to which he lacked access (but of which he was aware) had also moved far beyond the world of the sources, with the suspicion that, far from unravelling them, it left them locked up in their meaning even when in close examination of their opened pages. De Lubac was not the first to experience this perplexity of *distance* to what is needed to be known, and darkness in how to come near, but the question remains whether his answer – to read the texts for himself and unaided – sufficed to resolve the difficulty posed.

This acknowledged naïvety explains the character of the book, which at times even in the body of the text is no more than preparatory notes and an actual recollection of the research that gave rise to the conclusions attained in the final chapters. If this naïvety explains the book, it helps us as well to understand its reception. What de Lubac describes as his method of reading, the results of which are presented in this text, is exactly what Hans-Georg Gadamer has called *Horizontverschmelzung* – or 'fusion of horizons'. Gadamer reminds us that the character of this fusion of horizons – we might better say

---

2 H. Card. de Lubac, *Catholicisme: les aspects sociaux du dogme* (Paris, Éditions du Cerf 1947 [1938]) (E. T. by L. C. Sheppard, E. Englund, *Christ and the Common Destiny of Man* (San Francisco, Ignatius, 1988 [1950]).

3 H. Card. de Lubac, *Mémoire sur l'occasion de mes écrits*, p. 28. 'Je n'étais encombré d'aucune des catégories et des dichotomies classiques dans lequelles il m'aurait bien fallu tomber, si j'avais lu les historiens, à peu près tous alemands.'

worlds (our own and of that in which the text arose) is 'the central problem of hermeneutics'. He adds, 'it is the problem of *Anwendung* which is underlying in all understanding'.[4] The word *Anwendung* is usually translated as 'application' or 'use', but literally it means the directedness of a turning-in toward the matter at hand. The text presupposes a world from out of which it came, and it addresses the world in which the reader now stands: but this fusion can take place in one of two ways – either, as Gadamer says, in a dead end, a 'detour, on which we remain stuck',[5] or as a fusion in which the texts present themselves, not as an answer, but as a *question*, which, we may add, throws not only the world in which they arose open for us as a place to be interrrogated, but also throws our own world, our situation, open as a place in which we ourselves are opened to be questioned by the sources into which we enquire. Gadamer concludes that 'this is the basis for why all understanding is always more than mere comprehension of a distant viewpoint'.[6] The voices and texts of a world other than our own have the power to put *us* into question, and indeed, says Gadamer, they must do this if genuine understanding – intelligence – is to be possible: a *single* world arises hermeneutically, but one in which we who understand will stand out differently from how we did before.

De Lubac is himself well aware of the problem that Gadamer names – of the danger of a dead-end over against genuine understanding, and shows his sensitivity to what is at issue in how his own researches are to be read when he announced in the Preface to the second edition that 'no portion of our inheritance should be systematically despised'. For from the outset this text, with all its naïvety, has been used to justify an understanding of the past which is at best a caricature, very far from the understanding invited by de Lubac's actual words. The central thesis, that the singular *corpus mysticum* is at one and the same time a threefold: not just the *sacramentum* or signification of the Sacred Species, but also the body of the Church, and at the same time the very Body of Christ itself, has over and again been interpreted within the framework of the resistance to the fetishisation of objects that marks

---

4 H. G. Gadamer, *Wahrheit und Methode* in *Gesammelte Werke*, vol. 1 (Tübingen: Mohr Siebeck, 1990 [1960]), p. 312. 'Das zentrale Problem der Hermeneutik überhaupt. Es ist das Problem der *Anwendung*, die in allem Verstehen gelegen ist' (author's emphasis).

5 H. G. Gadamer, *Wahrheit und Methode*, p. 380. 'Ein Umweg, auf dem man steckenbleibt.'

6 H. G. Gadamer, *Wahrheit und Methode*, p. 381. 'Das ist der Grund, warum alles Verstehen immer mehr ist als bloßes Nachvollziehen einer fremden Meinung.'

the modern mind. This mind has – for entirely noble philosophical motives – sought to resist the production of the Sacred Species of the Holy Eucharist as a *mere* thing, whilst it simultaneously wanted to challenge the radical individualism that found expression so vigorously in the Catholic piety of the nineteenth century (although projecting its suspicion of this individualism back onto a much earlier age). Hans Urs von Balthasar sums up this challenge when, in describing *Corpus Mysticum*, he suggests that its 'point of departure' was that the accent of Eucharistic theology had been 'displaced from the social aspect to that of the real presence' so that 'individualistic eucharistic piety (won) a handhold'.[7] Even here, we must beware of von Balthasar's tendency to suggest a one-sided presentation of de Lubac's conclusions, which are in themselves far more subtle and in their very delicacy demand greater attentiveness. For de Lubac reminds us that only 'at one level' was there a question of 'an overly individualistic devotion'.[8] What other levels (*parts*) are at work? What degree of personal devotion is implied by de Lubac's understanding, that it be not 'overly' (*trop*) individual? Much more than individualism alone seems to be at issue in the book you have before you.

De Lubac, in reminding his readers only five years after the text appeared of the need for a historical perspicacity and reserve in interpreting his book, again draws attention to what is at issue: for whom is this fetish and individualism apparent, and so to whom does it appear as a danger? Is it, as has been routinely supposed in the whole vigorous drive to devalue the medieval (just to name an epoch in this manner is at the same time to mark out the boundaries of its objectification), the inversion that arose after the twelfth century (and which *Corpus Mysticum* attempts to name) – or is it a danger all too present for *us*, the readers and constitutors of this periodisation? Who would deny that our own lives are driven and constituted by the appearance of things as fetish, and at the same time by the appearance of an extreme individualism constituted *out of* the very things that mark out, isolate and individuate the human self? On top of the inversions and shifts that de Lubac actually traces must also be traced the one he did not:

---

7 H. U. Card. von Balthasar, *Henri de Lubac: Sein organisches Lebenswerk* (Einsiedeln, Johannes, 1976), p. 32. 'Hier zweigt die Fragestellung' . . . 'Der Akzent vom sozialen Aspekt auf den Realpräsenz verlagert wurde, gewann die individualistische Eucharistiefrömmigkeit eine Handhabe'. (E.T. by J. Fessio SJ, M. W. Waldstein, *The Theology of Henri de Lubac* [San Francisco, CA: Ignatius, 1991].)

8 See below, p. 259.

the inversions and shifts of modernity and postmodernity. De Lubac is himself sensitive to how the passage of time, and the passage of pedagogy itself, produces these shifts. Not arbitrarily does he name the distance between St. Thomas and Descartes as a period of the bastardisation of thought, and Descartes prepares the inception of modernity on the basis of the corruption, not the supercession, of the wisdom of antiquity and the Middle Ages.[9] This degeneration proceeds apace. *Objects* – and this means not just 'things', but also the matter of thinking, 'ideology' (ideas, slogans) – in these shifts and inversions have come to render selves as *subjects* and individuate them radically. The Marxist Louis Althusser refers to this as 'this very precise operation which we call *interpellation* or hailing . . . "Hey, you, down there"'.[10] A certain kind of hermeneutic in this tradition of interpretation takes for granted that the 'hoisting of the host', the elevation of the Sacred Species by the priest in the consecration of the Mass, has the power of an interpellative act, but it need not always have been so (or be so now). It is precisely here that de Lubac calls us to greater care in reading the past, and of not despising what we think we find there. De Lubac's research can (and has been) accounted for in versions that are mere caricatures of his original.

The 'shift' that these caricatures propose to 'solve' – the inversion that de Lubac traces in *Corpus Mysticum* – a correctional shift *away from* the appearance of the 'objectified' host *to* a concentration on the worshipping community – is one that the theology of the Schools could never have understood, and yet it has itself propelled much of the basis for liturgical reform from the point at which this was widely acclaimed. The difficulty is that the community that has assembled (as we now understand it, especially in an age when to be regularly at Mass is to make a choice *for* something and often *against* something else) is a community that has chosen to be there, not the community – the body proper – that we must assume has been chosen by God. The result – caricature indeed – has been the fetishisation, not of the Sacred Species, the host, but of the community itself, the one that has

---

9 See below, p. 329 'Philosophers compared Descartes with St. Thomas, without taking into account the interval of time that separates them, or all the undistinguished successors and all the bastard descendants who occupied that interval and defined Descartes's historical context.'

10 L. Althusser, *Idéologie et appareils idéologiques d'état* in *La pensée: revue du rationalisme moderne* (Paris: Livres de Poche, 1970), p. 31. 'Cette opération très précise que nous appelons *l'interpellation* [. . .] "hé, vous, là bas".' Emphasis in original.

assembled for the Eucharist, and so the *Anwendung* of the interpretation has been a turning-in on ourselves, to intensify the objectification of the subjects for whom the host has become mere object.[11] All of this arises, however, on the basis of the subject–object distinction, so much a category of the Enlightenment. This category is a necessity for the devaluation of the uppermost values, where objects become values whose valuations can be *changed* by those doing the valuing: subjects, who can therefore decide, or come to be convinced, that a *mere thing*, however sacred its former meaning, can be esteemed at nought. The paradox of Althusser's theory of interpellation is that when he wrote, he presumed that the invitation of the interpellative thing sufficed for subjection, but *now*, in postmodernity, what interpellates a subject is at the same time something to be overcome by that subject: it is the pretext for asserting my drive for the *triumph* of my subjection.

Is this what *Corpus Mysticum* makes possible – that one meaning is to be exchanged for another, supposedly older, but in fact entirely of the moment? De Lubac clearly thought not, and was aware by 1949 of both of the uses (*Anwendungen*) to which his conclusions could be put, and of the violence inherent in their ill-use.

The subject–object distinction is unknown to the sources into which de Lubac enquired. The production of the worshipping assembly as an end in itself was unthinkable in the patristic age, and that of the theology of the Schools, precisely because the Church here present (the assembly in whose midst I find myself) is always a thing unfinished, and whose immediate future is as yet to be decided. Who is saved, and so actually incorporated into the *corpus mysticum*, is a thing hoped for but actually unproven in the present. Judgement as a coming time is nothing less than the attestation of this. Only at the *end* of time is the Church in its entirety to be understood as fully present, and so only then is the identity of Church with the Body of Christ complete. At this point, sacraments, and above all the sacrament of the altar, cease to be, no longer needed as the mediation of the incompleteness of the *corpus*

---

11 It should be noted that – for just one example – St. Thomas Aquinas is acutely sensitive to the question of whether those assembled in a church for a particular Mass are synonymous with those constituted as the assembly – the *ecclesia Dei* – by the action of the Mass itself. Aquinas is clear that those who number the *ecclesia* are known only to God: there are those present unable or unfit to make their communion (and even if they do, do not do so 'spiritually', i.e. perfectly but only sacramentally); but there are also those *absent* or who do not actually communicate (or who cannot) but who by grace and desire nevertheless effectively (and so really) are joined to the body of Christ. cf. Aquinas, *Summa theologiæ*, IIIa; Q. 73, a. 3, resp.; Q. 80, a. 2, resp.

mysticum (the end of time and the glorification of Christ's mystical Body, the point at which the Body ceases to be mysterious, or a matter of significations, and so is completed). Von Balthasar himself emphasises the importance of this eschatological aspect in de Lubac's work, and notes: 'the Origenistic thought, which finds so strong an echo through history . . . that Christ and the blessed attain their ultimate beatitude only if the whole "Body of Christ", the redeemed creation, is gathered together in the transfiguration, is honoured in its lasting spiritual meaning'. This occurs, von Balthasar tells us, only in 'the heavenly Jerusalem'.[12]

On what basis is the transition and inversion from the patristic sources to the mid-twelfth century and the present day to be understood? Here we must part company with von Balthasar, and indeed with all the hermeneutical keys of de Lubac's work which provide quick or all-too-easy ways in to understanding his results. To understand the book you have here in your hands we must no longer be concerned with what de Lubac *said*, but must, in listening to de Lubac, concentrate on what he was speaking *of*. At the heart of this is the way in which philosophical perspicuity appears as the handmaiden to the discipline of theology, and so to the self-understanding to which Gadamer points. This understanding is required if we are to find our way back in to the place toward which de Lubac seeks to lead us. We must be willing to put to the sharpest possible questioning von Balthasar's claim that de Lubac's work is to be interpreted from a suspended place 'in which he could not practice any philosophy without its transcendence into theology, but also no theology without its essential inner substructure of philosophy'.[13] The danger is that this place names the very naïvety de Lubac himself spoke of with respect to this text, taken at the highest degree. Going by its other name of ontotheology, it runs the risk of being the manufacture of an erasure – the subjective and objective genitive is intended here – both of enacting an erasure (*erasing something*), and of being produced by an erasure

---

12 H. U. Card. von Balthasar, *Henri de Lubac: Sein organisches Lebenswerk* (Einsiedeln, Johannes, 1976), p. 32. 'Der origenistische Gedanke, der so starken Widerhall durch die Geschichte fand . . . daß Christus und die Seligen ihre letzte Seligkeit erst finden, wenn der ganze "Leib Christi", die erlöste Schöpfung in der Verklärung beisammen wird, wird in seiner bleibenden geistigen Bedeutung gewürdigt' . . . 'himmlisches Jerusalem'.

13 H. U. Card. von Balthasar, *Henri de Lubac: Sein organisches Lebenswerk* (Einsiedeln, Johannes, 1976), p. 12. 'In der er keine Philosophie ohne deren Übersteig in Theologie, aber auch keine Theologie ohne deren wesentliche, innere Substruktur von Philosophie treiben konnte.'

(*being erased*) at work elsewhere and from far outside the place of faith. The enquiry into past sources precisely has the task of illuminating and making intelligible not the world of the past but above all the world in which we ourselves stand out – and which is stood on the past. The erasure we are always most in danger of is a self-erasure, the erasure of the very world we inhabit. De Lubac's text, as naïve, names a *beginning*, from where we set out and seek maturity, not an *end*, a 'solution' to all our theological problems. Beginnings are filled with shortcomings and the lacunæ of understanding, which time slowly closes as understanding develops. The beginning, precisely because it is marked by gaps, teaches us a reserve towards what we do not know: to close these gaps too quickly is a temptation to be resisted. Taken as a beginning, de Lubac's work allows us to grow, and to learn, and to retrace the contours of previous ages. But taken as an end, it would do nothing other than name a point of ignorance, masquerading as deepest, most erudite, knowledge.

We to whom the truths of theology seem so self-evident, especially when couched in philosophical terms, must beware the erasure we thereby perform – the erasing of the age itself (and so the erasing of the hermeneutic most demanded, of allowing the past to put *us* into question, which is Gadamer's explicit concern). Our age indeed lives under a ban of nihilism that can be described philosophically only with the utmost difficulty, a period wherein the restriction to the self (as much as to the announced and self-appointed 'communities of selves') is being lived through to a euphoric, but still embittering end, and of which we also need an account. Too easy a conflation of philosophy and theology does just this, and makes our own philosophical perspicacity into a bid for domination because of the erasure it performs. For an erasure which erases the discussion of a thing, while not erasing the thing itself, is an annihilation of the most dreadful kind of all.

Precisely because the theologians of the patristic age and of the Schools had in view another end, an end to be consummated only at the end of time, they did not, and did not need, to undertake an erasure of this form – they were able to account for that period when Christ was not known to the pagans (in its philosophical heights and splendour) both with utmost generosity and with a decisive claim that even *this* past age could receive the gospel news of redemption, albeit through the medium of Hades or the figure of the harrowing of Hell. Nevertheless theirs was a roomier world than ours, since it was not restricted to them alone and to the moment of the restriction alone.

De Lubac himself seems to resist this erasure and conflation as a movement of thought, while applauding the performance of the excellent intertwining of thought and grace in the person of Augustine: 'He stands precisely at the point where intellectual research and spiritual tension coincide, participating in the same impetus and sketching the same curve.'[14] Thus the synthesis of grace and intellect is lived, and finds its pinnacles in the Doctors of the Church. Against this, and with dramatic sharpness, de Lubac reminds us that the despising of our inheritance – especially in the name of restoring supposedly more pristine things from an earlier age over things believed to be later and less 'pure' (what de Lubac is not alone in calling antiquarianism, the dangers of which he mentions)[15] – conceals within it the myth of progress. Citing Max Scheler, he notes, 'development is not only progress, but it is always and at the same time decadence'.[16]

Anyone familiar with the rites of the Church that pre-date the period of liturgical reform of the 1960s, and those familiar with the Breviary (especially in its pre-1911 form) will know that not a few of de Lubac's sources – St. Augustine's commentaries on St. John, above all – would have been most familiar as part of the daily office of the feast of Corpus Christi and its Octave, the seven days after the feast. We must never lose sight that it is prayer that makes the mystery, the *signification* of the *mystical body*, possible. Moreover these are not simply prayers that we can make, but rather are they prayers that are the making of us, and are given to us, and were given to us through the sacred liturgy, to make in Christ.

The translation we have prepared is offered in the midst of a time when the naïvety that marked this text and its reception is being tested, and the need acknowledged for it to be overcome – when there is demand for a return, not just to the sources themselves, but to the careful, patient, demanding, uncovering of how they are to be understood. This discovery brings to the fore the question of understanding itself – exactly as Gadamer proposes – as self-understanding of the most genuine kind. Not introspection, but rather of the way in which our own world can stand out and be intelligible *with respect to* that world of the sources with which de Lubac engages, so that a *singular* understanding can emerge. A second reading is required beyond the first – and therefore a return to this text a second time – one that does

---

14 See below, p. 234.

15 See below, p. 145, 256. Antiquarianism is the attempt to justify some contemporary change or innovation as the supposed reinstatement of more ancient foundations than those of what the innovation seeks to overcome.

16 See below, p. 236.

justice to de Lubac's own understanding of the intrinsic unity in the present of the *three* kinds of body signified in the Holy Eucharist. It is our earnest hope that this translation is, in part, the needed invitation.

Corpus Christi, 2006

Notes on the Translation

Corpus Mysticum is a work of intensive concentration on two words which, by its very nature, involves the close comparison of terms in Latin, Greek and French. We have sought to help the reader on occasion by giving the original Latin or Greek next to the English in order to make clear the interplay of words to which de Lubac is drawing attention, but for the most part the text that is in either Latin or Greek in the original has been translated. In the body of the text these translations are italicised. Rarely, de Lubac italicised words in French for emphasis, and these are also in italics in the translation. It is usually possible to tell from the context when an italicised word was in French or Latin (or even Greek) in the original. In the few places where it has been necessary to clarify the meaning by a note intruded by the editors or translators, these have been indicated with square brackets '[. . .]'

The literary French of de Lubac's generation often adopts a more grandiose tone than its English equivalent. This does not translate well into our more practical, modern tongue, so although we have endeavoured to give as close a rendering as possible of the original, the style is more sober in the English than the French. De Lubac writes of himself most often in the first person plural, but we have indicated this mainly in the singular.

Much of the material in the footnotes, often amounting to not more than de Lubac's notes (extensive Latin and Greek quotations from the Fathers), we have neither translated nor included, because we believed this material could either be available to a scholarly readership through familiarity with the texts and languages concerned, or (for a wider audience) otherwise constituted a distraction from the argument of the book. The full text of these notes, in their original languages, can be found in the 1949 edition, and the numbering of the notes in the present text exactly matches that of the 1949 edition. In some cases critical or more scholarly editions of the texts from which de Lubac worked have appeared since he prepared the text, but for sake of closeness to the original text we have indicated only de

Lubac's own sources. In many cases (as often as we felt able) we have suggested where English translations are to be found, and the editors' notes pointing to these also appear encased in square brackets.

Preface to the First Edition

[5]

'It would be running the risk of falling into error', wrote Fr. de Ghellinck, 'if, in the process of studying the history of a doctrine one were to be content with enquiring into the history of one particular word.' So let the reader of this study not be deceived regarding the intention of the pages that follow, nor seek in them a history of the Eucharist, even one that is limited to a single one of its attributes: the intention has only been to give direct consideration to the history of one or two words.

These reflections were developed out of a course given in the Faculty of Theology at Lyon during the winter of 1937–1938. They would certainly never have been edited had I not subsequently been forced to give up more worthy tasks. During this work, the reflections of St. Jerome have often come to my mind: '*Of what benefit our writing will be for others is a matter for God's judgement . . . It certainly benefits ourselves: for while we are doing this and thinking of nothing else, we attain understanding by stealth . . . The mind is nourished and forgets the tribulations of this life.*'

I hope that Fr. Victor Fontoynont, a teacher whom I greatly reverence and love, will accept the dedication of a book that, for so many reasons, is already his.

Lyon-Fourvière, 8th June 1939 on the Feast of Corpus Christi.

Preface to the Second Edition

The origin of this work was entirely fortuitous: a student wrote a thesis on Florus of Lyons, and as his designated examiner I had to prepare myself for my role; I did it by undertaking a close re-reading of the theologians of the ninth century. It was then that I was struck by the use of *corpus mysticum* in Paschasius Radbertus and Ratramnus, in Godescalc and Rabanus Maurus. Unravelling the exact sense of the words, tracking down their origin and following their destiny amid dusty texts was a painstaking task embarked upon during the enforced rest following an illness. At that time storm clouds were gathering over Europe: this occupation provided me with a haven of peace. When the book finally appeared, after the long delay caused by the war, how could I have known that a new storm was brewing, this time in the theological sky, to break over the modest joy I felt in having exhumed a treasure trove buried by tradition? Nevertheless it is that storm which necessitates my clarifying some points in this new preface.

Some readers imagined that in what I wrote they could detect, under cover of the praise of symbolism, my putting rationalist thought and classical theology on trial. I believe that the misunderstanding arose through their attributing to me far more ambitious intentions than I had. And I may inadvertently have been responsible for this. Seduced by all the riches that I discovered in this period of Christian antiquity, I may have rather forced the issue here or there. This cloud of minor witnesses, attesting to the vigour of a flourishing tradition by its sheer mass, more than any great name on its own could have done, threw me into a sort of amazed stupor. This was our family inheritance, and many people had hardly a suspicion of it! Some had even come to despise it, for want of having properly explored it! It was a matter, then, of restoring to it its proper value, and that could not be done without sharing as deeply as possible the same perspectives as the age that was being studied. I would have failed utterly, had I not at least been tempted in some way to induce a nostalgia for that lost age! But that was in no way to urge an imagined return to its methods or its way of thinking. My only ambition was to bring them to light and, if possible, to inspire a retrospective taste for them; and I continue to believe that such a result would not be without a certain profit for the theological project of our times. Because, without ever wishing simply to copy our forebears, a great deal can be gained from a better knowledge, not only of the fruits of their thinking but also of the interior sap which nourished them.

There have been so many new and interesting studies undertaken over the past thirty years, especially from the point of view of new schools of thought, that, in order to make for a more balanced historical judgement, it was perhaps also not without interest to sketch out a rather different approach, whose methodology reflected the perspective of traditional sources that were felt to be under threat. I am amazed that it should be necessary to stress that there was no question here of some antiquarian fantasy. Nor was there any intention either to denigrate or to question a more 'dialectical' understanding. It was not relevant to my subject to discuss in greater detail all that the changes that occurred towards the middle of the medieval period brought about in Christian thinking, by way of new and, in some areas, definitive resources. I nevertheless made a point of noting in passing that the Thomist synthesis, which was the culmination of these contributions, was open to future development. I also remarked that it needed to be 'tested against the same elements of tradition' as the theology which preceded it, and I expressed the regret that 'nourished by tradition and firmly balanced' as it was, it should so swiftly have been abandoned in favour of theories of the Church whose orientation was completely different. As for its general evolution, which I symbolized, admittedly in summary fashion, by two words borrowed from Fr. Mandonnet, it was, – I said it and I am happy to repeat it, – 'normal and therefore good'. Once certain problems have challenged our understanding, which is where they have their origin in the first place, nothing could or should prevent the mind from doing its proper job: it has to get to grips with them, and find a solution to them, even if that means overturning all that it has been familiar with, and from then on leaving fallow certain fields which up to then have been lovingly cultivated. I stated, as had others, that even the dialectical intemperance of someone like Berengar was 'a step in the right direction'. That is to say that I experience no difficulty whatsoever in subscribing to what the author proposes in his particularly well-intentioned account, any more than he himself would have experienced any in sharing what he would have called my 'discreet severity'. Indeed, 'the religious power of our understanding, moved by the mysterious light of faith, can take the rational faculties of our spirit a long way. That this can be a risky enterprise is witnessed by Berengar, and later Abelard and many others; but the likes of Anselm, Bonaventure and Thomas Aquinas, in widely varying veins that, we must admit, were different from an Augustinian understanding, were able through their curiosity and their "questions" to allow the mystery and its secret "intelligibility" to shine through naturally.' And many other theologians will find themselves in agreement with Chenu, as well as with me, in actively desiring 'that the mature age of the Schools will not cause us to lose the creative freshness of its youth, if it is true that faith, in all its mystery, assures the permanent youth of theology'.[17]

This presupposes that laziness does not incline us to accept too readily, within the heart of theological speculation, a certain myth of progress, which all the influences of our time have been contributing until recently to press upon us (and, despite appearances, it is not certain that this is not still the case today). In reacting against 'modern' self-sufficiency, which induces our contemporaries to attribute to themselves a better understanding than their forebears, simply because they were born after them, I see myself as reconnecting with a more traditional estimate of the matter, as shared not only by the patristic era and the high Middle Ages, but also by the centuries that followed them. Within these vast landscapes each person can carve out a chosen plot. But no portion of our common inheritance should be systematically despised. With good reason there has been talk of the 'dispossession, without which the attempt at historical understanding cannot begin'.[18] Historians must first of all make contrasts stand out, if they are not only to trade in banalities. But they should not close their eyes to more fundamental continuities! As for me, my gaze will always end up fixed on the history of human thinking itself, and even more on that of Christian theology. I will always find peace and joy in contemplating them. Amid so many varied riches that claim my attention, I will always seek to act like a child of Plato, that is to say, every time that there is at least the possibility of so acting, I will not make a choice. A unity that is too quickly affirmed has no power to inspire, while eclecticism has no impact. But the methodical welcoming of contrasts, once understood, can be fruitful: not only does it guard against

---

17 Chenu in *Dieu Vivant*, book I, pp. 141–3.
18 Paul Vignaux, *Nominalisme au XIVè siècle* (1948), p. 10.

over-eager partiality; not only does it open up to our understanding a deep underlying unity: it is also one of the preconditions that prepares us for new departures.[19]

---

19 It has not been possible for me to take into account the work of Fr. Jos. Andreas Jungmann, *Missarum solemnia, eine genetische Erklärung der römischen Messe* (2 vols, Vienna, 1948). But a translation is in preparation of this essential work, which we hope may soon appear in this same collection '*Théologie*'. [Translated into English by F. A. Brunner, *The Mass of the Roman Rite: Its Origin and Development* (2 vols, New York, 1951).]

I

THE EVOLUTION OF THE SENSE OF
CORPUS MYSTICUM

Introduction

In the preparatory outline of the *Constitutio de Ecclesia*, which the Vatican Council never had the time to finish, it says[1] that the Son of God became man in order that human beings 'should make up a mystical body, of which he himself would be the head' and that he instituted baptism 'in order to bring about that union of the mystical body'. This expression *corpus mysticum* was not an innovation. It can be found in numerous earlier Church documents.[2] The first chronological instance of its appearance would seem to be the famous Bull *Unam Sanctam* of Boniface VIII (18th November 1302): '*One holy Church . . . which represents the one mystical body, of which the head is Christ, just as the head of Christ is God.*'

Where does this expression come from? Nowadays, not only in works of theology, but even in works of pure history or exegesis, it is used concurrently with that of 'the mystical Christ', as if it were derived from St. Paul himself. But this is nevertheless not the case. It is also offered as the title of various patristic studies. It is quoted, sometimes in inverted commas, in the analysis, and even in literal translations of works of the Fathers, or of theologians of antiquity.[3] However, whatever the notes added to the Vatican outline might say in justification,[4] the Fathers were not familiar with the term. If one is to believe Erasmus, it is certainly to be found twice in the works of St. Cyprian, in chapters XXVIII and XXXVII in his study entitled *De duplici martyrio ad Fortunatum*.[5] But, as was proved some considerable time ago, this study is false. Published for the first time by Erasmus in his second

---

1 Ch. 1. 1, 2 (Mansi, LI, c. 53₉).

2 Fr. Tromp quotes a certain number in *Corpus Christi quod est Ecclesia*, I, pp. 161–6.

3 cf. St. Bernard, letter 244, to Emperor Conrad, translated by Paul Zunthor, *St. Bernard of Clairvaux*, p. 178 as 'he so intimately connected both of them to his mystical body . . .'.

4 '. . . in the common usage as received by the doctors of the Church', c. 554.

5 Hartel, III, pp. 240, 245. [This, along with many of St. Cyprian's works and letters, can be found in English in ANF V.]

edition of the works of Cyprian in 1530, allegedly found by him '*in an ancient library*', there is every reason to believe that its true author was the great humanist himself. He made use of this subterfuge in order to legitimise his point of view over the reform of the Church.[6]

The Fathers speak habitually, as does St. Paul, of the 'body of Christ', which is the Church. They speak of the 'whole body of Christ', of the 'universal body', or the 'full body' of Christ.[7] They speak of the 'body of the Church', or again, as with St. Basil, of the 'body of the Church of Christ'.[8] Through a word attributed to Jesus, they know of a 'perfect body' of Christ.[9] Tertullian[10] and Clement of Alexandria[11] and Zeno of Verona[12] also call it a 'spiritual body'.[13] Gregory the Great says that those within the Church who are governed by others, are, by

---

6 Hartel, p. LXIV: 'Certainly no one since Erasmus has managed to see the manuscript of this book.' Erasmus was a great enthusiast for the Pauline doctrine of the body of Christ (see above all his *Enchiridion* and *Preparation for Death*) and the expression '*corpus mysticum*' was familiar to him. [For the edited works of Erasmus in English, see the *Collected Works of Erasmus* series, University of Toronto Press.]

7 St. Augustine, *In psalmum 68*, s. 1, n. 11: 'his full body, the whole Church' (PL, 36, 850); *In psalmum 130*, n. 1 (37, 1704). [For St. Augustine's works in English, see NPNF, series 1, vols. –VIII.] cf. *Apostolic Constitutions*, 1. a, c. 41 and 43 (PG, 1, 697 B & 701 A). [For the *Apostolic Constitutions* in English, see ANF VII.] Origen, *In Joannem*, vol. 10, c. 43: 'In the great resurrection of all the body of Christ, by which should be understood, of his holy Church' (Preuschen, p. 29). St. Thomas, *In Jo.*, c. 2, p. 3, n. 4. [For St. Thomas Aquinas' commentary in English, see J. A. Weisheipl, *Commentary on the Gospel of John*, Aquinas Scripture Series, vol. 4 (Albany, 1980).]

8 St. Basil, *In Psalmum 29* (PG, 29, 308 A). [For the English, see Sr. A. C. Way, *The Fathers of the Church* series, vol. 46 (Washington, 1963). For selected works and letters of St. Basil translated into English, see B. Jackson (ed.), NPNF, series II. vol. 8; Sr. A. C. Way, *The Fathers of the Church* series, vols. 28 (New York, 1955) and 46, and *Saint Basil: the Letters*, R. J. Deferrari (tr.), 4 vols., Loeb Classical Library.]

9 'The Church, which is the perfect body of Christ and his clear image' (Resch, *Agrapha*, 2nd edn., 75).

10 *Adversus Marcionem*, 1. 5, c. 19 (Kroymann, pp. 644–5). *De virginibus velandis* (PL, 2, 89). *De monogamia*, c. 13 (PL, 2, 949). [For the works of Tertullian in English, see ANF vols. III–IV.]

11 *Stromates*, 1.7, c. 14 (Stählin, vol. 3, p. 62). [For St. Clement's works in English, see ANF, vol. II.]

12 1, tract. 13, n. 10 (PL, 11, 352 B).

13 This expression will sometimes be repeated in modern times. Du Perron *Replique à la Response du Serenissime Roy de la Grande Bretagne* (Paris, 1620), preface: God willed that we form 'under the authority of his name a type of spiritual body, and a sort of State and Republic'. Pius X, encyclical *Ad diem illum*, 2nd February 1904 (AAS, 36, pp. 452–3). [The Encyclical in English can be found in C. Carlen, *The Papal Encyclicals 1903–39* (Raleigh, 1981). All such papal documents from 1740 can be found in this series.]

that very fact, in the words of the apostle, 'members of a member' in the spiritual body of the Lord.[14] Others see in the Church 'the whole body of the saints in Christ', which, according to Origen, will at the end of time become 'the true and perfect body of Christ'.[15] 'The common body of Christ' writes St. Gregory Nazianzen, without any other qualification,[16] or again: 'the great and precious body of Christ'[17] and after him, Theodoret: 'the common body of the Church'.[18] The expression has its Latin parallel in the *'body in general'* engendered by the Church, that is both Virgin and Mother, as the individual body of the Saviour was engendered by the Virgin Mary.[19] In the sufferings of the infant Jesus fleeing into Egypt, Optatus of Milevus sees prefigured those of the *'body of Christians'*, of the *'body of the Church'*,[20] identical with the *'Church of the saints'*. Others, with St. Hilary,[21] St. Augustine[22] and St. Leo,[23] speak of the 'mystery' or of the 'sacrament of the body of Christ'. At the same time as a 'physical' and 'spiritual' union, the union of the faithful within this body is, for them, a 'mystical union'.[24] As 'spiritual members of the Church'[25] Christians are

---

14 *Moralia in Job*, 34, c. 4, n. 8 (PL, 76, 722 B). [English translation: J. H. Parker, *Library of the Fathers of the Holy Catholic Church* series (Oxford, 1844–50).]

15 *In Joannem*, vol X. c. 36 (Preuschen, p. 210). [For all of Origen's commentary on John in English, see R. E. Heine, *The Fathers of the Church* series, vols. 80, 89 (Washington, 1989, 1993).]

16 *Discourse 32*, c. 10 (PG, 36, 185 C). [For select works of St. Gregory in English, see C. G. Brown and J. E. Swallow, NPNF, series II, vol. 7; M. Vinson, *The Fathers of the Church* series, vol. 107 (Washington, 2003).]

17 *Discourse 6* (PG 35, 722 A): Analogous expressions can be found later, for example, in Gerhoh of Reichersberg: 'the great body' or 'the whole body' (PL, 193, 630 D, 1102 D, 1720 B, 1794 D, 1795 A; 194, 316 C, etc.).

18 *In I Cor.*, XII (PG, 82, 325 C). [For the English, see R. C. Hill, *Theodoret of Cyrus: Commentary on the Letters of St. Paul*, vol. 1 (Brookline, MA, 2001).]

19 Alcuin, *In Apocalypsin* (PL, 100, 1152 D).

20 *Sermon for Christmas* (Wilmart, *Revue des Sciences religieuses*, 1922, pp. 284, 288).

21 *In Psalmum 125*, n. 6 (Zingerle, p. 609).

22 *Annotationes in Job* (PL, 34, 873).

23 *Ep. 84*, c. 2 (PL, 54, 922). [For St. Leo's letters and sermons in English, see C. Lett Feltoe, NPNF, Series II, vol. 12; E. Hunt, *The Fathers of the Church* series, vol. 34 (New York, 1957). For further translations of his works, see F. W. Green, *The Œcumenical Documents of the Faith* (Westport, CN, 1980); E. H. Blakeney, *The Tome of Pope Leo the Great* (London, 1923).]

24 Cyril of Alexandria, *In Joannem* (PG, 73, 161, 1045, 1048). [For the Commentary in English, see P. E. Pusey, T. Randell, *A Library of the Fathers of the Holy Catholic Church* (London, 1885).] Thesaurus (PG, 75, 292). cf. Hubert du Manoir, *Dogme et spiritualité chez saint Cyrille d'Alexandrie*, pp. 299–301.

25 *In Romanos* (PL, 117, 472 A).

naturally therefore the 'mystical members'[26] of that body of which Christ is the 'mystical head'.[27] In the liturgies, the Church is sometimes described as the 'sacred body' of the only Son, gathered together by the apostles[28] and made beautiful through the virtues of the saints.[29] Paulinus of Nola saw 'the grace of the sacred body' growing through the diversity of the graces received by all its members.[30] St. Zeno of Verona celebrated the 'unique grace of the body of Christ', which gathers the elect into one,[31] and Florus of Lyon speaks in similar vein of the 'grace of the unity of the body'.[32] Contemplating the growth of the *body of Christ* which is the Church, John Scotus Erigena sees it, in its fulfilment, as an *intellectual body*.[33] Now *intellectual* or *intelligible* are often very closely akin to *mystical* and *intelligible* (μυστικὸς καὶ νοητός) as can be seen in the words of Erigena himself on the previous page *'mystical and intelligible days'*.[34] Once again, therefore, we come very close to the 'mystical body'. Nevertheless, there is no writer of Christian antiquity or of the high Middle Ages in whose work the word itself appears as a description of the Church. If it is found in certain titles or summaries, as is the case, for example, in a sermon of St. Leo the Great,[35] or with a chapter of the *Elucidarium* of Honorius of Autun,[36] it is always by the hand of later editors.[37]

There are, however, one or two apparent exceptions. The most notable of these is a text from Theodoret, in his fifth discourse on Providence:

Those who fly, free from all care for earthly things, and longing to attain to *the mystical body*, are called eagles in the holy Gospels.

---

26 Bede, *In Samuelem* (PL, 91, 657 B).

27 Ambrose, *In psalmum 118*, sermo 20, *De Elia et jejunio*, c. 10 (PL, 15, 1483 D, 14, 710 B). [For select works of St. Ambrose in English, see H. de Romestin, NPNF series II, vol. 10; for exegetical works, see M. P. McHugh, *The Fathers of The Church* series, vol. 65 (Washington, 1972). See also B. Ramsey, *Ambrose*, in the *Early Church Fathers* series (London: Routledge, 1997).]

28 Grimaldus, *Liber sacramentorum* (PL, 121, 907).

29 Gallican liturgy (Chardon, in Migne, *Theologiae cursus completus*, vol. 20, c. 344) [hereafter cited as Migne].

30 *Epistula 24*, n. 2 (PL, 61, 287 C).

31 *Tractoria 50* (PL, 11, 507).

32 *Adversus Amalarium*, I, n. 7 (PL, 119, 77).

33 *De divisione naturae*, I. 5, c. 38 (PL, 35, 1723).

34 *loc. cit.* (991B) cf. Augustine, *In Joannem*, tract. 45, n. 9 (PL, 35, 1723).

35 *Sermo 63*, c. 3 (PL, 54, compare 353 and 355).

36 Bk., I, c. 27 (PL, 172, 1128).

37 In the same way, tables of modern editions sometimes contain the rubric '*corpus mysticum*'.

Since, speaking of those saints who will be taken up into the heavens on the day of the resurrection, Christ states: where the body is, there will the eagles gather.[38]

There are two possible interpretations of this phrase: either the saints desire to obtain an individual glorious body of their own, or else they desire to enter into this one great glorious body which is the assembly of the blessed, gathered around Christ as one, and only made one with him. The second sense is far more likely,[39] but even this meaning is not identical with the contemporary understanding of the word. For Theodoret, the 'mystical body' is not the Church in general as is universally understood by the 'body of Christ' in St. Paul, but only the Church in Heaven, that society of the elect which St. Augustine, in around the same period, precisely called the 'mystical Church' in order to distinguish it from the one which is still journeying through this world: 'that blessed, mystical, great Church'.[40] This is what others have called either the celestial Church,[41] or the 'celestial body of Christ'.[42] The 'mystical body' is thus equivalent to the 'mystical Church', 'Church' being the equivalent of 'body', which brings us directly back to the terminology held in common by St. Paul and the Fathers.

It is worth noting, in addition, a passage from Eusebius, which also needs to be taken out of the reckoning:

In receiving the Scripture of the Gospels, you can see the whole of our Saviour's teaching, concerning what he said not of the body which he assumed, but of his *mystical body and blood*.[43]

It does not take much further analysis of the reading to realise that we are not dealing here with the mystical body in our sense of the term. Eusebius is commenting on the Bread of Life discourse. It is a *mystical discourse* (μυστικώτερον), he explains, which is to be understood in a spiritual sense. This body and blood are the truth taught by Christ,

---

38 PG, 83, 629. cf. Clement, *Excerpta ex Theodoto*, 58 and 63.

39 cf. Tromp, *Corpus Christi quod est Ecclesia*, I, p. 9. Hardy, *Onze sermons de Theodoret de la providence de Dieu* (1619), p. 600.

40 *Sermo* 252, n. 7 (PL, 38, 1175). cf. *Enchiridion*, c. 57, 58 (40, 259).

41 Pseudo-Primasius, *In Hebr.* (PL, 68, 783 B, 785 A–B).

42 Raoul of St. Germer, *In Leviticum*, 1, c. 5 (B.M.P., vol. 17, p. 58 C; cf. 5, c. 1, p. 91 C).

43 *On the Theology of the Church*, 3, c. 12 (PG, 24, 1021 B).

they are the Word of God.[44] This notion, which Eusebius principally owes to Clement[45] and to Origen[46] and which he shares with Basil,[47] Ambrose, Jerome,[48] Augustine and many others, is certainly not exclusive of other interpretations. If it focuses principally on Scripture, it does not rule out the Eucharist, that other nourishment of the soul, or even the Church, since each of these three mysteries is an aspect of the Mystery of Christ, who is the Logos.[49] But in the direct sense here, Eusebius is referring to the Church even less than he is speaking of the Eucharist.[50]

It is surprising that an expression, which seems so natural to us and which, from the very beginning of Christianity, has been suggested or almost demanded by a whole context of ideas and words, should have remained unknown for so many centuries. So exactly when and how did it make its first appearance? This is what, so far as I know, has not yet been determined in any specific way. Several historians have thought it necessary to go back to the thirteenth century to find it in the *Summa aurea* of William of Auxerre. Several times, in fact, in Book III of this Summa, William distinguishes precisely two bodies of Christ: the '*body of Christ by nature*', or '*true body*' and the '*mystical body of Christ through grace*'; the first of these two, which is the body born of the Virgin and present in the Eucharist, plays the role of '*sacra-*

---

44 *loc. cit.*, 1021–4.

45 *Paed.*, 1, c. 6.

46 *In Exodum*, hom. 13, n. 3 (Baehrens, p. 274). *In Leviticum*, hom. 7, n. 5 (pp. 386–7). *In Numeros*, hom.16, n. 9 (p. 152). *In Ecclesiasten* (PG, 23, 1033 B, 1039 A). *In Matthaeum*, c. 85 (Klostermann, pp. 196–9). [For selections of the homilies of Origen in English, see *The Fathers of The Church* series, vols. 71, 83, 94, 97, 103–5; R. P. Lawson, *Ancient Christian Writers* series, vol. 26 (London, 1957); ANF vol. 9, 4; *Ante-Nicene Christian Library* series, vol. 23, 2 Parts (Edinburgh, 1872); J. W. Trigg, *Origen*, in the *Early Church Fathers* series (London: Routledge, 1998).]

47 *Epistulae*, 1, *Ep.* 8, 4: 'Whoever eats will live through me. For we eat his flesh and drink his blood, having become, through his incarnation and his life in the senses, participants in the Logos and the Wisdom of God. For he has called body and blood all his "mystical" conversation' (PG, 32, 253). cf. *In psalmum* 44, n. 3 (29, 393 B).

48 *In Psalmos* 145, 147 (Morin, *Anecdota maredsolana*, III, 2, pp. 290, 301). *In Marcum* (*ibid.*, p. 342). *In Eccl.* (PL, 23, 1033, 1039). [For selections of St. Jerome's homilies in English, see M. Liguori Ewald, *The Fathers of the Church* series, vols. 48, 53, 57 (Washington, 1963, 1964, 1965). For a selection of his letters and other principal works, see W. H. Fremantle, NPNF, series II, vol. 6.]

49 H. U. von Balthasar, 'Le Mysterion d'Origène', *Recherches de Science religieuse*, 1936, pp. 523–5, 545–53, and 1937, p. 53. cf. Gaudentius of Brescia, *Tractatus* 2 (Glueck, pp. 24–32). Cassiodore, *In psalmum* 148 (PL, 70, 1039 C–D).

50 cf. *De solemnitate paschali*, n. 2 and n. 7 (PG 24, 696 B, 701 A–B).

ment' in relation to the second, which is none other than the Church.[51] Recently, following on from Lattey,[52] Father Tromp, whose learned patristic studies on the Church as body of Christ are well known, has tried to take it still further. From the thirteenth century, which he considers too conservative a date, he takes us in a giant leap back to the ninth century through a simple reference to two texts, one by Ratramnus, the other by St. Paschasius Radbertus.[53] Literally speaking, this assertion is entirely correct. In the two passages indicated by Fr. Tromp, we do indeed meet the expression *mystical body*. But in these two passages, as in several other texts of the same period, this expression cannot yet be understood to refer to the Church. As will be seen further on, it must be understood as referring to the Eucharist.

But Fr. Tromp is nevertheless on the right track. Research must certainly concentrate on those Latin authors of the high Middle Ages, who write about the Eucharist, although there will inevitably be a need to go on to a later period and also to cast an eye eastward. Because it is from its acceptance as a Eucharistic term, and in the unfolding of doctrines concerning the relationship between the Eucharist and the Church, that *mystical body*, thanks to an inversion that only came about by degrees, came to have the general meaning that it assumed after the mid-twelfth century and has preserved to this day.[54]

This is the fact retraced in the five chapters of the first division. The five chapters of the second division endeavour to account for it.

---

51 See *infra*, ch. v.
52 'The Church', *Papers from the Summer School of Catholic Studies* (1928), p. 7.
53 *op. cit.* (1937), p. 94.
54 Gregory the Great (PL, 75, 621).

FIRST PART

I

The Eucharist as Mystical Body

In the thinking of the whole of Christian antiquity, the Eucharist and the Church are linked. In St. Augustine, in the context of the Donatist controversy, this link is given especially particular force, and this can also be said of the Latin writers of the seventh century, eighth century and ninth century. For them, as for Augustine, on whom they are dependent either directly or through other writers, and whose formulations they endlessly reproduce, the Eucharist corresponds to the Church as cause to effect, as means to end, as sign to reality. However, they make the transition from the *sacrament* to the *power of the sacrament* or from *visible form* to the *reality itself* so swiftly,[1] and place the accent so strongly on the Church that if, in an explanation of the mystery of the Eucharist, we encounter the unqualified phrase 'the body of Christ', it is often not the Eucharist but the Church which is meant by the term.[2]

Here, for example, is St. Ildephonsus of Toledo († 669). In chapter 137 of his *De cognitione baptismi*, he sets out to comment on the affirmation of faith, '*bread is the body of Christ*'. Seeking understanding, faith enquires: '*How is bread his body?*' Ildephonsus then replies:

> *What is seen has bodily form; what is perceived mentally has spiritual fruit. Therefore if you want to grasp mentally the body of Christ, listen to the Apostle saying to the faithful, You are the body and members of Christ . . . Though many, we are one bread, one body.*[3]

---

1 Alcuin (PL, 100, 834 A). Leidrad (99, 867 B). Hetton (105, 763 B). Rabanus Maurus (107, 317–18; 112, 89 A). Florus (119, 78 A). Ratramnus (121, 150 A, 161). Adrevald of Fleury (124, 950 C), etc. cf. Bede, *In Joannem*: 'But what pertains to the power of the sacrament, not what pertains to the visible sacrament' (92, 717 D).

2 Bede, *In Leviticum* (PL, 91, 334 A). Rabanus Maurus, *De clericorum institutione* (107, 318 B); *In evangelica*, hom. 64 (110, 269–270). Walafrid Strabo, *De rebus ecclesiasticis*, c. 16 (114, 936 C). Also St. Thomas, *In Joannem*, c. 6, l. 6, n. 7.

3 PL, 96, 169 D. cf. Florus, *Expositio missae*, c. 62, n. 5 (Duc, p. 135). Hincmar of Reims, *De cavendis vitiis* (PL, 125, 919 A).

Not that Ildephonsus, or the writer from whom he takes his inspiration[4] and who is himself repeating an Augustinian formulation,[5] is thinking of denying the sacramental presence from which this 'spiritual fruit' will be the result, any more than by 'understanding' he is eliminating the need for faith. As much as Augustine himself, and as much as his nearer master, St. Isidore of Seville,[6] as well as his compatriot Gregory of Elvira,[7] he knows that in order to remain in this body of Christ, which is the holy Church, we must achieve true participation, through the sacrament, in the first body of Christ.[8] But no more than they does Augustine remain so fixated on the Eucharistic presence as to formulate an independent concept of it.[9] 'He discovers real union with Christ, not so much through the medium of the real presence, but through the medium of the sign, and this union is not so much individual union as that of individuals among one another in Christ.'[10] By a mental process which faithfully reproduces that of the great African doctor,[11] and which finds analogies with more than one of the Greek

---

4 It would appear that *De cognitione baptismi* is an adaptation of the *Liber responsionum* (now lost) of Justinian of Valence (c. 640). Séjourné, *Saint Isidore of Seville*, pp. 372–3.

5 Augustine, *Sermo 272* (PL, 38, 1247).

6 *De ecclesiasticis officiis*, Bk. 1, c. 18, no. 8: 'He ought not to separate himself from the medicine of the Lord's body, lest . . . he be separated from the body of Christ. . . . For it is manifest that they live who taste his body' (PL, 83,756B). These are formulations that derive from St. Cyprian, *De oratione dominica*, c. 18 (Hartel, pp. 280–1). Peter Chrysologus (PL, 52, 297 B). Etherius and Beatus, *Ad Elipandum* (96, 942 A–B). Jonas of Orléans, *De institutione laïcali*, 2, c. 18 (106, 203 B). Rudolph of Bourges, *Capitulum 28* (119, 717 D). Adrevald of Fleury (124, 953–4). Burchard of Worms (140, 756 B and 757 C), etc.

7 *Tractatus 17* (Batiffol-Wilmart, pp. 187–8).

8 *op. cit.*, c. 136 (PL, 96, 168–9). Augustine, *In psalmum 39*, n. 12 (36, 441–2); *Sermo 351*, n. 7 (38, 1542); *Contra duas epistulas Pelagianorum*, 1. 2, c. 4, n. 7 (44, 576).

9 For St. Augustine, see Karl Adam in *Theologische Quartalschrift*, 1931, pp. 490–536. The remark made by Bernold of Constance in *De sacramentis excommunicatorum* about the Fathers is still, generally speaking, valid for the first centuries of the Middle Ages (although the word 'sacramentum' is ambiguous, since Bernold understood by it the reality of the sacrament, the objective and substantial presence of Christ): 'Even though some of the early fathers paid little attention to a distinction of this kind between the sacrament and its effects . . .' (PL, 148, 1064 C–D).

10 F. van der Meer, *Sacramentum chez Saint Augustin*, in *La Maison-Dieu*, 13, p. 61.

11 Augustine, *In Joannem*, tract. 26, n. 11, 12 (PL, 35, 1611, 1612) *Ep. 185, ad Bonifacium*, n. 50 (33, 815). *Ep. 187* (33, 839). *De Civitate Dei*, 21, c. 25 (41, 741–2). *Sermones 57, 131, 234* (38, 839, 730, 1116). [For the works of St. Augustine in English, see NPNF series I, vols. I–VIII and *The Fathers of the Church* series, vols. 2, 3, 8, 14, 15 16, 24, 27, 30, 32, 25, 38, 45, 59, 60, 70, 78, 79, 81,

fathers,[12] Ildephonsus is therefore immediately looking to the 'spiritual fruit'. It is this alone which he is envisaging and analysing.

His contemporaries and his first successors most often follow him in this. In the following century Florus of Lyons is one example. He was a faithful Augustinian, very much on his guard against anything that could pass for an innovation. In his commentary on the Mass he took up again the formulation already given by Ildephonsus: '*What is seen is one thing, and what is grasped is another; what is seen, etc . . .*'.[13] He repeats it again in one of his tracts against Amalarius,[14] and in order to describe 'the saving and heavenly mystery' of the altar, he writes: '*Moreover the bread of the holy offering is the body of Christ not in matter or visible form but in power and spiritual potency.*'[15] Neither for him nor for any of the authors of that time who speak in the same way, was the real presence of the Eucharist truly in question. They are certainly neither 'dynamists' nor 'symbolists' in the explicitly restrictive sense that is commonly given to those words by historians of dogma. How could they forget the claims made so clearly by their great forebears, claims that they could not avoid quoting in their *florilegia* or making reference to,[16] either in prose or in verse? Above all, how could they contradict this *lex orandi*, which was finding such powerful expression in that era of the flowering of liturgy in the West?[17]

Come, you saints, and receive the body of Christ,
Drinking the sacred blood by which you are redeemed.[18]

86, 88, 90, 92.] Gregory the Great, *In I Regum*, 2, c. I (79, 83 C). [For the works of St. Gregory in English, see O. J. Zimmerman, *The Fathers of the Church* series, vol. 39 (Washington, 1959); J. Barmby, NPNF, vols. XII, XIII.]

12 cf. Irenaeus, *Adversus Haereses*, 3, 24, 1: 'In her (the Church) is made available communion with Christ, that is, with the Holy Spirit' (PG, 7, 966 B). Similarly, in Maximus the Confessor, 'the whole emphasis rests on the effect of the Eucharist, which seems to give the essential definition'. H. U. von Balthasar, *Liturgie cosmique*, p. 248. Or St. Ambrose, *De mysteriis*, c. 2, n. 6, on the sacraments in general (PL, 16, 391 A).

13 *Expositio missae*, c. 62, n. 5 (Duc, p. 135). cf. Hincmar of Rheims, *De cavendis vitiis* (PL, 125, 919 A).

14 *Adversus Amalarium* 2 (PL, 119, 83 D).

15 *Adversus Amalarium* 1 (PL, 119, 77 C–D).

16 Braulio of Saragossa, *Ep.* 42 (PL, 80, 690, A). Hesychius of Jerusalem, *In Leviticum* (PG 93, 1071 A, 1072 C). *Expositio* (PL, 147, 200 A). *Libri Carolini*, 2, c. 27 (PL, 98, 1095 B); I, c. 19 (c. 1047 D). Haimon (?), *In Hebr.* (117, 879 C–D). Pseudo-Bede, *In psalmum* 77 (PL, 93, 899, A–B).

17 E. Janot, 'L'Eucharistie dans les Sacramentaires occidentaux', *Recherches de Science religieuse* (1927).

18 Antiphonary of Bangor (seventh century).

Many of them were taught through a prayer from the Gregorian
sacramentary to pray 'so that they may be counted members of the one
whose body and blood we share'.[19] Like Jonas of Orleans, they also
knew how to say: '*We are the Temples of Christ, where his flesh and
blood are sacrificed*',[20] or even sometimes to repeat after Amalarius:
'*Here we believe that the simple nature of bread and mingled wine
are changed into a rational nature, namely, of the body and blood
of Christ.*'[21] None of them would have been surprised at the verses
which St. Remigius, according to his historiographer Hincmar, had
had engraved on a chalice:

> *Let the people draw from the sacred blood they receive*
> *The life which the eternal Christ poured from his wound.*[22]

From time to time they also went so far as to distinguish explicitly
between two sorts of participation in Christ.[23] The unity of the body
that they all received in communion appeared to them as the sign and
promise of the unity of the body, which they themselves must form.[24]
Nevertheless, this was not yet the era of logic-chopping, of objective
curiosity, nor even, at least among the first of them, of the necessary
struggles to ensure that the conditions for the efficacy of the sacrament
were met. For them the consecrated bread was certainly the body of
Christ – the expressions *sacramentum corporis* and *corpus* alternated
from their pens without any appreciable nuance to their sense – but
what they saw from the very beginning in this bread was a figure of
the Church:

> *Therefore he took the bread: he wanted this sacrament to involve*
> *bread since bread bears a likeness to his Church . . .*[25]

---

19 Lietzmann, n. 58, 3, p. 36; Wilson, p. 18. cf. Augustine, *In psalmum 33*,
n. 10, 25 (PL, 36, 313, 321).

20 *De institutione regia*, c. 13; c. 16 (Reviron, pp. 180, 191). cf. Godescalc, *De
praedestinatione* (Lambot, p. 195).

21 *Liber officialis*, 4, c. 24 (PL, 105, 1141 A–B).

22 Hincmar, *Vita Remigii* (MGH, *Scriptorum rerum merovingicarum*, vol. 3,
p. 262).

23 Pseudo-Primasius, *In Hebr.* (PL, 68, 708 B). Haimon, *In Hebr.* (117, 845 A,
cf. 839 A). Remigius of Auxerre, *In psalmos 21, 33* (131, 259, C–D, 314 D).

24 Feltoe, *Journal of Theological Studies* 11, p. 578.

25 Candidus of Fulda, *De passione Domini*, c. 5 (PL, 106, 68 C).

Thus the *bread of the sacrament* led them directly to the *unity of the body*.[26] In their eyes the Eucharist was essentially, as it was already for St. Paul and for the Fathers, the *mystery of unity*,[27] it was the *sacrament of conjunction, alliance, and unification*.[28] It was given to us '*to unite our race*'.[29] Was this not the truth inculcated in us by several of its rites and by the terms which described them, such as the word 'collect', to which Amalarius alerts us as having been given to the first prayer of the Mass, '*because it begins by binding the people into one*'?[30]

* * *

Is this not what is clearly signified by its other name of 'communion'? The *synaxis*, that is to say the mystery of communion.[31] So, at least, it is understood by the commentator of Auxerre writing on the First Letter to the Corinthians:[32]

---

26 Bede, *In Lucam*, 6 (PL, 92, 628, B) after Augustine, *De consensu evangelistarum*, 3, c. 25, n. 72 (34, 1206). Amalarius, *De ecclesiasticis officiis* (*Liber officialis*), 3, c. 34, (105, 1153 D).

27 Ildephonsus (PL, 96, 170 B). Haimon, *Homilia* 62 (118, 350 A). Remigius of Auxerre, *Expositio missae* (c. 40 of *Liber de divinis officiis* compiled under the name Alcuin; PL, 101 m 1260 C and D). cf. Hilary, *De Trinitate*, 3, c. 24 (10, 246 B); Augustine, *Ep. 185* n. 50 (33, 815). [For St. Hilary's *De Trinitate* in English, see S. McKenna, *Fathers of the Church* series, vol. 25 (Washington, 1954). For a further translation of this and other works, see E. W. Watson, L. Pullan, NPNF series II, vol. 9.]

28 Etherius and Beatus, *Ad Elipandum* (in 785) (PL, 96, 941 D). Amalarius (105, 1131 B). Rabanus Maurus, *De clericorum institutione* (107, 320 B); *In Numeros*, 3 (108, 744 B). Hincmar, *De cavendis vitiis*, c. 10 (125, 924 B, 925 A). Up to and including the thirteenth century, such expressions would be common; it is because it was *the sacrament of unity, the sacrament of fellowship* that, in the eyes of a certain number of theologians, schismatics could not have the Eucharist, since they had placed themselves outside that unity, outside that fellowship. See the texts quoted by Landgraf in *Scholastik*, 1940, pp. 210 and 211. cf. *infra*, conclusion.

29 Paschasius Radbertus, *Liber de corpore et sanguine Domini*, c. 10 (PL, 120, 1305 C).

30 Amalarius, *Eclogae de officio missae* (PL, 105, 1327 D). Remigius of Auxerre (101, 1249 D).

31 St. Maximus, *Scholia in Eccl. Hierarchiam*, c. 1–2 (PG, 66, 117 B). cf. Clement of Alexandria, *Strom.*, 3, c. 4 (Staehlin, vol. 2, pp. 208–9).

32 This commentary, along with several others, was mistakenly attributed, through a confusion of names, to Rabanus Maurus's friend Haymon, bishop of Halberstadt. Might it perhaps have been written by Haimon, a monk of Saint-Germain d'Auxerre towards the middle of the ninth century, or by his disciple and friend Remigius, 'the author *par excellence* and in some ways the popularizer of the theology of Auxerre' (Cappuyns)? See Cappuyns, in *Recherches de théologie ancienne et médiévale*, 1931, pp. 263–5, and Wilmart, in the same journal, 1936, pp. 325–30. M. E. Amann writes: 'It would seem that, out of charity, the writings of different authors were published in common at Saint-Germain' (*L'Eglise au pouvoir des laïques*, p. 505, n. 4).

Therefore the sacrament of the body of Christ is called supper because of the communion, since it ought to be celebrated in common by all the faithful and righteous. For the one bread signifies the wholeness of the Church.[33]

I could certainly also cite more than one case, in Christian antiquity, where *communio* – together with the Greek κοινώνια – implies no other idea except that of the reception of the sacrament.[34] We can nevertheless be sure that, as Duguet has written,[35] 'in the ancient custom of the Church there was no separation between reconciliation and participation in the sacraments, and when penitents were judged to have been made righteous, they were given the Eucharist, in such a way that communion signified both one and the other', that is to say, according to the context, either one or the other, or more often still, both at the same time. From this derives the complex sense encountered in many expressions such as '*to receive communion*', '*to be reconciled by communion*', '*to be separated from communion*', '*to be excluded from communion*', etc.[36] In their turn this is also the origin of discussions by several historians who, in varying degrees of over-enthusiasm, find differences of interpretation where the original documents present them as a unity. In addition, even in the context of the Eucharist, it is not unusual to find *communio* meaning union with the Church, the '*fellowship of Christians*' or the '*catholic communion*'[37] rather

---

33 *In I Cor*, XI (PL, 117, 570, 571). Remigius of Auxerre (101, 1259 A–B). Rabanus Maurus, *Liber de sacris ordinibus*, c. 19 (112, 1184 C). Also the *Roman Catechism*, 2, *De eucharistiae sacramento*, n. 5.

34 For example, Jerome, *Ep.* 49, n. 15 (Hilberg, vol. 1, p. 377); 77, n. 6 (vol. 2, p. 42). Cassian, *Collatio* 23, (PL, 49, 1279). [For the works of St. Cassian in English, see E. C. S. Gibson, NPNF, series II, vol. Gregory of Tours, *Vitae Patrum*, c. 17, n. 2 (71, 1080 A).] Council of Braga in 675, canon I (Mansi, vol. 11, 154). [For English translations of the major conciliar acts of the early councils, see Percival, NPNF, Series II, vol. 14; C. J. Hefele, *A History of the Christian Councils*, trans. W. R. Clark (Edinburgh 1871–96).] *Vita Alcuini* (Mabillon, *Praefationes et Dissertationes*, 1724, p. 697). Fortescue, The Mass, second edition (1937), p. 398; I Cor., 10.16; Acts of the Council in Trullo II. 42 (Mansi, vol. 11, 953, 983–7). Anastasius of Sinai (PG, 89, 208 D, 765 B).

35 *Conférences ecclésiastiques*, vol. 1 (Cologne, 1742), p. 287.

36 The Council of Elvira (v.300) *passim* (Héfélé-Leclercq, vol. 1, pp. 221–63). Council of Carthage (348), canon 3, etc. cf. Dom Ceillier, vol. 2, pp. 581, 603–8. On the broad sense of the word 'excommunicated' and similar words in Christian antiquity, as also on the difference between sinners and those correctly called excommunicated, see François Russo, *Penitence et excommunication (Recherches de Science religieuse*, 1946, p. 261). cf. Paul Hinschius, *System der Katholischen Kirchvaters*, vol. 4, pp. 701–3.

37 Possidius, *Vita sancti Augustini*, c. 14 (PL, 32, 45). [English in M. O'Connell, *Life of Saint Augustine* (Villanova, PA, 1988).]

than the actual receiving of the sacrament.[38] When there is a desire to distinguish reception from the effect which it is the sacrament's mission to express and bring about, there is often recourse to certain subtle nuances of language. For example, instead of *communio*, we often find instead *communicatio*: thus in the work of Walafrid Strabo, the first of these two words indicates the bond within the body of the Church, whereas the second is reserved for the act of sacramental communion.[39] Does not the derivation of both these nouns, from the single verb *communicare*, underline in its own way the central truth of this mystery?

This same truth is equally evident from another distinction, which was already conventional by about the ninth century, above all in the customary language of the precepts of Church councils. For particularly in their penitential legislation, they rarely used *communio* without an attribute, in a complex and integral sense. To go into detail, their custom was to list two sorts of communion to which a penitent could be readmitted in two successive stages:[40] first of all there was simple communion, which comprised only communion in prayer or at most communion in the offerings, which entailed admission to the ceremonies of the Church, then, subsequently, full or perfect communion, which in addition consisted of full sacramental reception of the body of Christ: the *sharing in the mysteries*,[41] or *sharing in the bread*.[42] This second form found an effective sign at the same time as it acquired a profound reality in this full participation of the reconciled penitent in the holy mysteries.[43] It was, according to the double formula of Pope Gregory III,

---

38 cf. Dom Claude de Vert, *Dissertation sur les mots de messe et de communion* (1694), p. 159: 'How many councils equate the Mass and communion together in one same canon, and equate them with the day of Sunday, without it being possible, for all that, to understand this communion in a sacramental sense.' The thesis of the erudite Benedictine, who had an excessively systematic mind, is nevertheless somewhat exaggerated.

39 *De rebus ecclesiasticis*, c. 22 (PL, 114, 950 C, 948 D). William of Auvergne, *De sacramento ordinis*, c. 11, 12 (*Opera omnia*, vol. 1. pp. 545–8). *Liber Pancrisis* (Lottin, *Bulletin de théologie ancienne et médiévale*, vol. 3, p. 526).

40 I am clearly only retaining the distinction which is of interest for the present subject within this frequently complicated legislation, certain of whose expressions remain obscure.

41 Ambrose, *In Lucam*, 7, n. 232 (PL, 15, 1761 C).

42 Fulgentius, *Ep. 12*, n. 26 (PL, 65, 392 C–D).

43 A ninth-century text, mistakenly attributed to a Council of Nantes in 658, would rule as follows on the case of manslaughter: 'He is to be excluded from the prayer of the faithful for two years, and is neither to communicate nor take part in the offering; after two years he is to take part in the offering of prayer, but without communicating; after five years he is to be received back into full communion'

'*communion in the offering*' and '*communion in the Eucharist*'.[44] The terms '*holy communion*' or '*sacred communion*' were still sometimes used for the first form;[45] and, for the second: '*lawful communion*',[46] '*the Lord's communion*',[47] '*communion of the altar*', '*communion of the Lord's sacraments*',[48] '*communion of the most holy mystery . . .*'.[49]

The same united duality or, if preferred, the same organic unity is found in the famous expression in the Symbol (or Creed) of the Apostles, 'the communion of saints', notably as presented in a sermon of the Carolingian era, entitled *Symbolum graeca lingua*:

> *The communion of saints. This is holy communion through the invocation of the Father and the Son and the Holy Spirit, at which all the faithful should communicate every Sunday.*[50]

The first testimony to this article that has come down to us dates from the fifth century. It can be found in the *Explanation of the Symbol*, attributed to Nicetas of Remesiana. *Of the Saints* is in the masculine, and covers not only all the just who lived '*from the beginning of the world*', but also the angels and celestial powers, all united within the same Church.[51] This is the antithesis of the '*communion of the impious*' mentioned by the apostolic constitutions.[52] But whatever is meant by the original sense of the expression,[53] the sense given to it by our Carolingian sermon represents neither an innovation nor an isolated instance. If there is any case where the theory of synthesis pro-

---

(canon 18; cf. canon 17, on manslaughter; Hardouin, 6, 1, 641). Paulinus, *Vita Ambrosii*, n. 31 (PL, 14, 37 D).

44 Mansi, vol. 12, 29 A.

45 Felix III (fifth century). Hormisdas (sixth century).

46 Council of Orange (441), canon 3 (Mansi, vol. 4. 437).

47 Gregory III (Mansi, vol. 12. 294 E). Council of Elvira, canon 78 (Héfélé-Leclercq, vol. 1, p. 262). Augustine, *Ep. 228, ad Honoratum*, n. 8 (PL, 33, 1017).

48 Council of Vannes (465) (Hardouin, vol. 2. 797). Augustine, *Ep. 149*, n. 3 (PL, 33, 631).

49 Felix III (fifth century). The more general attributes 'sacred' and 'holy' also sometimes qualify sacramental communion; but sometimes, as with Gregory II, there is stronger emphasis elsewhere: 'To become unworthy of the holy communion of the body and blood' (Mansi, vol. 12. 259 D).

50 Ed. Burn, *Zeitschrift fur Kirchengeschichte*, vol. 21, p. 129.

51 Caspari, *Kirchenhistorischen Anekdota*, vol. 1, pp. 355–7; PL, 52, 871 A–B: *Explanatio Symboli*, n. 10.

52 Bk. 8, c. 15, n. 3 (Funk, p. 518).

53 cf. Dom Morin, *Revue d'histoire et de literature religieuses* (1904), p. 216; F. J. Badcock, 'Sanctorum communion as an article in the Creed', *Journal of Theological Studies* 21. cf. Rom. XII, 13, old Vulgate.

posed by Kattensbusch[54] is best proved, it would seem to be this one. Here we have the *communion of saints*, simultaneously and indivisibly described as *communion of the sacraments* and *the society or fellowship of the blessed*, that is to say, it is the communion of saints in its current sense, or communion with the saints or among the saints – *one fellowship in communion*[55] – in the common sharing in the sacrament, in the *holy things* (= *holy mysteries*) and through the effect of this participation.[56] It is, as St. Augustine said, the *fellowship of the sacraments*.[57] Union with the Church began with admission to the common prayer, the *community of prayer*: admission to the sacred banquet, the *communion of saints*, brought it to completion. In the latter we truly have, according to the ancient expression of the Council of Ancyra, the fulfilment (τὸ τέλειον).[58] So also the venerable formula of our Creed helps us to see more clearly how the word *communion* has, fundamentally, only one sense. For, in the same way that sacramental communion (*communion in the body and the blood*) is always at the same time an ecclesial communion (*communion within the Church, of the Church, for the Church . . .*), so also ecclesial communion always includes, in its fulfilment, sacramental communion. Being in communion with someone means to receive the body of the Lord with them.[59] Being united with the saints in the Church and participating in the Eucharist, being part of the common Kingdom, and sharing in the holy mysteries go together in tandem[60] and it can be said that they are one and the same thing. It is what will later be succinctly expressed in the formulation: *Christian communion*.[61]

It is therefore clear that through the unique bread of the sacrifice,

---

54 *Das apostolische Symbol* (2 vols., 1894, 1900) vol. 2, pp. 927–50.

55 Optatus, *De schismate donatistarum*, I. 2, c. 3 (PL, II, 949 A). [For Optatus's work against the Donatists in English, see M. J. Edwards, *Optatus, Against the Donatists* (Liverpool, 1997).] Paulinus, *Vita Ambrosii*, n. 19 (14, 33 C).

56 Paulinus, *Vita Ambrosii*, n. 24, (PL, 14, 35 C). Augustine, *Contra Cresconium grammaticum*, 2, c. 36, n. 45; 4, c. 1 (PL, 43, 439, 547). St. Leo, *Sermo* 42, c. 5 (54, 280). C. Callewaert, *Sacris Erudiri*, p. 283, and *supra*, note 23.

57 *In psalmum* 67, n. 39 (PL, 36, 837); *Ep*. 93, c. 9, n. 28 (33, 335); *Quaestiones evangeliorum*, 2, c. 40 (35, 1356). cf. Cyril of Alexandria (PG, 68, 417 A). Genade, *Liber ecclesisticorum dogmatum* (PL, 58, 994). Florus, *Liber adversus Joannem Scotum*, c. 13 (161, 181 A). Alan of Lille, *Contra haereticos*, 1, c. 59 (210, 363 B–C).

58 Canons 4, 5, 6, 8, 9, 22 (Mansi, vol. 2. 515–20). [E.T. Percival, NPNF XIV.]

59 John of Ephesus, *HE*, (*Scr. Syri*, ser. 3, vol. 3, p. 51).

60 *Apostolic Constitutions*, 8, c. 6, n. 13 and c. 8, n. 2 (Funk, pp. 480, 484).

61 *Concilium Gerund.*, 1101 (Mansi, vol. 20, 1134 E). cf. the letter of Emperor Henry to the king of France, Louis, in 1106 (1204 B).

every one of the faithful who is in communion with the body of Christ is also by that same fact in communion with the Church.[62] By receiving the Eucharist, each one 'passes into the body of Christ',[63] each one participates in the body of Christ, that is always to say, in the Church:

> *For just as by receiving of the one bread and the one cup we share and participate in the Lord's body . . .*[64]

But let there be no mistake: this '*Lord's body*' that Rabanus Maurus is referring to here is not, or at least does not mean either exclusively or even principally what we would call the sacramental body. It is already the ecclesial body, which also includes the sense of the sacramental body. If the '*one bread*', an expression borrowed from St. Paul, were not already a sufficiently clear warning, if the following formulation: 'companions *in the body of Christ*' did not confirm it for us,[65] we would nevertheless receive any necessary assurance from the parallel and more explicit formulation which again comes from St. Augustine,[66] and which Amalarius borrows from him through the mediation of Bede:[67]

> *Let no one think that he has recognized Christ, if he does not share in his body, that is, the Church.*[68]

'*Communicating*', '*to sharing*', '*being participants and companions*': I repeat yet again, the complexity of the sense of these expressions is in exact accordance with the complexity of the sense of the word '*body*'.

---

62 Origen, *In psalmum* 37, v. 6 (PG, 12, 1386 D). Dionysius of Alexandria, in Eusebius, *HE*, 7, c. 9, n. 5. [For Eusebius's history in English and Greek, see K. Lake, J. E. L Oulton, *Loeb Classical Library*, vols. 153, 265 (London, 2001, 2000). For the English alone, alongside further significant works of Eusebius, see A. Cushman, NPNF, series II, vol. 1.]

63 Theodulphus of Orléans, *Liber de ordine baptismi*, c. 18 (PL, 105, 239–40). cf. Augustine, *Quaest. evang.*, 2, c. 39 (35, 1353).

64 Rabanus Maurus, *In I Cor.* (PL, 112, 94 A).

65 *ibid.* (94 C, and following 94 D). cf. Augustine, *Contra Adimantum manichaeum*, c. 14, n. 3 (42, 152). Remigius of Auxerre, *De celebratione missae* (101, 1262–3). Gallican sacramentary (72, 498 A); *Missale Francorum* (72, 336 C). Nicholas I, *Ep.* 26, (119, 810 C). I Cor. 10. Augustine, *Contra adversarium legis et prophetarum*, 1, n. 38 (42, 625–6).

66 *De consensus evangelistarum*, 3, n. 72 (PL, 34, 1206). cf. Tertullian, *De oratione*, c. 6 (Reiffersched-Wissowa, p. 185).

67 PL, 92, 628 B; 105, 1153 D.

68 The text is cited by Peter Lombard (192, 858). cf. Lombard, *In I Cor.*, X (191, 1624–5).

Fundamentally, they are not so much used to describe two successive objects as two simultaneous things that make one whole. For the body of Christ that is the Church is in no way *other* than the body and the blood of the mystery. And properly speaking, this is not a piece of word-play.[69] Through the Eucharist each person is truly placed within the one body. It unites all the members of it among themselves, as it unites them to their one head. This is what is explained, at the beginning of the ninth century, in the *Expositio missae 'Primum in ordine'*, the most ancient of these anonymous 'explanations', written in the tradition of Isidore of Seville:

> 'So that it may become for us the body and blood of the beloved Son': that is, so that we may be made his body, and that in the mystery of divine grace he may give to us from God the bread which came down from heaven.[70]

In this way, little by little, the *'whole Christ'*[71] comes into being, who is always in our minds as the ultimate end of the mystery. So much so that, in this perspective of totality and of unity, there is virtually no need to search for formulations or expressions to distinguish one 'body' from the other.[72]

*   *   *

From one point of view, it would be possible, in this unique and complete *Body of Christ*, to make a firm distinction between its several aspects; but on the other hand one could also argue exclusively, or at least more vigorously, in favour of its unity. To give one example, this was the basis of the duel, in the first half of the ninth century, between Amalarius of Metz and Florus of Lyon. Several years later, with regard to another type of distinction, which will concern us further on, a long and somewhat confused discussion was raised around the treatise of St. Paschasius Radbertus. But the *body par excellence*, the one that

---

69 cf. M. Comeau, *Les prédications pascales de saint Augustin (Recherches de Science religieuse*, 1933, p. 268): 'It is thus in playing on the word body, understood successively in different senses, that Augustine constructs his sermon.' On '*communicare*' in Christian antiquity, see H. Pétré, *'Caritas', etude sur le vocabulaire latin de la charité chrétienne*, pp. 267–9.

70 PL, 138, 1180 D.

71 Etherius and Beatus (PL, 96, 938 D).

72 The continuity from one sense to another is again expressed in the text from *De Civitate Dei*, 10, c. 19 (PL, 41, 298) that Florus quotes, *Expositio Missae*, c. 57, n. 4 (Duc, p. 130).

always comes first to mind,[73] the one that needs no other designation, is the Church. Despite disagreements, which were often distinguished more for their liveliness of expression than for their depth of content, the mysterious continuity linking the incarnation to the Church was strongly felt by all, even if it has to be admitted that it was not always clearly analysed. Is the Church not the continuation of Christ? *Christ is transferred to the Church*: these simple words are pregnant with significance. And the passing of Christ into his Church was itself prepared, or even prefigured by an earlier passing, that of the Church into Christ: is the Church not in fact the greater body from which Christ drew his body? This last point strikes the monk of Fulda, Candidus, as essential:

> '*Take and eat.' That is, Gentiles, make up my body, which you already are. This is the body which is given for you. What he took from that mass of the human race, he broke by his passion, and raised up after breaking. . . Therefore what he took from us he handed over for us. You are to 'eat', that is, perfect the body of the Church, so that, whole and perfect, she may become the one bread, with Christ as its head . . . Bread, therefore, is the body of Christ, which he took from the body, his Church . . .*'[74]

Although, from a certain point of view, the Church could be one among the three bodies normally distinguished from one another, in fact in reality it is not 'another body' in relation to the first two. Understood in this sense, it is simply '*the other body*',[75] '*the rest of the body*',[76] that is to say, in contrast to the head. Since if it is envisaged in its totality, that is to say, with its head, it is itself the body that, in the last analysis, contains within itself all the bodies that can be said to be of Christ. '*The bread is one because of the unity of the body of Christ*', was the expression of Amalarius himself, who was the

---

73 As M. H. Peltier observed in *Pascase Radbert, abbé de Corbie* (1938), pp. 215–16, this can even be verified in Paschasius Radbertus. cf. the prayer of consecration of the newly-ordained priest (PL,73, 221).

74 *De passione Domini*, c. 5 (PL, 106, 68–9) and c. 6 (71 B). Etherius and Beatus (96, 938 A). Rabanus Maurus, *In I Cor.*, X (112, 94 D). Ivo of Chartres (161, 135 A–B). Gratian, *De consecratione*, 2, c. 36 (Freidberg, 1326).

75 Augustine, *Sermo 361*, n. 3 (PL, 39, 1600).

76 Jerome, *In psalmum 7*, (Morin, *Anecdota Maredsolana*, vol 3, p. 2, p. 24). Joannes monachus (PL, 166, 1514 C). Helinandus (212, 522 D). cf. Origen, *In Ephes.*, I, 23 (*Journal of Theological Studies*, vol III, p. 401). Hesychius, *In psalmum 39*, (PG, 93, 1191–2 D).

author of the theory of the *threefold body*,[77] which was so bitterly contested from the outset, yet nevertheless proved so tenacious. For his
part, when Florus reproached him in terms of utmost vehemence with
having ruined the unity of the body of Christ with this theory, he did
not only mean by this the sacrament only, nor even the connection
between the sacrament and the personal body of Jesus. He meant the
ruin of the unity of the Church. Amalarius, in the words of Florus, was
'*the greatest enemy of the unity of the Church*'. Opposing him meant
working to safeguard that unity proclaimed by the apostle and for
which the Saviour died:

> *Indeed no one should ever call the body of Christ triple or three-*
> *fold, since the Apostle always calls it one and unique, when he says:*
> *'Though many, we are one bread, one body', etc. Indeed since it has*
> *Christ as its one head the body of all the elect is one. . . . How could*
> *one divide one heavenly bread into three? We are all . . . one bread in*
> *Christ, incorporated and united in Christ. This unity of the Church,*
> *that is, of his body, the Lord Jesus. . . indicated, when he said:*
> *'I have other sheep, etc.' It was for this unification and unity of his*
> *body that he underwent death. . . This is the ineffably miraculous*
> *union between the Lord Jesus and his body. . . which no one may*
> *violate or divide. . . He does his best to separate and scatter it when*
> *he divides it into three parts, three forms, and three bodies.*[78]

And a little further on, in the course of the same diatribe, after recalling that in the mystery it is Christ himself, in his body and in his flesh
who is received, Florus calls to witness, in favour of his principal assertion, the words of St. Cyprian in his *De Ecclesiae unitate*: '*the mystery*
of Christ, that is, of his body, ought not to be divided'; then he calls
upon his usual mentor St. Augustine to establish to the same end that
'the entire universal Church is but one single sacrifice to God and one
single body of Christ'.[79]

---

77 *Eclogae de officio missae* (PL, 105, 1328 C); *De ecclesiasticis officiis* (1154–
5). Here we have an explanation of the unity of the Eucharistic body derived
from the unity of the Church, parallel to the explanation (possibly from Erigena),
derived from the unity of the Word, such as the one we find, for example, in *In*
I Cor. (PL, 117, 564 C), *In Hebr.* (117, 889 B–C), Gezonius of Tortona (137, 406
B–C), Hériger of Lobbes (139, 187 A–B), etc. cf. Gratian and Peter Lombard (192,
863). Rupert unites these two explanations (see *infra*, ch. iv). Amalarius, *Eclogue*
(1316 C, 1318 A).

78 *Adversus Amalarium*, I, n. 7 (PL, 119, 76–7) and II, n. 7 (85–7). *Discours au*
Concile de Kierzy (MGH, Concilia, vol. II, p. 772). cf. I, n. 3 (74 A) and *Expositio*
missae, c. 45 (Duc, pp. 122, 123).

79 MGH, *Concilia*, vol. 2, pp. 773–5.

Dicta cujusdam sapientis de corpore et sanguine domini adversus Radbertum is a document once thought to have been a letter by Rabanus Maurus, but Dom Morin and Dom Cappuyns have successfully proved it to have been written by Godescalc of Orbais,[80] and we must thank Dom Lambot for his recent critical edition of it.[81] In it the author expresses astonishment at the confidence with which Paschasius Radbertus quotes texts from Ambrose and 'Augustine', one after the other, without apparently realising that, at least on first reading, they contradict one another. Indeed the first of these two Fathers identifies the body born of the Virgin with the sacramental body, while the second distinguishes between the two.[82] Godescalc sets himself the task of finding a formulation that reconciles the two opinions. From the outset, and several times further on, he affirms that in the Eucharist we have the true body and true blood of the Lord;[83] but he then asks if we are not nevertheless in some sense obliged to distinguish with Saint Augustine between the three bodies of Christ? For one is the body born of the Virgin and ascended into heaven, another is the body created and consecrated anew each day, and finally another is the body that we ourselves are, and that receives the sacrament . . .[84] Only just as Paschasius, by affirming the unity, was not therefore failing to distinguish the three modes, so Godescalc, by affirming the three modes, was not less resolute in establishing the unity. He insists upon the need to distinguish the three bodies of which Paschasius was writing *by species* more firmly than Paschasius himself had done: but this was only in order to add, still within the same sentence, that *by nature* the three bodies make up one single body alone: '*different in species, and yet one in nature*'.[85] This is the origin of an entire series of subtle formulations, or, in a jangle of words, the triple distinction that, so to speak, weaves a plait around the unity:

---

80 Mabillon, who did not fail to observe the similarity between his language and that of Godescalc (*De controversies eucharisticis saeculi noni*, c. 4, in Zaccaria, *Thesaurus theologicus*, vol. 10, p. 881) had nevertheless identified it by conjecture with the *Letter to Egil*, to which Rabanus Maurus referred himself in order to refute Paschasius (*Paenitentiale ad Heribaldum*, PL, 110, 493 A). cf. Hériger of Lobbes (PL, 139, 179 A). Following Vacant, Geiselmann rejects this identification: *Die Eucharistielehre der Vorscholastik* (1926), pp. 222–9. For the attribution to Godescalc, see Morin, *Revue bénédictine* (1931) p. 310; Cappuyns, *John Scotus Eriugena* (1933), p. 87; Peltier, DTC, vol. XIII, c. 1630.

81 *Œuvres théologiques et grammaticales de Godescalc d'Orbais* (*Spicilegium sacrum lovaniese*, 1945).

82 *op. cit.*, pp. 325–6.

83 pp. 324, 325, 329, 332, 334.

84 p. 326.

85 pp. 335–6; cf. p. 327, 337.

*Therefore if it is now clear and agreed that there is a difference in
species between the flesh that is not to be consumed, the flesh that
is received, and the flesh that is corruptible, and yet the flesh that
receives the flesh that is given by the flesh that gives, will by receiving wholesomely become incorruptible, nevertheless it should also
be clear and agreed that one in nature are the flesh that gives, the
flesh that is given, and the flesh that receives: in other words, the
inedible, the edible, and the one eating; the non-consumable, the
consumable, the consumer. . .*[86]

And this is how Ambrose, as explained by 'Augustine', can now be
interpreted: '*It is in nature the flesh itself, without excluding difference
in form.*'[87]

Similar formulations can be widely found among those writing at the
same time about the Eucharist. '*That flesh which he assumed and the
bread, and the whole Church do not make up three bodies of Christ,
but one body*' writes the author from Auxerre in his commentary on
the First Letter to the Corinthians.[88] '*Threeness, but united*' Hériger of
Lobbes was soon to write, in his short treatise *De corpore et sanguine
Domini*,[89] thus endeavouring to reconcile those in favour of distinc-

---

86 p. 335. cf. pp. 333–4.

87 p. 337. It is clear that we should not strain too much to translate Godescalc's two adverbs, as does Dom Paul Renaudin, by: 'with regard to substance,
with regard to appearance' (*Questions théologiques et canoniques*, I, 1913, p. 10).
Nevertheless, these last words could only be an anachronistic equivalent of them,
and besides we would do well not to forget that every time Godescalc affirms this
identity, he is speaking of the identity of the *three* bodies.

88 PL, 117, 564 D; 571 A. Mabillon, *De controversies saeculi noni* (Zaccaria,
vol. X, p. 873).

89 Designated first of all as 'the anonymous work of Cellot', after the name
of its first editor, this brief work was attributed by Mabillon (*De Controversiis
saeculi noni*, c. 3, *loc. cit.*, pp. 876–8) to Hériger, abbot of Lobbes († 1007),
while others, with B. Pez, attributed it to Gerbert, among whose works it figures
in Migne. More recently, R. Astier puts forward the name of Scotus Erigena. In
1908, Dom Morin once more suggested the name of Hériger, and Dom Cappuyus
backed up this suggestion. This opinion is shared by Heurlevent in *Durand de
Troarn et les origines de l' hérésie bérengarienne* (1912). In 1933, impressed by
his reading of a C12th manuscript that quoted copious extracts from the work in
connection with the name 'Joannes Scotus', Dom Morin believed that the problem needed to be reconsidered (*Bulletin de théologie ancienne et médiévale*, 2,
p. 179). But an important study by Geiselmann that has appeared since then,
*Der Einfluss des Remigius von Auxerre auf die Eucharistielehre des Hériger von
Lobbes (Theologische, Quartalschrift*, 1934, pp. 222–44) obliges us to abandon the hypothesis of John Scotus definitively, and it confirms the attribution to
Hériger. cf. Cappuyus, *Bulletin*, 3, pp. 86, 333. Hériger is dependent on Remigius
via Gezonius of Tortona: Lebon, *Sur la doctrine Eucharistique d' H. de Lobbes* in
Studia Maedievalia, p. 64.

tion and those in favour of unity. He would later add: '*there is not diversity where there is one, since there are not two or three bodies, but one*' and, following Godescalc: '*the body of Christ is one in nature*'.[90]

This was not a passing form of expression. While exploring and making slight modifications to the theory of Amalarius in his turn, Hugh of St. Victor would repeat the following definition, which would be reproduced by several authors in the second half of the twelfth century, notably the future Innocent III:

> For the body of Christ is the whole Church, namely the head with its members, and there are found in this body as it were three parts, which make up the whole body.[91]

Whether understood historically or sacramentally, the particular body of Christ is therefore still included by Hugh within the whole body, that unique body in which three parts are distinguished.[92] It is understood in the same way by Baldwin of Canterbury[93] and the author of the *Sententiae divinitatis*. In a discussion on the same rite of fraction, they once again elaborate the same doctrine in similar terms: '*the body of Christ is divided sacramentally in three parts, yet there are nevertheless not three Christs, but one Christ only*'.[94]

* * *

Nevertheless, despite the fact that this unity always ends up by being affirmed, the 'parts', 'types', 'forms' or aspects which could not avoid being distinguished within the one body often found themselves described by this same word *corpus*. '*The first is the body, the second is the body and the third is the body*', said Amalarius, for example.[95] If

---

90 5.7, 8 (PL, 139, 183 C, 185–186) Later on Wycliffe would say on the contrary, in comparing the Eucharist to the individual body, *Sermonum Pars IIIa*, I, 61 (Loserth, p. 457).

91 *De sacramentis* (PL, 176, 468 D). Innocent III, *De sacro altaris mysterio* (217, 907–8). Meter Comestor, *Sententiae de sacramentis* (Martin, p. 57).

92 According to another transformation of Amalarius's theory, this would not be thus any longer.

93 *Liber de sacramento altaris* (PL, 204, 771 D).

94 *Tractatus 5* (Geyer, p. 138). Beyond the three pieces of the host, which alone is divided, the assertion envisages, like the definition of Hugh, the three parts of the body of Christ, of which these three pieces are the sign, and which the author proceeds to enumerate under a double formulation (only the first of which is of interest to us here).

95 *De ecclesiasticis officiis*, 3, c. 35 (PL, 105, 1154 D). Algerius of Liége, *De sacramentis corporis et sanguinis Domini*, 1, c. 17 (180, 791).

it were felt that this system of enumeration was unsatisfactory, since it tended to smack of a certain scrupulosity, particular turns of phrase would have to be found that would prevent confusion. This is where *corpus mysticum* comes into service in order to specify the sacramental body. It is not the trade mark of any particular author or school. During the conflict over the Eucharist to which I have already made reference, we will see it being used in the same context and in the same sense by all four of the original protagonists, that is to say by Paschasius Radbertus and his three adversaries: Ratramnus, Rabanus Maurus and Godescalc.

Sometimes a mistaken confusion takes place between the two triple divisions of Paschasius and Amalarius. The scriptural exegesis of the abbot of Corbia and the liturgical exegesis of the deacon of Metz do not in any way contradict one another, but neither do they meet each other half way. Paschasius, writing after Amalarius, owes nothing to the latter's speculations about the *threefold body*. Indeed he appears very critical towards them, doubtless under the influence of Florus's criticism.[96] His point of departure and his point of view are completely different. In chapter VII of the *Liber de corpore et sanguine Domini* he observes that in Scripture there are three different accepted interpretations of *corpus Christi*; he then explains them and sets them in the strictest order in relation to one another on the following page:

> *Because assuredly the universal Church of Christ is his body, where Christ is the head, and all the elect are called members, from whom one body is assembled daily to form the perfect man . . . , from this (body) whoever removes a member of Christ and makes it the member of a prostitute . . . is assuredly no longer in the body of Christ*

---

96 In his commentary on St. Matthew he says: 'Christ, in leaving his body, is not divided within himself by the mystery, nor in any way made into three parts' (PL, 120, 962 B), and in his *Letter to Frudegard*: 'do not follow the nonsense of the body of Christ divided into three' (1365 a) – What remains true is that Amalarius, like Paschasius, but in another way, and to a lesser degree, is conscious of the 'real presence' and sometimes finds formulations for expressing this that are in advance of his time. cf. *De ecclesiasticis officiis, 1.3, c. 25,* and *Epistula 4 ad Rantgarium* (PL, 105, 1141 and 1334–5). Historians, bogged down by the external detail of his symbolism, do not always give him the benefit of the doubt, as if it were understood in advance that the more symbolism is found in an author's work, the less realism there is in it . . . *La Perpetuité* said, with greater justice, though not without some exaggeration in the opposite sense: 'No one ever taught the real presence more formally' (ed. Migne, vol. 3). Is Florus not making a protest in relation to Amalarius, as Ratramnus is in relation to Paschasius, although the former is doing so in the name of unity and the latter in the name of distinction?

... Therefore he has no right to eat of this mystical body of Christ, the body which, in order to be the true flesh of Christ, is consecrated daily through the Holy Spirit for the life of the world ... They feed on it worthily, who are in his body, with the result that only the body of Christ, while it is on pilgrimage, is nourished by his flesh ...

That other body is that which is born of the Virgin Mary and into which this body is transformed, ... and now the one who has become priest for ever daily intercedes for us; if we rightly communicate with him, we so direct our minds that we, his body, take his flesh from him and out of him, while he remains entire: which flesh he indeed is, and the fruit of this flesh, so that he always remains the same and feeds all those who are in the body.[97]

While making these distinctions and balancing these formulations against one another, Paschasius Radbertus continued to insist on the truth of the sacramental body, which earlier on he called '*the mystical body and blood of Christ*'[98] at the same time as he insisted on its identification with the historical and heavenly body: '*his own body*', '*true flesh*', '*one flesh of Christ*'.[99] He was no less attached, on the other hand, to the real unity of the three bodies. The page we have just read, with all its subtle interconnections, is ample evidence of this. In the lines that follow on immediately afterwards, he explains himself even more clearly: the '*three designations of the body*' did not obscure for him the '*unity of that body*'.[100] He returned to this several years later, towards 851, in his commentary on St. Matthew, Chapter 26: '*so that they might recognize more clearly how great is the oneness of the body*' he wrote, and: '*whoever wishes to live in the oneness of the body must realize that these three are mystically one body*'.[101]

97 PL, 120, 1284–6. In his extended analysis of the treatise, Dom Ceillier only consecrates a short sentence to this chapter, whose terminology is inexact (*Histoire générale des auteurs sacrés et ecclésiastiques*, 12, p. 536). A more exact resume can be found in Jacquin, *Revue des Sciences philosophiques et théologiques*, 1914, p. 85. It would seem that M. H. Pellier did not dare to repeat a terminology that had nevertheless not escaped him: see DTC, vol. 13, c. 1635, and Paschasius Radbertus, pp. 200, 210, 251–217, 233, 246, 266.

98 c. 2 (PL, 120, 1273 A.)

99 c. 4, 5, 7 (1278 A, 1279 B, 1281 D, 1285 A). *In Matthaeum* (896 C), Letter to Frudegard (1361 A). *In I Cor.*, (PL, 117, 564 B–C).

100 c. 7 (PL, 120, 1286 A).

101 PL, 120, 896 C and D. It should be noted how the attribute 'mystical' while designating above all the sacramental body, is ultimately applied to the three bodies, and even in a certain way to the third, considered with reference to the final and total unity of the body that includes the head and its members: no

The first of these two points, above all, was contested as we know by Ratramnus. The same, at least in a certain sense, is true of the second, contested by Rabanus Maurus and by Godescalc. This did not prevent these three adversaries of the abbot of Corbia, who were far from being in agreement among themselves, from being at one with him in using 'corpus mysticum' as a term for the Eucharist. '*About this mystical body*', said Ratramnus;[102] and again, contrasting the Eucharist to the historical body:

> How much difference there is between the body in which Christ suffered, and this body which is for the commemoration of his passion or death . . . For the former is proper and true, containing nothing either mystical or figurative, while the latter is indeed mystical.[103]

The same language is used by Rabanus Maurus, who writes in his *De clericorum institutione*:

> . . . Now in the Church his mystical body, created by the oil of sacred prayer, is administered in sacred vessels for the reception of the faithful through the ministry of priests.[104]

The work was edited by Rabanus when he was still in charge of the school at Fulda, around 819, and therefore about twelve years before the first edition of the treatise of Paschasius Radbertus, which dates back to 831. Godescalc, on the other hand, is dependent on Paschasius. In the study in which he vigorously takes up the challenge, he begins by using his own terms without finding any need to restate them:

> Here we reach another point which is far more troublesome, and extremely difficult, the point namely . . . where the body of Christ is spoken of in three ways, that is, the Church, and the mystical one, and that which is seated at the right hand of God.[105]

---

longer only the unity as it is constituting itself, nor only the unity of the Church as the body of Christ, but the unity accomplished between Christ and the Church 'in one flesh'. As real as they are in themselves, each in its own order and according to is proper mode, all the other aspects of the body of Christ have as their purpose to bring about and to signify 'mystically' this ultimate and 'solid' reality while, as it were, waiting to be absorbed in it.

102 *De Corporae et sanguine domini*, c. 95 (PL, 121, 168 A). Trans. W. F. Taylor (London, 1880) and W. Hopkins (London, 1688).
103 c. 92 (167 A). cf. c. 97, 98 (169 A and B).
104 LI, c. 33 (PL, 107, 324).
105 *Dicta cujusdam sapientis* (PL, 112, 1513 C).

What we have here is a form of words that was common at the time. The ninth century itself still bears witness to this. The Church of Lyon once possessed a book of sermons in which Mabillon, who quotes it from extracts sent to him by Baluze,[106] thinks he recognizes the hand of Florus.[107] There was a commentary on the Maundy Thursday Epistle in the following terms:

> 'This is my body.' The body that spoke is one thing, and the body that is given up is another. The body that speaks is substantial, while the body that is 'given up' is mystical. The body of the Lord died, was buried, and ascended into heaven. But the body which was entrusted to the apostles in a mystery[108] is consecrated daily by the hands of the priest.[109]

* * *

Our homilist from Lyon is certainly nearer to Ratramnus than to Paschasius from the point of view of the doctrine. But he speaks like both of them. Such uniformity of vocabulary perhaps invites us to seek a common source, or at least some earlier example. Without leaving the ninth century, a closer reading of Rabanus Maurus will make our research easier. The passage quoted earlier from *De Clericorum insitutione* is not the only one, in fact, where Rabanus Maurus describes the Eucharist as *corpus mysticum*. If we consult his *Expositiones in Leviticum* we find:

> The rational daughter of the priest, that is, every soul regenerated by him through baptism, if it is conjoined to an alien, doing the

---

106 This book of sermons was part of the collection of manuscripts drawn up by Baluze, which was acquired on his death by the Royal Library and which can be found today in the National Library. Auray-Poupardin, *Bibliotheque nationale, Catalogue des manuscrits de la collection Baluze* (1921), p. 422, no. 379, fol. 159–66: homilies extracted from a manuscript of the Church of Lyon. For its own part, the municipal library of Lyon possesses a book of Sermons on the epistles and gospels for the year, a manuscript dating back to the ninth century (Molinier-Desvernay, vol. 1, 1900, p. 172, n. 628).

107 We know that one of the poems of Florus is in praise of the book of Sermons: *Epigramma libri homelarum totius anni ex diversorum Patrum tractatibus ordinati* (MGH, *Poetae latini aevi carolini*, vol. 2, pp. 530–5).

108 Note the equivalence of '*mysticum*' and '*in mysterio*'. cf. Florus's poem on the Gospel of St. Matthew, v. 236: '*Corporis ipse sui sanctis mysteria tradit*' (*loc. cit.*, p. 515).

109 Mabillon, *Praefationes in Acta SS. Ordinis S. Benedicti* (1724), p. 331. The quotation is reproduced by Alexander Natalis (in Zaccaria, *Thesaurus theologicus*, vol. 10, p. 891).

things which pertain to aliens, such as, for example, Jews, pagans or
heretics, and embracing their company, should not feed on the first
fruits of the sanctified, that is, the mystical body.[110]

This allegorical exegesis of Leviticus chapter 22, verse 12 was not an
invention of the abbot of Fulda. We know that his commentaries on
Scripture, as were most of them at that time, were scarcely more than
collections of chosen extracts. For Leviticus, he used above all the commentary attributed to Hesychius of Jerusalem.[111] After his own works
on Genesis and on Exodus, he confides to us that he even thought
simply of referring his readers to it.[112] The passage that we have just
read is a quotation from this actual text,[113] and the same can be said
about the 'mystical blood' which we read about in another passage of
these same *Expositiones.*[114]

Rabanus Maurus naturally read Hesychius in the Latin version,
which was widely distributed at the time. The author and date of this
version have remained unknown to date, and it has even been supposed – but certainly wrongly[115] – that it was an original Latin work.
It would seem beyond doubt that '*mystical body*' and '*mystical blood*'
are the faithful reproduction of σῶμα μυστικόν and of μυστικὸν αἷμα,
although we no longer have the Greek text. For Hesychius, who was
a prodigious exegete, also wrote several commentaries on the psalms.
However, in one of the fragments of his great commentary, which
were edited by Cordier and reproduced in Migne, we can read the following reflections on Psalm 103, verse 32:

'And wine brings joy to the human heart.' This is talking about the
mystical wine. Therefore it brings joy not to the body but to the
heart . . . You see how the psalmist speaks of the mystical bread and
wine . . . But how does this mystical bread make us strong, if not
by bringing surety to our hearts? We ourselves become the body of

---

110 l. 6, c. 18 (PL, 108, 492 D).

111 *In Leviticum* (PG, 93).

112 *Expositiones in Leviticum, Praefatio* (PL, 108, 247 A).

113 Hesychius, 6, c. 22 (PG, 93, 1070 C–D).

114 *Expositiones*, 5, c. 8 (PL, 108, 432 C). Hesychius 5, c. 17 (PG, 93, 1005
D).

115 As Tillemont already noted with greater acuity, the Latin appears in several places to have been translated. As for the 'semi-barbaric' character that some
thought to recognize in it (Labbe, *De scriptoribus ecclesiasticis*, vol. 1, p. 637) it
is doubtless nothing more than the result of an effort at literary faithfulness. We
might remember that critics refused to attribute the translations of the homilies of
Origen on Isaiah to St. Jerome, as being too barbaric for their tastes.

Christ by partaking in his mystical body: σῶμα καὶ ἡμεῖς Χριστοῦ τῇ τοῦ μυστικοῦ σώματος μεταλήψει γενόμεθα.[116]

Corpus mysticum, still in its Eucharistic sense, can be found again in the life of a holy bishop of the Merovingian period, Austregesilus (or Austrilegius), abbot of St-Nizier in Lyon, and subsequently archbishop of Bourges (551–624). The saint, nearing death, is determined to celebrate Mass one last time:

> *Taking the bread and cup, in the accustomed way, offering spiritual sacrifices to the Lord, he confects by a prayer the mystical body of the Lord.*[117]

The author of this account is a contemporary of the saint, which takes us back to the seventh century. But did he really write '*mystical body*'? It might be difficult to verify it. Reading this phrase recalls unfailingly to mind the '*mystical prayer*' of St. Augustine in his *De Trinitate,*[118] a text so often repeated in the following centuries, that one wonders if the authentic text of our hagiographer might not rather have read: '*he confects the body by a mystical prayer*'. The phrase seems to ring more naturally like this. Despite the '*to make a prayer*' in the *Vita Melaniae,*[119] despite the '*soon after the prayer*' of St. Gregory,[120] which is the same as the '*soon after the canon*' of his biographer, John the Deacon[121] and several analogous expressions,[122] one cannot help finding rather strange, in the present context, the use of this indeterminate '*prayer*', whereas '*to confect the body*' was, on the contrary, a simple and common expression. At any rate, Hesychius, who died in 438, takes precedence, just as it seems that he had the major influence over the language used by Latin writers of the ninth century.

The patronage of the man whom Tillemont was to call 'the great Hesychius'[123] was not the only authority on which *corpus mysticum*

---

116 l. 3, c. 4, n. 10 (PL, 42, 874). See *infra,* ch. ii, note 7.

117 *Vita sancti Austregisili,* 1, c. 2, n. 16 (ed. Heuschenius, *Acta Sanctorum* (Anvers, 1685) vol. 5, p. 232).

118 l. 3, c. 4, n. 10 (PL, 42, 874). See *infra,* ch. ii, note 7.

119 n. 66 (Rampolla, p. 38).

120 *Epistularum,* 9, *Ep.* 12. Gregory had just written, which explains his abbreviated term: '. . . *ut precem quam scolasticus composuerat super oblationem diceremus*' (PL, 77, 956–7).

121 *Vita Gregorii,* 2, c. 20 (PL, 75, 94).

122 Marius Victorinus, *Adversus Arium,* 2, c. 8 (PL, 8, 1094 B). Vigilus, *Letter to the bishop of Braga* (Jaffe, 907).

123 *Mémoires . . . ,* vol. 14, p. 227.

was to call. In a strange *quid pro quo* it effectively received that of St. Augustine via its use by Paschasius Radbertus. The section of the chapter in Paschasius where we encountered it met with an extraordinary fate: it was almost immediately transferred, with several other fragments from the same treatise, into a Eucharistic *florilegia*, from which Godescalc extracted it in order to set it in opposition, in St. Augustine's name, to the doctrine which Paschasius develops in the same chapter.[124] Nevertheless, despite this impressive pedigree, it would seem that the expression did not remain in common use, once the controversies of the ninth century were over. It would seem more prudent not to refer overmuch to a text that can already be found in Florus[125] and in Remigius of Auxerre,[126] which both authors may have borrowed from some earlier *Expositio*, and where it is said of the Eucharist: '*this body, this blood . . . become mystical through consecration*'. Because the words '*body*' and '*blood*' to which the word '*mystical*' had just been added as an attribute were possibly copied mistakenly instead of the original '*bread*' and '*cup*'. These are, in fact, the words that can be read in St. Augustine in the passage in *Contra Faustum*[127] from which this text is clearly derived. Other authors, including Hincmar, in the ninth century,[128] quote it in its authentic form, which is, in addition, the only one that seems to offer an acceptable understanding.[129] But the text of Florus and of Remigius was taken up again in the eleventh century by John of Fécamp, who introduced it, with some variants, into his *Confessio Fidei*:[130]

---

124 Lambot, p. 326: '*this is disputed by the blessed Augustine*' (PL 112, 1513 C). This operation was carried out shortly after the first edition of Paschasius's treatise. See M. Lepin, *L'idée du sacrifice de la Messe . . .* , pp. 759–86.

125 *Expositio missae*, c. 59, n. 9.

126 *Expositio missae* (ed. Frobenius), (PL, 101, 1260 A–B).

127 Bk. 20, c. 13 (PL, 42, 379). Gregory of Nyssa, *Life of Moses* (PG, 44, 368 C). [For the English, see A. J. Malherbe, *Life of Moses* (New York, 1978). For a selection of St. Gregory's further works in English, see W. Moore and H. A. Wilson, NPNF, series II, vol. 5.] L. Delisle, 'Anciens manuscrits de la Bibliothèque de Lyon', *Notices et extraits des manuscrits*, vol. 29 (1880), p. 390.

128 Hincmar (PL, 125, 925 A–B). Ivo of Chatres (161, 135 A, 1071 C). Algerius of Liége (180, 764 C). Gratian, *Decretum*, p. 3; *De consecratione*, 2.39 (Friedberg, 1328). Huguccio (Geiselmann, *Die Abendmahlslehre . . .* , p. 154).

129 With '*corpus*' and '*sanguis*' as its subjects, the expression '*non in spicis colligitur*' makes little sense.

130 This completes the demonstration offered by Geiselmann to show that this work, far from being of Alcuin's authorship, presupposes the Berengarian controversy. Dom Wilmart added it to the literary works of John of Fécamp († 1079): *Auteurs spirituels et texts dévots du moyen âge latin*, p. 196.

This body and this blood are not gathered in ears and shoots, but through indubitable consecration become mystical for us and are not born, when created bread and wine are transformed into the sacrament of flesh and blood through ineffable sanctification by the Holy Spirit.[131]

In the tenth century Hériger of Lobbes quotes in passing the expression of Paschasius Radbertus, still believing it to be one of St. Augustine's: in the Paschasian text, which Godescalc used in opposition to Paschasius, in the name of Augustine, he now thinks he has found a formulation which reconciles Paschasius and Godescalc![132] The imbroglio has reached its peak . . . We find the same quotation yet again in the twelfth century in Algerius of Liège.[133] Nevertheless Algerius does not go on to use the expression on his own account any more than Hériger does. On the other hand, Gilbert of Nogent adopts it: in the *De pignoribus sanctorum* (c. 1120), '*mystical body*' is used in tandem with '*figurative body*' and set in opposition to '*principal body*'.[134] The expression survives almost to the end of the century. Jean Béleth picks it up again, around 1165, in his *Rationale divinorum officiorum*:

This question, why Christ gave his mystical body to the disciples before he had offered it in truth, has been adequately discussed by others.[135]

---

131 p. 4, c. 3 (PL, 101, 1088 C).
132 *op. cit.*, n. 3 (PL, 139, 181 B).
133 PL, 180, 790 D. cf. Godescalc (112, 1513 C).
134 Bk. 2 (PL, 156, 629, 634 C, 650).
135 c. 99 (PL, 202, 104 C). The edited Béleth text departs in many details from the manuscript text (Hauréau, *Notices et extraits des manuscrits* . . . , vol. 32, 1888, p. 188). But it is hardly likely that this attribute is the work of the editor, Corneille Laurimann, whose mania for correction would have been more likely to lead him in the opposite direction.

2

'Mystery'

Such usage, which is so different from our own, might well surprise us. But on reflection, it is understandable, and there appear to be more reasons in justification of it than those used in modification of it later on.

In the Christian tradition, both Greek and Latin, and in the liturgies as well as in 'theological' works, everything that touches on the mystery of the altar is broadly and almost without differentiation qualified as mystical. Nothing could therefore appear more normal, even discounting a specific influence such as the one possibly exercised by Hesychius, than to call 'mystical' the body of Christ present in the Eucharist; it is so normal that the practice seems to have come about all by itself, as it were, without any conscious intention. In addition, during the ninth century the reading of authors such as Augustine, Hesychius and Bede had particularly spread the use of this expression.

Could it not be said that tradition showed the body of Christ present on the altar through the effect of 'mystical words'[1] and of 'mystical blessings'?[2] And did these not accompany the 'mystical signs'[3] and the 'mystical gestures'[4] that the priest enacted in a 'mystical mingling'[5] of the water and wine, after the mystical reading of the sacred diptychs?[6] Did the action of the Holy Spirit not come as a response to the 'mystical

---

1 Severus of Antioch (Brooks, *The Sixth Book*, vol II, pp. 234–5). Durandus of Troarn (PL, 149, 1380 A). Hervé of Bourg-Dieu (191, 934 B). Peter Cantor (Giesekmann, *Die Abendmahlslehre . . .* , p.135).

2 Cyril of Alexandria, *Letter of the Council of Egypt to Nestorius* (Mansi, vol. 4, 1077).

3 Hildebert (PL, 171, 1179 A, 1184 B, 1186 C). Peter Cantor (171, 1205 D). Stephen of Baugé (172, 1301 D). *Speculum Ecclesiae* (177, 370 A).

4 Pseudo-Germain of Constantinople (PG, 98, 449 D). Ivo of Chatres (PL, 162, 553B).

5 Algerius of Liége (PL, 180, 795 D) Anselm of Havelberg (188, 1244 A).

6 Pseudo-Dionysius (PG, 3, 425 C, 437 A).

prayer'[7] of the celebrant in order to 'give life mystically'[8] to the offerings and thus to produce, thanks to a 'mystical consecration'[9] or a 'mystical sanctification',[10] a 'conversion' or 'mystical change'?[11] In contrast to what the presence of Jesus had been to his contemporaries in Palestine, was the presence in the sacrament not a presence in 'mystical form',[12] that is to say hidden beneath 'mystical symbols'?[13] During this 'mystical liturgy',[14] of the 'mystical rite',[15] in the 'mystical ceremonial'[16] of this 'mystical sacrifice'[17] which is the Mass, is not Christ, once sacrificed on the cross, once again 'mystically sacrificed'[18] in order to offer himself once more to his Father in a 'mystic obla-

---

7 Augustine (PL, 42, 874). Isidore (82, 255 B). Florus (119, 77 D). *Expositio* (138, 1178 D). Rabanus Maurus (107, 321 D; 111, 131 A). Ratramnus (121, 144 C). *Council of Arras*, text of Gerard of Cambrai (Mansi, vol. 19. 431 A; PL, 142, 1278 C). Hugh of Langres (142, 1329 V). Gratian, *Decretum*, p. 3, [DD. 1–20, trans. K. Christensen, J. Gardley, A. Thompson, *Studies in Medieval and Early Modern Canon Law* series, vol. 2 (Washington, 1993).] *De consecratione* d. 2, c. 60 (Friedberg, 1337). Peter Lombard (192, 862, 867). Baldwin of Canterbury (204, 715 C). Peter Comestor, *Sententiae de Sacramentis* (Martin, p. 32). cf. Ambrose (PL, 16, 641 A), Durandus of Troarn (149, 1403 C), Lanfranc, Gregory of Bergamo (Hürter, p. 14).

8 Isidore (PL, 82, 255 D). Rabanus Maurus (111, 133 A–B).

9 Augustine, *Contra Faustum* (PL, 42, 379). Paschasius (PL, 120, 1278, A). Godesalc (Lambot, p. 325). Ratramnus (121, 131 B). Druthmar (106, 1326, B). Algerius (180, 788 B). Abelard (178, 1530 C). Gilbert, *In cantica, sermo 7* (184, 47A). Peter Lombard (192, 861).

10 Adam, *Life of Hugh of Lincoln* (Gieselmann, *op. cit.*, p. 120).

11 Baldwin of Canterbury (PL, 204, 678 A, 680 A, 681 B).

12 Algerius of Liége (PL, 180, 764 D).

13 Theodoret (PG, 83, 165–9). Nicholas of Méthone, *Treatise on the unleavened* (Allatius, vol. 6, p. 432). cf. Erasmus, *In Lucam* (Basle, 1535, p. 218); *In Joannem* (p. 78).

14 Eusebius (PG, 20, 1196 B). Theodoret (82, 736 B). Cyril of Alexandria (69, 109 C). Nicholas of Méthone (135, 509 A). cf. Pseudo-Dionysius (3, 441 D).

15 *Apostolic Constitutions*, 8, c. 15, n. 11 (Funk, p. 521).

16 Gilbert of Nogent (PL, 156, 632 D).

17 *Apostolic Constitutions*, 6, c. 23, (Funk, p. 361). Chrysostom (PG, 50, 459). Pseudo-Chrysostom (55, 741). Proclus (65, 849 C). Eutychius of Constantinople (86, 2393, 2396). Anastasius of Sinai (89, 209 A). Hesychius (93, 1071 D). *Historia mystagogica* (Brightman, *Journal of Theological Studies* 9, p. 258). Latin in Mai-Cozza, NPB, vol. 10, p. 2, pp. 10, 11). *Vita Sancti Marae* (*Acta Sanctorum*, vol. II, p. 268). Rabanus Maurus (PL, 108, 494 A). Paschasius (120, 1274 B). Gerhoh (193, 957 D).

18 Augustine (PL, 33, 363). Abelard (178, 1530 C). Rabanus Maurus (PL, 108, 504 D), Paschasius (120, 1277 D, 1294 A, 1343 A), Godescalc (Lambot, p. 325), Ascelin (Hardouin, *Concilia*, vol. 6, c. 1021), Anselm, *Ep. 107* (PL, 159, 257 A), Algerius (180, 788 B). Hesychius (PG, 93, 1085 B–C). cf. Gregory the Great (PL, 77, 425 D), Paschasius (120, 1274 C and 1355 A), Guitmond (149, 1474 A), Algerius (180, 788 C). Gratian, *De consecratione*, 2.72 (Friedberg, 1342).

tion'?[19] As the 'mystical host',[20] did he not show at the altar, for those with eyes to see them, the 'mystical signs of his Passion'?[21] Was he not subsequently, as 'mystical manna',[22] 'mystically multiplied'[23] through a 'mystical fraction',[24] and then 'mystically shared out'[25] to all with a view to 'mystical participation'?[26] Was he not in this way 'mystically received'[27] by the faithful gathered around the 'mystical table'?[28] Did every day not see renewed in this way the 'mystical banquet',[29] celebrated by our Saviour on the eve of his Passion and mystically prepared by him for his Church?[30] Did not this body, the 'mystical gift',[31]

---

19 *Gelasium* (Wilson, pp. 242, 359). *Gregorianum* (Lietzmann, p. 97). *Liber mozarabicus sacramentorum* (Férotin, c. 585). Gerhoh (PL, 193, 953 D).

20 Paschasius, *In Lamentationes Jeremiae* (PL, 120, 1119 B).

21 Algerius of Liége (PL, 180, 759 A).

22 Peter Damian (PL, 145, 717 D).

23 Paschasius, *Liber de corpore* (PL, 120, 1335–6). cf. Pseudo-Dionysius (PG, 3, 444 A).

24 Hildebert (PL, 171, 1192). *Speculum Ecclesiae* (177, 373 B). Peter of Celle (202, 767 D).

25 Pseudo-Dionysius (PG, 3, 445 A). St. Leo (PL, 54, 868 B). Inscription of Marinus, Vienne-en-Dauphiné (DACL, vol. 3, c. 168). Hincmar, *Vita Remigii* (MGH Script. Rerum merov., vol. 3, p. 278). Gratian, *De consecratione*, 2.38 (Friedberg, 1327).

26 Cyril of Alexandria (PG, 73, 521 A; 74, 560 B). Leontius Byzantinus (86, 1765). Theophylactus (123, 1308 B, 1312 C). Grimaldus, *Liber sacramentorum* (PL, 121, 818 B).

27 Hesychius (PG, 93. 852 A). Rabanus Maurus (PL, 108. 299 A).

28 Cyril of Jerusalem (PG, 33, 1101 G). Gregory Nazianzen (36, 404 A, 37, 1161 A). Gregory of Nyssa (46, 692). John Damascene (94, 1149). Cyril of Alexandria (68, 284 B; cf. 604 C; 77, 1017 C). Isidore of Péluse (78, 256). Anastasius of Sinai (89, 297 B, 836 C, 840 B). Théophylacte (124, 704 D). Hesychius (93, 1102 D, 1103 and *In Isaiam*, Faulhaber, pp. 1, 61, 111, 175). Ambrose (PL, 14, 708 D). Rabanus Maurus (108, 517 C). Hildebert (171, 1185 C). *Liturgie de Jacques d'Edesse* (Renaudot, vol. 2, p. 373).

29 Chrysostom (PG, 61, 204), Cyril of Alexandria (77, 1016 C, 1017 A, 1024 A). Hesychius, *In Isaiam* (Faulhaber, p. 105). *In Leviticum* (PG, 93, 883 A, 886 B, 888 C, 891 C). Maximus (4, 137 B). Eutchius (86, 2400 B). Anastasius (89, 297 B). Pseudo-Germain (98, 449 C). Nicetas David (105, 105 D). *Historia mystagogica* (Brightman, p. 264; Mai-Cozza, p. 16). Michael Glykas (*Eustratiadès*, vol. 2, p. 348). Greek Mass (Mercenier-Paris, vol. I, pp. 290, 306, 307). St. Leo (PL, 54, 333 B). *Libri sacramentorum* (Feltoe, p. 165; PL, 121, 885 D; 151, 331 B). Alcuin (MGH, *Epistularum*, vol. IV, pp. 336, 472). Rabanus Maurus (*ibid.*, vol. 5, p. 436, PL, 107, 319 A). *Missale gothicum* (PL, 72, 286 D). Bruno of Wurzburg (142, 383 A). Gerard of Cambrai (142, 1279 A). Card. Humbert (143, 938 C). Gerhoh (193, 952).

30 Paschasius (PL, 120, 1336 C).

31 Cyril of Alexandria (PG, 72, 908 B). Hildebert (PL, 171, 1181 A, 1182 A, 1183 A, 1188 B). Peter of Blois (207, 1138 B). *Liturgica Jacobi Baradati* (Renaudot, vol. 2, p. 336).

the 'mystical thing',[32] constitute the most efficacious of the 'mystical remedies'?[33] Did not those who received it worthily taste the 'mystical flavour'[34] of this 'mystical food'[35] and of this 'mystical drink'? Were they not nourished by the 'mystical bread',[36] inebriated by the 'mystical wine'[37] poured out for them by a 'mystical cup'?[38] Did they not know the infinite price of this 'mystical libation'?[39] Did they not for a long time afterwards preserve its 'mystical effect'?[40] This 'mystical eucharist' had a 'mystic power'.[41] On the other hand, had this mystery not often, and in many ways, both in the Old Testament and in the Gospel, been mystically announced,[42] mystically prefigured?[43] Had it not been the object of mystical hope?[44] Finally, did it not itself bear, and in more than one sense, a 'mystical significance'?[45] In a word, was the Eucharist, this 'divine mystagogia',[46] not the culmination of the Christian religion, the chief of its three great mystical rites?[47] Was it not the mystery *par excellence*, of them all, the most secret as well as the most sacred, the sign itself of a reality that is at the same time both secret and sacred? *The Christian mystery, in which so many and such great mysteries are involved.*[48] Did not everything take place *'mystically'*[49] during it? Was not everything in it accomplished *'by the*

32　Hildebert, *Liber de sacra eucharistica* (PL, 171, 1201 A).

33　*Letter to Charlemagne* (PL, 98, 940 A). cf. Gezonius of Tortona (137, 388 A).

34　Fulbert of Chartres (PL, 141, 202 C).

35　See *infra*, Chapter 3, n. 15.

36　*ibid*, n. 17.

37　Hesychius, *In psalmos* (PG, 93, 1229 D).

38　Hesychius, *In Isaiam* (Faulhaber, pp. 28, 72, 202). Ambrose, (PL, 16, 142 A). Ambrosiaster (17, 243 B). Rabanus Maurus (112, 103 C). Gezonius of Tortona (137, 388 B). Abelard (178, 1350 B). cf. Nestorius (Loofs, *Nestoriana*, p. 230; PG, 76, 205 B). Gregory of Bergamo (Hürter, pp. 75, 78).

39　*Liber de canone mystici libaminis* (PL, 177, 956).

40　*Gelasianum* (Wilson, p. 35).

41　cf. Gerhoh, *In psalmos* (PL, 193, 1058 A, 1102 B).

42　Augustine (PL, 35, 1616; 41, 301). Alcuin (100, 836 D). Walafrid Strabo (114, 936 B).

43　Cassiodorus (PL, 70, 797 B). Remigius of Lyon (121, 1129 C).

44　Eustathius of Thessalonica (PG, 135, 728 A).

45　Hugh of St. Victor (PL, 176, 468, D, 469 B). *Sermo de excellentia*, n. 13 (184, 988 B). Peter Lombard (192, 866). Baldwin (204, 656 D, 658 B, 663 A, 680 A). Gregory of Bergamo (Hürter, pp. 65, 74, etc.). cf. Dionysius Bar Salibi (CSCO, vol. XCXIII, p. 73).

46　Gregory of Nyssa (PG, 44, 625).

47　John Scotus Erigena (PL, 122, 308).

48　Cyril of Alexandria (PG, 76, 189 D). Jerome (PL, 22, 484). Innocent III (217, 913 D).

49　Hesychius (PG, 93, 1085 C). *Leonianum* (Feltoe, p. 3). Paschasius (PL, 120, 892 A, 1277 D, 1294 A, 1336 C, 1358 C). *Speculum Ecclesiae* (177, 359 A). Raoul Ardent (155, 1836), etc.

mystery',[50] 'through the mystery'?[51] Was not everything contained there 'within the mystery'[52] hidden 'under the mystery'?[53] In short, in this 'mystical action', was not everything mystical?[54]

> . . . It reveals nothing earthly, but instead the mysteries of Heaven.[55]

* * *

It is clear that speaking of a 'mystical body' in the context of the Eucharist is nothing more than conforming to the logic of the most traditional and universal language. Among so many other analogous expressions, so commonly used, how could this particular one not come one day to fall from the pen of some ecclesiastical writer? Even if, when all is said and done, it only became widespread quite late in the day, it is not that an expression was lacking for the name, but it is no exaggeration to say that a name was lacking for the expression. No doubt it is possible to find many instances of the Eucharistic use of 'body' (σῶμα) starting from the time of St. Paul and the Synoptic Gospels. But as common as it was, that use was not specific. From St. Paul onward, even in the context of the Eucharist, the name evoked a vaster doctrine, and in cases where it is a question simultaneously

---

50 Grimaldus, *Liber sacramentorum* (PL, 121, 805 A) etc.

51 Faustus of Riez (Pseudo Eusebius of Emesa, PL, 30, 272 A). Gregory the Great (77, 425 C). Florus, Remigius of Auxerre, Gezonius, Adrevald, Fulbert of Chatres, Durandus of Troarn, Lanfranc, Guitmond, John of Fécamp, Pseudo-Haimon, Algerius, Gregory of Bergamo, Ivo of Chartres, Gratian (*De consecratione* 2.35), *Sermo de excellentia* (PL, 184, 985 B).

52 Hesychius, *In psalmos* (PG, 93, 1297 B). Gaudentius of Brescia (Gleuck, p. 26). Ambrosiaster (PL, 17, 243 D). Pseudo-Jerome (26, 1259 A). Gregory (76, 1279 A; 77, 425 D). Isidore, 83, 755 A). Florus (119, 49 B). Paschasius (120, 896 C, 962 B, 1281 A, 1302 B). Ratramnus (121, 129 B, 136 A, 114 B, 159 A and B). Haimon (118, 363 C–D). Anastasius (149, 434 B). Guitmond (149, 1473 D). Anselm of Laon (159, 257 A). Franco (166, 776 D and 778 B). Hildebert (171, 1192 A). Hervé (181, 934 D). Gratian (c. 72, 74; Fr., 1342, 1344). Peter Lombard (192, 862), etc.

53 Hilary (PL, 10, 246). Ratramnus (121, 128 A). Hincmar, *Vita Remigii*, (MGH, *Scr. Rer. Merov.*, vol. 3, p. 334). Durandus of Troarn (PL, 149, 1891 B). Guitmond (149, 1474 D). Ivo of Chartres, *Décrit* (161, 139 A). Gratian, *De consecratione*, 2.82 (Fr., 1346). Isaac of Stella (194, 1891 B). cf. Heriger (139, 184 B).

54 Gregory of Nyssa (PG, 46, 581 A). Hesychius (93, 391 C). Paschasius (PL, 120, 1274 A, 1332 B, 1353 A). St. Bruno (152, 725 C). Peter Cantor (Pseudo-Hildebert, 171, 1201 A, 1205 A; Peter of Blois, PL, 207), etc.

55 Paschasius, *Ad carolum regem*, 17 (PL, 120, 1260 B). Reinier of St. Laurent, *De milite captive* (204, 87 D).

of both the Eucharist and the Church, and where the author is concerned to vary the expression used for both one and the other, there is a noticeable tendency within the tradition to preserve *corpus* for designating the Church. Was there not another, equally Scriptural word: *caro* (σάρξ) for the Eucharist? This word, which never carried in Scripture the second sense which *corpus* has in St. Paul, perhaps came to bear more strongly and, so to speak, more specifically in Eucharistic theology.[56] It was certainly the word best adapted to the Eucharist envisaged as food.[57] The body of Christ – composed of all the faithful as of so many members – was to nourish itself from the flesh of Christ: '*so that we may be in his body, under the head itself, in his members, eating his flesh*'. So said St. Augustine,[58] whose language was vulgarised by both Bede and Alcuin.[59] As a marvellous extension of the incarnation, the Eucharist was given to us for the same purpose: just as, according to St. Leo, the Lord Jesus had become one flesh with us through being born, so that we might become his body through being reborn,[60] so, following his loving plan, he delivered over to us his flesh as food in order to hasten that rebirth in his body.[61] If we re-read that page where Paschasius Radbertus specifically designates the Eucharist as *mystical body*, we find that '*body*' is inserted there for symmetry, to create a balance with the two other '*bodies*' on either side of it; but in the subsequent development it is immediately replaced by '*flesh*',

---

56 Ignatius of Antioch, for whom Johannine influence is a determining factor, always used σάρξ: Rom. 7:3, Phil. 4:1, Smyrn. 7,1; cf. Trall. 8,1 with regard to faith (Lelong pp. 64, 72, 88). According to Fr. J. Bonsirven, '*Hoc est corpus meum*', *recherches sur l'original araméen* (Biblica, 1948, pp. 205–319), σάρξ is the word that corresponds with Jesus's own word at the Last Supper.

57 cf. St. Thomas, *In IV Sent.*, 8.2.1 (Moos, p. 335).

58 *In Joannem*, tract. 27, n. 1 (PL, 35, 1616). Cyril of Alexandria, *In Joannem*, 11 (PG, 72, 236 D).

59 Bede, *In Leviticum* (PL, 91, 341 B and C). Alcuin, *In Joannem* (100, 836 D).

60 *Sermo 23*, c. 5 (PL, 54, 203 A). Bede, *Homiliae*, 1.22 (91, 119 A). Alcuin, *In Joannem* (100, 777 A). cf. Augustine, *De anima et ejus origine*, 4.36.

61 In the inverse sense from that found in c. 1:21 (cf. 2:11) and that found in most commentators on St. Paul, it would appear that St. Hilary is playing with the opposition of the two formulations '*caro corporis*' and '*corpus carnis*' in order to underline both the distinction and the continuity of the historical and sacramental body and the ecclesial body. *In psalmos* (Zingerle, pp. 352–3 and 609); *De Trinitate* (PL, 10, 282 and 246 A–B). This last text would often be quoted in the Middle Ages. *Missale gothicum* (Bannister, 1, 1, p. 18). On this compilation of Frankish origin, no doubt destined 'for some Church of Merovingian Gaul' towards the end of the seventh century, see G. Morin *Sur la provenance du 'Missale gothicum'* (*Revue d' histoire ecclésiastique*, 37, 1941, pp. 24–30). cf. Atton of Vercelli, *In Coloss* (PL, 134, 624 B); *In Ephes.* (571 A). cf. Augustine, *De Trinitate*, 14, n. 22 (PL, 42, 1053).

which is repeated as many as five times on the same page. In the following chapters, other formulations recall that of St. Augustine:

> *So we now as the members of Christ are fed with his flesh, so that we may be found to be nothing other than his body and blood, which are the source of our life . . . The flesh and blood are made into our eternal food, so that we may be his body.*[62]

A similar tendency can be found in such writers as Hériger of Lobbes, and others.[63] In the same way, they write: *'the sacrament of the body of Christ'* but if they choose a more succinct phrase, they write: *'the flesh of Christ'.*[64] The significance of this point, to which I will return later, should not be exaggerated. But thanks to this observation it will be no surprise to meet, possibly as an anticipation of *'mystical body'*, the expression *'mystical flesh'.* Strictly speaking, this only constitutes an approximate equivalent, as will be seen in the second part of this study. But it is right to bring it up at this point.

I also mention, as a reminder, the paschal hymn, whose date, though uncertain, cannot be very late:

> *. . . Now on the table of the life of our leader*
> *Let us eat, together with bitter herbs,*
> *The mystical flesh of the lamb.*[65]

Here there is talk of flesh only because there is talk of a lamb. It is the oldest and most approved image of all, which has a subsequent history. The mystical fleshes of the lamb (and note the use of the plural) signify here the fleshes of the mystical Lamb. But St. Jerome will offer us a far more ancient and more interesting case.

In Book XV of his commentary on Isaiah, St. Jerome compares Isaiah 45:1, which speaks of bread and water, to Genesis 49:12, which mentions wine and milk. Both passages naturally seem to him to

---

62 PL, 120, 1297 A, 1311–12, etc. (But cf. 891 A and B). M. H. Peltier, *op. cit.*, pp. 214, 229–30, has signalled, perhaps by exaggerating it a little, Paschasius's personal predilection for *caro*.

63 In the expositions of chapters 7 and 8, we always find *caro*, with one exception (PL, 139, 184–6).

64 Lanfranc (PL, 150, 425 A and 423 D; cf. 430 D). See *infra*, Chapter 4.

65 Mai, *Hymni inediti* (PNB, vol. I, 1852, p. 2). Hymn 28 (p. 208). cf. *Vita sancti Conradi altera*, c. 20 (MGH, Script., vol. 4, p. 439). Paschasius Radbertus, *In Matthaeum* (PL, 120, 889). Lanfranc, *Liber de corpore*, c. 10 (150, 421 C). Hugh of St. Victor, *De sacramentis*, l. 2, p. 8, c. 5 (176, 465 B) etc. cf. Gaudentius of Brescia, *Tract.* 2 (Glueck, p. 26).

contain allusions to the Eucharist (we know that most of the Fathers were not particularly concerned about this topic). On this point he observes that in the Septuagint the 'milk' of Genesis is replaced by 'fat'. From this he draws a series of other ingenious comparisons, which further reinforce the Eucharistic sense of the prophecy:

> *Moses, understanding the wine and milk to relate to the passion of Christ, witnesses in mystical speech, 'Gracious are his eyes from wine, and bright his teeth from milk' (Gen 49:12). For 'milk' in this passage the Septuagint gives 'fat', about which the holy David says in a psalm, 'May my soul be filled as with fat and richness' (Ps 62:6), and in another passage, 'He fed them with the fat of the corn and filled them with honey from the rock' (Ps 80:17). This fat means nothing other than the mystical flesh, in relation to which the Lord exhorted his disciples, when he taught them, 'Unless you eat my flesh and drink my blood, you will not have life in you' (Jn 6:54). This is why he was betrayed at Gethsemane, since the name means valley of fat, or richness . . .*[66]

Despite the analogy of other passages where Jerome, following the line of Origen, applies texts of this type to the Scriptures as Bread of Life,[67] he is certainly thinking here of the Eucharist. The theologians of the Eucharist cannot have failed to notice these lines. They figure in the short collection of documents appended by William of St. Thierry to his treatise *De corpore et sanguine Domini*, and they can already be found, in the form of an implicit quotation, in chapter VI of the work itself.[68] But from the seventh century we have an exact copy from a Greek author, Anastasios of Sinai:

> 'Whoever eats my flesh and drinks my blood remains in me, and I in him.' He is not speaking here of his visible flesh and blood (ὁρωμένης): because Judas and Simon Magus received the body and the blood of the Eucharist, the bread and the wine, but nevertheless Christ did not live in them, and did not remain in them, nor they in him. But I leave it to those more skilled and more learned than myself to explain how this mystical flesh of Christ (ἡ ἀληθὴς βρῶσις τῆς μυστικῆς σαρκὸς τοῦ Χριστοῦ) is truly ingested, and

---

66 PL, 24, 529–30. cf. *In Ezechielem* (25, 432, 435).

67 PL, 25, 115 D, 140 C, 343 A–B, 475 C, 1028 B, 1083–4, 1408 D, 1489, 1548–9, 1571 D; 23 1033 B, 1039 A. *Anecdota maredsolana*, vol. III, p. 2, pp. 73–74, 290, 301, etc.

68 PL, 180, 363 B, 353; 184, 387 B.

what is the nature of the ineffable blood that is hidden within it' (τὸ ἐν αὐτῇ κρυπτόμενον ἀπορρητον αἷμα αὐτοῦ).[69]

* * *

Perhaps after this series of simple verbal comparisons, we are better prepared to understand in which sense or rather in which precise sense the Eucharist can be called the mystical body.

The adjective 'mystical' depends on the noun 'mystery', μυστήριον, to which both the Latin *mysterium* and *sacramentum* correspond. For *sacramentum* the classical definitions of a St. Augustine or a St. Isidore of Seville are well known and have been endlessly repeated. The word *sacramentum* essentially means a sign. But either, or rather primarily, St. Augustine insists on using its first adjective *sacred*, which brings it near to *sacrifice: sacrifice, as if made sacred*; or else Isidore underlines its second adjective *secret*, which makes it look more intimately akin to *mystery*. Already in St. Cyprian both senses can be found. The definition of Isidore, with the etymology which supports it –'*sacraments are called after . . . secret power*' is therefore less of an innovation than some might have thought: it barely does anything but take note of an already ancient usage and make sense of it. In the language of the liturgy, as with that of exegesis, *mystery* and *sacrament* are often used interchangeably.[70] The Latin versions of the New Testament translate μυστήριον equally by either word.[71] In the ninth century, if John Scotus Erigena, translating Denis, twice translates the Greek word by *mysterium*, his immediate predecessor Hilduin once uses *mysterium* and once *sacramentum*.[72] '*Sacrament or mystery*:'[73] this equivalence in practice comes well before Isidore's definition. The translations of Rufinus bear witness to it.[74] It is found throughout the work of St. Augustine himself.[75] In reverse, Commodianus was already using *mysterium* or *secreta* in places where *sacramentum* or *sacramenta* would

---

69 *In Hexaemeron* (PG, 89, 1069). cf. Macarius Magnes, l. 3, c. 32 (Blondel, p.104).

70 cf. Hilary, *De Trinitate*, l. 9, c. 55 (PL, 10, 326 B; cf. A) etc.

71 J. de Ghellinck, etc., *Pour l'histoire du mot 'sacramentum'*, I, pp. 30, 51, 55. cf. Dom O. Casel, *Jahrbuch für Liturgiewiss*, 8, 1928, p. 232

72 Théry, *Études dionysiennes*, vol. 2, p. 466.

73 Paschasius (PL, 120, 1277 A). *In Ephes* (117, 704 B, 712 D, 730–731). Gregory of Bergamo (Hüter, p. 18). Hugh of Rouen (PL, 192, 1203 B–C). cf. Hilary, *De Trinitate*, 9.62 (10, 331 A).

74 cf. Origen *In Jesu Nave*, hom. 20, n. 4: The things that the Bible teaches us are true and divine, but 'because of the weakness of human nature they are disguised by symbols (*sacramenta*) and wrapped in mysteries' (Baehrens, p. 422).

75 *De vera religione*, c. 17, n. 33 (PL, 34, 36). *In psalmum* 120, n. 4 (37, 1607). See also PL, 35, 1451, 1512; 36, 858; 38, 29, 516.

rather have been expected.[76] This does not go as far as the sense of the classical Latin word, a sense which is apparently far removed from the one it was to develop in Christian language, whose analogies with μυστήριον we cannot recognize today.[77]

As for *mysterium* itself, its history appears to be equally complex. Few words, if even one, were subject down the centuries to such current usage and such wide and flexible, not to say fluid acceptance. It is like a huge confluence, where the waters of several rivers come together to intermingle, only to separate again into a multiplicity of tributaries. Nevertheless, without having to go back to its origins or insisting on those aspects which have less direct bearing on this study, it does not seem impossible to delineate more or less the basic extent of the word, determining the two major areas which are in turn distinct and interchangeable, but always closely linked, within which it is most normally used. And the same is true for *sacramentum*: on the one hand there is the area which, to avoid using the tautology 'mysterious' [*mystérique*] and in order not to seem to presume certain debatable analogies, I will call ritual or ceremonial.[78] And on the other hand there is the area that I will describe as scriptural, understanding by that not Scripture itself, but the vast array of speculation on Scripture, on its spiritual significance and the links between the two Testaments. Between both areas the conjunctions are all the more numerous and the connections all the more profound because the two *Testamenta* are unanimously considered in tradition as the centre of operation of all the *sacramenta*, the secret refuge of all the *mysteria*: '*two breasts of the spouse, from which is sucked the milk of all the sacraments*'.[79] Therefore on the one hand and on the other, both in exegesis and in the liturgy, the word 'mystery' and its derivations or its close relations retain two essential constants. They always appear – beyond the permanent allusion to something sacred ('*divine and mystical*', '*sacred and mystical*') and all the resonances which such an allusion comprises – with the two fundamental senses, united in variable proportions, of

---

76 PL, 5, 230. *Carmen apologeticum* (Dombart, p. 148).

77 Thus DBC (Capelle): 'From before its use among Christians, *sacramentum*, while continuing to designate very specifically a military oath, sometimes also embraced a whole world of mysterious things, which relegated to the background the precise reality that had justified its use' (*Bulletin de théologie ancienne et médiévale*, 1, pp. 154–5; O. Casel's review, *Zum Worte Sacramentum*).

78 cf. Pseudo-Alcuin, *Disputatio puerorum*, c. 10 (PL, 101, 1135 B).

79 William of St. Thierry, *Expositio altera in Cantica* (PL, 180, 488 C). cf. Augustine, *In Joannem* (35, 1998) and Origen, *In Ezechielem* (PG, 13, 809 C). Sicard of Cremona, *Mitrale*, l. 2, c. 5 (PL, 213, 79). Augustine, *In psalmum 74*, n. 12 (36, 954).

sign and secret – '*arcanum*'[80] – which are still the two senses attached respectively to our two words sacrament and mystery. This is how '*the sacrament of the incarnation of the Lord's day*' will mean rather the mystery of the Word incarnate in so far as it is the sign or the sacrament of the Godhead, whereas the '*mystery of the Incarnation*' will mean rather the same mystery in so far as it is itself mysterious and is signified by its '*sacraments*', in Scripture.[81] The mystery of the altar, which is prefigured by the offering of Melchizedek, is in its turn, within its visible aspect, a sign: it could therefore be said that the bread and wine of the king of Salem '*were sacraments of the sacrament*'.[82] The *sacramentum* would therefore play the role of container, or envelope,[83] with regard to the *mysterium* hidden within it.[84] In this way, according to Paschasius Radbertus, the purple cloak in which the soldiers clothed Jesus is the mystery of which the scarlet thread of Rahab was the sign.[85] The ordained series of the different *sacramenta* leads us as if by so many stages right to the ultimate mysteries, which are no longer sacraments at all: the '*mysteries of the Godhead*'.[86]

St. Ambrose clearly underlines the opposition of the two terms when he writes: '*The symbol [sacramentum] preceded in figure, but now the mystery is complete in truth.*'[87] All the same, this opposition should not be exaggerated. Most of the time it is only a matter of nuances. If *mysterium* mainly evokes the idea of depth and obscurity, it nearly always also evokes at the same time that of 'type' or of 'symbol'; and

---

80 *Gelasianum* (Wilson, pp. 17–18). Amalarius (PL, 105, 1294 D). Bruno of Wurzburg (142, *passim*). Gilbert of Nogent (156, 531 C), etc. – cf. Ratramnus, *De corpore . . .*, c. 9 (121, 131 A).

81 MGH, *Poetae latini aevi carolini*, vol. 2, p. 164. Herbert Losinga (Goulburn-Symonds, p. 20). Peter Lombard (PL, 192, 222), etc. cf. Hilary, *De Trinitate* 4.27 (PL, 10, 117 B).

82 Baldwin of Canterbury (PL, 204, 650 A).

83 Rabanus Maurus (PL, 108, 1099 B). Jerome (25, 1177 C). Paschasius Radbertus, *In Matthaeum* (120, 916 D), but: (902 D). St. Bernard, *In Cantica, sermo* 23, n. 3 (183, 952 D).

84 Ambrose (PL, 15, 1605 B, 1663 C, 1770 A). Gaudentius (Glueck, p. 27). Origen, *In Numeros*, hom. 4, n. 3 (Baehrens, pp. 23–4).

85 *In Matthaeum* 12 (PL, 120, 941 B).

86 Origen, *In Lucam* (Rauer, p. 229). Ambrose (PL, 15, 1626 C; 16, 1381 A). Pseudo-Jerome (26, 1009 A). Cassiodorus (70, 9 D). Gregory (76, 1018 C). Isidore (82, 255). Pseudo-Primasius, *In Hebr.* (68, 719 B). Ratramnus (121, 131 A). John Scotus (122, 284 C). Odo of Cambrai (160, 1063 B–C). Gregory of Bergamo (Hürter, pp. 44–7), etc.

87 *In Lucam*, 7.96 (PL, 15, 1724 B).

as for *sacramentum*, that word hides as much as it reveals of the thing that it signifies. It implies it mysteriously,[88] '*it prefigures secretly*',[89] '*it prefigures mystically*'.[90] This is what emerges from common expressions such as '*mystical sense*', '*mystical understanding*' or '*to speak in mystery*'. The two adverbs '*sacramentally*' and '*mystically*' have the same meaning in a number of cases.[91] The *mysteria* are in fact *types of mysteries*,[92] *mystical figures*,[93] *mystical sacraments*,[94] *secret sacraments*,[95] just as the *sacramenta* are *mystical types*,[96] or *sacred mysteries*.[97] The *sacramenta* are the *bodily mysteries*, as the *mysteria* are the *spiritual sacraments*. Also the adjectives that serve as attributes for the nature of *mysterium* (*deep, mysterious, high, shadowy, secret, hidden, veiled . . .*) are at least naturally complementary to *sacramentum*.[98]

All of this can be verified in a number of cases as much for the Eucharist as for the Scriptures, and the mystery which is enacted at the altar can be described as: '*this mystical sacrament of the chalice*'.[99] A text from Algerius of Liège gives us a good summary both of the

---

88 St. Leo, *Sermo* 4, c. 4 (PL, 54, 152 A).

89 cf. Augustine, *In Joannem*, tract. 28, n. 9 (PL, 35, 1627). Isidore, PL, 83, 337 c. Paschasius, PL, 120, 1342 A. cf. *Libri Carolini* (98, 1094 C). Abelard, *In Ephes.*, III (Landgraf, vol. 2, p. 403).

90 Rupert (PL, 167, 643 B). cf. Jerome (25, 1198 B).

91 Wycliffe, *De Ecclesia*, c. 18 (Loserth, p. 440). [For an edited edition with English notes, see J. Loserth, *Ioannes Wyclife Tractatus de ecclesia* (London, 1886). For translations of Wycliffe's works on the Church, see J. H. Todd, *Three Treatises . . .* , (Dublin, 1851) and *The Last Age of the Church* (Dublin, 1840).]

92 Ermenrich of Ellwangen, *Epistola ad Grimaldum* (MGH, *Epistularum*, vol. V, p. 575).

93 Bede (PL, 92, 275 A). Paschasius (120, 63 B, 95 A). *Liber mozarabicus ordinum* (Férotin, c. 291). Adhelmus (MGH, Ehwald, pp. 312, 251). Algerius of Liège, *De sacramentis*, 3.14 (PL, 180, 852 C).

94 Jerome, *In psalmum* 86 (Morin, p. 100); *In Ezechielem* (PL, 25, 433 A). Pseudo-Jerome (26, 1081 D). *Leonianum* (Feltoe, p. 122). *Gregorianum* (Lietzmann, p. 7). *Liber mozarabicus ordinum* (Férotin, 291). Councils of Fréjus and Aix-la-Chapelle (MGH, Concila, vol. 2, pp. 195, 242). Paschasius Radbertus (PL, 120, 51 C, 55A, 65 D, 67 D, 112 C, 133 B, 145 D, 310 D, 228 A, 236 B, 318 A, 393 C, 540 A, 894 C, 964 A, 1108 D, 1119 B, 1175 B). John Scotus (122, 267 B). Gozechin (143, 899 A). *Missale Francorum* (72, 322 B). Gerhoh (193, 1196 D), etc. St. Thomas, *In Joannem*, c. 2, l. 3, n. 1 and 2.

95 Gregory, *Moralia in Job*, 13.19 (PL, 75, 1026–7).

96 Peter Damian (PL, 145, 282 C; cf. 395 C). Baldwin (204, 707 A), etc. Algerius, *De sacramentis*, I. 5 (PL, 180, 753 B), etc.

97 Algerius, *De sacramentis*, 1, c. 5 (PL, 180, 753 B) etc.

98 Augustine (PL, 36, 301; 37, 1265). cf. Arnobius (5, 24 A), etc. Otho of Lucques, *Summa sententiarum*, tract. 4, c. 1 (PL, 176, 117 C).

99 cf. Gratian, *De consecratione*, 2.72 (Friedberg, 1342).

differences and the similarities between these two words, and of their constant interconnectedness:

> *A sacrament and a mystery differ in this respect that sacrament is a visible sign signifying something, while a mystery is something hidden that it signifies. However one can be used for the other . . . , with the consequence that a mystery is both concealing and concealed, and a sacrament both signifying and signified.*[100]

* * *

Nevertheless, in order to unravel the sense of that simple phrase *corpus mysticum*, which is more complex than appears at first sight, it is important to note further two particularly essential features.

In the first place – and this is the other note which tends to differentiate *mysterium* from *sacramentum* – a mystery, in the old sense of the word, is more of an action than a thing. This active nuance already has an effect on the word in St. Paul, although he also highlights its intellectual aspect. This can often be found in later works: 'When the mystery of my incarnation is accomplished, I shall return to the Father.'[101] This is also the dominant application of the word to the Eucharist.[102] Thus we still speak today of celebrating the holy Mysteries, but, on the contrary, of the adoration of the Blessed Sacrament. Here again, there will certainly be no difficulty in putting forward numerous exceptions: there are redundant formulations where the two words are synonymous; there are sentences where one or other is used haphazardly, in a general sense; there is the alternating of the two words with the sole apparent aim of avoiding verbal repetition; finally, and more rarely, there are the instances when the nuances which I have been pointing out are found in the reverse sense. The most notable exception is undoubtedly the Augustinian use of the *celebration of the sacrament*.[103] Nevertheless, if we are in any way to respect the rule of statistics, we should say that, while the *sacramentum* is 'confected', carried, deposed, kept, divided, broken, distributed, received,

---

100 Algerius, *De sacramentis*, 1, c. 5 (PL, 180, 753 B), etc.

101 Paul the Deacon, *Hom. 103 de tempore* (PL, 95, 1308 D).

102 cf. O. Casel, *Le Mystère du culte dans christianisme* (trans. Hild), pp. 109, 112, 116.

103 PL, 33, 205, 363, 364; 42, 35, 44, 124, etc.). Ambrose, *De oficiis ministrorum*, 1, c. 50, n. 248 (16, 98 A). Bede, *De Tabernaculo* (91, 428 A). Godescalc (Lambot, p. 329). Peter of Poitiers, *Allegoriae super Tabernaculum Moysi* (Moore-Corbett, p. 112). cf. Paschasius Radbertus, *Liber de corpore*, c. 3 (PL, 120, 1275 A).

absorbed, eaten and drunk,[104] the *mysterium* itself is 'done', worked, celebrated, offered, completed, interrupted, re-started, frequented.[105] By the first we are nourished, purified, fortified, vivified; we assist, serve and officiate at the second.[106] It is the accomplishment of the mystery which produces the sacrament.[107] *In the enacting of the mysteries.*[108] Rabanus Maurus calls the Mass the '*mystery of the celebration of the Lord*'[109] and Florus writes in one of his liturgical poems:

> . . . *while the sacred mysteries are being performed in a pious rite* . . . [110]

And later Hildebert of Lavardin writes:

> *It is not someone else who celebrates, even though another appears: it is God the Word who performs this sacred mystery.*[111]

'*Celebrating the sacred mystery* . . . , *he receives the sacrament itself*' says the author of the *Instructio sacerdotalis*, which was attributed to Saint Bernard.[112] As with other words such as sacrifice,[113] or eucharist,[114] or offering,[115] or even communion,[116] it certainly seems as if

---

104 'Sacramentum (sacramenta), conficere, gerere, deponere, frangere, dividere, accipere, sumere, percipere, manducare, bibere, portare, edere, consequi, dispensare, custodire, distribuere, largiri, assumere, projicere' etc . . .'.

105 'Mysterium (mysteria) celebrare, agree, peragere, operari, offerre, complere, implore, absolvere, consummare, perficere, iterare, frequentare . . .'.

106 'Sacramento (sacramentis) refici, vegetari, muniri, reparari, purificari, vivificari . . . Mysteriis interesse, assistere, ministrare, servire, deservire, exsequi . . .'.

107 cf. Athanasius (PG, 26, 1289 B, 1325 C, 1328 C).

108 Gelasius (Routh, *Scriptorum ecclesiasticorum opuscula*, vol. II, p. 139. Hesychius, *In Leviticum* (PG, 93, 891 B–C). Walafrid Strabo (PL, 114, 946 C), etc. Batiffol, *Leçons sur la Messe*, 5th edn., p. 170. cf. Remigius of Auxerre (PL, 109, 1271).

109 *De clericorum institutione*, 1, c. 33 (PL, 107, 322 D); cf. c. 31 (319 C). *Missale gothicum* (Bannister, n. 30, 321). St. Thomas, IIIa, q.83, a. 4.

110 *De cereo paschali* (*Poetae latini aevi carolini*, vol II, p. 565).

111 *Liber de sacra eucharistica* (PL, 171, 1202 A). cf. Hugh of Rouen, *Dialogues*, 5, 11 (192, 1204 B and C).

112 p. 2, c. 12, n. 30 (PL, 184, 789 A).

113 There are numerous examples of liturgical, canonical and other types: *Sacrificium comedere, custodire, accipere, evomere* etc. Roman Mass: *Haec dona, haec munera, haec sancta sacrificia illibata*. The same observation can be made of the Pasch, which can mean either the feast or, in addition, the paschal lamb (or Christ).

114 Already in the objective sense in Ignatius of Antioch, Clement of Alexandria, Cyprian, Irenaeus, the *Acts of Peter* . . . Justin and Origen have both senses.

115 Card. Humbert, *Adversus Graecorum calumnies*, c. 33 (PL, 143, 951 D).

116 Pseudo-Clement (PG, 1, 510 A). Card. Humbert, *loc. cit.*

the objective and static sense of mystery, from its earliest appearance comes from the noun-driven instinct of the language, but is nevertheless nothing other than a sense derived from the active and ritual sense which, in liturgical parlance, came first.[117] *'According to the rite of the mystery and the mode of the sacrament'* also says William of St. Thierry, to explain the presence of Christ at the altar.[118] Now, despite occasionally contradictory appearances, the same will occur with regard to certain objects described as 'mystical'. It is clear enough in the case of such expressions as 'mystical eulogy', where the noun itself is active in origin: the expression alludes to the blessing which makes the Eucharist, before becoming the term for the Eucharistic action, the blessing in some way solidified, that is to say the blessed, consecrated bread, 'eucharisted', the 'mystical bread'.[119] It is also true, in some sense, of the 'mystical body', an expression in which we will discover at least an implicit and indirect reference to the action, whatever it is, in which this 'body' is engaged.[120]

But in the second place, it is not only in its content, because of what it designates, that the mystery is essentially an action. We see this again, and in more radical, though less tangible fashion, in its form. We are presented here, in the original sense of the words, with something unclear and fluid. It conveys dynamism and synthesis. It focuses less on the apparent sign, or rather the hidden reality, than on both at the same time: on their mutual relationship, union and implications, on the way in which one passes into the other, or is penetrated by the other. It focuses on the appeal which the first term makes to the second, or better, on the hidden presence of the second term within the first,

---

117 Although it could be the case for the Greek word, in a primitive local sense, as attested by the suffix – τήριον: τελεστήριον, θυσιαστήριον, etc.

118 *Disputatio adversus Abelardum* (PL, 180, 280 C; cf. 343 D). Pseudo-Isidore, *Letter to Redemptus* (83, 905 C, 906 B). Othon of Lucques (176, 141 D). Peter Comestor, *Sententiae de sacramentis* (Martin, p. 53). Jerome, *Ep. 51*, n. 3 (translation of the letter of Epiphanius to John of Jerusalem; Hilberg, vol. 1, p. 399).

119 I Cor. 10:16; cf. Eph.1:3. We find this first sense upheld in Origen, the *Martyrium Matthaei*. Gregory of Nyssa, Basil, Pseudo-Dionysius, Theophylactus, etc; the same is true for 'benedictio' in Augustine, the Mozarabic liturgy . . . By extension, it covers the entire holy action: Sophronius of Jerusalem (PG, 87, 3989). The second sense is first attested, above all, in Egypt: we find it used frequently in Cyril of Alexandria, who says 'to receive mystical praise' in the way that we would say 'to receive communion'; an inscription from fifth-century Alexandria (Wilpert, *Fractio panis*, p. 10); a synodal letter from the Council of Egypt in 430 (Mansi, vol. 4, 1077); the Greek Mass (Mercenier, Paris, p. 296).

120 We even find abridged expressions such as 'the body to be celebrated' (Hincmar; PL, 125, 921 C).

already at work secretly but effectively. Thus what is properly and primarily mystical here is the secret and dynamic link within the *allusion*, the *significance*:[121] '*mystical figuration*',[122] '*mystical similitude*',[123] '*the mystery of the internal meaning*'.[124] Father Simonin has already correctly remarked on this with regard to Origen: the Mysterion, he explains, 'designates precisely the mutual relationship of the one with the other (= of the sensible sign to that which it signifies), a relationship which is hidden from the eyes of the profane (wherein lies the mystery), but progressively revealed to the believers who choose to submit themselves deliberately to the school of the Logos. This mystery lies in the aptitude for being revealed, with regard to the thing itself, and in the aptitude for revealing effectively with regard to the sign.'[125]

I would add that, as the basis of this double aptitude, this is the *ratio mystica*[126] through which the thing lies within the sign, and the sign, in some way, and to different degrees depending on the case, participates in the higher reality of the thing. Or again, if we concentrate less on the text than on the rites, we could say that it is the *secret power*[127] by which the thing operates across the sign and through which the sign participates, here again in widely differing ways, in the higher efficacy of the thing. This is the origin of the adverbial form *mystically*,[128] (or *in the mystery*), which is so frequently used, but determines in an exclusive sense neither one or other of the terms which the verb places in conjunction, but rather the relationship itself which the verb is expressing: '*the bread is mystically turned into the body of Christ*'.[129] This is

---

121 Augustine (PL, 35, 1458). Cassiodorus (70, 24 A, 45 B, 581 A, 797 B, 1038 D). Paschasius (120, 1344 A). *Speculum Ecclesiae* (177, 358 D). Baldwin (204, 645D, 712C, 731, 741), Gregory of Bergamo (Hürter, p. 65). Gandulph of Bologna (J. de Walter, p. 455), etc.

122 Amalarius (PL, 105, 1106 B).

123 Pseudo-Haimon (PL, 116, 650–1). Atton of Vercelli (134, 755 B). Rupert (168, 1620 D), etc.

124 Peter Damian (PL, 145, 282 C).

125 *Revue des Sciences philosophiques et théologiques*, 1938, p. 266.

126 Optatus, *Christmas Sermon* (Wilmart, *Revue des Sciences religieuses*, 1922, p. 284). Origen, *In Leviticum* (Baehrens, p. 364). Maximus, *Ambiguorum liber* (PG, 91, 1133 A, 1136 B). Ambrose (PL, 16, 562 A). Cyril of Alexandria (PG, 73, 456 C). Innocent IV, encyclical *Eger in levia* (Winkelmann, *Acta imper. inedita*, vol. II, n. 1053, p. 698. See *infra*, Chapter 10, n. 38.

127 Cardinal Humbert, *Adversus Simoniacos*, 2.39 (MGH, *Libelli de lite*, vol. I, pp. 188–9). cf. Paschasius Radbertus, *In Matthaeum* (PL, 120, 663).

128 '*Mystice fieri, dici, vocari, innui, referri, esse, designari, intelligi, significari, sonare*', etc.

129 Rabanus Maurus (PL, 107, 1106 C) Bede (92, 272 C, 597 A). Haimon, *Homilia 66* (118, 398 A). See *infra*, Chapter 5.

also the source for some authors' use of the verb *to make mystical, to be made mystical*,[130] or *to mysticize*.[131] This is also the source of such subtle interchanges as the sacrament of the mystery and the mystery of the sacrament.[132] Finally this is the origin of the phenomenon, which is frequently observed in exemplarist vocabulary[133] and especially with the adjective *spiritual*, which is so close to *mystical*,[134] but which is never so frequent except in the case of mystical itself, and of mystery: it is the phenomenon of a transfer of attributes, of an exchange or a 'communication of idioms', between the two poles of attraction and location of the '*mystery*', between the τύπος and the ἀλήθεια.[135] While resolving any equivocation which might result from it, this is the phenomenon which was to be expressed by a whole series of formulations which achieved classical status within the twelfth century, when our sacramental theology became elaborated with precision: these formulations distinguished, for example, '*concealing the mystery*' and '*the concealed mystery*', '*sacrament in the active or passive sense*', *sign signifying* and *sign signified* (*or secret sign*), etc.[136] They are useful formulations that shed light on, but perhaps also challenge a weakened understanding of the reality that they are translating by dislocating it. Hidden in the 'depths of God', before being revealed within Christ, the mystery of our salvation had already been prefigured in the numerous

---

130 Rupert of Tuy, *In Joannem* (PL, 169, 795 B). *Speculum Ecclesiae* (177, 359 C, 369 A). Gilbert of Tournai, *De officio episcopi* (B.M.P., vol 25, p. 408 B). cf. Ermenrich of Ellwangen (MGH, *Epistularum*, vol. 5, p. 397).

131 Arno of Reichesberg, *Liber apologeticus contra Folmarum* (Weichert, p. 193).

132 See *infra*, Note A.

133 For example, 'type' substituting itself for 'antitype', 'exemplar' meaning in turn both the model and its copy, etc. Note also the hesitation in using formulations such as '*in typo*' or '*in typum*' . . . the same is true for *figuraliter*, Remigius of Auxerre, *In Psalmos* (PL, 131, 159 B and 570 B; cf. 166 B, 554 D). Augustine (PL, 34, 703). Rupert (167, 1661 A). On Origen, see H. U. von Balthasar, *loc. cit.*, p. 515.

134 cf. Chrysostom, *In I Cor.*, hom. 23 (PG, 61, 191), etc. [Trans. T.W. Chambers, *NPNF* series I, vol. 12. For St. Chrysostom's wider works, see vols. IX–XIV and W. Mayer, P. Allen, *John Chrysostom*, Routledge *Early Church Fathers* series (London, 2000).]

135 Another cause of these uncertainties of language and these interchangeable attributes should also be noted, namely the disturbance brought about in the language of antiquity through its application to the novelty of Christianity. cf. *Catholicisme* (1938), Chapter 6.

136 William of St. Thierry (180, 362 B–C), Otho of Lucques (176, 144), Innocent III (217, 881). Dhanis, *Revue d'histoire ecclésiastique*, 1930, pp. 920–2. Algerius of Liége, cited in *supra*, p. 58. *De sacramentis*, 1, c. 4 (PG, 180, 751–2).

mysteries contained in the Scriptures.[137] The 'great mystery' of which St. Paul spoke to the Ephesians is the union of Adam and Eve in relation to Christ and to the Church, but it is equally the union of Christ with the Church, which that original union signified.[138] The number of the Fathers of Nicaea is a *mystical number* both because it is signified by the three hundred and eighteen servants of Abraham, and because it signifies in itself the cross and the victorious name of Jesus, and for both of these reasons at the same time.[139] The *mystical gifts* offered to the infant God can be the Magi's presents themselves or the things which those presents signify; they are *sacraments of the gifts*.[140] The same ambivalence can be observed with mystical lamb and mystical passover, which touch so closely on our subject. The 'mystical lamb' can equally be the one who designates or the one who is designated: whether the 'typological' or the figurative or symbolic lamb, the 'legal' lamb of the Jewish Passover, sacrificed each springtime *'figuratively and through imagination'*,[141] or, on the other hand, our Paschal Lamb, the 'true Lamb', the 'archetypal', 'intelligible and spiritual' Lamb, the unique Lamb, the 'truth' behind this 'figure'.[142]

---

137 Cyril of Alexandria (PG, 73, 428 A; cf. 433 A), etc. Pseudo-Primasius, *In Hebr.*, (PL, 68, 740 C, 741 D, 749 B). Pseudo-Haimon (116, 246 C; 117, 882 C). Aldhelm (Ehwald, p. 65), etc.

138 Not only for *sacramentum*, but even for *mysterium*, the first understanding is more frequent. What makes the second possible is precisely the nature of a sacred object not to be open to being fully revealed: it always remains partly secret, always 'mysterious' in itself. A mystery that was not revealed or open to revelation would be totally unknowable (Simonin, *loc. cit.*), but on the other hand a mystery that was fully unveiled would no longer be worthy of the name.

139 J. Rivière, '"Trois cent dix-huit." Un cas de symbolisme arithmétique chez saint Ambroise', *Recherches de théologie ancienne et médiévale*, 1934, pp. 349–67. cf. *De pascha computus*, n. 10 (PL, 4, 954 A–B). Rupert (167, 380–1).

140 Jerome, *In Matthaeum*, c. 2 (PL, 26, 26 B).

141 Hesychius (PG, 93, 882, 1081, 1082,). *Liber mozarabicus ordinum* (Férotin, 225). Isidore (PL, 83, 754 C). Etherius and Beatus (96, 940 D). Rabanus Maurus (108, 499–555, 1100 B; MGH, *Epistularum*, vol. 5, p. 466). Paschasius (PL, 120, 893 B, 1330). Werner (157, 209 D. Rupert (167, 1662, 168, 1533 D; 169, 500–501 et 794 D). Honorius of Autun (172, 552 A, 666 A, 923 C). Raoul Ardent (155, 1842 A), etc. cf. Victorinus of Peltan, *In Apoc.* (Hansleiter, p. 72).

142 Hesychius (PG, 93, 1421, D). Jerome, *Ep 52* (Hilberg, vol. I, p. 432; cf. vol. 3, pp. 359, 360). John Scotus, *In Joannem*, frag. 1 (PL, 122, 310 A, 311 A–B). Rupert (167, 613–14). Hugh of Rouen, *Tractatus de memoria*, 1, 11 (192, 1304 C). Hildebert, *Versus de mysterio missae* (171, 1177 A. cf. Paschasius, *In Matthaeum* (120, 988 C), Augustine, *De catechizandis rudibus*, n. 41 (40, 340). Card. Humbert, *Adversus graecorum calumnies*, c. 9 (143, 938 D). St. Thomas, *In Joannem*, c. 12, l. 1, n. 1.

3

Memorial, Anticipation, Presence

[67]

Given this sense of *mystery* and of *mystical,* and without implying that any given case is exclusive, it will first of all be necessary to distinguish as many interpretations of the words 'mystical body', applied to the Eucharist, as possible, with regard to the Eucharist, to distinguish the relationship between the sign and the thing signified. Besides this, we will always be dealing with a body envisaged as the end or, inversely, as the *initiation* of a mystery. Beneath the objectified and, as it were, solidified expression *mystical body,* we will need to discern the process of a *sacrament of the body,*[1] or of a *mystery of the body.*[2] The cases differ and are distinguished one from another by hundreds of subtle nuances, which could be analysed *ad infinitum.* But it would seem that, schematically, they can all be listed under the following three headings, which correspond to the three essential aspects of the Eucharistic mystery.

* * *

1. *The mystical body* can first of all be envisaged, within the sphere which I have called ceremonial, as a term for a mystical action, of the *'celebration of the body'.*[3] In the Eucharist the body of Christ is therefore called mystical, whatever the kind of existence or the degree of reality which is attributed to it elsewhere, simply because it is found within the mystery, that is to say, within the sacrament.[4] It is a mystical body, therefore, primarily because it is hidden – *mystically, secretly* – under the material or ritual appearances that mystically signify

---

1 Compare, in Paschasius Radbertus, the two expressions (PL, 120, 1285 A, 1276 D, 1346 A).

2 Humbert, *Adversus graecorum calumnies,* c. 20 (PL, 143, 946 A).

3 Augustine (PL, 34, 71). cf. *Gregorianum* (Lietzmann, p. 45). Ratramnus (PL, 121, 128 A). Guitmond (149, 1454 C, 1455 B–D, 1457 C). Gregory of Bergamo (Hürter, pp. 13–14), etc.

4 Algerius of Liége (PL, 180, 791 B). Pseudo-Algerius, *De sacrificio missae* (180, 855 D), etc.

it:[5] *the hidden body of Christ.*[6] A gloss on the fourth book of the Sentences explains: '*In a mystery, that is, in figure, that is, under the species which is called concealed, because the body of Christ is hidden and concealed.*'[7] To say mystical body, is also and at the same time to say sacred body – *consecrated body*;[8] sacrosanct body,[9] brought forth in the course of a sacred ceremony,[10] *through the mystery of sacred prayer*,[11] received, as holy nourishment, at a holy table. In liturgical usage as well as in literary texts, *mysterious* and *holy* are, to all extents and purposes, synonyms.[12] Finally, in a more general fashion, and without having to dig for a sharper nuance, we have the body of the mystery, the sacramental body,[13] celebrated in the sacrament.[14] This description is valid, furthermore, for all the sacraments.[15] Thus to designate the grace of baptism, which today we would call sacramental grace, someone like Gregory of Nyssa would say: 'mystical grace'.[16]

Therefore our expression can be explained quite naturally, although it came about by a circuitous route. In its first phase the dominant expressions are those based on more synthetic expressions, such as 'mystical food',[17] or 'mystical eulogy', or again, 'mystical things'.[18] These terms imply, in a confused fashion, both what will later be called

---

5 *Expositio 'Quotiens'* (PL, 96, 1496 B). Rabanus Maurus (111, 133). Guitmond (149, 1430 D). Gratian, *De consecratione*, 2.48 (Friedberg, 1332).

6 Gerhoh of Reichersberg, *Liber de simoniacis* (MGH, *Libelli de lite*, vol. 3, p. 267). Roland, *Sentences* (Gietl, p. 216).

7 H. Weisweiler, *Mélanges Grabmann*, vol. 1, p. 393.

8 Ambrose, *Hymn of the Dedication* (PL, 17, 1257). Cassiodorus (70, 801). Raoul of St. Germer (B.M.P., vol. 17, p. 182 F).

9 *Leonianum* (Feltoe, pp. 59, 67). *Missale gothicum* (Bannister, vol. 1, n. 154).

10 Bede, *In Marcum* (PL, 92, 270 B, 271 C and D). *Glose in Lucam* (114, 338 C), etc. Citing Bede, Hincmar of Rheims. cf. William of St. Thierry (PL, 180, 355 C).

11 Ambrose, *De fide* 4, c. 3 (PL, 16, 641 A); cf. Berengar, *Profession of faith*, Lateran, 1050 (Mansi, vol. 19, 762 E) and 1079 (vol. 20, 524 D), etc.

12 Note also, without any appreciable difference in meaning, 'mystical table' and 'holy table'. The same for oblation, food, bread, banquet, etc.

13 Wycliffe, *Sermonum Pars IIIa*, s. 25 (Loserth, p. 194). cf. Augustine, *Ep.* 98, n. 9 (PL, 33, 364).

14 Rupert (PL, 168, 1035 C–D).

15 Gilbert of Nogent, *Liber quo ordine sermo fieri debat* (PL, 156, 23 C).

16 PG, 44, 596 A.

17 Hesychius, *In Leviticum* (PG, 93, 1072 A). Rabanus Maurus, *De ecclesiastica disciplina*, 3 (PL, 112, 1246 C). Gerhoh, *In psalmos* (193, 953 B).

18 Clement of Alexandria (Stählin, vol. 2, p. 10). Hippolytus, *Elenchos* (Wendland, p. 77). Hesychius, *In Isaiam* (Faulhaber, p. 70). Rabanus Maurus (PL, 108, 493 D).

the 'sacramental species' and the 'substance of the body'. From that starting point are born a couple of differentiated expressions: *'mystical bread'*[19] on the one hand and, on the other, *'mystical body'*. These expressions will react against each other and even replace one another, by virtue of the communication (or rather the reversal) of terms: we see both of them used by Hesychius of Jerusalem, on the same page of his *Commentary on Leviticus*.[20] It is mystical body because it is *in the form of bread* (ἐν τύπῳ ἄρτου).[21] It is a body that is both referred to and contained mystically in the symbol of bread. According to a formulation of Durandus of Troarn and of Lanfranc, which in the twelfth century was taken to be an Augustinian formulation: *'the flesh is hidden under the form of bread'*;[22] or, according to a parallel formulation by Gilbert of Nogent: *'the body confected under the shadow of bread'*.[23] Thus we have the primacy of the act and of the synthesis, stemming from which the vocabulary extends through analytical divergence. This is once again paralleled in the case of baptism. It is a 'mystical action', comprising a 'mystical cleansing'[24] from a 'mystical spring'[25] with a view to 'mystical regeneration'.[26] Now, are we not speaking here in the same way, when treating of this topic and of 'mystical water',[27] that is to say of the water of the sacrament, by which

---

19 Origen, *In Genesim, In Leviticum* (Baehrens, pp. 52, 477). Macarius Magnes 3, c. 23 (Blondel, p. 106). Eutherius of Tyana (Batiffol, *L'Eucharistie*, 5th edn., pp. 445–59). Hesychius, *In Isiam* (F., pp. 11, 63, 95). Maximus (PG, 4, 137 C). Anastasius of Sinai (PG, 89, 829 C). Procopius of Gaza, *In Genesim*. Augustine (PL, 42, 370). Rabanus Maurus (108, 492 C). Lanfranc (150, 416 C). Algerius (180, 764 C). Photius (PG, 101, 420).

20 PG, 93, 1070 B and C.

21 Cyril of Jerusalem, *Fourth Mystagogical Lecture* (PG, 33, 1100 A). [For the lectures in English, see L. P. McCauley and A. A. Stephenson, *Fathers of the Church* series, vol. 63 (Washington, 1970). For the Catecheses and further works of St. Cyril, see the same volume, and vol. 61 (Washington, 1968) and the *Early Church Fathers* series, E. J. Yarnold, *Cyril of Jerusalem* (London: Routledge, 2000).]

22 Lanfranc (PL, 150, 423 D), cited by Ivo of Chartres, *Decretum* (PL, 161, 153 D). The *Panormia* attributed to St. Augustine (*ex sententiis Prosperii*; 161, 1076 A). Likewise, Algerius, Abelard, Gratian, Peter Lombard. cf. M. Lepin, *L'idée du sacrifice de la messe*, pp. 786–97. Durandus of Troarn, *proœmium* (149, 1375).

23 Gilbert of Nogent (PL, 156, 634 C).

24 Leo, *Sermo* 24, c. 3 (PL, 54, 206 A). Walafrid Strabon, *De rebus ecclesiasticis*, c. 26 (114, 957 D). Origen, *In Jesu Nave*, hom. 4, n. 1 (Baehrens, p. 37). Gregory of Nyssa (PG, 46, 581 A).

25 *Ordo baptismi* of Severus of Antioch (Assemani, vol. 2, pp. 285, 286).

26 Gregory of Nyssa, *In Cantica* (PG, 44, 626).

27 Gregory of Nyssa, *Catechetical Discourse* (Méridier, p. 190). Theophilus of Alexandria, translated by Jerome (Hilberg, vol. 2, p. 196). Sophronius of Jerusalem (cf, *Greek liturgy*, Mercenier, Paris, vol. 2, p. 173). Ambrose (PL, 15, 1627 B).

the grace is conferred, and of the 'mystical grace', that is to say of the grace which is mysteriously conferred by this cleansing and mysteriously contained in this water?[28]

* * *

2. *Mystical body* can also be considered as the *initiation* of a process of mystical signification, within the sphere that I have previously called 'scriptural'. Here above all, however useful and soundly based it may be in other contexts, we will need to forget the separation inserted in so many modern treatises between 'the Eucharist as sacrifice' and 'the Eucharist as sacrament'. Because the sacrament cannot be understood apart from the sacrifice during which it comes into being and to which, in its permanent state, it must retain a reference: '*In the sacrament of the body of Christ his death is announced*';[29] and for its part, the sacrifice is itself a sacrament: '*For the sacrifice is a sacrament.*'[30] Ritual sacrifice and sacramental sacrifice, they are one and the same. There is nothing contained within it that is not essentially related to the Passion of our Saviour: '*What is performed in the celebration of the Mass is performed in the sacrament of the Lord's passion.*'[31] It is the daily sacrament whose 'substance' is the unique Sacrifice accomplished by Christ in the days of his flesh: '*Of this reality he wished the sacrifice of the Church to be a daily sacrament.*'[32] This total symbolism can be understood in a variety of ways, as there are different ways of understanding the total symbolism of Scripture, some of which will be more quantitative and superficial, others more profound, more flexible or more concise. But it would not be possible to separate it out in a way that imposed limits on it. In the words, once again, of St. Augustine: '*the sacrament of the sacrifice, the mystery of the sacrifice*'.[33] '*In the likeness of a sacrifice*', says Paschasius Radbertus.[34] '*In the sacrament of the Mass*', says Rabanus Maurus;[35] and Rupert says: '*the sacra-*

---

28 Amalarius, (PL, 105, 1022 D), Laurence of Novare (66, 92 C), Gregory of Bergamo (Hürter, p. 59), etc.

29 Lanfranc, *In I Cor.* (PL, 150, 194 B).

30 Deusdedit, *Libellus contra invasores et simoniacos* (*Libelli de lite*, vol. 2, p. 325). cf. Peter Lombard, *Sentences* 4 (192, 840), etc.

31 Amalarius, *De ecclesiasticis officiis*, praefatio (PL, 105, 989 A). Ambrose, *In psalmum* 43, n. 36 (14, 1107 B). cf. Gratian, *De consecratione*, 2.60 (Fr. 1337).

32 Augustine, *De Civ. Dei*, 10, c. 20 (PL, 41, 298). Haimon, *In Hebr.* (117, 874 C). Pseudo-Primasius, *In Hebr.* (68, 734 B).

33 See *infra*, Note A.

34 *In Matthaeum* 7 (PL, 120, 518 C).

35 *In Josue* (PL, 108, 1106 A).

ments of the Masses'.[36] Was the missal *par excellence,* the 'liturgical book of the celebrant at the altar',[37] where prayers, preface and canon were to be read, not a '*sacramentary*', a '*book of the sacraments*' or '*book of the mysteries*'?[38] Just as the sacrifices of the ancient Law were symbolic prefigurations, the Eucharist in its entirety, as the rite of the new Law, is a 'sacrament of remembrance':[39]

Commemorating and celebrating the passion . . .[40]

Without this commemoration we do not confect the sacrament of the Lord's body and blood.[41]
In the wonderful sacrament you have left a commemoration of your passion . . .

In its very reality, although through the mediation of the external rite, the Eucharist therefore signifies a thing, or rather an action, which is past.[42] It is a mystery of commemoration.[43] It commemorates and reproduces, that is to say renders once again present – *makes present by representing*[44] – but in the mystery – *represents in the mystery*[45] – and through the mystery – *renews through the mystery*[46] – this

---

36 *Chronicon sancti Laurentii Leodiensis,* n. 21 (MGH, Scriptores, vol. 8, p. 269).

37 V. Leroquais, *Sacramentaires et Missels des bibliothèques publiques de France,* vol. 1, p. xi.

38 Florus, *Expositio missae,* c. 1, n. 2 (Duc, p. 87). Paschasius Radbertus, Paul and Gebehard of Ratisbon, *Third Letter to Martin of Milan* (v. 1132), cited by Le Brun, *Explication des ceremonies de la messe,* new edn., vol. 2, 1860, p. 162.

39 Augustine, *Contra Faustum* 20, c. 21 (PL, 42, 385); c. 18 (383) and 6, c. 5 (231). Alcuin, *Ep.* 307 (MGH, *Epistularum,* vol. 4, p. 470). Urban IV, bull instituting Corpus Christi in 1264.

40 *Missale gothicum* (B., vol. 1, n. 33). Pseudo-Germain (PL, 72, 89, 93). *Libri Carolini* (98, 1093, 1214), etc. cf. Gregory the Great, *Diologues,* IV, c. 59 (77, 428 A).

41 Odo of Cambrai (PL, 160, 1063 C–D). cf. Cyprian, *Ep.* 63, c. 17, n. 1 (Bayard, vol. 2, p. 211). Rabanus Maurus (PL, 107, 321 D; 111, 131 A).

42 Guitmond, 2 (PL, 149, 1455 B). cf. Eusebius (PG, 22, 89–92; 24, 701; *HE* 1, 10, Grapin, vol. 3, pp. 78–9).

43 William of St. Thierry, *Ep. ad Fratres de Monte Dei,* n. 55 (Davy, p. 103).

44 Algerius (PL, 180, 787 A). Jerome, *In Matthaeum* (26, 195). Rupert, *De devinis officiis* (170, 15 A). Baldwin (204, 732 D). Peter of Poitiers, *Sentences,* 5, c. 13 (211, 1256 C–D).

45 Pseudo-Algerius (PL, 180, 853 D). Theophrid of Echternach, *Flores epitaphii sanctorum* (157, 368 A).

46 Gregory the Great, *In evangelia,* hom. 37 (PL, 76, 1279 A); *Dialogues* 4, c. 58 (77, 425 C). Lepin, *op. cit.,* pp. 40–1. Hincmar, *Vita Remigii* (MGH, *Script. Rerum merov.,* vol. 3, p. 300).

same and unique historical Sacrifice which, equally within the mystery, the ancient rites prefigured.[47] It is not necessary to imagine a plethora of symbolic details, after the manner of Amalarius (or earlier of Pseudo-Germanus of Paris), in order to say with him, as with the whole tradition: '*In the sacrament . . . the passion of Christ is manifest.*'[48] This essential point cannot be too heavily stressed. The Mass is still 'the Passover of the Lord'.[49] The sacrifice of the Church and the memorial of the Passion cannot be separated, in the strictest terms they are one and the same. Everything happens at the altar 'in the sacrament of his precious death'.[50] As St. Cyprian had already written, 'The sacrifice which we offer is the Passion of the Lord.'[51] The *celebration of the body* that we were considering earlier is therefore a *celebration of the passion.*[52] It is '*the rite of the passion of the Lord*'.[53] In the same way the *sacrifice of the body* is the *sacrifice of the passion,*[54] and the *communion of the body* is the *communion of the passion.*[55] This is the derivation of the new sense contained in the simplest expression, although it still does not lose the original sense attributed to it: the *mystery of the body is the mystery of the passion,*[56]

---

47 Ambrose, *In psalmum* 43, n. 36 (PL, 14, 1107).

48 Amalarius, *De ecclesiasticis officiis* (PL, 105, 1141 B). cf. E. de Moreau, 'Les explanations allégoriques des ceremonies de la sainte messe au moyen âge', *Nouvelle revue théologique* 48 (1921) pp. 123 ff. *Gregorianum* (L., p. 44). Remigius of Auxerre, *Homilia 8* (PL, 131, 909 D). Rupert, *In Malachiam* (168, 821 C).

49 Paschasius Radbertus, *In Matthaeum*, 6 (PL, 120, 415 A and C).

50 *Sermo de excellentia SS. Sacramenti*, n. 7 (PL, 184, 986 A). cf. St. Leo, *Sermo* 42, c. 1 (54, 275).

51 *Ep.* 63, c. 17, n. 1 (Bayard, vol. 2, p. 211). Tertullian, *De oratione*, c. 14 (PL, 1, 1170).

52 Raoul of St. Germer, *In Leviticum* (B.M.P., vol. 17, p. 201 C). Hugh of St. Victor, *De sacramentis* (PL, 176, 429 D). cf. Serapion of Thmuis (Brightman, *Journal of Theological Studies*, vol. 1, p. 105).

53 Jerome, *Ep.*114, n. 2 (Hilberg, vol. 2, p. 395).

54 Florus, *Expositio missae*, c. 53, n. 3 (Duc, p. 127), and c. 60, n. 7 (p. 156). cf. Gregory of Bergamo, c. 3, 4 (Hürter, pp. 13–14, 16).

55 *Responsio cujusdam* (d'Achery, *Spicilegium*, vol. 1, p. 149).

56 Augustine, (PL, 35, 1353). Gregory (76, 1178 B; 77, 426 A), cited by Jonas of Orléans, Florus, Hincmar, Gezon, Lanfranc, Algerius, Gerhoh . . . *Gelasianum* (W., p. 62). Florus, Expositio missae (Duc, p. 134). Rabanus Maurus (PL, 107, 319 C, 111, 131 A and 171 B). Ratramnus, *De corporae . . .* (121, 145 A, 169 B, 170 A). Hincmar (125, 918 B, 919 B). Pseudo-Isidore (83, 906 C). *Expositio 'Dominus vobiscum'* (147, 197 A–B). St. Bruno (152, 725 B). *Glose in Matthaeum* (114, 169 A). Rupert (167, 616 D). Honorius of Autun, *Elucidarium* (172, 1130 A). William of St. Thierry, *Ep. ad Fratres de Monte Dei* (184, 327 A–B), etc. Bede (PL, 94, 75 A); Paschasius (120, 1294 C); Hincmar (125, 95 C); Rupert (167, 1246 A). cf. Florus, *Expositio missae* (Duc, p. 156). Rupert, *In Joannem* (PL, 169, 803 D; cf. 170, 49–50).

the invisible sacrament of the passion.[57] It is the *mystery of redemption.*[58]

This connection is so essential that it finds expression in strangely realist formulations. The Eucharistic cup, says St. Fulgentius of Ruspe, is *'the cup of the bodily passion'.*[59] A decree attributed to Pope Alexander declares that: *'In the offering of the sacraments . . . the passion of the Lord is to be mixed.'*[60] In a more ancient source from St. Cyprian, the Last Supper itself was called the *passion.*[61] In language reminiscent of the Greek and Oriental traditions,[62] Rupert of Tuy explains that, through the effect of the consecration, just as a metal is penetrated by fire, the bread offered on the altar becomes *'immersed in the awesome and ineffable mystery of the passion'*, and this is the reason why it continues to be the Christ in very truth.[63] The Church, says Peter Damian, is the place *'in which through the mystery of the life-giving passion, the body of Christ is offered'.*[64] Just as the holy mysteries are celebrated as a *type of the passion,*[65] so within them the mystical chalice is also drunk as a *type of the blood poured out.*[66] To partake in communion is to take into oneself the memory of the Passion,[67] or in some way to receive the cross of Christ as nourishment:[68] *'We feed off the cross of the Lord, because we eat his body.'*[69]

57 Rupert, *In Cantica*, 7 (PL, 168, 952 A). Franco, *De gratia Dei* 10, 11 (166, 776 D and 784 B).

58 *Roman Missal.* Florus, *Adversus Amalarium* 2, n. 16 (PL, 119, 91 C). *Gregorianum* (W., p. 107). Cyprian, *Ep.* 63, c. 14).

59 *Contra Fabianum*, frag. 28 (PL, 65, 790 A).

60 Burchard (PL, 140, 753). Ivo of Chartres, *Decretum*, p. 2, c. 15 (1661, 164 B). cf. *Liber pontificalis*, vol. 1, p. 127. [For much of the *Liber Pontificalis* translated into English, see R. Davis, Liverpool *Translated Texts for Historians* series, vols. 6, 13, 20 (Liverpool, 1989, 1992, 1995), and his revised 2nd edn (Liverpool, 2000).]

61 *Ep. 63*, passim. cf. Batiffol, *Leçons sur la Messe*, 5th edn., p. 176.

62 Cyril of Jerusalem (PG, 33, 1116 B). Chrysostom (61, 203, 527; 63, 898), etc.

63 *In Genesim* (PL, 167, 431 C). Peter Damian, *Opusculum* 39, c. 2 (145, 644 C). Cardinal Humbert, *Adversus Graecorum calumnies*, c. 65 (143, 644 C).

64 *Opusculum 39*, c. 2 (PL, 145, 645 B).

65 Jerome, *Adversus Jovinianum* (PL, 23, 391 A).

66 Ambrosiaster, *In I Cor.* (PL, 23, 391 A).

67 Rabanus Maurus, *In Leviticum* (PL, 108, 259 D). Hesychius, *In Leviticum* (PG, 93, 808 B). Gennadius (PL, 58, 997 C). cf. Theodore of Mopsuestia, *Fifth Mystagogical Leture* (Mingana, p. 73)

68 *Missale gothicum* (B., vol. 1, n. 214). *Liber mozarabicus sacramentorum* (F., 25)

69 Augustine (PL, 37, 1920). Rupert, *In Joannem* (169, 468). [Trans. G. McCracken, A. Cabaniss, *Library of Christian Classics* series, vol. 9, *Early Medieval Theology* (Philadelphia, 1957).]

With reference to this doctrine, the *mystical body*, which is the body mystically sacrificed and mystically offered, will therefore be the body which symbolizes the one which was once truly sacrificed and truly offered up on Calvary (without threatening in any way their particular identity). It will no longer simply be, as in the first instance, '*the body in the mystery*' but '*the body in the mystery of the passion*'.[70] It will be the body as the object of a mystical sacrifice, itself entirely relative to that sacrifice which Christ made of himself at the end of his earthly life;[71] the body engaged in a mystical action, a ritual echo, endlessly reverberating in time and space, of the unique action from which it takes its sense; and finally it is the body which is received as we proclaim the death of the Lord: '*the reception of the Eucharist is the commemoration of the Lord's passion*'. [72] It is the body by which we share in the Passion of the Lord. '*Take in the bread that which hung on the tree; take in the chalice that which poured from his side*': this Augustinian formulation, quoted by Paschasius Radbertus,[73] is something quite other than a certificate of identity; it helps us to penetrate into the intimate meaning of the mystery.

* * *

We will see this second meaning of *mystical body* in a clearer light if, in the interests of thoroughness, and following the implications and invitation of so many texts, we picture the Eucharist within the whole spectrum of its relationship to the sacrifices of the ancient Law and the Patriarchs. To study the symmetrical opposition between the 'prophecy' and the 'memory',[74] the *presentation* and the *representation*, the *preformation* or *prefiguration* or *adumbration* and the *refiguration*[75]

---

70 Ratramnus (PL, 121, 155 A). Grimaldus, *Liber sacramentorum*.

71 Gregory (PL, 77, 425 D). Remigius of Lyon, *De tenenda Scripturae veritate* (121, 1126).

72 Robert Puyllen (PL, 186, 773–4). Rupert (167, 1664 A; 169, 1472 C). Gregory of Bergamo (H., p. 14). Augustine (PL, 42, 873), cited by Hugh of Langres (142, 1329 B), Durandus of Troarn (149, 1379 C–D), Peter Lombard (192, 862), Gandolph of Bologna (Walter, p. 448), etc.

73 Augustine (PL, 120, 1354 A). J. Turmel, *Histoire de la théologie positive*, vol. 1, pp. 435–6. Augustine, *Contra Faustum* 12, c. 20 (PL, 42, 265). Third sermon of the collection of Denis (PL, 46, 827. Dom Morin, *Sermones post Maurinos reperti*, p. 19). J. Claude, *Réponse aux deux traités . . .* (Charenton, 1667), p. 479.

74 Augustine, *Contra Faustum* 20, c. 18 (PL, 42, 382–3).

75 And perhaps, in its primitive acceptance, *transformatio*. Another example of these words which are part of the two vocabularies at the same time, both eucharistic and 'scriptural'.

or the *reparation*,[76] or again between the *type, protype, prototype* and the *antitype*, each one linked in its completeness (though quite differently) to the unique summit which towers above everything, the *Very Truth of the Sacrifice of Christ*, would be to make a study not only of a privileged case, but, in its very essence, of the link between the Old Testament and the New. '*Then, the mystery of the truth to be accomplished; but now, the mystery of the truth that has been accomplished.*'[77] The Last Supper is the defining moment of both the one and the other: '*on that day the New Covenant was inaugurated*'.[78] Or still more precisely: '*the beginning of the Gospel and the sacraments of his body and blood*'.[79] As the words of institution as given by Saint Paul: '*this cup is the new covenant in my blood*'. The two cups which St. Luke mentions one after the other during that last meal should be understood as the two Testaments,[80] since the second is the Eucharistic cup, and the Eucharist is itself, as it were, a résumé of the New Testament: '*A new covenant, which he gave us of bread and the wine.*'[81] To take part in it is to have a part in the '*mystery of newness*'.[82] The new wine of this mystery is drunk 'not in the decrepitude of the letter, but in the newness of the spirit'.[83] This is the idea developed by St. Avitus of Vienne in one of the all-too-rare fragments of his sermons that have come down to us:

> *When about to accomplish the sacrament of the assumed flesh, our Redeemer . . . made a covenant by which through his gifts he made us his heirs . . . This covenant we call the new covenant . . . On the completion of the old covenant, the new one is duly and properly performed and is celebrated by mysteries of the greatest sureness.*

---

76 *Missale gothicum* (Bannister, vol. 1, p. 103), etc. Hesychius, *In Leviticum* (PG, 93, 891 B). cf. Gratian, *De consecratione*, 2.88 (Friedberg, 1350).

77 cf. Paschasius Radbertus (PL, 120, 1280 B–C). Augustine, *Contra adversarium legis et prophetarum* 1, c. 20, n. 39 (PL, 42, 66).

78 Abbon, *Sermo* 2 (PL, 132, 765 A). Amalarius, *Liber officialis* 1, c. 12 (105, 1023 B). Bruno of Segni (165, 1001 A). Garnier of Rochefort (205, 674 A). cf. Anselm of Laon, *In Matthaeum* (162, 1470 C).

79 Rupert, *In Ecclesiasten* (PL, 168, 1214 A). Honorius of Autun, *sacramentarium* (172, 745–6). Bonizo, *Decretum* (Mai, *N.P.B.*, vol. 7, p. 3, p. 20). Pseudo-Hugh, *Miscellanea* 7, t. 37 (PL, 177, 886 D). Peter Lombard (191, 1299 A).

80 Fulgentius, *Ep. 14*, n. 43 (PL, 65, 431). Paschasius, *In Matthaeum*, 12, c. 26 (120, 893 C).

81 Hincmar (PL, 135, 913 A–B). Florus, *Expositio missae*, c. 61 (Duc, pp. 133–4). *Apostolic Constitutions* 8, c. 5, n. 7; c. 12, n. 36 (Funk, pp. 477, 508). Pseudo-Athanasius, *On the unleavened* (PG, 26, 1329 C and 1331 A). cf. Luke 22.20 and I Cor. 11.25.

82 Paschasius, *In Matthaeum* 9, c. 19 (PL, 120, 669 C).

83 cf. Ivo of Chartres, *Decretum*, p. 2, c. 5, after Jerome (PL, 161, 141 A).

*This covenant our ineffable Redeemer . . . composed by his betrayal,
sealed by his passion, and opened up by his resurrection . . . This
clearly is the covenant which, at the supper of the apostles, instituted and consecrated an everlasting offering. And so we see that he
removed nothing from the fullness of his substance, since what he
had assumed for us he bequeathed to us in its totality. Others leave
their property to their heirs, but he left his very self, that is, the flesh
and blood of his body.*[84]

Within the ancient tradition of the Church, the idea of the two
Testaments, of what divides and what unites them, is a fundamental
category. It is a constantly present factor, especially in sacramental
doctrine. Of course not only are the Old and the New Testaments
not to be considered as two books, but essentially they are not even
two histories: they are to be seen above all, as their name suggests,
as two instruments of salvation, two legislations, two 'institutions',[85]
which are, both one and the other, although in different manner,
sacramental institutions. Moreover, to speak of the Old and the New
Testaments is to speak of the sacraments which define them in some
way; to speak of the relationship between one and the other, of the
relationship between their respective sacraments. And reciprocally, it
would not be possible to speak of the sacraments without, in a more or
less explicit fashion, bringing into consideration the Testaments from
which they are derived.[86] Considerably late in the history of theology,
when the sense of the word *sacramentum* has already become firmly
restricted and specialized, a treatise on the sacraments will be called
De sacramentis novae legis, and will include an obligatory introduction on the 'sacraments of the ancient law'. It holds together, as it
were, by explaining the transformation of the latter into the former,[87]
and, inversely, the passage from one Testament to the other is understood as a *transformation of sacraments*:[88]

---

84 *Ex sermone die natali calicis* (MGH, *Auctores antiquissimi*, vol. 6, p. 2). cf.
Pseudo-Dionysius, *Ecclesiastical Hierarchy*, c. 3, n. 5 (PG, 3, 432). [The *Hierarchy*
can be found in English alongside Pseudo-Dionysius's other works in C. Luibhéid
and P. Rorem, *Pseudo-Dionysius: the Complete Works* (New York, 1987).] Sicard
of Cremona, *Mitrale*, 3, c. 6 (PL, 213, 130).

85 Augustine, *De gestis Pelagii*, c. 5, n. 4, 15 (PL, 44, 327–9); *Contra duas
epistulas Pelagianorum* 3, c. 4, n. 12 (44, 595–6).

86 Augustine, *De spiritu et littera*, c. 8, n. 14 (PL, 44, 208). [English trans.
NPNF, vol. 5.]

87 *ibid.*, c. 25, n. 42 (PL, 44, 226).

88 See also *Liber de peccato originali*, c. 32, n. 37 (PL, 44, 403); *In psalmum*
73, n. 2 (36, 931); *Ep. 138*, n. 7 (33, 528).

The victim prescribed by the law passes away, as the reality con-
cealed by figures is revealed. . . No longer is a roasted lamb given
to the people through Moses, but Christ is present as the lamb who
suffered on the cross for us.[89]

Given these conditions, it is not surprising that in order to gain a sound
understanding of certain terms in Eucharistic vocabulary, recourse
has to be had to what, for want of a better name, I have called the
'scriptural sphere', that is to say to the theories elaborated in the first
Christian centuries with regard to Scripture and its interpretation. For
just as the reflection of the Fathers on the Eucharistic mystery cannot
be separated from their reflection on the entire Christian economy [of
salvation], which they find revealed in Scripture, so also their reflection on this same Scripture breaks well beyond the limits of exegesis:
its aim is to include in its grasp the totality of the work of God in the
world. Now the Middle Ages had to live for a long time off the rations
of thought derived from this source, and only slowly modified the
vocabulary which came out of this reflection. It would seem, in any
case, that a good number of texts concerning the Eucharist would be
more thoroughly understood, and some of them would offer fewer
exegetical problems to defenders of the 'real presence' if the two following points were taken into consideration more resolutely than has
perhaps been the case up till now. On the one hand, the essential perspective of these texts is not that of a presence or of an object, but that
of an action and of a sacrifice: *'the celebration as a sign imitates his*
death';[90] and, on the other hand, the vocabulary relative to this action
and this sacrifice is driven in great part by the vocabulary relative to
the two Testaments:

> *. . . ancient documents have their ending,*
> *for the newer rite is here.*

In the texts being alluded to, it is the entire 'Eucharistic complex', if I
may use such a term – action and presence, sacrifice and sacrament,

---

89 Pseudo-Hildebert. Hauréau, 'Notice sur les mélanges poétiques d'Hildebert
de Lavardin', *Notices et extraits des manuscrits de la Bibliothèque nationale*
. . . , 28 (1878) pp. 408–9. See *infra*, Chapter 9.

90 Augustine, *Ad Bonifacium* (PL, 33, 363) or Gregory, Dialogues (77, 425).
Lanfranc (150, 423), Guitmond (149, 1457). Pseudo-Bede, *In psalmos* (93, 600
B–C, and 1035 C–D), Gilbert of Nogent, *Ep. de buccella Judae data*, c. 3 (156,
531 A–C).

tangible sign and profound reality – which is being brought into juxta-position either with Calvary – *the sacrament of the body which hung on the tree* – or with the Mosaic rites or the sacrifices of the patriarchal era. In no way is a direct link between the body of Christ, considered 'in itself' and the 'sacramental species' being envisaged here.[91]

* * *

3. The *mystical body* can finally be understood as the *initiation* of a process in reverse of the one above: a process that is no longer looking backward but looking forward, and a process which simultaneously signifies and effects. In this third case, more than in the previous two, our two spheres, both the 'ceremonial' and the 'scriptural', become enmeshed.

This means that the Eucharist is not simply oriented towards the past, dependent on Calvary. It is also oriented towards a future, which in turn depends on it: the building up of the Church and the coming of the 'Truth'.[92] Thus it has a double symbolism. It is a sacrament of memory but also a sacrament of hope.[93] *A pledge and image of the reality to come.*[94] It does not only reproduce, it also anticipates: *pre-signs, pre-figures, pre-demonstrates.*[95] In its own turn it also makes present and makes present by signifying. It is the effective sign, most particularly, of the *body of Christ which is the Church*; it is the effec-tive sign of the fraternal charity which binds its members: '*fraternal charity, which is signified by this sacrament*';[96] it is the effective sign of the peace and unity for which Christ died and towards which we are reaching, moved by his Spirit: '*the sign of unity, the sign of con-cord and of peace*'.[97] It therefore signifies us to ourselves – *our own mystery,*[98] *a figure of ourselves*[99] – in what we have already begun to

---

91 *Sententiae divinitatis*, tract. 5 (Geyer, p. 135).

92 Drogon (PL, 166, 1562 C–D). cf. *Expositio officiorum Ecclesiae* attributed to George of Arbella (trans. Connelly, CSCO, *Scriptores Syri*, series II, vol. 92).

93 Augustine, *Contra Faustum* 12, c. 20 (PL, 42, 265). Hincmar, *De cavendis vitiis*, c. 9 (125, 920 A).

94 Ratramnus (PL, 121, 163 A). cf. Hilary, *In Matthaeum* (9, 1065 B–C).

95 *Roman Missal.*

96 Gilbert the Universal, *Glosula in psalmum* 21 (Smalley, *Recherches de théo-logie ancienne et médiévale*, 1936, p. 58).

97 Ernulf of Rochester (d'Achéry, Spicilegium, vol. 3, p. 472). Rupert, *In Joannem* (PL, 169, 482). Gregory of Bergamo (H., pp. 44, 74, 78), etc.

98 Augustine (PL, 38, 1247). Pseudo-Haimon, *De corporae et sanguine Domini* (118, 81 A). St. Bruno (152, 725), etc. Jerome, *Liber hebraïcarum quaestionum in Genesim*, c. 14 (PL, 23, 961 B).

99 Gilbert the Universal (*loc. cit.* p. 57).

be through baptism (*one baptism*), but above all in what we ought to become: in this sacrament of unity, *is prefigured what we will become in the future.*[100]

Here once again, if we do not wish to misinterpret ancient Christian tradition, the Eucharist has to be seen as a whole. It has to be seen indivisibly as sacrifice and sacrament, sacramental sacrifice or sacrament of sacrifice: *the sacrifice of his body, the sacrament of the faithful.*[101] The external sacrifice and ritual is also the sacrament of the 'true' sacrifice, of that interior and spiritual sacrifice by which the holy society of all those who belong to God is brought into being:

> *Every work we perform in order to cleave to God in holy fellowship is a true sacrifice . . . A visible sacrifice is the sacrament of an invisible sacrifice.*[102]

Posited by St. Augustine with regard to the rites of the old covenant, the thinking behind this principle covers every sacrifice in which there is a ritual element. It also covers the Mass, whose aim is to lead us '*to the fellowship of union*'. Therefore it has to be said that every time they participate worthily in the mysteries, the members of Christ do not only proclaim, in the words of St. Paul, the past death of their Lord. They also proclaim, by means of that same death,[103] the future fulfilment of the great Body of which they are members: 'until he comes', as the Apostle added.[104]

In this third and final sense, the sacramental body of Christ can still be called mystical, because it is still in this context that it is called a sign.[105] '*It conveys something mystical.*'[106] Just as we say 'mystical bread' because we are speaking of bread with which a mystery is enacted, the mystery of the altar, so we will also say 'mystical body' because, on the altar, it is the body through which 'our mystery' is enacted. And just as the manna was a *mystical thing* in relation to

---

100 Augustine, *In psalmum 26*, sermo 2, n. 2 (PL, 36, 200).

101 Augustine, *Ep.* 140, n. 61 (PL, 41, 238; cf. 655). Amalarius (105, 1138 C–D).

102 Augustine, *De civitate Dei*, 10, c. 6 (PL, 41, 238; cf. 655).

103 Cyprian, *De passione Christi*, c. 6.

104 Ambrosian Rite (DACL, vol. 1, 1418). cf. *De sacramentis*, 4, c. 6, n. 26 (PL, 16, 445 A).

105 Remigius of Auxerre, *In psalmum 21* (PL, 131, 259 D). St. Bruno, *Expositio in psalmum 21* (152, 725). Pseudo-Haimon, *De corporae et sanguine Domini* (118, 817 A).

106 Guitmond (PL, 149, 1500 B–C).

the Eucharist of which it was the promise and the sign,[107] so also the Eucharistic mystery, which is the truth prefigured here, exists as such in relation to its ultimate fruit. It is a mystical body, a body 'as type and symbol',[108] this time signifying, either in itself or by virtue of the elements which already signify it – not only the 'real body', once born of the Virgin, but the 'true body', the total and definitive body, the one for whose redemption the Saviour sacrificed his body of flesh, the one which is sufficiently solid, in the spiritual sense, not to be the sign of any other. This is the origin of the connection made by many authors between the *breaking of the host* and the *opening of the Scriptures*. This was supported by the Emmaus story, itself brought into connection with the Eucharistic action by certain liturgies,[109] at the same time as by the traditional assimilation of the divine Word to the Bread of Life. In this is illustrated in a striking fashion that old idea of an 'understanding of faith', which was a search for the *rationale of the sacraments*, an understanding of the mysteries contained both in the Scriptures and in the liturgy, *the understanding of the Scriptures and of the sacraments of God*.[110] Therefore we should not be surprised by its fate:

> *The breaking is to be understood as revelation. He 'broke', that is, he made them understand what his body signified, namely, the Church of which he is the head . . . The breaking, as I have said, is the revelation of the mystery. Of this breaking it is said, 'The little ones have sought for bread'. This bread is Scripture, which has crusts and crumbs; the crust is the letter; the crumbs are the meaning that lies hidden in it. This is 'broken' when it is expounded. This breaking of Scripture is alluded to by the Apostle: 'The bread which we break . . .'*[111]

---

107 Peter of Blois (PL, 207, 1145; cf. 1141 A), etc.

108 Origen, *In Matthaeum*, vol. 11, n.14 (Klostermann, p. 58); *In Joannem*, vol. 10 (Preuschen, p. 209).

109 Celtic Mass (DTC, vol. 10. 1385). cf. Augustine (PL, 38, 1106, 1118, 1127).

110 William of St. Thierry, *Liber de natura et dignitate amoris*, c. 10, n. 31 (PL, 184, 399 A). cf. Hilary, *In psalmum* 64, n. 15 (Zingerle, p. 246). Ambrose, *De mysteriis*, c. 1, n. 2 (PL, 16, 389; cf. De sacramentis: 417). Alcuin, *Ep. 137* (MGH, *Epistularum*, vol. 4, p. 214).

111 *Sententiae Parisienses* (Landgraf, p. 42). Master Herman, *Epitome theologiae christianae* (PL, 178, 1742–3). *Sententiae divinitatis* (Geyer, p. 134). cf. Abbaudus, *De fractione* (PL, 166, 1341–8). Honorius of Autun (172, 563 D). John of Salisbury, *Polycraticus* 7, c. 13 (199, 667 C). Baldwin (204, 762 D). Ivo of Chartres (PL, 162, 559); Amalarius (105, 1328 C); Bede (92, 628 B); Augustine (34, 1206); Ambrose (15, 1692 C and *In psalmos*, Petschenig, p. 237); Origen, *In Genesim* (B., p. 112) and *In Leviticum* (p. 331).

The supper at Emmaus made possible an identical and more natural bringing together of the two, given the explanation of the Scriptures which had preceded the moment of recognition.[112] And the same lesson could be learned from the first breaking of bread at the hands of our Saviour on the day when he multiplied the loaves. It was a prefiguration of the Eucharist, but also, by virtue of that, of the breaking open of the Gospel. The seven loaves on that occasion signify the Book of the seven mysterious seals. The gesture of breaking them was the same as the breaking open of the seals of the Book. And who was able do it, who was able in the same way to break open for us the bread of the word for which we were starving, in order to bring us into the very heart of the mystery, if not He who is the Word itself and the Bread of Life come down from Heaven?[113] This is as much about the Eucharist as about the Scriptures. Neither one is sufficient in itself in its literal sense, although faith must first of all be rooted within them. It must be accessed in its fullness by means of a 'spiritual understanding' or a 'mystical understanding', which is the work of the Spirit of Christ[114] if it is to be understood in its fullest meaning. *The bread that we break, that is whose mystery we break open.*[115] One day, this double mystery, the one that is hidden beneath the word and the one that is hidden beneath the rite, the mystery of the Word and the mystery of the Church, will be revealed to us in its unity. Adored today through the same faith in the Scriptures and in the Eucharist, this unique Mystery of Christ will shine before the eyes of all when Christ comes to perfect stature within the Church, which is his body, and he appears in glory with all his saints. Then, says the Apostle, we will no longer know in figures, and we will no longer know in part: *when he who has been made perfect will come.*[116]

* * *

---

112 Otho of Lucques (PL, 176, 144–145). Stephen of Baugé (172, 1303). Master Simon (Weisweiler, p. 38). cf. Albert the Great, *In IV Sent* (Vivès, vol. 29, p. 337).

113 Paschasius Radbertus, *In Matthaeum* 7, c. 16 (PL, 120, 549 A–B).

114 cf. Grimaldus, *Liber Sacramentorum* (PL, 121 835 C).

115 *Commentarius Catabringiensis in epistulas Pauli e schola Petri Abaelardi, In I Cor.*, X (Landgraf, vol. 2, p. 257; cf. p. 265). cf. Richard of St. Victor, *De eruditione hominis interioris*, I, c. 20 (PL, 196, 1264 B).

116 I Cor. 13.9–12. cf. Augustine (PL, 38, 389–90). Rupert (168, 1612 C). Algerius (180, 764 A). Drogon (166, 1562 C–D).

Memorial, anticipation and presence: in each of these three essential aspects,[117] which it possesses from the outset, the Eucharist is indeed a mystery,[118] and although each in turn can be thrown into sharper relief, they remain inseparable. The body of Christ that the Church offers through it – *in the mystery of bread, in the mystery of the passion, in our mystery* – could with good reason be described as mystical.

If we now refer back to one or other of the passages quoted above, which makes use of the Eucharistic terms *mystical body* or *mystical flesh*, it will be easy to determine its sense, which is not always identical.

For someone like Paschasius Radbertus, for example, the mystical body is either, in a general fashion, the body which is present and received '*in the mystery*' (the first case), or more specifically (the second case) a figure of the historical body: this is what is being expressed by saying that, in the Eucharist, Christ is '*the figure of himself*', '*the sacrament of himself*'.[119] This formulation recalls another from St. Augustine, which relates to the Last Supper: '*Christ was carried in his own hands*.'[120] It should have enjoyed greater success, although it was hotly contested by several people,[121] because it was open to differing

---

117 St. Thomas would summarize these in the office of the Blessed Sacrament: '*The memory of his passion is contemplated, the mind is filled with grace, and a pledge of future glory is given to us.*'

118 The memorial aspect would be built on a double foundation. It would emerge further in both the 'scriptural' and the 'ceremonial' spheres at the same time, if it could be established with certainty, according to Dom Casel and Dölger, that the word μυστήριον, to the extent that it depends on pagan language, originates in the vocabulary of meals and funeral offerings, where the μυστήρια were ceremonies of commemoration, 'memorials' (anamneses).

119 Lanfranc, *Liber de corporae*, c. 14 (PL, 150, 424). Ivo of Chartres (161, 154 B); Algerius (180, 792 B–D and 793 B), etc. cf. Paschasius (120, 1279 B). Gregory of Bergamo, *De veritate corporis Christi*, c. 18 (Hürter, pp. 75–6).

120 *In psalmum 33* (PL, 36, 306, 308). Pseudo-Bede (93, 652–653), Hincmar (125, 921 A), Remigius of Auxerre (131, 312 B), Hériger (139, 186 A–B), Theoduin of Liége (146, 1441 B), Durandus of Troarn (149, 1401 D), Guitmond (149, 1469 T), Odo of Cambrai (160, 1062 A), Rupert (167, 1105; 169, 465 C; 170, 15 A), Hugh of St. Victor (176, 464 A), Gerhoh, *In psalmos* (193, 815 D and 1328 C), Gratian, *De consecratione* 2.92 (Friedberg, 1351). cf. *Sermo de excellentia* (PL, 184, 984 A–B), etc. St. Bonaventure, *In cena Domini*, sermo 2 (Quaracchi, vol. 9, p. 251). [For the works of St. Bonaventure in English, see G. Marcil and Z. Hayes, eds., *Works of Saint Bonaventure* (New York, 1978–); J. de Vinck, *The Works of Bonaventure*, cf. *I Reg.* 21.13.]

121 How, it was objected, can an invisible body be the sign of a body which is in itself visible? This objection would be taken up again by Aubertin and examined in *Perpetuité* (Migne, vol. 2, pp. 795–6). Or again, albeit rarely: 'This cannot be, that the form and the formed thing are the same' (*Florilegia of Saint-Amand*,

interpretations. In his Eucharistic mystery, Christ can indeed signify himself, either in his earthly life and his historical sacrifice, or in his existence at the right hand of the Father,[122] or in his spiritual work[123] and above all in his Church.[124] Each individual could therefore, in using the same formulation, either underline a preferred aspect of this complex symbolism, or unite them all in the same interpretation.[125] Scholasticism will say: '*Nothing prevents the same thing from being understood in different ways, either as a sign or as a figure for the thing itself.*'[126]

For Ratramnus, although Paschasius's second sense is not excluded – indeed it is even mentioned explicitly – there is another aspect which is dominant. For him, the Eucharist is above all a mystical body in that it symbolizes, as Saint Augustine so often repeated, the body of Christ which we ourselves are, or should be: the '*body of the people that believes*', the '*body of the people that receives*', the '*body of the people reborn in Christ*', '*the body of believers*'.[127] It is, reproduced on the altar, the mystery of ourselves (the third case).

As for the text of Saint Jerome on the *mystical flesh*, it allows us to verify in more tangible fashion certain effects of this phrase on the language of exegesis. It is certainly in terms of being Eucharistic, as food for the faithful soul, that the flesh of Christ is called mystical here: if Jerome had spoken of Christ in the context of his earthly existence, he would never have thought of using such an attribute. Nevertheless it does not seem to be uniquely, or even especially so described through Eucharistic considerations. Note that in the preceding lines it is already linked twice to other words: '*about which the prophet proclaimed in mystical speech*', '*Moses. . . testifies in mystical speech*'.[128] This repeated use of a familiar formulation[129] will have

---

loc. cit., n. 89). cf. Gerhoh of Reichersberg, *Liber de simoniacis* (MGH, *Libelli de lite*, vol. 3, p. 267).

122 Otho of Lucques (PL, 176, 144).

123 Gregory of Bergamo (H., p. 81) or the *Florilegia of Saint-Amand*, (School of Anselm of Laon) (Lottin, *Recherches de théologie ancienne et médiévale*, 1939, p. 309).

124 Guitmond (PL, 149, 1460 D; cf. 1461 C). *Deus de cujus principo* of the school of Laon (Weisweiler, *Recherches de théologie ancienne et médiévale*, 1933, p. 269).

125 Lanfranc (PL, 150, 415 A) and Robert Puyllen (189, 965 A–B).

126 Albert the Great, *In IV Sent.* (Vivès, vol. 29, p. 178). William of St. Thierry (PL, 180, 356).

127 PL, 121, 167–9, 159.

128 PL, 24, 529 A and D.

129 In the same commentary on Isaiah, c. 149 C, 633 B, 638 C; cf. 875 D and 25, 1478 B. *In psalmum* 96 (Morin, p. 142). *Ep. 78*, n. 17 (Hilberg, vol. 2, p. 67); 119, n. 7 (p. 456); 129, n. 2 (t. III, p. 166), etc.

made it spring spontaneously, once again, from the pen of Jerome. Here we find ourselves at the very centre of the 'scriptural sphere', and we could certainly, without sacrificing a single appreciable nuance, translate: '*Which fat refers mystically to nothing other than the flesh*' in the way in which Saint Augustine wrote: '*speaking mystically of eating his flesh*'. [130] Here the *mystical flesh* is the flesh that Christ, either by himself in the Gospel, or in the Old Testament through its prophets, *mystically commends* to us.

Finally, there is Jean Béleth. For all that his formulation appears facile and apparently banal, it is nevertheless instructive. Béleth is speaking of the institution of the Eucharist. At the Last Supper, he says, our Saviour 'first of all gave his body mystically, before offering it in truth'. The contrast *in truth – mystically* is what strikes us initially. It obliges us to understand *mystically* by *in mystery*, seeing it rather as an attribute than as an apposition, and we would therefore express it thus: '*first of all he gave us his body through the mystery, which he would then offer in truth*'. *Mystically and proleptically* (Μυστικῶς καὶ προληπτικῶς), said Eutychius of Constantinople:[131] and Isidore of Seville, still speaking of the Last Supper said: '*This was then performed in mystery*.'[132] This 'mystery' in which Christ gives himself to his Apostles is of course the rite, the 'sacrament' (first case). As Christian Druthmar said, in his commentary on Saint Matthew's narrative: '*this is my body, that is, he says, in the sacrament*'.[133] And as Rupert of Tuy said: '*First in the sacrament of bread and wine, then in its own form.*'[134] But, in the second place, it is clear that the gift *in mystery* is contrasted with the offering *in truth*. Now, the *truth* with which we are dealing here is not the final truth, the fullness of Christ in which everything must be brought to completion, but the first truth, the truth of the sacrifice from which everything else flows. It is the historical reality of the cross. The 'mystical' body is thus made dependent on the 'true' body, which hung on the cross (second case). This is the origin of the classical problem, to which, following on from many others, Jean Béleth precisely aludes, the problem posed by the apparent contrast with the Eucharist distributed to the apostles before the Passion.

Jean Béleth's phrase gives us a further example of this reference to

---

130 *De civitate Dei* (PL, 41, 301). cf. Ambrose, *In Lucam* 6, n. 82 (15, 1690).
131 PG, 86, 2397 A.
132 PL, 83, 755 A.
133 *In Matthaeum* (PL, 106, 1476).
134 *In Reg.* (PL, 167, 1171 D). Peter of Poitiers, *Sentences*, 5, c. 12 (PL, 211, 1249 B), etc.

the action which I said was still implied to some degree: and not only to a 'real' action, that was historically accomplished, but to a ritual action that was engaged in immediately. Indeed, in order to translate fully the adjective *mystical*, on top of the reconstituted formulation 'given in the mystery', we need here to presume yet another: '*offered in mystery*'. Symmetry demands it, and it is required in order to give the full sense to '*offered in truth*'. The body that is mystically shared out is therefore, and it should have been from the beginning, the body that was mystically offered. The 'presence' of this body is not denied, not even neglected: quite the contrary. But it appears to follow on logically from the affirmation of the offering and the gift, an offering and a gift that are acts, and the mystical manner of this presence will be likewise determined by the mystical manner of the acts. This 'pragmatic' aspect can first of all be found in a passage from Hesychius that is parallel to the one from Béleth. To finish this chapter, let us therefore allow our first witness to *the mystical body* to comment on our last witness:

> He did not only say, '*I have power to lay down my soul*', but in anticipation he offered up himself at the supper of the apostles, as is known by those who perceive the power of the mysteries . . . [The Passion] *was accomplished first in his hands at the mystical supper, when he took and broke the bread, and then on the cross, when he was fastened to the tree.*[135]

Whatever we make of these nuances, it is clear that there is no point our searching in the use of *mystical body* or of *mystical flesh* for some indication or other of the degree of 'realism' or of 'symbolism' in the Eucharistic doctrines where they appear. The fact that such people as Paschasius Radbertus, Ratramnus, Rabanus Maurus or Godescalc can be brought together in their use of it should be enough to dissuade us from attempting any such research. No doubt the intentions of Ratramnus and the homilist from Lyon go some way to smoothing things out. But their use of it is a question of context, not of the meaning of the word itself. It nevertheless stands that, in this early stage of its history, and particularly in the ninth century, *mystical body* is in some sense a technical expression that serves, inadequately at times, to distinguish the Eucharist from the 'body born of the Virgin', or from the '*body of the Church*', while at the same time placing it in relation with both one and the other. By what curious cross-country route the

---

135 *In Leviticum* (PG, 93, 821 D).

'body of the Church' came in its turn, and precisely in opposition to the Eucharistic body, to take the name of *mystical body*, is what we will see in the next two chapters.

4

Sacramental Body and Ecclesial Body

[89–90]

The Pauline and traditional terminology maintained its simple interpretation for a long time. The Church is the body of Christ. It is
pre-eminently so, and it is so in all truth. There is no intention of
tempering this affirmation with any gloss or attribute, as still happens
with the Eucharist when it is seen in relation to the historical body of
the Redeemer. So we find it in that anonymous epistle of the eleventh
century or twelfth century on the sacraments of the heretics, which
takes up the classic division of the three bodies in the following terms:
'the Body of Christ in person – the sacrament of the body – his body,
which is the Church'.[1] So we find in Honorius of Autun, who writes:
'Melchizedek expressed the sacrifice of Christ with bread and wine,
which Christ transformed into the *sacrament of his body* and blood
. . . This sacrifice they confirmed with his blood, and so deserved to be
numbered *in the body of Christ*.'[2] So we find, above all, in Gilbert of
Nogent and Rupert of Tuy.

In his work on saints' relics, Gilbert of Nogent, finding himself led
to commenting on the Eucharist, speaks of the sacramental body as of
a '*relative body*', a '*derived body*', a '*vicarious body*', which in relation
to the '*principal body*', that is, with the historical body, could only
have a '*vicarious identity*' and which could distinguish itself from it as
'*other*' or '*quasi-other*'.[3] By allusion to the '*sacrificed flesh*' of the Old
Testament[4] and in a natural correlation with the expression '*sacrificial
bread*',[5] Rupert of Tuy, for his part, forms the short-lived expression
'*sacrificial body*',[6] which perhaps takes its inspiration from certain

---

1 MGH, *Libelli de lite*, vol. 3, p. 17.

2 *Gemma animae*, c. 106, 108 (PL, 172, 579 B, 580 A). Gerard of Cambrai,
Acta synodi abretac (142, 1280 B). Rupert, (168, 448 D, 1543 B and D, etc. . . .).

3 *De pignoribus sanctorum*, 2, c. 1, 2 (PL, 156, 629–31). See J. de Ghellinck,
L'essor de la literature latine au XIIe siècle, vol. 2, pp. 117, 170.

4 Levit., 7.20. Hesychius, *In Leviticum* (PG, 93, 855 D, 856 A, 862 C, 886 B).

5 Rabanus Maurus (PL, 107 A, 319 A).

6 *De divinis officiis*, 2, c. 9 (PL, 170, 41 B); *In Genesim* 4, c. 5 (167, 329 D);
cf. *In Leviticum* 1, c. 16 (167, 759).

passages in which Saint Augustine spoke of the '*flesh and blood of the sacrifice*',[7] which can be approximated to the '*through the sacrificed flesh*' of the poems of Hildebert.[8]

These last distinctions do not altogether correspond to those to which we have become accustomed through the theologians of the ninth century or tenth century. If, indeed, the body present on the altar is still clearly distinct from the 'body born of the Virgin' in its earthly existence in the flesh, it is far less distinct from the resurrected and glorious body, seated at the right hand of the Father. It is between these last two, the historical body and the heavenly body, that the abbot of Nogent and the abbot of Tuy place the principal division. In speaking of a *vicarious identification*, the former does not in the least intend to undervalue the mystery of the Eucharist, but, on the contrary, he wishes to exalt it in the face of the pseudo-relics of Christ to which a doubly ill-informed piety accorded such value.[9] If he insists on maintaining a certain duality between the historical body and the sacramental body, it is with a view to suppressing any duality between the sacramental body and the celestial body: for the one can be accepted without scandal, since it can be understood by reason of the temporal difference, while the other – as happens with those who venerate material relics of the Saviour – would be *a perverse duality*. It would ruin the essential unity that, above all distinctions, we must acknowledge in Christ. From the sacramental body to the glorified body, there is therefore a perfect conformity and harmony.[10] Besides this, Gilbert protests that it would not be possible to express his idea differently, given that, in the context, '*the identity is often expressed by number*'. In addition he asks if it means undermining the divinity of the Logos, or his nature with regard to the Father when, along with Scripture itself, we call him Splendour, Figure or Image?[11] As for Rupert's *sacrificial body*, if it does not appear to be purely and simply identical to the '*indi-*

---

7 *Contra Faustum* 20, c. 21 (PL, 42, 385); cited by Florus, *Expositio Missae*, c. 4, n. 25 (Duc, p. 92). But here Augustine is speaking of Christ's sacrifice in general, not particularly of the Eucharist. The same in Etherius and Beatus, *Ad Elipandum*, I, c. 67 (PL, 96, 936 C). See also Augustine, *Quaestiones in Heptateuchum*, 3, c. 57 (34, 704).

8 *Versus de sacramento altaris* (PL, 171, 1193 B). *Missale Francorum* (72, 336 D).

9 Geiselmann, 'Die Stellung des Guibert von Nogent in der Eucharistlehre der Frühscholastik', *Theologische Quartalschrift*, 1929. cf. Gerard of Cambrai (PL, 142, 1282–1283). *Vita S. Eudociae martyris*, c. 12, n. 44; c. 13, n. 49 (*Acta Sanctorum*, martii, vol. 1, pp. 20, 21).

10 *De pignoribus sanctorum* (PL, 156, 648–650, 643 D).

11 *Epistula mancupatoria*, n. 1 (PL, 156, 609).

vidual body of the Lord', this is not because it is any less truly the body of the Lord. Above all it would seem that if this is the case, it is because it is a body that has been set free from the bondage of purely animal life. It is this sacrificed flesh, stripped down beforehand of its grosser elements, its *hide and hair*, to an altogether spiritual flesh, reduced to its pure essence, but all the more alive and vivifying for that; it is a flesh that has been liberated from all that is corruptible and wretched in humanity, fired in the forge of the Passion, which allowed nothing to survive but that pure and substantial *'fat and richness'* exalted by the Psalmist.[12] The bread and wine of the sacrifice are therefore in no way less than flesh and blood; they are in fact more: they are spirit and life, because the true Logos and the true Godhead are contained within them.[13] Since nothing mortal remains in them any longer, they have become bearers of all the grace and all the truth of the Word incarnate. And Rupert concludes: *'In name, reality and effect, it is true flesh and true blood.'* Everything that constitutes the true essence of the body of Christ is there, for the nourishment of the faithful soul.[14] It remains no less true, however, that such ways of speaking carry a restrictive nuance within their very content, a nuance that it is almost impossible to eliminate, and which anyway their authors do not entirely deny. We can see this clearly in the addition that Rupert himself tacks onto his first explanations:

> *Animal life . . . is fleshly, is flesh. But the Lord said, 'The flesh is of no avail.'. . . It was fitting that his wisdom should administer to us through the sacrifice spiritual life alone . . . This spiritual life is in the sacrificial body, though without animal life, just as the light of the sun, without its heat, is present to us in the body of the moon.*[15]

If it was only a matter of the contrast between the body in its carnal state and the glorified body, Rupert would certainly have made a point of finding a more adequate comparison, just as he would not have employed, as he does several times deliberately to designate the Eucharist with regard to the Victim of Calvary, the neuter form *holy*

---

12 Psalm 19.4; 62.6. cf. St. Bernard, *In Cantica*, sermo 23, n. 3 (PL, 183, 952 D). *Sermo de excellentia*, n. 8 (184, 986 B).

13 *In Genesim* 4, c. 5 (PL, 167, 329 C–D). cf. *In Matthaeum*, 11 (168, 1583).

14 *In Leviticum* I, c. 16 (PL, 167, 759–60) there is a parallel between the holocaust and the Eucharist. We must judge it in the same way as 'whether the body is true, whether the flesh is true, which we consume' (167, 662 A); 'truly the body of Christ and the blood' (168, 818–20), etc.

15 *De divinis officiis*, 2, c. 9 (PL, 170, 41 D); cf. c. 12 (49–50).

of holies. He does this deliberately, because more than once he moves in this way from the masculine to the neuter forms in the same sentence.[16] And certainly once again these two expressions, so dear to the abbot of Tuy, are not without strong connotations, both traditional and scriptural. His concept of the '*sacrificial body*' does not exactly recapture our concept of the real presence;[17] it more comfortably approximates to the Cyrilian concept of 'mystical eulogy', from which not all connotations of 'species' are absent, and in which we can also immediately see the link between his '*holy of holies*' and the '*holy things*' or '*holy of holies*' of the liturgy.[18] Saint Cyprian had already called the Eucharist '*the holy thing of the Lord*';[19] and, like Rupert himself, Remigius of Auxerre spoke of '*the holy of holies*'.[20] Was this language significantly different from the '*holy of holies*' of the realist Paschasius?[21] But this persistence of archaic concepts joined to the use of the word '*body*' was precisely what would begin, at the start of the twelfth century, to cause astonishment and eventually anxiety. The author of the *Sermo de excellentia SS. Sacramenti* would say once again, though significantly later: '*this holy of holies and sacrament of sacraments*',[22] but the context is no longer the same, and this redundancy is in itself reassuring. For its part, Gilbert of Nogent's '*vicarious body*' still retains some connection with the vocabulary of the cult of images; its correlative '*principal body*' translates the Greek πρωτότυπον, by which was meant the original, of which the image was the

---

16 *In Leviticum* (PL, 167, 760; cf. 779 D; 168, 927 D, 928 B). *Ad Cunonem* (169, 203). *De Spiritu sancto*, 3, c .21 (167, 1663 A–B).

17 To make this clear we would need to develop this in a way that would be inappropriate here. cf. *De divinis officiis*, 2, c. 9 (PL, 170, 41 B); *In Genesim*, 4, c. 5 (167, 329). Dom Séjourné, 'Rupert de Deutz', (DTC).

18 Cyril of Jerusalem, *Fifth Mystagogical Lecture*, c. 19 (PG, 33, 1124); *Apostolic Constitutions*, 8, c. 13, n. 12–13 (Funk, p. 516). *Didache*, c. 9, n. 5 (Quasten, p. 11). [For the Didache in English translation, see the Loeb series, K. Lake, *The Apostolic Fathers* (London, 1970), vols. 24–5. See also K. Niederwimmer, *The Didache: a commentary* (Minneapolis, 1998).] Cyril of Alexandria (PG, 74, 696 C). cf. Chrysostom, *In Hebr.*, hom. 17 (63, 128) [English translation in NPNF, series I, vol XIV]. *Leonianum* (Feltoe, pp. 108, 127). Gregory the Great, *Epist.* 10, *Ep.* 35 (PL, 77, 1092 B). Augustine (PL, 36, 828) after Daniel 9.24. Gregory (77, 1159 A). Paschasius Radbertus (120, 177 C). Rupert (PL, 167, 561 D, 674 D, 789 A, 1057 B, 1064 D, 1368 D, 1500 A, 1519 D, 1651 D, 1663 A–B; 168, 422 B, 673 A, 870 C, etc.). Gerhoh (PL, 193, 1791 A; 194, 418 B) on the Eucharist (193, 702–3). Peter Alfonsi, *Dialogue* (157, 666 C; cf. 625 B).

19 Hartel, pp. 248, 256, 562.

20 *Homilia 8* (PL, 131, 909 D).

21 *Liber de corporae*, c. 8, n. 1; n. 5–6 (PL, 120, 1286 B, 1290 B–C). cf. Gezonius of Tortona (137, 394 D).

22 n. 10 (PL, 184, 987 B).

copy.[23] Despite the sincere and irenic commentary that accompanies it, it still appears – and all the other uses of '*vicarious*' contribute to this impression[24] – rather like a delegate, a substitute, almost a provisional replacement. This is certainly infinitely better than any reference to materiality would be, but – and here I again use Gilbert's word – the suspicion remains that it constitutes something *provisional*.[25]

* * *

At the very least, expression of this sort specified the Eucharistic body by distinguishing it from any other type of 'body'. Of the Church, in contrast, both in the context of the Eucharist and elsewhere, we still commonly use, without any further explanation, in the ancient and Carolingian fashion: '*the body of Christ*', '*the body of the Lord*',[26] '*the body which is the Church*', '*the true body of the Church*'.[27] Whenever it is a question of 'the unity of the body of Christ',[28] everyone still understands, as they did in the time of Florus and Amalarius, which unity is being talked about. The same is true whenever 'being transformed into the body of Christ'[29] or even 'into the flesh of Christ'[30] is under discussion. We sometimes still find the *flesh–body* succession, in which case the word *body* means the Church, or at least the Eucharist in its specific relation to the Church. So we find it in the formulation of Gerald of Cambrai that is analogous to those of Augustine and

---

23　*Acts of the Second Council of Nicaea* (Mansi, vol. 13. 325–6) [trans. NPNF series II., vol XIV]. *Libri Carolini*, 3, c. 16 (PL, 98, 1147 B).

24　Peter Damian, *Sermo 63* (PL, 144, 858 C). Peter of Celle (202, 1108 D), etc. cf. Origen, *In Lucam*, hom. 22 (trans. by Jerome) (Rauer, p. 142). Rupert (167, 634 D, 635 A).

25　*De pignoribus sanctorum* (PL, 156, 640 A).

26　Gilbert of Nogent, *Liber quo ordine sermo fieri debeat* (PL, 156, 24 B).

27　Guitmond (PL, 149, 1459, 1460). Peter Damian (145, 94 A, 834 A). Cardinal Humbert (*Libelli de lite*, vol. 1. p. 195). *Liber canonum contra Henricum* (*ibid.*, p. 480). Bruno of Segni (vol. 2, p. 195). Yves of Chartres (PL, 162, 543 C). Rupert (167, 555 C, 564 D, 759 C; 168, 39 A, 496 D, 560 B, 807 D; 169, 301 A and D, 802 A). Stephen of Baugé (172, 1289 B). Honorius of Autun (172, 271, 554, 794, 1128 D, 1129 B). Hermann of Tours (180, 30 A, 34 A–B). Abelard (180, 331 A). William of St. Thierry (184, 398 A). Arnold of Bonneval (189, 1643–1644). Baldwin (204, 697 A and 771). *Sententiae Parisienses* (Landgraf, p. 42). *Causa Decretalium* (Landgraf, *Scholastik*, 1940, p. 211; cf. *ibid.*, p. 215), etc.

28　Robert of Melun, *In I Cor.* (Martin, p. 215; cf. p. 211).

29　Augustine (PL, 35, 1353; 37, 1804). Faustus of Riez (30, 272 C). Theodulphus of Orléans (105, 239 C, 240 B). Rabanus Maurus (107, 660 D). Paschasius (120, 895 C, 1306 B, 1312 B, 1345 C). Gerard of Cambrai (142, 1280 A). Fulbert (141, 202 B). Algerius (180, 741 B), etc.

30　Leo, *Ep. 59* (PL, 54, 868 B; cf. 357 C). Hincmar (125, 925 D). *Glose in Jo.* IV (114, 384 D).

Paschasius: '*I give my flesh to those who believe, I transfer them into my body.*'[31] Or again, Lanfranc says, with more subtlety: '*The cup of blessing and the bread that is broken (become) for those who receive them the flesh and blood of Christ; for the one bread and the one body signify love.*'[32]

Little by little, however, this same word *body*, in its accepted Eucharistic sense, would come to impose itself, thereby supplanting more complex formulations, such as '*sacrament of the body*' or '*mystery of the body*' which had been so common up to then. The watershed, as we will see further on, must be situated in the years immediately following on from the scandal caused by Berengar. Up to the middle of the eleventh century, in chronicles, in lives of the saints, in canons of councils as well as in doctrinal works, there is frequent reference to the '*sacrament of the body of the Lord*'.[33] A theologian as scrupulous about realist precision as Hincmar of Rheims experienced no repugnance in recalling the transformation of the bread and wine '*into the sacrament of flesh and blood*'.[34] And now suddenly '*the sacrament of the body*' is retreating on all sides before '*body*'. There are some exceptions here and there:[35] but there is a very clear change of proportions. Now this minute linguistic quibble is a matter of importance for our story: this is because, in its Eucharistic sense, '*mystical body*' was more or less the equivalent, as we have seen, to '*the sacrament (the mystery) of the body*'. To abandon the one is to abandon the other. And indeed we can note the following: in proportion to how much *body* dominates here, it becomes divested of the attributes that formerly determined it in its Eucharistic sense, particularly with reference to *mystical*. Furthermore, the distinctions between one 'body' and another, in the way that people like Paschasius, Godescalc or Hériger loved to underline them, fall apart. From now on, as Church

---

31 PL, 142, 1280 A, cf. 1281. Alcuin cites Bede (100, 777A). Pseudo-Bede, *In psalmos* (93, 1088 A). cf. Paschasius (Pseudo-Augustine) (120, 1285 B).

32 PL, 150, 189 A–B; cf. 425 A, 423 D.

33 *Vita Joannis abbatis*, c. 9, 10 (MGH, *Script. Rer. Merov.*, vol. 3, p. 511). Ratramnus (PL, 121, 309 B and 312 B). Ruotger, *Vita Brunonis*, c. 44 (MGH, *Script.*, vol. 4, p. 272). Odilo of Cluny, *Epitaphium Adalheidae*, c. 21 (p. 644). Thaugmarus, *Vita Bernwardi*, c. 37 (p. 775). *Hugonis Chronicon* (vol. 8, p. 472). *Liber legume ecclesiasticarum*, c. 44 (Mansi, vol. 19, 192 D), etc. Othlo of St. Emmeran, *Dialogus de tribus quaetionibus* (PL, 146, 128 B–D).

34 *Vita Remigii* (MGH, *Script. rer. merov.*, vol. III, p. 335).

35 Hincmar, *ibid.*, pp. 290, 333, 335–6; see *supra*, p. 66, n. 10. Werner of St. Blaise, *Sermo in cena Domini* (PL, 157, 911 B). St. Hildegard, *Ep.* 47 (197, 225 B and C) [Trans. J. L. Baird and R. K. Ehrman, *The Letters of Hildegard of Bingen* (Oxford, 1998)].

and Eucharist continue to be intimately associated in the explanation of doctrine, it can be said that at every moment, and not only on the same page but even in the same sentence, the words *'body of Christ'* will be repeated with no further explanation, to denote both the one and the other. It will become part of traditional teaching, for example, that it is necessary to be part of the body of Christ in order to receive the body of Christ worthily.[36] Or again, at the time of the Gregorian reform and for a long time after it, it will become an object of heated discussion to determine if someone separated from the body of Christ on account of simony or of heresy can nevertheless validly consecrate the body of Christ: *'How will they confect the body of Christ, who have separated themselves from the body of Christ?'*[37] and Ivo of Chartres will say, adapting a text of Saint Isidore in his sermon for Maundy Thursday:

> On that day none of the faithful should be in exile from the body of Christ, which is the Church, for on this day the Church received her remedy of reconciliation, namely the body and blood.[38]

At the end of the twelfth century, we can still find the following phrase from Hesychius being copied: *'He poured out his intelligible blood on the altar, that is, his body. But the Church is the body of Christ.'*[39] This is how the ambiguity of certain Augustinian Formulations,[40] of which many examples could be seen in the preceding centuries, was kept alive: *'to be fed on the body, and be made the body'*;[41] *'the memorial of the body of Christ is not lacking to the body of Christ'*;[42] *'while we share in his body and blood, we eagerly confess ourselves to be trans-*

---

36 Ivo of Chartres (PL, 161, 167 B). cf. Isidore (83, 756 B). Rabanus Maurus (107, 321 B), etc.

37 Bernald, *De damnatione schismaticorum* (*Libelli de lite*, vol. 2, p. 39). *Liber canonum contra Henricum* (vol. 1, p. 479).

38 *Sermo 17* (PL, 162, 588). For the antecedents, *supra*, Chapter 1, nn. 47–51.

39 *In Leviticum* (PG, 93, 883 A–B). Odo of Ourscamp (Pitra, *Analecta novissima*, p. 38). Gandulph of Bologna (Walter, p. 439).

40 *In Joannem* (PL, 35, 1612). *Sermones 57*, 227, 272 (38, 389, 1099, 1247). Sermo Denis, 6 (Morin, p. 30). Sermo Guelf., 7 (p. 463). *De anima et ejus origine*, 2, c. 15 (PL, 44, 508), etc. cf. Chrysostom, *In I Cor.*, hom. 24, n. 2 (PG, 61, 200). John Damascene (94, 1152 B). Fulgentius (PL, 65, 188 C). Rabanus Maurus (110, 269 D). Remigius of Lyon (121, 1129 A, cf. 1127 C). Hincmar (125, 924 B and 928 C). Godescalc (Lambot, pp. 329, 330, 335). cf. Faustus of Riez, *Sermo 3* (PL, 58, 876).

41 Ancient Gallican liturgy (Neale-Forbes, p. 154). *Liber mozarabicus ordinum* (F., p. 398).

42 Bonizo of Sutri, *Liber de vita Christiana* (Mai, *N.P.B.*, vol. 7, p. 3, p. 21).

ferred into his body';[43] '*to eat the body of Christ is nothing other than to be made the body of Christ*',[44] '*by eating the body of Christ they become the body of Christ*'.[45] etc. Here we have a deliberate and significant ambiguity with important doctrinal implications. In the sense that ended up being dominant, although this is not consistent with the original sense of its formulation, the idea that is being affirmed here is still that of the '*sacramental body of the body*'.[46] More fundamentally, it is the idea of the real continuity that exists between the Head and the members of the one Body: '*He embodies his body in the Church as his body*';[47] '*(The Church) becomes the body of Christ by sharing in his most integral body*.'[48] Thus *body* has interpretations that are distinct without being separate: the word is therefore not used equivocally. Furthermore, this ambiguity was not generally open to misunderstanding, since the context made its meaning quite clear. Despite all this, in the long run it was capable of inducing a level of confusion in certain minds, and could even, for those paying insufficient attention to the underlying intention, risk causing, or at least covering up, mistakes.

It is worth commenting on other intentional or instinctive connections. For the Eucharist as for the Church – and here they are indeed one and the same, since we are talking about the Eucharist inasmuch as it bears fruit, the traditional expression is used: '*to receive a part, to participate*'.[49] Just as bread and wine are 'consecrated' by the priest in order to be changed into the body and blood of Christ, so communion consecrates us:

> *The Lord's body which we take at the altar is rightly called the sacrament of union because by that visible food . . . we are invisibly consecrated into the one Church of Christ, which is his body.*[50]

---

43 *Fulbert of Chartres, Ep.* 5 (PL, 141, 202 B).

44 William of St. Thierry (PL, 184, 403; cf. 180, 362–363). Honorius of Autun (172, 1252). Algerius (180, 806 A). Wycliffe, *De Ecclesia*, c. 1 (Loserth, p. 4).

45 Gerhoh, *In psalmum* 9 (PL, 193, 780 D).

46 See *supra*, Chapter 3, n. 103. Gregory of Bergamo (H., pp. 74–8). William of St. Thierry (PL, 180, 355 C). Garnier of Rochefort (205, 687 A–B). Ernulf, *Ep.* 2 (d'Achéry, vol. 3, p. 472), etc.

47 Algerius (PL, 180, 774 D; cf. 806 A). Fulbert (141, 203 D). St. Anselm, *Oratio* 34 (158, 927 B).

48 Card. Humbert, *Adversus graecorum calumnias*, c. 32 (PL, 143, 951 A).

49 See *supra*, ch. I, notes 47, 51. *Liber mozarabicus ordinum* (F., 100). Honorius of Autun (PL, 172, 561 B), etc.

50 Rupert (PL, 169, 483 A). Innocent III (217, 848 A–B; cf. 907 D).

The verbs '*to be changed*',[51] '*to pass*', '*to be transferred*', '*to be transfigured*' – in anticipation of '*to be transubstantiated*'[52] – indicate, and sometimes in the writing of the same author, both the change undergone by the bread and wine, and – as with the verb '*to be transferred*'[53] – our being brought into the body of Christ.[54] The verb '*to confect*', '*to be confected*' in some sense provides the technical term for the 'confection' of the Eucharist,[55] is also commonly used for the 'confection' of the Church in this mystery: '*one body is confected, which is both Christ and the Church*'.[56] Gregory of Bergamo underlines this identification of one word with another, saying first of all of the Eucharist, and then of the Church: '*the body of Christ – equally the body of Christ*'.[57]

* * *

Nevertheless some nuances survive, while at the same time others emerge, influenced by a variety of different factors. First of all, in a number of cases, the ecclesial body was from the outset accompanied by an adjective that, in the same context, was not always explicitly given to the sacramental body. Following Saint Paul's own expression, it was said to be '*one body*', since it came about through the sacrament whose fruit is the '*unity of the Church*'.[58] Thus, during the

---

51 Rabanus Maurus, *De clericorum institutione* (PL, 107, 318 A).

52 Thomas Waldensis, *Doctinale fidei catholicae* 2, c. 16 (edn. of 1757, vol. 1, p. 319).

53 Augustine, *In psalmum 88*, s. 1, n. 24 (PL, 37, 1129). Paschasius (120, 54 A, 209 D). Gerhoh (194, 253 D, 828 C). Compare Amalarius, PL, 105, 1035 A and 1060 D.

54 *Transire* is found in the first sense in Isidore, Theodolphus, Paschasius, commentary on I Cor., Guitmond of Aversa, William of St. Thierry, Stephen of Baugé, Robert Puyllen. In the second sense in St. Leo, Theodulphus, Paschasius, Hincmar, Remigius of Auxerre, Gerhoh. cf. Gregory of Bergamo (H., p. 76; PL, 30, 632 A). Augustine, *In psalmum 68*, n. 7 (PL, 36, 859). Faustus of Riez, *Homilia de corporae et sanguine Christi*, c. 3, 11 (PL, 30, 272 C, 275 C). Hincmar, *Vita Remigii* (MGH, *Script. rer. merov.*, vol. 3, p. 278).

55 cf. M. de la Taille, *Mysterium fidei*, edn. 3 a, pp. 407–408, note B. Botte, 'Conficere corpus Christi', *Année théologique* 8 (1947), pp. 309–15. Ambrose, *De mysteriis*, c. 9, n. 52 (PL, 16, 406 C). *Missale Francorum* (72, 329 C), etc.

56 Stephen of Baugé (PL, 172, 1285 B and C). St. Bruno (132, 725). Algerius (180, 847 B). Honorius of Autun (172, 561 C–D). Odo of Ourscamp (Pitra, p. 38), etc. cf. Rupert (PL, 170, 49–50).

57 Hürter, p. 78. Ehrard of Béthune, *Against the Waldensians*, c. 8 (B.M.P., vol. 24, p. 1547 C).

58 Gerhoh (*Libelli de lite*, vol. 3, p. 261). Algerius (PL, 180, 751 A). Stephen of Baugé (172, 1285 C). Honorius of Autun (172, 791 C, 795 B). Isaac of Stella (194, 1892). Gratian cites Hilary, *De cobsecratione*, 2.82 (Fr. 1346–8). Baldwin (204, 716–17, etc. Albert the Great, *In IV Sent.*, d. 8, a. 1, q. 1).

earlier period, Paschasius Radbertus, following 'Eusebius of Emesus' says: *'and we in Christ naturally become one body'.*[59] And thus afterwards Saint Peter Damian,[60] Gebhard of Salzburg,[61] or Saint Bruno the Carthusian (?) say: *'we are made one body, that is, of Christ'.*[62] Formulations of this type occur frequently in liturgies. This is the case, for example, in the preface of the Gelasian sacramentary, which Guitmond of Aversa reproduced textually during the course of a theological exposition:

> *We who communicate in this holy bread and cup are made one in the body of Christ.*[63]

But equally that *one* could often not play its specifying role, since it qualified just as much the sacramental body, which it was important to show as not having been multiplied by the multiplication of species through time and space:

> *All of us who partake of the one bread are, though many, one body. For so great is the unity of the Church in Christ that, just as there is one faith, one baptism and one altar . . . , so there is everywhere one bread of the body of Christ and one cup of his blood.*[64]

Does this not mean that we are dealing here with some sort of double *'unity of the body'*? There again, we can hardly say double, since through the mediating term 'unity of sacrifice', this duality itself is restored to unity, the unity of the sacramental body, by means of a reciprocal causality, and this in its own turn brings about a greater unity of the ecclesial body. *'All Christians are one body on account of the oneness of the body of Christ.'*[65] There is another expression which responded better to the gradually felt need for greater clarity. In conformity with the tradition of the *'body of the people'*, the *'body of*

---

59 PL, 120, 1296, 1276 B, 1324 A. Faustus (30, 275 B). Gregory of Bergamo (H., p. 74).

60 *Opusc.* 11, c. 8 (PL, 145, 238 A).

61 *Libelli de lite*, vol. 1, p. 267.

62 *In psalmum* 21 (PL, 152, 725 D).

63 Mohlberg, n. 196. Guitmond (PL, 149, 1434 C, 1468 B). Paschasius (120, 1364 B). Werner of St. Blaise (PL, 157, 911 B).

64 Florus, *Expositio Missae* (Duc, p. 133). Fulbert (PL, 141, 194 C). John of Fécamp (101, 1088 B). Peter Damian (145, 238 A). Odo of Cambrai (160, 1062 C). cf. Amalarius (105, 1328). Hervé (181, 917 D), etc. See, *supra*, Chapter 1, n. 64.

65 Remigius of Auxerre, *In psalmum* 103 (PL, 131, 672 D).

Christ which we are', we often find: '*our body, which is the Church*', or more simply, again with Saint Paul: '*the body of the Church*'.[66] Or else, combining this expression with the one before it: '*the one body of the Church*', '*the oneness of the body of the Church*'. Through the Eucharist, says Rupert, we are all '*joined in the one body of the Church*'.[67] Robert of Melun was to write: '*The body of Christ signifies . . . the body of the Church*.'[68] Since if the body that is formed by us, the members of Christ, is the body that belongs to Christ, the body of which Christ is the head – the body of Christ – it is also the body of which the Church consists, it is the organic unity, the totality that defines it: *the body of the Church*.

Only this *body of the Church* could be nothing more than a huge collection, called a body by use of a banal metaphor. This is what we are dealing with when, to describe a collection of the lives of the saints, we find: *the body of texts*,[69] or the way in which people used *juridical body*, or spoke of the body of the week, which had the Sabbath for its head,[70] without the addition of attributes such as *sacred* or *holy*, which would have been enough to give the expression a more significant meaning. Speaking of the body of the Church could therefore be nothing more than a slightly more descriptive way of talking about the 'body of Christians', as the Romans used to speak of the 'body of the Greeks', or the 'body of the Jews'.[71] Even the idea of the ἐκκλησία, which from the earliest beginnings of Christianity had embraced the idea of the οἰκουμένη, the '*body of the whole Church*', the '*universal body of the Churches of Christ dispersed throughout the world*',[72]

---

66 Guitmond (PL, 149, 1459). Algerius (180, 750 A). Robert Paululus (177, 430). *Sententiae divinitatis* (G., p. 136), etc. cf. Colos. 1. 18.

67 PL, 170, 38 D. Sometimes, like 'Church' itself, 'the body of the Church' designates humanity as a whole considered even before its effective union with Christ. This is how we find it in Robert Paululus, who compares it to the goat, whereas the 'body born of the virgin' is the spotless lamb (PL, 177, 450). cf. Amalarius (105, 1025 A–B).

68 *In I Cor.* (Martin, p. 207). *Sententiae Parisienses* (L., p. 41). Baldwin (PL, 204, 770), etc.

69 Gaudentius (Glueck, p. 26. Eucher (PL, 50, 773 B). Ratramnus (121, 87 C, cf. 92 D). Lanfranc (150, 429 A). Raoul of St. Germer (B.M.P., vol. 8, p. 207 D), etc. Rupert (PL, 168, 881 D). Jerome, *In Marcum* (Morin, p. 342). cf. Claude of Turin (PL, 104, 617 A–B).

70 Chrysostom (PG, 55, 519). Paulinus of Nola on St. Paul. Adhelmus, *De metris et aenigmatibus*, c. 9 (Ehwald, p. 81). Amalarius (PL, 105, 1314 B); *De ordine antiphonarii* (105, 1244 C).

71 cf. *Journal of Theological Studies*, 1936, p. 385; 1937, p. 165.

72 Ratramnus, *Contra graecorum opposita* 4, c. 2 (PL, 121, 308 D).

had to follow on naturally from the '*body of the entire universe*'.[73] Once the Church had triumphed over the empire and in some way succeeded to its title, Christian Rome made wider use of this metaphor, but always in a sense that was analogous to that of pagan Rome, contenting itself with replacing it and its Caesar, in the role of head, with regard to the universe – or rather now with regard to the universal Church – which played the role of body. We are familiar with the famous formulations of Saint Prosper,[74] Saint Leo the Great[75] and the Council of Chalcedon,[76] dating back to the fifth century. They are frequently repeated by the Popes of the eighth and ninth: '*the head of the whole body, the head of all the churches of God, the holy Roman church*'.[77] The *Donation of Constantine* could not avoid making use of it: '*The head and summit of all the churches in the whole world*.'[78] John VIII would exhort King Michael of Bulgaria to return to the Roman Church, '*which possesses primacy over all the nations, and to which flock the nations of the whole world, as if to one mother and one head*'.[79] Such types of expression remained common throughout the entire Middle Ages.[80] After a period of theoretical alliance and of the separation of powers under the sole rule of Christ, the only argument that arose concerned whether it was the Pope or the emperor who, as the true heir of the former imperial power, deserved in practi-

---

73 W. L. Knox, *Parallels to the N.T. use of* σῶμα (same review, 1938, pp. 243–6). John the Deacon, *Vita Gregorii*, 2, c. 54 (PL, 75, 111 A–B). Gregory II (Mansi, vol. 12, 259 B). Possidius, *Vita Augustini*, c. 7 (PL, 32, 39).

74 *Carmen de ingratis* (PL, 51, 97). *De vocatione omnium gentium* (51, 704 A).

75 *Sermo 82* (PL, 54, 422–4).

76 Letter of the Council to St. Leo, *in fine* (Mansi, vol. 6, 153). Declaration of the legates of the Pope at the start of the Council (580–1).

77 Paul, letter to Pippin (MGH, *Epistularum*, vol. 3, p. 549). Hadrian, letters to Charles (pp. 575, 636). Lothaire and Leo IV. cf. Gregory II (p. 268) and Pseudo-Gregory IV (vol. 5, pp. 78, 606, 609). Nicholas I, *Ep.* 12, to Photius, *Ep.* 13, to the emperor Michael (PL, 119, 786 A and B, 790 C). Hadrian (Mansi, vol. 12, 1081).

78 Leo IX, bull of excommunication of Michael Cerularius (in 1054). Gregory VII, *Licet ex praeteritis* (Caspar, p. 31). Gregory IX, letter to Frederick II (in 1236), etc.

79 MGH, *Epist.*, vol. 7, p. 159. cf. Charles the Bald (PL, 126, 715 B).

80 Alcuin (MGH, *Poetae latini . . .* , vol. 1, pp. 245, 258). Council of Paris in 829 (*Concilia*, vol. 2, p. 610). Ratramnus (PL, 121, 267). *Gallican Sacramentary* (72, 473 A). *Missale gothicum* (72, 292 B, 256 B and D). Peter Damian (145, 150 B, 161 A, 166, 203). Hugh of Fleury (*Libelli de lite*, vol. 2, p. 467). Rupert (PL, 168, 431 D). Honorius (173, 1182 A). Paululus (177, 419 B), etc. Council of Florence, discourse of John of Montenegro (Mansi, vol. 31, 1667–1668). Alcuin, *loc. cit.*, p. 251; Amalarius (PL, 105, 1324 D). Council of Mâcon in 585 (*Concilia*, vol. 1, p. 164).

cal terms to be the head of this great universal body[81] which today, somewhat in retrospect, we call Christianity[82] and which, for centuries, was for the most part simply called the Church. And the Roman Church or the '*chair of Peter*' would also be called '*the head of the body of the Church*', as it would be called '*the mother and teacher of all the Churches*', '*the head and teacher of all Christendom*'.[83]

There is nothing mysterious in this, nothing 'mystical', any more in the '*body of the Church*' than in the '*body of Scripture*'. But if we consider Scripture from within and with the eyes of faith, not as a collection of more or less unified works, but as the *doctrinal word*, and if we are to see it as *sacra doctrina* rather than as *sacra pagina*, and at the same time to remember that Christ was the Logos, that is to say the Word of the Father, could it not be said that this *body of Scripture* appears truly as a *body of Christ*? From there, does it not follow that this immanence of the unique Word at the heart of these multi-faceted words makes of them a real and living unity? This was the opinion of many of the Fathers, whose teaching on the matter was not lost on their readers.[84] It was the same, but only more so, with the *body of the*

---

81 Gregory of Catino (*Libelli de lite*, vol. 2, pp. 536–537). Thierry of Verdun (Jaffé, *Monum. Bamberg.*, p. 130). Anselm of Havelberg (PL, 188, 1225 A–B, 1226 A). Boniface VIII, bull *Ausculta fili*. Matthew of Aquasparta, consistory of 24 June 1302. Alan of Wales (Martin, *Les origines du gallicanisme*, vol. 1, p. 121). cf. Innocent III, letter to Peter of Compostella (PL, 214, 680 B); Letter to the archbishop of Bourges (106 A); to Basil of Zagora (1117 A).

82 In the first part of the Middle Ages, when it was not simply an honorific title (cf. the letters of Stephen II or Paul I to Pippin: Mansi, 12, 540, 550, 601), *christianitas* sometimes on the contrary had a more purely religious meaning than 'Church' and rather than 'Christendom' it was 'Christianity' that would come close to it. . . cf. Nicetas of Remesiana, *De psalmodiae bono* (Burn, p. 80). Amalarius (PL, 105, 1036 D, 1324 D). The word also designated the profession of Christian faith, or baptism . . . (Origen, *In Matt.* series, c. 14, 33, 39, 45, 48, 63, 68) or even priesthood. In the *Chanson de Roland* 'Christianity' would signify Christian faith or baptism. It seems that it is with Nicholas I that we find the first use of *christianitas* in a social sense; from the twelfth century onwards, a juridical nuance would be added to it (Alexander III); this is how a meaning similar to the one it carries today was gradually introduced. . . . (*Opera Omnia*, Anvers, 1706, vol. 1, p. 120). cf. Jean Rupp, *L'idée de chrétienté dans la pensée pontificale, des origins à Innocent III* (1939), and Joseph Lecler, 'Qu'est-ce que le cléricalisme?', *Construire* 7, pp. 71–2. In some texts in which M. Rupp sees *christianitas* already distinguished from the *ecclesia*, I only find it distinct from the *ecclesia romana*: it is the body of the Church of which Rome is the head.

83 cf. Innocent III (PL, 214, 59 A, 21 D; 215, 710, etc.). Rupp, pp. 103–4.

84 Ambrose (PL, 15, 1677 A). Gaudentius (Glueck, p. 27). Jerome, *In psalmum* 147 (Morin, p. 301; cf. Breviarium *in psalmos*, PL, 26, 1251 A). Hesychius, *In Leviticum* (PG, 93, 969 B–C, cf. 985 A–B). Etherius and Beatus (PL, 96, 947–955, 962–963). Abelard (178, 1528–1529). cf. Origen, *In Jeremiam*, hom. 39 (PG, 13, 513).

Church. Over and above the institutional unity that was clear to any observer, from the time of St. Paul faith recognized within it an internal unity.[85] It assigned to it a mysterious source of life: the very Spirit of Christ. Such was the teaching behind the *lex orandi*,[86] repeated over and over again by theologians:

> *The holy Church is the body of Christ, made alive by the one Spirit ... the holy Church, that is, the totality of the faithful, is called the body of Christ because of the Spirit of Christ, which she receives.*[87]

But in order thus to bypass the sociological order and to become in all truth this *'body of the Church made alive by the Spirit'*,[88] the ecclesial body has to become in all reality the body of Christ: *'let it be made the body of the* Church',[89] *'the* Church, *made into the body of Christ'*.[90] Now, the Eucharist is the mystical principle, permanently at work at the heart of Christian society, which gives concrete form to this miracle. It is the universal bond, it is the ever-springing source of life. Nourished by the body and blood of the Saviour, his faithful people thus all 'drink of the one Spirit', who truly makes them into one single body.[91] Literally speaking, therefore, the Eucharist makes the Church. It makes of it an inner reality. By its hidden power, the members of the body come to unite themselves by becoming more fully members of Christ, and their unity with one another is part and parcel of their unity with the one single Head. This unity of the head and of all the rest of the body, the unity of Christ and of his Church – *He is her head, she is his body*[92] – is more than what is normally called '*the whole body of the Church*' or even '*the body of Christ in general*'.[93] It

---

85 cf. Ambrose, *In psalmum 61* (Petschenig, p. 397). Hesychius, *In Leviticum* (PG, 93, 982 A), etc.

86 *Gelasianum* (W., pp. 76, 120), etc.

87 Hugh of St. Victor (PL, 176, 416). Isaac of Stella (194, 1801). cf. Fulgentius, *Ad Monimum* (65, 189 C). Cardinal Humbert (*Libelli de lite*, vol. 1, p. 235).

88 Anselm of Havelberg (PL, 188, 1144 A–C).

89 Odo of Ourscamp (Pitra, p. 38). cf. Fulbert, after Faustus of Riez (PL, 141, 203 C). *Supra*, note 44.

90 Placidus (*libelli de lite*, vol. 2, p. 576). Arnold of Bonneval (PL, 189, 1644), etc.

91 Chrysostom, *In I Cor.*, hom. 30, n. 2 (PG, 61, 251).

92 Algerius (PL, 180, 747 C, 749 B).

93 Leonianum (F., p. 20). St. Leo, Sermo 4, c. 1 (PL, 54, 149 A). Nicholas I, *Ep.* 35 (PL, 119, 833 A). *De unitate Ecclesiae conservanda* (*Libelli de lite*, vol. 2, p. 191). Bruno of Segni (PL, 165, 445 C). Jean le Moine (166, 1513 B). Hervé (181, 1325 A). Isaac of Stella (194, 1801), etc.

constitutes a real being. It is what Algerius of Liège designated as 'the universal body of Christ', 'entirely the Lord's body':

> *Since the sacrifice of the altar, by signifying the union of the Church herself and Christ, is the sacrament of the entire body of Christ, Christ is not confected there without a confection of the whole body. And so the Eucharist does not occur there without a bestowal of the grace of the union of the entire body of the Lord.*[94]

* * *

On the other hand, and here we are dealing with something more recent, the same Algerius of Liège felt the need to provide a reassuring exegesis of a phrase from Lanfranc, which, along with all his contemporaries, he believed to be one of Saint Augustine's.[95] '*The heavenly bread*' as Lanfranc had written in his treatise against Berengar '*is called in its own manner the body of Christ.*'[96] '*In its own manner*', Algerius explains to us, certainly in an effort to convince himself, '*that is, that is, in one singular to itself . . . not in an ordinary manner, but one that is its own and as if proper to itself.*'[97] Another formulation – this time authentically one of Augustine's – seems even more resistant to any realist interpretation. In a letter to his brother Bishop Boniface, Saint Augustine had said:

> *If the sacraments did not have a certain similarity to those realities of which they are the sacraments, they would not be sacraments at all. From this similarity they generally receive the names of the realities themselves. Therefore, just as in a certain manner the sacrament of the body of Christ is the body of Christ, so the sacrament of faith is faith.*[98]

Under Augustine's authorship, that *in a certain manner* did not have as restrictive a sense as could be imagined.[99] Nevertheless, it could not

---

94 PL, 180, 847 A–B, cf. 750 B–C. Hugh of St. Victor (176, 468, 506). Peter Lombard (192, 262 A).

95 M. Lepin, *op. cit.*, pp. 786–97. cf. Gratian, *De consecratione* 2.48 (Fr. 1332).

96 PL, 150, 425 A.

97 *De sacramentis* I, c. 18 (PL, 180, 793 B and D).

98 *Ep.* 98., n. 9 (PL, 33, 364). cf. Amalarius (105, 1043 C, 1334–5). Rupert, *De Spiritu sancto*, I, c. 18 (PL, 167, 1588 C). Augustine, *De Trin.*, I, c. 10, n. 20 (PL, 42, 834).

99 Compare *Sermo* 90, n. 2 (38, 559). cf. Florus, *Liber adversus J. Scotum*, c. 13 (PL, 119, 181 A).

fail to prove awkward at first sight for theologians of the 'realist' tendency. Thus, while Ratramnus naturally found it pleasing, Paschasius Radbertus had already had to comment on it with the help of other texts in which the reality of the Eucharistic body is declared in plain terms in order to smooth over the anxiety that his disciple Frudegard had confided to him.[100] Insofar as points of view were changing, it proved fatal that the word was subject to more and more misunderstanding. Some wielded it as a formidable weapon against the new forms of orthodoxy, while others 'brought it into line' with explanations that were no less lacking in objectivity. The opponents of Berengar, in the eleventh and twelfth centuries came to grief over it. Lanfranc evaded the difficulty: he contented himself with demonstrating in general how it was possible, without mounting an assault on realism, to designate the flesh of Christ as the sacrament of his body.[101] Guitmond of Aversa proposed two interpretations, according to the preference of the reader, each one as improbable as the other: he suggested that by *sacrament of the body* Augustine would have understood the Eucharistic figures of the Old Testament, or else Christ himself, as a figure of the Church.[102] Algerius's commentary is a failure: for him, Saint Augustine was only thinking of the sacramental species, of the '*form of bread*', which can indeed '*not truly, but figuratively and in name*' be called '*the body of Christ*'.[103] Gregory of Bergamo got elegantly out of the tight spot by making different use of the formulation: he used it to explain that in the Eucharist the body of Christ can also be called the sacrament of the body – whether of the historical body in its visible state or of that body which is the Church.[104] Thus once again we fall back into the most classic developments. None of these exegeses managed to impose its authority. Their very proliferation only served to make clear the awkwardness that they sought to cover over. Consequently there was no further temptation to take up that questionable '*in a certain manner*', any more than Lanfranc's '*in its own way*', although both of them had been included in the anthologies of Ivo of Chartres[105] and Abelard,[106]

---

100 PL, 120, 1353.

101 PL, 150, 423–5.

102 PL, 149, 1465.

103 *De sacramentis*, I, c. 18 (PL, 180, 793); cf. c. 5 (753–4). Algerius, *De sacramento Eucharistiae*, 2, c. 24.

104 Hürter, p. 80.

105 *Decretum* (PL, 178, 1524, 1534).

106 *Sic et Non* (PL, 178, 1524, 1534). [See B. B. Boyer and R. McKeon, *Sic et non: A Critical Edition* (London, 1976–7).]

and Lanfranc's had also been included in Gratian's *Decrees*.[107] Peter Lombard, who was to offer an explanation that was substantially analogous to Algerius's, appears to have taken care to avoid the very mention of either compromising formulation.[108]

The same general tendency would soon condemn the language of Gilbert of Nogent and Rupert of Tuy. We know that Gilbert was obliged to present an apology for his *'vicarious body'*.[109] In a friendly reproach to Rupert for an expression that struck him as dangerous, William of Saint-Thierry wrote to him:

> I do not at all advert to what name you give here to the body of sacrifice . . . By *'the body of sacrifice'* I understand nothing other than that which is dead and rose again – which we do not call the body of sacrifice but, as it truly is, the body of the Lord.[110]

In the same way, no one would any longer use the expression *'the same and not the same'*, although that expression survived through its inclusion in the *Decretum* of Ivo of Chartres[111] and in those of Gratian.[112] More and more willingly we find repeated in terms of the Eucharist not only *'the true body'*, which had been a tradition since antiquity, but also *'the very same body'*, which, up till then, except in the case of Augustine, had been rare;[113] and not only *'his own body'*, known already in antiquity as in the Carolingian era:

> He taught the disciples that he would hand over his own body . . .[114]

> The Lamb, the light of the world, feeding us with his own body . . .[115]

---

107 *De consecratione*, 2.48 (Fr. 1332).

108 PL, 192, 860–1.

109 *Epistula nuncupatoria* (PL, 156, 609).

110 PL, 180, 341 C, 342 A–B. *Histoire literature de la France*, vol. 11, pp. 554–5; vol. 12, p. 325.

111 p. 2, c. 9 (PL, 161, 156 B).

112 *De consecratione*, 2.45 (Friedberg, 1331).

113 Lanfranc (PL, 150, 427 C). Algerius (180, 783 A). Gregory of Bergamo (H., p. 75). *Sententiae Parisienses* (L., p. 41). *Ysagoge in theologiam* (L., p. 205). Otho of Lucques (PL, 176, 140). Baldwin (204, 770), etc. cf. Florus (MGH, *Concilia*, vol. 2, p. 773). Augustine, *In psalmum 98*, n. 9 (PL, 37, 1264, 1265). cf. *infra*, p. 93. Fulgentius, *Ad Monimum*, 2, c. 11 (PL, 65, 190 B). Peter Chrysologus, *Sermo 34* (PL, 52, 297 B).

114 Juvencus (PL, 19, 310 A). cf. Chrysostom, *In Matthaeum*, hom. 82, n. 5 (PG, 58, 744). Isidore of Peluse, I, *Ep. 109* (78, 256 C). Macarius Magnes, 3., c. 23 (Blondel, pp. 105, 106).

115 Hincmar, *Ferculum Salomonis* (MGH, *Potae latini*, vol. 3, p. 414).

but also *'his very own body'*,[116] *'his own true body'*,[117] etc. *'The same body'* no longer seemed to be enough, as it once was enough for Ratherius of Verona,[118] but it was reinforced by saying *'the very same body'*, *'the very same blood'*, *'one and the same'*, *'simply the same'*, *'entirely the same'*, *'the very same individual body'*, *'always the very same'*, *'the same and not another'*, *'the very same and not another'*.[119] Except in the way they were repeated, these formulations were not new, but they became far more universally and more insistently used. They were above all the subject of a school of their own,[120] and Hériger of Lobbes was able to establish on their account a sort of *Sic et Non*.[121] Nowadays, we no longer question them within orthodox discourse. Neither there, nor in previous usage, is there a suggestion by means of antithesis of a minimisation of the reality of the *Church-body*. In most cases, it is not to this ecclesial body that they oppose the sacramental body: as in the parallel expressions which include the word *flesh*,[122] they tend more simply to underline the perfect identity, within the

---

Ratramnus, c. 28 (PL, 121, 139 C). Irenaeus, *Adv. Haer.* 5, c. 2 (PG, 7, 1126). [For St. Irenaeus's works in English, see J. Donaldson, A. Robertson, A. Cleveland Coxe, ANF, vol. 1; R. M. Grant, *Irenaeus of Lyons*, *Early Church Fathers* series (London: Routledge, 1997). Gaudentius (Glueck, p. 26); R. Grant, *Irenaeus of Lyons* (London, 1997); D. N. Power, *Irenaeus of Lyons on Baptism and Eucharist* (Bramcote, 1991).]

116 Guitmond (PL, 149, 1459 B, 1460 B–C, cf. 1444 B). *Sententiae Florianenses* (O., p. 30). Peter Lombard (PL, 192, 859). Pseudo-Damian (145, 881 C). Innocent III (214, 1120 A), etc.

117 Durandus of Troarn, *cit.* Hincmar (PL, 149, 1407 D). Guitmond (149, 1451 B). *Speculum Ecclesiae* (177, 362 A). Gerard of Cambrai, Council of Arras of 1025 (Mansi, vol. 19, 431 B).

118 *Ex dialogo confesionali* (PL, 136, 403 C).

119 Hugh of Langres (PL, 142, 1329 A). Durandus of Troarn (149, 1413 A). Ivo of Chartres (161, 143 B). Otho of Lucques (176, 139 D). Bruno of Segni (165, 219 A). Honorius of Autun (172, 1252–1253). Hugh of Rouen (192, 1209 B, 1306 A). Gerhoh (1051 A).

120 Paschasius (PL, 120, 891 A, 1361 A, 1361 C, etc.). Rabanus Maurus (110, 493 A).

121 PL, 139, 179 A–C.

122 Geoffrey (PL, 157, 213). Bruno of Segni (165, 1006 B). Peter Lombard (191, 1642). Peter of Blois (207, 1138 C), etc. cf. Augustine, *Sermo 71*, n. 17 (PL, 38, 453). Cyril of Alexandria, *Adversus Nestoriam* 4, c. 5, 6 (PG, 76, 192–193, 201 C). Cyril's 11th anathema, recalling Paschasius (Mansi, vol. 4, 1077, 1094). [For the works of St. Cyril against Nestorius in English, see selections in N. Russell, Cyril of Alexandria (London, 2000); selections in W. H. C. Frend, J. Stevenson, Creeds, *Councils and Controversies*, revised edn (London, 1989); *Library of the Fathers of the Holy Catholic Church* series, vols. 43, 47, 48 (Oxford, 1874, 1881, 1885). See also N. Russell, *Cyril of Alexandria*, in the *Early Church Fathers* series (London: Routledge, 2000).] cf. Ivo of Chartres, PL, 161, 138 C; Gratian, *De consecratione* 2.80 (Fr. 1346).

differences according to state, between the sacramental body and the
'body born of a virgin':[123]

> *. . . the flesh that was then born of the Virgin is the same as the flesh
> that is now consecrated from bread by the word of life.*[124]

Other changes, which are scarcely perceptible, have the same intention, or at least, since they can barely have been conscious, lead to the
same result. This is why Algerius of Liège, distinguishing in his turn
between the three traditional bodies, no longer says, as does the *Letter
on the Sacraments of the Heretics* quoted at the beginning of this chapter: '*the body in person*' and '*the sacrament of the body*'; instead he
says: '*the body in human form*', and '*the body in the sacrament*'. Only
his last term remains unchanged: '*the body which is the Church*'.[125]

Not that we are without occasional remnants of the earlier terminology. We find traces in the first group of the opponents of Berengar.
A whole dialectic needs to operate with regard to another text of Saint
Augustine, who seems to have discouraged in advance any attempt
to distinguish the first two bodies: '*What you will eat is not this body
which you see.*'[126] It was all the more impossible to avoid it since
Berengar had also taken issue with it. But the very thing that seemed set
to create difficulties for the new formulations ended up as the foundation of their success, since it forced the commentators to become more
precise in order to justify themselves. If Durandus of Troarn set aside
the difficulty without resolving it, in reading *nam* instead of '*non*',[127]
if Lanfranc appealed principally to other, less ambiguous passages in
Saint Augustine (as he was justified in doing by the immediate context itself),[128] Guitmond of Aversa did something more definitive. As
Berengar had done, but in opposition to him, he exploited the dialectical and grammatical resources that Lanfranc had used in a still more
subtle fashion, and through the strictest analysis of the Augustinian
formulation, put forward distinctions of a perfect clarity:

---

123 Ratramnus (PL, 121, 167 A; but 139 C). Paschasius (120, 1315, etc.).
124 Hildebert (?), *Liber de sacra eucharistia* (PL, 171, 1199 B).
125 PL, 180, 791.
126 *In psalmum* 98, n. 9 (PL, 37, 1265). Yves (161, 150 C, 156 B, 1075 B).
Gratian, *De consecratione* 2.44, 45 (Fr., 1330). *In psalmum* 33, s. 1, n. 8 (36,
305). Sermo 131, n. 1 (38, 729). Augustine (42, 843).
127 PL, 149, 1412–13.
128 PL, 150, 430 C, 433–434 (cf. 424 B). cf. Ivo of Chartres, *Ep.* 287 (162,
287–288). Augustine (37, 1264).

He gives us to eat the flesh itself in the same substance, but not this
body, that is, in the same form. It is as if he said, 'I shall indeed give
you my body, but . . . not in this form which you see.' Moreover,
why did he add 'which you see', when it would have been enough
to say 'not this', unless it is because he meant [that we will eat] *this*
body in respect of essence but not this body in respect to what is
seen?[129]

The Lord's body is true not qualitatively but substantially.[130]

These distinctions, which were to become classics in themselves,[131]
allayed any scruples that could have arisen from the differences between
the new language and the old. They are not that different, for example,
from Godescalc's '*in nature – in form*'. Nor can it be said that they
work in opposition to one another – far from it. Nevertheless, they
serve as 'explanations' that St. Augustine would never have dreamed
of offering. If, by some double miracle, he had both travelled forward
into the eleventh century and been fully informed of all that had happened in between that time and his own, he would no doubt have
approved of them, but less as an exegesis of his text than as protective
measures which, in his era, would have served no purpose. For they
presuppose not only new errors and dangers, but an entire 'problematic' that is completely different from any that could have assailed a
fifth-century mind, or even the general run of those of the ninth or tenth
century. The old homilist of Lyon, in whose work we read '*mystical*
body' was being no forerunner of Berengar when he explained to the
faithful: '*The body that was spoken is one thing, and the body which*
was handed over is another.' He was simply being true to the language
of his master Augustine, and he could be so without astonishing his
audience. Taking this language even further, though we have no need
to see in this any indication of incipient heretical tendencies, one of the
texts of Aelfric of Canterbury quoted in Bede's *History* tells us: '*There*
is a great difference between the body in which Christ suffered, and
the body which is consecrated in the Eucharist.'[132] In company with

---

129 PL, 149, 1462 B–C; cf. 1463–4.
130 *Confessio* (PL, 149, 1500 D).
131 Algerius (PL, 180, 772 B–C). Hervé (181, 933–934). School of Laon
(Weisweiler, *Recherches de théologie ancienne et médiévale*, 1933, p. 269). Ivo
of Chartres (PL, 162, 286–7). Peter Lombard, *In I Cor.* (191, 1640 D), etc. cf.
Gregory of Bergamo, c. 8 (H., pp. 31–5). *Compare with Augustine* (PL, 42, 843).
132 Bede, *Historia Ecclesia*, 5, c. 22 (ed. A. Whelocus, 1664). [For Bede's
Church History and letters in English, see the *Penguin Classics* edition, L. Sherley-

Lanfranc and Guitmond, we are far from that '*one thing and another*', far from that '*great difference*'.

It is the same with the author of the *Letter to Abbot Gerald*, who offered his profession of faith shortly after the storm raised by Berengar:

> I believe that the sacred body of the Lord which is consecrated daily on the altar by the ministry of the priest is, without any doubt at all, the true flesh of Christ which suffered on the cross and the true blood which flowed from his side . . . Just as I know that no body was handed over for our salvation apart from his own, so I believe that no flesh of his other than that which was born of the Virgin Mary and rose from the tomb is eaten for the forgiveness of sins, and I am certain that no blood is drunk other than that which flowed from his side.[133]

From then on, the matter was sealed: the first two 'bodies' were moulded into one.

* * *

But what we gained through this on the one hand was perhaps beginning to be lost on the other. However necessary progress may be, it cannot be absolute. Unwittingly, with the spread of these new customs, the distinctions that had hitherto defined the 'third body' became blurred, or at least ceased to occupy their previously dominant position in the economy of the mystery. Admittedly the Church still occupied a central position in any account. They were still far from imagining a treatise on the Eucharist that could fail to acknowledge it, or a treatise on the Church that made no reference to the position of the Eucharist. The mystery of the Eucharist still appeared essentially as the *mystery of union*.[134] It was, according to Saint Peter Damian, *the sacrament of inseparable union*.[135] Eucharistic communion was

---

Price and R. E. Latham, *Historia ecclesiastica gentis Anglorum* (London, 1990).] cf. Ratramnus, *Liber de corpore*, c. 69 (PL, 121, 155, 156 A).

133 PL, 149, 434. St. Anastasius of Cluny († 1085)? cf. P. Fournier, in Baudrillart, DHGE, vol. 2, col. 1469.

134 Ivo of Chartres (PL, 162, 512 B, 506 A). Peter Lombard, *In I Cor.* (191, 1624 C). Gratian, *cit.* Augustine, *De consecratione*, 2.36, 58 (Fr., 1326, 1336). Anselm of Laon, *In Matthaeum*, c. 26 (162, 1462 B). Baldwin (204, 695). Sicard of Cremona, *Summa in Decretum Gratiani* (Teetaert, *La confession aux laïques dans l'Église latine . . .*, p. 218, n. 1), etc.

135 PL, 145, 238 B.

also still conceived of as a communion with the Church. The very
term communion, which, we are occasionally reminded, is a translation of the Greek '*synaxis*',[136] retained the ecclesial sense which it had
in preceding eras.[137] It would retain it for some considerable time to
come.[138] The sacramental act would continue to be placed in relation
to the necessary union with the body of the Church.[139] In thought as
in words, the mystery of the altar would remain close to the mystery
of the communion of saints: '*the solemnity of the Eucharist, to which
pertains the communion of saints*'.[140] Despite all this, however, slowly
and imperceptibly a dissociation began to occur. While up till recently, after the enumeration of the three bodies, there would be some
emphatic insistence on the unity of the second and third, now it was
above all the distinction between them that was demonstrated. The
doctrinal interest was shifting. The need for unity was being replaced
by a need for analysis, and what had been the object of mystic fer-
vour was increasingly perceived as a source of dangerous confusion.
Algerius of Liège would soon state this, at the beginning of his *De
sacramentis*:

> Because the saints wrote variously about the body and blood of
> the lord, sometimes speaking of the whole Christ, namely head and
> members, and sometimes of either the head or the members, simple
> people have fallen into error (as on an ineffable subject that is not
> understood), while those who wish to be more wise than they should
> have given birth to heresies . . . For some ascribe to the head which

---

136 We should observe, furthermore, that *synaxis* itself, as well as κοινωνία, is
sometimes lacking in any ecclesial connotation. This is how we find it in Pseudo-
Dionysius, who never gives any other sense to these two words, at least explicitly,
than that of being united to Christ and to God. We find the same with Anastasios
the Synaite (PG, 89, 208 D, 765 B). In the thirteenth century, his commentator,
Pachymeros, protested against the contrary interpretation given to him by some
. . . : *In Hierarchiam ecclesiasticam*, c. 3 (PG, 3, 452 B). Cf, Bessarion, *De sacramento Eucharistiae* (PG, 161, 497 B).

137 Honorius of Autun (*Libelli de lite*, vol. 3, p. 56). Raoul Ardent (PL, 155,
1834). Baldwin (204, 715 D). Odo of Ourscamp (Pitra, p. 37).

138 Albert the Great (Vivès, vol. 21, p. 162; vol. 24, p. 228; vol. 38, p. 97).
St. Thomas, *Summa theologiæ*, IIIa, q. 73, a. 4. [For the Latin and English of the
Summa in parallel, see T. Gilby, *Summa theologiæ: Latin text and English translation* (London, 1964–81).] St. Peter Canisius, *Catechismus major* (*Chatechismi
latini*, vol. 1, pp. 35, 130–1).

139 Odo of Cambrai (PL, 160, 1058 D, cf. 1061 D). St. Bonaventure (Q., vol.
9, p. 247), etc.

140 Gilbert of Tournai, *Tractatus de officio episcopi*, c. 25 (B.M.P., vol. 25,
p. 409 C).

is said of the members, while others apply to the members what is said of the head; and they hold such confused opinions about one or both of these that they exaggerate either the lowliness of the head or the glory of the members.[141]

As a remedy to these abuses, therefore, *another body* came to be placed in opposition to *his own body*.[142] While maintaining the link between them of their sacramental significance, they were presented as *one thing* and *another thing*. Thus once again Algerius: '*He wished it to signify another body of his, namely the Church*',[143] or Abelard's commentary on the First Letter to the Corinthians.[144] Thus when Gregory of Bergamo said, as we have seen above: '*equally the body*', he was as much distinguishing their duality in the new way, as he was affirming the identity contained within their name in the old way. Thus also Gerhoh of Reichersberg:

The bread is one thing, and signifies another . . . It is 'the Lord's body', but it signifies the one Church. Although the Church is herself the Lord's body, the Lord's body that redeems is one thing, and the Lord's body that is redeemed is another. The Lord's body which is the Lord of whom Mary said, 'They have taken away my Lord . . .', is one thing, and the Lord's body which cannot be called Lord or God, even though it is the body of the Lord, is another. The Lord's body by which we are redeemed is that individual body of which Christ said, 'This is my body. . .' But the Lord's body that is the Church is not an individual body nor is it the body that redeems, but it is one body because of one faith, and is the one Church in many individuals or persons, redeemed by the body of Christ.[145]

The example of Rupert, himself carried along by the general movement, is particularly symptomatic. Unlike Gerhoh, he would certainly not voluntarily have called the Eucharistic body '*the individual body itself*'. He would not perhaps have refused so categorically to attribute to the ecclesial body the qualifying *undivided* whose original sense he would have preserved, as in the formulation '*the undivided Trinity*',

---

141 PL, 180, 739.
142 Guitmond (PL, 149, 1465 D). William of St. Thierry (180, 357 C). *Sententiae Florianenses* (p. 30).
143 PL, 180, 794 c.
144 *In I Cor.*, X (Landgraf., vol. 2, pp. 257–8).
145 *Libelli de lite*, vol. 3, p. 26. Algerius (PL, 180, 783 B).

or with Peter Damian, when speaking of the '*sacrament of undivided unity*'. Nevertheless, he also insisted, as much as and even more than any other, on the presence within the sacrament of that same body 'which was given up for us'.[146] He refused to allow that the Eucharist could be the same as the historical body,[147] while in contrast, on a number of different occasions he was frequently at pains to allay any confusion concerning the ecclesial body. For example he made clear that the Church could only be called the body of Christ '*in another respect*'.[148] And again:

> *The oneness of the Word makes the body of Christ one, with the result that the body that then hung on the cross and the body which the faith of the Church now confects through sacred speech are one body... The Church is the body of Christ, but not that body which was handed over for us, if indeed the Church was not handed over for herself... Although the holy Church is the body of Christ, she is not the very same body of Christ that was handed over for us...*[149]

Once again, nothing in this is fundamentally new. These are elementary distinctions. The opposition of the fleshly body to the spiritual body, of the individual body to the ecclesial body, of the body sacrificed by Christ to the 'more precious', 'more lovable' body for which he sacrificed it has its roots in the first centuries of Christianity. We find it in Tertullian[150] and in Gregory of Elvira,[151] it had passed into the Middle Ages via Etherius and Beatus,[152] then via the commentary from Auxerre on the Epistle to the Ephesians,[153] and St. Bernard would repeat it again.[154] But up to this point, such an opposition had not been formulated with regard to the Eucharist. Its introduction in this new

---

146 *In Joannem*, I, 6 (PL, 169, 463 A).

147 *De divinis officiis*, 2, c. 2 (PL, 170, 35).

148 *In Joannem* (PL, 169, 494 A-B).

149 PL, 169, 469, 483 D, 463 C.

150 *Adversus Marcionem* 5, c. 19 (Kroymann, p. 645). [In Latin and English together, see. E. Evans, *Adversus Marcionem* (Oxford, 1972).]

151 *In Cantica*, sermo 12, n. 7 (PL, 183, 831); *Sermo de diversis* 90, n. 5 (c. 710).

152 2, c. 80 (PL, 96, 1019 B).

153 PL, 117, 730 B.

154 *In Cantica*, sermo 12, n. 7 (PL, 183, 831); *Sermo de diversis* 90, n. 5 (c. 710).

domain is nothing short of revolutionary: if Eucharistic doctrine had to make such distinctions in order to protect itself against error, it cannot be said to have altered in any essentials. But neither the accent nor the perspective remains altogether identical. Above all, with regard to the Church, it has to be admitted that all this already constitutes a certain relaxing of the old expressions, perhaps in some long-term preparation for a certain attenuation of the ideas themselves.

So eventually, some time later, towards the middle of the twelfth century, an old expression reappeared with a new sense, which thus served to distinguish the 'third body'. It foretold and prepared for the re-emergence, in an equally new sense, of *mystical body*. The Eucharist was called – and these expressions can be understood in their own terms: *the flesh of the sacrament,*[155] *the invisible flesh.*[156] It was also called *the intelligible flesh.*[157] To this invisible and 'intelligible' flesh, to this flesh of the sacrament, Peter Lombard also opposed another, a *spiritual flesh*, the object of spiritual understanding and of spiritual reception (or rather already the result of that spiritual reception), in which the union of all communicants was realized:

> . . . *the spiritual flesh of Christ, which is the union of the faithful.*[158]

And, shortly afterwards, Peter of Poitiers was to say: '*Note that ecclesiastical union is called the spiritual flesh of Christ.*'[159]

Thus, up till now, I have only prepared the ground for this first stage. We will have to investigate some details more closely, at the same time as searching for the roots of the adjective 'mystical', which we have seen, along with a series of other more or less analogous expressions, gradually separating from the sacramental body, while a certain number of expressions or adjectives have already begun to determine and in some sense particularize the ecclesial body. The latter, in the course of a second stage, would come to have attributed to it more and more the adjective 'mystical', which fell into disuse to

---

155 Stephen of Baugé (PL, 172, 1296 B–C), etc.

156 Hugh of Langres (PL, 142, 1330 D). *Sententiae Anselmi* (Bliemetsrieder, p. 118). Algerius (PL, 180, 814 C). Peter Lombard (192, 860). *Speculum Eccesiae* (177, 365), etc.

157 Peter Lombard (PL, 192, 860). Otho of Lucques (176, 144). Odo of Ourscamp (Pitra, p. 38). Gandulph of Bologne (W., p. 439), etc. Godescalc (Lambot, p. 328). See *infra*, Chapter 7, p. 156.

158 *In I Cor.* (PL, 191, 1643 C); *Sentences* (192, 859).

159 *Sentences* (PL, 211, 1252–3; 1252 D).

the extent that the sacramental body shed it; so much so that the day would come when 'mystical' would be definitively joined to 'body' as a designation for the Church.[160]

---

160 Of course, these two stages cross over one another. They had some fore-runners and some descendants. Writings about the Eucharist are too many and too varied for the evolution of their language to have had a chance of being a matter of perfect regularity. It is nonetheless true that a certain curve can be clearly distinguished. Whoever takes an overview can trace a logical sequence that I will try to reproduce before commenting on it.

5

The Church as Mystical Body

There existed at least one precedent. Was it not true that by the ninth century, Rabanus Maurus, while reserving the name *mystical body* for the Eucharist, had also said of the Church: 'the Catholic Church, which is mystically the body'?[1] That adverb, or at least one of its most common equivalents, was to be repeated some two or three centuries later by Lanfranc, and then by the author of the *Speculum Ecclesiae*:

> Since the Church of Christ is called the one bread and one body as a type . . .[2]

> . . . In another respect the bread and wine signify the body of Christ, which is the Church. For just as bread is from many grains and wine from many clusters, so the one Church, which is typically the body of Christ, is formed by a union of many persons.[3]

Shortly before the *Speculum*, Gregory of Bergamo made use of an intermediate formulation, which is particularly revealing for us:

> . . . That the one body, which we many are, through the life-giving power of the Holy Spirit, is designated mystically by this sacrament, was clearly expressed in these words by the Apostle. In the Eucharist . . . the body of Christ, which is the Church, . . . is intimated mystically, or sacramentally.[4]

What we have captured here is the moment when the adjective *mystical* passed from being the signifier to the signified, from the Eucharist to the Church, borrowing, for the purposes of this passage, the adverbial form in which its dual significance is at once condensed and brought together.

---

1 *De Universo*, 5, c. 10 (PL, 111, 131).
2 Lanfranc, *In I Cor.*, X (PL, 150, 189 B).
3 *Speculum Ecclesiae*, c. 7 (PL, 177, 363 A).
4 c. 18, 19 (Hürter, pp. 74, 80).

Nevertheless, before finally being called *mystical body*, the Church would sometimes find itself being called *mystical flesh*. Is it necessary to call attention to the Eucharistic origin of such an expression? We will need to return to the texts of St. Jerome and William of Saint-Thierry where we have already met it. In its ecclesial sense, it can be found in Peter Lombard, always in a context where the Eucharist is under discussion. It alternates with *spiritual flesh*. The equivalence is quite natural, since in the transformation from the signifier to the signified, it passes from 'type' to 'spirit'. 'To know mystical and spiritual things', as Paschasius Radbertus was already saying.[5] In his commentary on the First Letter to the Corinthians, the Lombard distinguishes, in a specific reference to St. Jerome, but in a different way from his, a *twofold flesh of Christ*: the first, the '*sacrament and reality*', which he calls *proper flesh*, and the second, '*reality and not sacrament*', which he calls *the mystical flesh*. We find the same distinction, and the same terms in the fourth book of the *Sentences*. Now, in both works, this *mystical flesh* is the Church: the '*unity of the faithful*', the '*ecclesial union*', the '*unity of the Church in those predestined*'.[6]

If the expression was not exactly new, it nevertheless would appear that it cannot be found anywhere else with such clear ecclesial significance before the time of Peter Lombard. Was he truly the first to use it in this way, or did he inherit this usage from some immediate predecessor? Whatever the case, the gloss on Saint Paul, which he both quotes and completes, already contains an approximate formulation:

> That visible form . . . has a similarity to the mystical reality, which is the unity of the faithful.[7]

It would not have been impossible for that same gloss to have included in it somewhere the specific words '*mystical flesh*'. But 'in the current state of the editions, no proper study of the sources' which Lombard used for his commentary on Saint Paul 'could be based on printed texts'.[8] This minor problem could only be resolved by a study of the

---

5 PL, 120, 1274 B. cf. Cyril of Alexandria (PG, 73, 460 B). Pseudo-Chrysostom, *In psalmum 95* (55, 623). Bede, *Ep. 13* (PL, 94, 698 C), etc.

6 PL, 191, 1642; 192, 857. cf. 192, 58.

7 *In I Cor.*, X. *Sentences* (PL, 192, 857).

8 J. de Ghellinck, DTC, vol. IX 9, col.1956. cf. Dom Wilmart: 'In order to say something useful about the Gloss, it would be essential to have recourse to a trustworthy edition; the manuscripts which I have seen convinced me that it was dangerous to rely on printed texts' (*Recherches de théologie ancienne et médiévale* (1936), p. 340).

manuscript translation or by research into unpublished material of the time. I think, however, that the literary habits of the author in question, and what could be called his genius for eclectic compilation, predisposed him towards this slight innovation.

A short time later, Peter of Troyes, known as Peter Comestor, was to express himself in similar terms to those of his illustrious predecessor. In his *Sentences* on the Sacraments, which must have been written sometime between 1165 and 1170, he too was to make a distinction, based on the same text of St. Jerome, between the two forms of Christ's flesh. To the first he attributed in turn three adjectives, each of which was already traditional by then: *true*, in order to safeguard realism; *proper*, in order to emphasize more precisely its identity with the flesh, 'born of the Virgin'; and *sacramental*, since he was treating of the Eucharist body. The second flesh, which was the fruit of the first, would be the *mystical flesh*, that is to say the Church insofar as it is unified, gathered together in Christ by virtue of the sacrament: '*the Church, whose unity is faithfulness*', or more simply: '*the unity of the Church*'.[9] It would be noted that *sacramental* and *mystical*, which until recently had still been considered synonymous, and are basically the same word, were now separated and placed in opposition to one another.

The English Carmelite Herbert of Bosham, first secretary and then historiographer of Thomas Becket, also made highly interesting use of *mystical flesh*, though this time without any Eucharistic reference. In his strange *Liber Malorum*, which must have been written shortly after 1180,[10] he still habitually designates the Church as the *body of Christ*, without any further qualification.[11] At one point he even says that it is Christ's *body proper*.[12] For him as for Saint Augustine, the '*integral Christ*' is the '*head with the body*'. But this whole Christ, this total Christ seems to him to be 'completely mystical', like a 'completely mystical man', that is to say that he recognizes within him a 'mystery'.[13] Under his authorship the Pauline image of the bridegroom and the bride would soon lead to the word *flesh*. Thus comparing the incarnation of the Word and the union of the Church with Christ he writes:

---

9 Martin, pp. 35, 36.

10 The book is a sort of appendix to the *Life of Thomas Becket*, which was addressed to Archbishop Baldwin, who was raised to the see of Canterbury in 1180.

11 PL, 190, 1398 B, 1399 D, etc. cf. *Ep. 29* (1463 A).

12 2 (PL, 190, 1329 C).

13 2 (1329–1330) and 3 (1398 B–D).

*Who would dare to put the union of the Spouse and the bride above
or on a par with the union between the Supreme Word himself, the
unifier, and the flesh that was united to him? Or, from a different
point of view . . . , who would presume to put it in second place?
For the (fellowship?) of the Word and the flesh is for the sake of the
union of the Spouse and the bride, and it is agreed that the mystical
and invisible flesh of the Emperor, which is the union of the faithful, is of a much higher dignity and much more dear to the Emperor
himself than the visible flesh of the Christ, heavy and corporeal,
which he drew from the Virgin. Among the reasons for this the following appears one of the most cogent, that it was for the sake of
this his mystical and invisible flesh that he took visible flesh and
united it to himself.*[14]

Mystical body would follow on closely from *mystical flesh*. It was
as if one called forth the other. Here we have it at last, and also in a
Eucharistic context, in the *Tractatus de sacramentis* written by a certain Master Simon:

> *In the sacrament of the altar there are two (bodies): that is, the true
> body of Christ and also that which it signifies, namely, his mystical
> body, which is the Church.*

And a little further on:

> *In this sacrament two (bodies) are to be noted: one that is hidden,
> that is, the true body of Christ, which is concealed under the form
> of bread and the accidents; and another one which is signified, that
> is, the mystical body of Christ, which is the Church.*[15]

This 'Master Simon', whose *Tractatus* has recently been brought to
light, is unknown in any other context. Therefore the exact date of his
work is difficult to determine. After comparing his work closely with
Peter Lombard's *Sentences*, Father Dhanis made a very strong case
for the latter's being an earlier work, and suggested dating Simon's
De Sacramentis around 1170.[16] Following on from this, the editor
of Master Simon's text, Father Weisweiler, was led by an analogous
comparison with the *Sententiae Divinitatis* to conclude that they

---

14 3 (1392 C).
15 Weisweiler, *Maître Simon et son groupe* (1937), pp. 27, 34.
16 *Revue d'histoire ecclésiastique*, 1930, p. 947.

were dependent on Master Simon.[17] But the date of the *Sententiae Divinitatis* is no less uncertain. Geyer, their editor, had suggested the years 1141–1147, but since then this date has been recognized as being too late, and in fact if the suggestions on this matter made by Father Pelster[18] are to be accepted, it should be set considerably earlier. Therefore even if we were to accept Father Weisweiler's opinion on its relationship to the *Sententiae Divinitatis*, nothing would oblige us to date our *De Sacramentis* before Peter Lombard's *Sentences*, which were finished in 1152. Perhaps the very use that Master Simon makes of *'mystical body'*, a use that I would not wish to contradict, provides fresh evidence for the conclusions of Father Dhanis. For his part Father Weisweiler, who adopts 'around 1145' as the date for Master Simon's now lost principal source, authorizes us to date the Treatise itself between that date and 1160.[19]

The anonymous treatise on the seven sacraments, called the *Treatise of Madrid*, which comes from the same school or the same 'group' as Master Simon's, and which must have been written shortly afterwards, around 1170, uses almost the identical expressions:

> *The Lord . . . wanted to give his body in a sacrament . . . and through such a sacrament that by the true body is signified the mystical body, that is to say, the Church.*[20]

Also at around the same time, but in a quite other context, Abbot Isaac of Stella used the word 'mystical body' in the course of an instruction that he addressed to his monks. Speaking of the Church as the body of Christ, Isaac naturally compares it to the human organism. But this in turn, in its complex unity, is itself compared to an inverted tree. And again in the same way the Church:

> *There is a similar structure in the mystical body, where, under the one head that is Christ and the one root . . . , there are many members . . . Moreover, just as the life of the root is the sole source of the greenness, strength and life of the entire body of the tree, so the Holy Spirit of Christ and our God is the sole source of the life, consciousness and movement of the entire body of the Church.*[21]

---

17 Introduction, pp. XLVI–LXII. Lottin, *Bulletin de théologie ancienne et médiévale*, vol. 3, n. 472, and Bergh, *Nouvelle Revue théologique*, 1938, p. 367.

18 *Zeitschrift für katholische Theologie*, 1929, p. 575.

19 *op. cit.* p. ccxiv, 1145–60. F. Stegmüller, *Reptorium commentariorum in Sententias Petri Lombardi* (1947), vol. 2 (*Indices*, p. 710).

20 ed. Weisweiler, p. 91.

21 PL, 194, 1801.

In the second half of the twelfth century, the Church therefore began to be called a '*mystical body*', and it would appear that from then on this expression spread rapidly. It made particular headway in the *Glossa*, and then in the Commentaries on Peter Lombard's *Sentences*:

> The similarity of wine to the blood of Christ you will find above, in the text of that chapter which treats those three, namely, the form of wine, the mystical body of the Church of Christ, and true body of Christ.[22]

. . . This sacrament represents of itself this triple union within the mystical body . . .[23]

We also find it in one of the many sermons falsely attributed to Hugh of Saint Victor, precisely the one *in festivitate paschali et corporis Christi*; it could not be said, however, that the immediate context was Eucharistic, as it is in the quotation above:

> The first (Easter) was in the striking of Egypt, the second in the passion of the Lord, the third in the justification of the wicked, the fourth in the death of the righteous, the fifth in the assumption and glorification of the whole Church, which is the mystical body of Christ.[24]

*   *   *

It has to be admitted, however, that in this new formulation we are still not dealing with a complete expression, nor with a technical description. '*Mystical*' is still not a natural adjective for the '*body which is the Church*'. As we have just read, the abbot of Stella certainly says at one point, for example, '*this* mystical body', in a sentence where the Church is compared both to the human body and to a tree. But he never says anywhere else '*the* mystical body', nor even: 'the mystical body of Christ'. Like the generations that went before him, he says: '*the body of the Church*' or '*the body of Christ*'. This last expression is repeated up to three times on the same page of the sermon that I quoted,[25] and this is the one that Isaac uses in his *Epistola de offi-*

---

22 MS. of Munich, cited by H. Weisweiler, *Mélanges Grabmann*, vol. 1, p. 393.

23 Commentary (MS of Paris) cited by A. Landgraf, *Scholastik*, 1940, pp. 220–1.

24 Pseudo-Hugh, *Sermo* 27 (PL, 177, 960 A).

25 PL, 194, 1801–2.

cio missae.[26] Master Simon does not automatically join '*mystical*' to '*body*' either, when talking about the Church. The two cases that can be found in his writing remain isolated instances, although he had other opportunities to repeat them.

He says, for example, that whoever receives the Sacrament worthily becomes '*one aggregated to the unity of the body of Christ*'; or else, through the Eucharistic species, '*is represented the body of Christ, that is, the Church*'.[27] Other authors who were contemporary with Master Simon, or who wrote shortly after him, such as Baldwin of Canterbury (†1190), remained faithful to the simple formulations of the past. Peter Comestor, who used '*mystical flesh*', also used elsewhere '*the body of Christ*'.[28] It would not be until the dawn of the thirteenth century, and perhaps even a little later, that the new expression could be found in general use and definitively fixed. Simon of Tournai, who taught in Paris around 1200, preferred to go back to the ancient '*spiritual body*':

> *The sixth question is, how are we to understand the words of the canon, 'Bid these be taken to your altar on high . . .'? For if this refers to the body which is there confected, how can it be taken to the altar on high when it is there already? The answer is as follows. There are two bodies of Christ: one is material, taken from the Virgin, and the other is spiritual fellowship, ecclesiastical fellowship. But the spiritual one so cleaves to Christ in a bond of love that the con-fection of the material body occurs for the sake of the salvation of the spiritual one. So these words request the spiritual body of Christ to be taken away to the altar on high, where it is not yet, after being celebrated here by means of the material confection. This is implied by the following words of the canon, 'Whoever of us . . .': these are to be understood to refer to our being taken up to the altar on high.*[29]

In this extract Simon of Tournai demonstrates that cast of mind, both original and conservative, which was to keep him somewhat on the margins of the current thinking of his day. His terminology did not

---

26 c. 1894–5

27 *op. cit.*, pp. 25, 28.

28 p. 57.

29 *Disputatio 71* (Warichez, pp. 202–3). On Simon of Tournai, see J. de Ghellinck, *L'essoir de la literature latine au XIIe siècle*, vol. 1, pp. 85–6. On the history of the explanation, see B. Botte, 'L'Ange du Sacrifice', *Recherches de théologie ancienne et médiévale*, 1929, pp. 285–308.

found a school. The '*spiritual body*' that he was attempting to resuscitate now suggested, as if in antithesis, a '*material body*' (coupled with a '*material confection*'!) which, despite the example given by William of Saint-Thierry, and despite the progressive abandonment of spiritualizing vocabulary in Eucharistic matters, still found itself inspiring a certain repugnance.[30] It would only be found once in a while in subsequent tradition.[31] It appears once in the writing of Peter of Poitiers: for him the Church is the spiritual body of Christ, as it is also the 'spiritual tabernacle'.[32] But in the passage where, among others, he repeated in substance the same explanation given for the enigmatic prayer of the Canon by Simon of Tournai, Peter of Poitiers once more said simply, as was his custom, '*body of Christ*':

> . . . or, '*Bid your body be taken away to your altar on high to be joined to the body of Christ*', that is, so that the union of the Church which is signified and brought into being by the body of Christ that is here may be joined to the body of Christ; that is, so that the Church militant may be joined to the Church triumphant. There is a figure by which properties of what is represented are attributed to that which represents.[33]

Other theologians, who were already familiar with '*mystical body*', nevertheless did not make exclusive use of it. Thus Lothaire di Segni, composing his great treatise *De sacro altaris mysterio* around 1195, during the enforced rest that preceded his elevation to the papacy, did indeed oppose the '*mystical body of Christ*' to the '*true body of Christ*' in his work, but it was only in one passage. Elsewhere, and exactly in the same sense, he was to say: '*the mystical flesh of Christ*'; and elsewhere again, on several occasions: '*the body of Christ*'.[34] With the liturgist Sicard of Cremona († 1215), it is similarly a question of the '*mystical body*' which is the Church, as opposed to the '*personal body*' or '*partial body*' which is the Eucharist;[35] but, as with Master Simon, and as with Abbot Isaac and Innocent III, this is only said in passing. Sicard only uses the word once, whereas on two occasions, in the same

---

30 See *infra*, Chapter 7. Wycliffe, *De Ecclesia*, c. 6 (Loserth, p. 137).

31 cf. *infra*, n. 59.

32 *Allegoriae super tabernaculum Moysi* (Moore-Corbett, p. 145). Gregory, Moralia in Job, 28, n. 14 (PL, 76, 455 D; 113, 280 A). *ibid*, p. 174. Also, *Vitis mystica*, n. 128 (PL, 184, 712, 713).

33 *Sentences*, 5, c. 12 (PL, 211, 1251–2); cf. Alegoriae, p. 57, 85.

34 PL, 217, 866 B, 879 B, 907 D.

35 *Mitrale*, 3 (PL, 213, 141).

context, he uses the more symmetrically pleasing expression '*univer-sal body*'.[36] We already know that William of Auxerre would put the '*mystical*' or body of Christ '*by grace*' in opposition to the '*true*' or '*natural*' body of Christ. He not only says this in the fourth book of his *Summa Aurea*, in the treatise on the Eucharist,[37] but he also does it in the third book, in his treatise *On the Incarnation*,[38] and this is no doubt why he was taken to be the inventor of the expression: because the original link between the two mysteries of the Eucharist and the Church had become so tenuous that it no longer occurred to anyone to search for it within the developments around the Eucharist. What is more, that '*mystical body*', which is synonymous for '*the Church as the one Church*' and which William also calls '*the mystical flesh of Christ*',[39] would appear again so rarely, during his lifetime, as a cur-rent expression in its application to the Church, that he would at one point take the trouble to explain to his reader: '*mystical body, that is the mystical Church*'. This is in the passage where he himself also com-ments, in the same way as Peter of Poitiers and Simon of Tournai, on the words '*Bid these be taken*':

> *The pronoun 'these' refers to the signifier, but with reference to that which is signified in final place, namely the mystical body of Christ. For it is common in sacred Scripture for the signifier to stand for the signified ... So the meaning is: 'Bid these be taken', that is, bid your mystical body, that is, the mystical Church, be taken 'by the hand', that is, the operation, of the holy angels who assist at the sacrifice of the altar, 'to your altar on high', that is, to the triumphant Church in heaven; that is, bid the Church militant to be joined to the Church triumphant.*[40]

We can see both the link between this text and that of Peter of Poitiers and, from our point of view, its novelty in relation to it. In order to underline the effect of communion, William says once again, and three

---

36 *op. cit.* (PL, 213, 117).
37 edn. of 1500, fol. 257 v°, 259 r°, 262 v°.
38 Tract. 1, c. 4, qq. 5 and 6 (fol. 116 v°).
39 Fol. 258 v° and 259 r°.
40 Fol. 262 r°. It is noticeable that '*mystical body*' and '*mystical Church*' have the opposite sense here to the one found in Theodoret and Augustine (*Introduc-tion*, nn. 31, 33). In the analogous explanation that they give for the same text, Sicard of Cremona (PL, 213, 132) and Prevostinus of Cremona still do not use the adjective '*mystical*'; see, in contrast, the *Summa* of Alexander, St. Thomas and Peter of Tarentaise.

times subsequently: '*to be mystically incorporated into the body of Christ*', and this expression, at the same time as it marks the transition from the former Eucharistic usage to the new ecclesial usage of *mystical body*, emphasizes the bond of continuity that faith recognizes between one body and the other, from one 'mystery' to the other:

> To take the body of Christ spirituality is to be mystically incorporated in the body of Christ. Being incorporated in the body of Christ mystically occurs in two ways, etc.[41]

The *Summa Aurea* dates from the first third of the thirteenth century.[42] A manuscript from Douai that contains a series of *Quaestiones*, which must have been composed in the 1230s, gives as the title to one of these questions: '*On the mystical body*'.[43] William of Auvergne, in his treatise *De sacramento Eucharistiae*, which clearly dates from the same time,[44] uses indifferently either '*the mystical body of Christ*' or '*the body of the Church*', but this second expression still remains his principal one: thus it appears four times on the same page, but the first appears only once.[45] In *De sacramento ordinis*,[46] William also writes: '*the mystical body of Christ, which is the Church*', which is yet another transitional formulation. Luke of Tuy (†1249), writing against the Albigensians, repeated the traditional doctrine without any linguistic innovation:

> By the sacrament of communion of the body and blood of Christ the faithful people are made one body, joined to Christ as the head.[47]

* * *

---

41 Fol. 359 r°.

42 Not before 1215; perhaps even after 1222. William of Auxerre died in 1231 or 1232.

43 The question turns on Jn. 16: 'Father, I pray that they might be one'. Glorieux, *Recherches de théologie ancienne et médiévale*, 1938, p. 131. The *Questiones* in this manuscript seem mostly to belong to the period around 1230–7 (pp. 123–34).

44 This treatise is part of a *De Sacramentis* whose composition is dated by a fifteenth-century manuscript as 1234. 'One wonders what such information is worth', wrote F. Vernet (DTC, vol. 6, c. 1969), who was inclined to think that most of William's writings preceded his episcopacy (1228).

45 c. 4 (*Opera*, 1674, vol. 1, pp. 441–2).

46 c. 11 (*ibid.*, p. 545).

47 *Adversus Albigenses*, 1. 2, c. 1 (1612 edn., p. 69).

We have scant knowledge of the works, most of which are still unedited, that immediately preceded the generation of the great Scholastics. In any case, from their time onwards, *mystical body*, in its new interpretation, became both the technical and the common term. In their unanimity on this point, they succeeded in consigning to oblivion the long 'prehistory' whose remains my preceding pages have tried to exhume. There is no appreciable difference in this regard between Saint Albert the Great,[48] whose long discourses on the mystery of the Eucharist play such a crucial role in the traditional viewpoint, Saint Bonaventure,[49] Saint Thomas Aquinas,[50] the *Summa* of Alexander of Hales,[51] or popularizers such as Hugh Ripelin of Strasbourg. Take the latter for example. In his work, as in that of all the others, '*true body of Christ*' and '*mystical body of Christ*', describing respectively the sacramental body and the ecclesial body, are at the same time associated and opposed:

> *In the Eucharist there is something that is purely a sacrament, as the form of bread and wine, there is something that is purely a reality, as the mystical body of Christ, and there is something that is reality and sacrament, as the true body of Christ which he drew from the Virgin, which is the reality that the first of these relates to and the sacrament of the second of them.*[52]

Understood in this context, the expression became so established that Saint Bonaventure, without realizing it, attributed it to Peter Lombard.[53] It would often appear subsequently, notably in treatises on Ordination, regarding the double power conferred on the priest by the sacrament over the '*true body of Christ*' and over the '*mystical body*

---

48 *In Mattheum*, 36 (Vivès, vol. 21, p. 6). *In IV Sent.* (vol. 29, pp. 91, 206–11, 251, 300, 381, 392–3 etc.). cf. A. Piolanti, *Il Corpo Mistico et le sue Relazioni con l'Eucaristia in S. Alberto Magno* (Rome, 1939).

49 *In III Sent.* (Quaracchi, vol. 3, pp. 164, 209, 210). *In IV Sent.* (vol. 4, pp. 184, 191, 196, 208, 286, 440). *Breviloquium* (vol. 5, pp. 273–5). *In Lucam* (vol. 7, p. 546). cf. Richard of Middleton, *In III Sent.*, d. 13 (Hocedez, pp. 293, 294).

50 *In IV Sent.*, d. 12, 13 (Vivès, vol. 10, pp. 305, 322).

51 *Summa theologiæ*, IIIa, q. 12, m. 2, a. 2, n. 3 (Venice 1575, mol. 40 v°).

52 *Compendium theologicae veritatis*, 6, c. 6; cf. c. 18 (Lyon, 1649, pp. 457, 473, under the name Albert the Great). cf. Bessarion, *De sacramento Eucharistiae* (PG, 161, 495–8).

53 Q., vol. 4, p. 196.

of Christ': we find it thus in Gerson,[54] or in the Roman Catechism.[55] In fact it is already poised to detach itself from the context in which it originally arose and by which it is explained. Nevertheless, it is not yet a *fait accompli*. Although it is already widespread, and almost obligatory in treatises on the Eucharist, the use of *mystical body* remains rare outside this context. Saint Bonaventure apparently offers only one example, in his treatise on Penance, where it appears with regard to restitution to others:

> We see in a body of an animal that one member exposes itself to receive a wound directed at another, as when the arm exposes itself on behalf of the head. If, then, the mystical body is connected by similarity to the natural body, it appears likewise that one member can and ought to bear the burdens of another.[56]

Here we have a direct inference from *'natural body'* to *'mystical body'*. The analogy is taken, not from Christ or from the sacramental elements, but from the body in general. The expression is not used in a commentary on the tenth or eleventh chapters of the First Letter to the Corinthians, but on the twelfth chapter, or the parallel passage in the Epistle to the Romans, where Saint Paul repeated and expanded on the old apologia of the head and its members. What appears only as an exception in Saint Bonaventure is also an exception[57] in St. Albert the Great[58] and in the *Summa* of Alexander. In the two questions that the third part of that *Summa* devotes to the grace of Christ, *'mystical body'* can only be found three times among a great many other formulations such as *'body of the Church'*, *'one body'*, *'member of the body'*, etc. The third of these three still constitutes a sort of parenthesis, a little entity in itself, transported just as it was from the treatise on the Eucharist.[59]

In Saint Thomas, who also uses *'mystical person'*,[60] we already

---

54 *De examinatione doctrinarum* (*Opera*, vol. 1, p. 10; Anvers, 1706) and *De potestate ecclesiastica*, consideration 7 (Goldast, vol. 2, p. 1390). See also Antonius de Rosellis, *Monarchia*, p. 2, c. 12 (Goldast, pp. 341–2). cf. Bonaventure, *In IV Sent.*, d. 17 (Q., IV, p. 440).

55 However, the Roman Catechism speaks more habitually of the Church as *'body of Christ'*, as in antiquity.

56 *In IV Sent.*, d. 20 (Q., vol. 4, p. 530).

57 Even then it is within the context of sacramental doctrine.

58 *Quaestiones de incarnatione, De unione capitis quod est Christus et corporis, scilicet Ecclesiae* (Backes, pp. 19, 23).

59 Fol. 40 v°.

60 *In Colos.* (Vivès, vol. 21, p. 390). *Summa theologiæ*, IIIa, q. 48, a. 2, ad 1 (vol. 5, p. 242); q. 19, a. 4 (p. 2). *De Veritate*, q. 29, a. 7, ad 11, cf. ad 10 (vol.

find this independent usage a little more frequently.[61] In several texts *'mystical body'* appears to be explained by its analogy in contrast to *'natural body'*: we find this in commentaries on the First Letter to the Corinthians and the Letter to the Ephesians.[62] In the Third Part of the *Summa* the first article on the eighth question even says specifically: *'Just as the whole Church is called one mystical body through its similarity to the natural body of man . . .'* The fact that the *Summa* willingly uses *'mystical body of the Church'* instead of *'mystical body of Christ'*[63] is also an indication of an advanced evolution. Nevertheless, we also find there: *'the true body of Christ represents the mystical body'*,[64] which takes us back to the origins of the phrase as it is used by Master Simon and the *Treatise of Madrid*. Furthermore, in Saint Thomas as in many of his contemporaries, we find cases where *'mystical body'* is not used, whereas it would seem to be indispensably called for by *'natural body'*.[65] The fact is that in reality these two expressions do not explain one another. Besides, in most cases, in order to speak of the 'mystical body', most of these authors simply say, as people had been saying for twelve centuries: *'the body of Christ'*, *'the body of the Church'*, *'one body'*,[66] etc. When they add an adjective, it is not always *'mystical'*. To *'natural body'* or *'material body'* there corresponds more frequently, by means of a simple relationship of analogy, a *'spiritual body'*,[67] whose head is the *'spiritual head'*,[68] whose

---

15, p. 352. cf. *Summa theologiæ*, IIIa, q. 49, a. 1; *In III Sent.*, d. 18, a. 6, sol. 1, ad 2.

61 *Summa theologiæ*, IIIa, q. 8, a. 1 (Vivès, vol. 4, p. 630). cf. a. 3 and 4 (pp. 632, 634). Q. 49, a.1 (vol. 5, p. 246). Q. 82, a. 1, ad 4 (p. 506). *De Veritate*, q. 29, a. 5 (vol. 15, p. 347). *In III Sent.*, d. 13, 18 (vol. 9, pp. 203, 283). *In Rom.*, XII (vol. 20, p. 552). *In I Cor.*, xii (pp. 747, 750). *In Ephes.* (vol. 21, pp. 131–314). St. Thomas, *In I Cor.* 12 and 10–11 (p. 741).

62 *In I Cor.*, xii (vol. 20, p. 747); *In Ephes.*, iv (vol XXI, p. 000); *Summa theologiæ* IIa IIae, q.183, a.2, ad 3 (vol. 4, pp. 383–4); *Summa theologiæ*, IIIa, q. 48, a.1 (vol. 4, p. 630). cf. M.-J. Congar, *Esquisses du Mystère de l'Église*, p. 65, n. 2.

63 *Summa theologiæ*, IIIa, q. 8, a. 3 and 4 (vol. 4, pp. 632–4).

64 *Summa theologiæ*, IIIa, q. 82, a.9, 2; cf. q. 80, a. 4 (vol. 5 pp. 512, 488). *In IV Sent.*, d. 8, q. 1, a. 1, 3.(Moos, pp. 304, 3–5, 317); q. 2, a. 1 (p. 335).

65 Bonaventure, *In III Sent.* (Q., vol. 3, p. 27). Thomas, *In III Sent.* (vol. 9, p. 201; *In IV Sent.* (vol. 10, p. 325); *De Veritate*, q. 29, a. 4 (vol. 15, pp. 343–6); *In Ephes.* (vol. 21 pp. 277–8, cf. pp. 288, 306). Ulrich of Strasbourg, *Summa de Bono*, vol. 5, tr. I, c. 13 (Backes, pp. 29–30), etc. cf. *Perpetuité* (Migne, vol. 2, 784).

66 Ulrich of Strasbourg, *Summa de Bono* (Backes, p. 29), etc.

67 Alexander of Hales, *loc. cit.* Albert, *In III sent.*, d. 13, a. 2 (vol. 28, pp. 238, 240). St. Thomas, *Summa theologiæ*, IIIa, q. 69, a. 5 (vol. 5, p. 393).

68 Alexander of Hales, *loc. cit.* Albert, *In III Sent.*, d. 13, a. 2 (vol. 28, pp. 238, 240). St. Thomas, *Summa theologiæ*, IIIa, q. 69, a. 5 (t. V, p. 393).

members are '*spiritual members*',[69] and which is gifted with '*spiritual senses*'.[70] In contrast there is a genuine bond of 'mystical' meaning that joins the '*mystical body of Christ*'[71] with the '*true body of Christ*' or the '*natural body of Christ*'. Thus we come to understand how, despite the secondary tradition whose precursor we find in Isaac of Stella, and one of whose principal initiators seems to have been William of Auxerre, it took a long time for the custom to arise whereby *mystical body* was uprooted from its 'natural place' in order to be planted in an independent location.

* * *

Nevertheless, we are fast approaching the time when this custom would take root. It would become common to speak of 'mystical body' without any reference to the Eucharist, to the same extent that theories concerning the Church, whether in its visible form or in its hidden life, would develop outside the sacramental framework. This is how we already find it in 'the most ancient treatise on the Church', the *De regimine christiano* published by James of Viterbo at the beginning of the fourteenth century.[72] James of Viterbo preferred the Gospel metaphor of the reign of God to the Pauline metaphor of the body. Nevertheless he had recourse to it in order to give an account of the unity that in his view was the principal mark of the *reign of the Church*: for him, therefore, the Church is a *mystical body* and Christ is its *spiritual and mystical head*.[73] It is the same for John of Paris, although his theology is considerably different in other senses.[74] This mystical body would now be thought of not only in terms of the analogy with the natural human body, but also in terms of the analogy with human society, according to the famous comparison that Aristotle had established in his *Politics*,[75] and thus they would more or less fall back on the antique and banal formulation: *body of the Church*. But here again it would still only be a matter of analogy: and this is what was all too often forgotten. We are only too familiar with the use – some might

---

69 Albert (vol. 28, pp. 239, 240).

70 Albert, *loc. cit.*

71 William of Auxerre, *Summa aurea* (fol. 116, vᵒ). St. Thomas, *In Ephes.* (vol. 21, pp. 311, 312), etc.

72 Y. Congar, 'L'idée thomiste de l'Église', *Esquisses*, pp. 59–61, 90.

73 pp. 109, 152, 199, 201.

74 cf. Dom John Leclercq, *Jean de Paris et l'ecclésiologie du XIIIe siècle*, p. 113.

75 cf. G. de Lagarde, *La Naissance de l'ésprit laic*, vol. 3, *Secteur social de la Scolastique*, pp. 170–5.

perhaps even call it abuse – made of the expression by some of the theologians in the circle of Boniface VIII, in order to claim power. While at the beginning of the thirteenth century the canonist Alun of Wales was still saying in the glosses which he added to his compilation of the *Decretals*: '*For there is one body of the Church*',[76] the likes of Giles of Rome,[77] Matthew of Aquasparta, and Alvaro Pelayo,[78] would say: '*the mystical body is one*'. But in thus applying to the juridical and social order a word whose resonances were entirely 'mystical' and spiritual, their doctrine would mark a sort of degeneration of the *mystical body*, exposing ecclesiastical power to the resentment of secular rulers and to the polemics of their theologians. This is the origin of the bitter and prolonged arguments that dominated the final centuries of the Middle Ages, reviving in another guise the old struggle between the priesthood and the empire. In a certain way these arguments turned on the unity between the mystical body and its head. The time was certainly past when someone like Peter Damian could still speak of the kingdom and the priesthood as of the two heads of the world.[79] Now such language was universally condemned. The papal theologians said: for fear of creating a monster, a single body can only have a single head: its one and only head is the Pope.[80] To which the royal theologians gave a threefold response. Either, admitting the premises of their adversaries, they insisted, in terms of the analogy with the human body, on a role for the heart as essential as that of the head: and would not that heart of the mystical body be the prince, king or emperor, who had sovereignty over temporal matters?[81] Or else it was the unity of the body itself that they opposed: next to the *mystical body* that is the Church, and before it, was there not another great collective body, that *natural body* formed by the human race?[82] And if it could be said of the Pope that he is the '*head of the Church*', should it not then be said of the

---

76 Around 1208.

77 *De ecclesiastica potestate* (Schloz, pp. 50, 132, 152), etc. Commentary on Romans, lectio 39, (Rome, 1555, fol. 76 v°, in Rom., xii).

78 *Collyricum adversus haereses.* Cited by N. Jung, *Alvaro Pelayo*, pp. 215–6.

79 *Disceptatio synodalis* (*Libelli de lite*, vol. 1, pp. 77ff.).

80 Antonius de Rosellis, *Monarchia* (about 1440) in Goldast, vol. 1, pp. 254–5, 308, 315, etc. Hostiensis, *Summa super titulis Decretalium.* Anonymous fragment published by Scholz, p. 471. Henry of Cremona, *De potestate papae*, p. 466. (See Carlyle, *A History of the mediaeval political Theory in the West*, vol. 5, pp. 328, 395, 401.) cf. St. Thomas, *De regimine principum*, 3, c. 10. Fr. Petrach., *Epistolae de juribus imperii romani* (Goldast, vol. 2, p. 1355). Paschasius Radbertus, *In Matthaeum* (PL, 120, 565 D).

81 *Songe du Vergier*, c. 38 (Goldast, pp. 71, cf. p. 73 and 165). Antonius de Rosellis, pp. 308, 440. cf. Claudel, *La Ville*, act 3.

82 cf. Wycliffe, *Sermonum*, p. 2, pp. 84–6 (Loserth).

emperor that he is *head of the world*?[83] Could not the body of the laity and the body of the clergy therefore each have its own head, without risking any talk of monsters?[84] Lastly, and more radically, others refused to envisage for the mystical body any head other than Christ himself,[85] and, in a spirited counter-offensive, it was the partisans of papal imperialism whom they accused of having given birth to an intellectual monster. Thus we have Marsilius of Padua, writing that Roman pretensions to absolute power '*have infected the entire mystical body of Christ*'.[86]

This last reproach would be found shortly afterwards on the lips both of the precursors and then of the instigators of the Reformation. They would not only take issue with the Roman curia's pretensions to the temporal power of princes, but they would object to the primacy of Peter itself. It expresses a reaction against the very idea of a visible Church. What started off as the simple articulation of a power struggle, once it had begun to dissolve the social edifice of Christendom, finally played a role in the breaking up of the Church itself. An exaggerated attempt had been made to assimilate the 'mystical body' with the 'visible body',[87] chiefly to the benefit of the most exterior element of the Church in its most contingent forms – that is the power claimed by the papacy over temporal matters. This lack of prudence would exact a heavy price. Beyond any of these abuses, the objections of the likes of Wycliffe,[88] Jan Huss,[89] Luther or Calvin[90] would assail Catholicism itself, and the inverted excesses of their 'spiritualist' reaction would lead to the total dissociation of the mystical body of Christ from the

---

83　John of Paris, *Tractatus de potestate regia et papali* (edn. of 1618, p. 19).

84　*Songe du Vergier*, c. 307 (p. 200). Ockham, *Octo quaestiones*, I (Goldast, vol. 2, pp. 314, 319). [For a selection of Ockham's works in English, see A. J. Freddoso and F. E. Kelley, *Quodlibetal questions* (London, 1991); P. Boehner, S. F. Brown, *Philosophical Writings: a selection*, revised edn. (Indianapolis, 1990); M. Adams, N. Kretzmann, *Predestination, God's foreknowledge, and future contingents* (New York, 1969).]

85　cf. *Quaestio de utraque potestate* (Goldast, vol. 2, p. 103). John of Paris, *loc. cit.* Gregory of Heimburg (Goldast, vol. 2, p. 1629). Panormitanus, *Lectura super V libros decretalium* (Basle, 1488).

86　*Defensor Pacis*, 2, c. 24, n. 2.

87　Albert the Great, *In IV Sent.*, d. 13, a. 28 (Vivès, vol. 29, p. 381). St. Thomas, *Summa theologiæ*, IIIa, q. 8, a. 3, 6.

88　*De Ecclesia*, c. 1, 2 (Loserth, pp. 5ff.), etc. See the four volumes of sermons (Loserth), *passim.* cf. vol. 4, p. 77 and p. 298.

89　Several texts in W. Wagner, 'Die Kirche als Corpus Christi mysticum beim jungen Luther', *Zeitschrift für Katholische Theologie* (1937), p. 63.

90　See the refutation of Bellarmine, *De romano Pontifice*, 1, c. 9 (Vivès, vol. 1, p. 486).

visible body of the Church. In its own turn, and in spite of more than one notable exception, Catholic theology itself would not avoid experiencing the repercussions of such a dissociation. At times it would even seem to accept it. When we read, for example, the observations made by the Fathers of the First Vatican Council on the plan put before them, whereby the Church was defined from the outset as being the *mystical body*, we note that a good number of them were astonished. Not only did they object to this notion in its 'obscurity',[91] or else its overly metaphorical character,[92] or that, in contrast, it was too abstract.[93] Some of them wanted to outlaw it as a possible source of dangerous error: the sole fact that the Jansenists had used it seemed to them to call for its condemnation without further appeal.[94] Without going to such excessive lengths, several of them estimated that, valid as it was for mystical theology, it was out of place in a dogmatic exposition on the Church,[95] where there was a need to define its essence, rather than to offer nourishment to the life of piety . . .[96] Others, expressing a fairer, if not a more current view of the time, nonetheless felt that it would be an awkward task for them to unite in a harmonious synthesis the doctrine of the mystical body, whose traditional importance they could perceive or guess at, and the necessary teaching on the institution of the Church . . .[97] We know how these different scruples were definitively swept aside by the publication of Pius XII's encyclical *Mystici Corporis* on the 29th June 1943.[98]

All these deviations, these polemics, these exclusions and these hesitations would have had less reason to exist had the historical origins of the expression *mystical body* not been consigned to oblivion so early on, at the same time as the spirit of the doctrine at whose heart it had developed. Be that as it may, the expression itself, with its variations, passed from that time onward into Christian discourse, and it can be said that from the thirteenth century onwards, whether correctly or incorrectly understood, it never fell into decline. To recall but a

---

91 Mansi, vol. 51, pp. 738–9 (n. 26), 745 (63), 751 (95).
92 *ibid.*, pp. 760, 763 (n. 128, 132, 140).
93 *ibid.*, pp. 741, 745 (n. 43, 63).
94 *ibid.*, p. 761, n. 133.
95 *ibid.*, p. 760 (n. 128, 130).
96 *ibid.*, p. 760 (n. 128, 130).
97 *ibid.*, pp. 744, 753, 755, 762; n. 57, 105, 111, 135.
98 cf. D.-C. Lialine, *Une étape en eclésiologie, réflexions sur l'encyclique 'Mysici corporis'* (*Irenicon*, 1946–7). L. Malevez, 'Quelques enseignements de l'encyclique "Mystici corporis Christi"', *Nouvelle Revue théologique* 67 (1945), pp. 993–1015. On the history of the theology of the mystical body in the nineteenth century, see in the same review pp. 1025–38.

few examples, we know the enthusiasm with which St. Catherine of Siena, at the time of the Great Schism, celebrated the 'mystical body of the holy Church', for whose ills she implored God's mercy[99] and for whose unity she fought and died.[100] Some years later, in the sentence of condemnation of Joan of Arc, Pierre Cauchon declared that the Maid had to be cut off, like a rotten branch, from the *mystical body of Christ*.[101] In the sixteenth century, Scholastics, Humanists and Protestants spoke repeatedly of the mystical body. As an exception to this, Calvin preferred to replace it with any of several analogous turns of phrase: when he does not simply say, in the ancient manner: '*the body of Christ*', he opposes the '*spiritual and secret body of Christ*' to the '*merely political body, as far as it applies*', or else he speaks of the 'sacred union' that reigns between Christ and his members, who will in time come to form an '*entire and perfect body*'.[102] But Erasmus[103] and Luther[104] in contrast both contributed to the success of the modern formulation. Since then, it has remained the common property of both Catholic and Protestant theologians. Fénelon made good use of it in his *Traité du ministère des pasteurs*.[105] From theology it would even make some inroads into the world of philosophy: Suárez would say that people grouped into society formed: '*a mystical body that morally can be called one in itself*',[106] and, in his *Critique of Pure Reason*, Kant would address his readers on the *mystical body* of reasonable beings formed by the free submission of each one to the rule of moral laws.[107]

We do not have to pursue our expression as far as this new phase in its history. Its sense could still vary, sometimes profoundly, according to the general context of the doctrines of which it was a part – the examples given above make the point sufficiently – but its orientation was fixed from then onwards. There remains only to observe that, at

---

99 cf. *Diologue* (tr. Hutaud, vol. 2, p. 323).

100 She wrote also to Peter de Luna, 'Have passion for truth, that you may become a column in the mystical body of the holy Church'.

101 Champion, vol. 1 (1920), p. 390.

102 *Opera*, vol. 49, c. 501-7; vol. 51, c. 282.

103 *Supra*, Introduction, n. 5.

104 Commentary on the letter to the Romans (Ficker, p. 55, 111), etc. Sermon on the Eucharist, December 1519 (Strohl, *L'épanouissement de la pensée religieuse de Luther*, pp. 341, 344). [For Luther's works in English, see *Luther's Works* series (St. Louis, MO: Concordia Publishing House).]

105 Ch. II (Œuvres, edn. of Paris, vol. 1, pp. 154, 155).

106 *De legibus*, 3, c. 2, n. 4 (*Opera omnia*, Vivès, vol. 5, p. 181). What Rousseau calls 'collective moral body': Émile 5; cf. *De l'Économie politique*, in *Encyclopédie*.

107 *Transcendental Methodology* (Barni-Archambault, vol. 2, p. 276).

the end of the thirteenth century, in the fourth book of his famous *Rationale*, the liturgist Durandus of Mende uses *mystical flesh* in the same sense, that is, in the new sense, in one chapter, and *mystical body* in another.[108] It might be supposed that some subtle reason governed this change of vocabulary: for example, *mystical flesh* might describe more precisely the unity that is the 'power' of the sacrament, while *mystical body* might be taken for the Church in general. The preceding history of these two words suggests a hypothesis of this sort. But in fact there is a simpler explanation. William Durandus was eclectic, choosing his material from whatever source came to hand. The authors he cites bear witness to an age where vocabulary had not yet been fixed. The first of his two chapters, the one in which *mystical flesh* features, was copied straight from Innocent III, who was writing a century earlier.[109] The second is an adaptation of it: the text of Innocent said simply '*body of Christ*'; in the new manner, and probably without even thinking, William added: '*mystical*'.[110]

---

108 *Rationale divinorum officiorum* 4, c. 42, n. 21–2; c. 51, n. 20 (edn. of 1672, pp. 176, 198).

109 Compare c. 42 and Innocent, 4, c. 36 (*supra*, n. 34).

110 Compare c. 31 and Innocent 6, c. 3. See also Bonaventure, *In IV Sent.*, 12 (Q., vol. 4, p. 286).

SECOND PART

6

'Spiritual Flesh'

[139]

Spiritual flesh, *mystical flesh*, *mystical body*: these three expressions formed a chain and, with the passage of time, became practically equivalent, but only if readers restricted themselves to certain texts and did not look too closely. Certain additional indications are indispensable if we wish to discern the nuances more clearly. They will help us to understand the verbal evolution which up till now I have been satisfied merely to trace, but which it is now time I attempted to explain.

We have seen that, from the beginning, *flesh* was used more specifically of the Eucharist than *body*. This can easily be understood, because since Saint Paul the word *body* had a further dogmatic function of supreme importance to which *flesh* could not aspire.[1] There is indeed, in the current acceptance of the word 'body', an idea of totality which is both unified and diversified, and which is essential in the Pauline concept of the Church. A 'body' is an organism, it is the exchange between members whose functions simultaneously differ and work together. It also represents plenitude. The theologians of the thirteenth century would not fail to observe that, if the Eucharist were to be considered by itself alone, independently of its significance, it would be more proper to call it *flesh of Christ*.[2] Furthermore *flesh* was the word used for the sacrifices of the ancient law where the bodies of animal victims prefigured the flesh of the divine Victim.[3] In St. John's Gospel, it not only appeared in chapter six, in the Bread of Life discourse – and we know that many of the first Christians did not understand this discourse as referring, at least directly, to the Eucharist – but it already figured in the Prologue: *the Word became flesh*. It was the proper word for the Incarnation. It is a word that contains a double paradox, a word which flesh could not comprehend: '*that which flesh*

---

1 Nevertheless, Gregory of Elvira, *Tractatus* 9 (B. W., p. 99). But if the Church is called to be flesh of Christ, this is rather as his spouse than as his body. cf. Godescalc, *De corporae et sanguine Domini* (Lambot, p. 335).

2 See the *Somme d'Alexandre*, IV^a, q.10, m. 4, a. 2. cf. m. 3, a. 3.

3 Bede, *In Leviticum* (PL, 91, 341 B).

does not understand is called flesh, and flesh does not understand all the more because it is called flesh'.[4] It is a word that denotes weakness and death – '*Does flesh give life?*'[5] – to which the idea of resurrection was attached,[6] the idea of spiritual and life-giving food: *flesh that is food. Flesh of Christ, body of life.*[7] One ninth-century homily, which is little more than an adaptation of a sermon of Saint Augustine on Saint John, says:

> It is through spirit that the flesh avails, since in itself it does not avail . . . For it was through the flesh that the spirit did something for our salvation. Flesh was its vessel, by means of which spirit saved us, using the instrument of flesh for the salvation of the human race.[8]

Flesh full of sacrament would be the song of Pseudo-Hildebert in the ninth century . . .[9]

Now, among the patristic texts known to the Middle Ages that deal with the question of the *flesh of Christ*, there was one that was particularly famous. It is a sentence taken from Saint Jerome's commentary on the Letter to the Ephesians:

> The blood and flesh of Christ are understood in two ways: they are either that spiritual and divine flesh and blood, of which he said, '*my flesh is truly food*' and '*unless you eat . . .*', or the flesh and blood of which the first was crucified and the latter made to pour forth by the soldier's lance.[10]

---

4 Augustine (PL, 35, 1612). Pseudo-Bede (92, 718 A). Alcuin (100, 834 D). Rabanus Maurus (110, 269 D). Adrevald of Fleury (124, 950 D). Durandus of Troarn (149, 1402 B). William of St. Thierry (180, 357 C). cf. Rom. 8.3.

5 Augustine, *In psalm. 98*, 9 (PL, 37, 1264).

6 cf. Jo., 6. St. Bernard, *In vigilia Nativitatis Domini sermo 1*, n. 6 (PL, 183, 89 D). [For selections of St. Bernard's sermons and letters in English, see G. R. Evans, *Bernard of Clairvaux: selected works* (New York, 1987); *Cistercian Fathers series*, vol. 1, 3, 4, 7, 13, 19, 31, 37, 55, 62; H. C. Backhouse, *The Song of Songs* (London, 1990).]

7 Ambrose, *De mysteriis*, c. 8, n. 48 (PL, 16, 405 A). Lanfranc (150, 430 D). Cyril of Alexandria, *In Joannem* (PG, 73, 568 C) and *Adversus Nestorium* (76, 189 D, etc.). (Cyril also says *soma* often: PG, 73, 601 B, 604 B and D; 76, 193 B). cf. Athanasius (26, 1011) and John Damascene (94, 1152). Ivo of Chartres, *Decretum*, p. 2, c. 4 (PL, 161, 138 D); Gratian, *De consecratione* 2.80 (Fr., 1346).

8 Haimon (PL, 118, 351 B). Augustine (35, 1616, 1617–18). Alcuin (100, 838 A–B).

9 PL, 171, 1199 B; 207, 1138 B (Peter Cantor).

10 *In Ephes.*, 1, c. 1 (PL, 26, 451). After often having been quoted, this text will be inserted in Abelard (178, 1530), in the *Decretum* of Ivo of Chartres, p. 2, c. 5

The text that follows on from this sheds light on the implications of this distinction:

> In accordance with this distinction his saints too accept a diversity of blood and flesh, such that the flesh which will behold the salvation of God is one thing and the flesh and blood which are not able to possess the kingdom of God are another.[11]

Notice first of all that, despite the repetition of the words 'one flesh, another flesh', it is less a question of two different fleshes designated by the same word as of two different ways of understanding one and the same text: 'it is to be doubly understood'.[12] Therefore there is no duality of substance here. Could we speak, along with Algerius of Liège and many others, of a duality of 'forms' or of states? Strictly speaking, not any more than we could of substance. At least this is not what interests Jerome most. His idea includes this, but goes beyond it. In the second part of the text that we have just read, he is less speaking of an objective duality than expressing an opposition of connections; the opposition is analogous to the one that Jesus himself taught when he said: 'Flesh and blood have not revealed this to you . . . the flesh is of no avail . . . my words are spirit and they are life.' Consequently it appears that, from the first part of the text this mysterious 'spiritual and divine flesh' does not simply define the Eucharistic mystery 'in itself'. The expression does not only aim to describe the condition of Christ in this mystery, to qualify what will later be called a 'mode of presence'. But, like the ripened corn and the mystical flesh of the commentary on Isaiah, like the mystical flesh (μυστικὴ σάρξ) of Anastasius of Sinai, and also a little like the heavenly bread of many other ancient texts, it insists first and foremost on the life-giving power of the Eucharist, a power linked in actual fact to the faith and the dispositions of the communicant. The intention appears even more explicit here than it does elsewhere, thanks to the contrast demonstrated by the mention of the other flesh, alia caro. Jerome's text reminds us of the liturgical expressions that celebrate the 'saving body', the 'life-giving' body,

---

(161, 141 A–B), in the Panormia (161, 1076 B–C), in Gratian, De consecratione 2.49 (Fr., 1332). cf. Berengarian text (Matronola, p. 112).

11 cf. Clement, Paed., Bk. 2, c. 2 (Stählin, vol. 1, pp. 167 ff.). Origen, In Leviticum, hom. 9, n. 10 (Baehrens, p. 438). For the opposition of flesh and of spirit: Jerome, In Galat., 5 (PL, 26, 406–22).

12 cf. In Isaiam (PL, 24, 309 D). Ep. 78, n. 18 (Hilberg, vol. 2, p. 67). Compare the Latin version of Irenaeus, Adv. Haer., 4, c. 41, n .2 (PG, 7, 1115).

the '*salvific body, the vivifying body, the body that is alive and gives life*' . . .[13] What is more, it comes close to various Augustinian texts, though their original perspective is not always exactly identical. The first of the two terms that Jerome sets in opposition to one another is the flesh in its sensible aspect, in its purely 'carnal' reality, whereas Saint Augustine usually starts from the '*visible sacrament*'. But this difference does not prevent Jerome's '*spiritual flesh*' from coinciding more or less with Augustine's '*sacrament spiritually understood*'.[14] According to yet another expression of Augustine's, it is also the flesh of Christ insofar as it is received, or ought to be received in truth – '*eaten spiritually in truth itself*' – that is to say, '*not only in a sacrament but involving a sharing in the spirit*'.[15] Or again, according to an expression of Paschasius Radbertus repeated by Hériger of Lobbes: '*flesh spiritually mingled with flesh*'.[16]

Nevertheless, in the ninth century, by gleaning scarce facts within the tradition, a quite different point of view arose in the form of the theory that I analysed in the first chapter on the 'triple body of Christ'. In the thought of its first author, the aim of this theory was above all to separate out and organize the different texts of Scripture where the word 'body' is used with reference to Christ. Soon, thanks to a mistaken attribution, itself apparently reinforced by a mistaken interpretation, it came to be thought of as coming from Saint Augustine, a fact that contributed considerably to its success. We already know of the strange misunderstanding in which a previously edited text of Paschasius came to be attributed to the great African doctor, and primarily used against the very doctrine that Paschasius was defending in his passage. As for the mistaken interpretation, it was based on a passage, this time an authentic one, from a sermon where Saint Augustine is explaining how Christ '*is understood and named in three ways*'.[17] But this triple mode of being of Christ's – as God, as Incarnate, and '*in the fullness of the Church*' – is not remotely the 'triple body' of Paschasius's theory. That, as M. Lepin[18] has observed with consider-

---

13 Expressions seen frequently in Syriac liturgies (Renaudot, vol. 2, *passim*). cf. Peter Comestor, *Sententiae de sacramentis*, n. 17 (Martin, p. 48).

14 *In psalmum 98* (PL, 37, 1264). cf. Lanfranc (140, 433–4), etc.

15 *De verbis Apostoli sermo 2*, cited by Algerius (PL, 180, 798 A). *In Joannem*, tract. 27 (35, 1616), etc. cf. Geoffrey (157, 213). Abelard, *Sic et Non*, c. 117 (178, 1533 C and 1535 B). Algerius (180, 798 D, 895 D).

16 Hériger (PL, 139, 188 A). Paschasius (120, 1327 A). cf. Peter Lombard, *In I Cor.* (191, 1623 C).

17 *Sermo 341* (PL, 39, 1493). cf. Baldwin (204, 695 B–C).

18 *op. cit.*, p. 766.

able justification, certainly 'imitates Saint Augustine', but only in its
form, and not in its 'idea'. It could more properly have made claims on
Saint Ambrose, who in his commentary on Luke 17:37 had written:

> '*Where the body will be, there the eagles will be gathered together.*'
> *If we have understood the eagles, we cannot now be in doubt about
> the body, particularly if we remember that Joseph received the body
> from Pilate . . . There is also a body of which it is said, 'My flesh is
> truly food' . . . There is also the body that is the Church.*[19]

Whatever the case, the conviction that held at the time made it necessary to confront the 'triple body' with the 'double flesh'. Jerome and
'Augustine' had to be made to agree with one another. It was impossible to permit of any supposed 'disagreement' between two such great
authorities, and it was deemed only proper to establish, according to
the prevailing custom, that their apparent diversity was not a contradiction: '*they are spoken of in ways that vary but do not contradict
one another*'.[20] The work did not demand any extended effort and the
two theories were not long in coming together. Hot on the heels of the
Paschasian controversy, Jerome and 'Augustine' were quoted side by
side to the same end,[21] and for a long time afterwards Jerome and his
'double flesh' would be called upon to introduce any development of
the 'triple body'.[22] If the need arose, in order to reinforce the analogy,
the technical terms would be lightly touched up: in Hériger of Lobbes,
and then in Algerius of Liège, the '*three modes*' of Pseudo-Augustine
became a '*triple*' that balanced with Jerome's '*double*', and on the
other hand, Jerome's '*twofold flesh*' becomes a '*twofold body*'.[23] But
this fully conscious juxtaposition naturally took place at the expense
of the most recent theory. If *flesh* and *body* were still willingly being
interchanged or eclectically fused together, even if *flesh* was still preferred for a time over *body*, nevertheless the Paschasian view of the
objective presence cast something of a shadow over Jerome's view of

---

19 *In Lucam*, 8 (PL, 15, 1781–2).

20 Hériger of Lobbes (PL, 139, 180 A, 183 B–C). Algerius (180, 790 C).
Bernold, *De sacramentis haereticorum* (*Libelli de lite*, vol. 2, pp. 89–90).

21 Hériger (PL, 139, 181 B). Algerius (180, 363 A).

22 Hériger, Algerius, William of St. Thierry (PL, 180, 363 A). Peter Lombard
(192, 857; cf. 191, 1642 A–B). Peter Comestor (Martin, p. 35).

23 Hériger (PL, 139, 179, 183 C). Gratian, *De consecratione* 2.62 (Friedberg,
1337); compare c. 49 (1332). Algerius, *De sacramentis* I, title of Chapter 17 (PL,
180, 790 B). M. Brigué, *Alger de Liége*, p. 25.

the life-giving communion. It was not enough to sing, together with Hincmar of Rheims or John of Fécamp:

The nourishing flesh is eaten and the consecrated blood is drunk,[24]

but in a number of churches, long before Saint Thomas Aquinas had composed the *Ave verum corpus*, people were singing:

Hail, most sacred flesh . . .[25]

Thus the two 'fleshes' that Jerome distinguished were purely and simply assimilated to the first two 'bodies' of Pseudo-Augustine, that is to say to the historical body and the sacramental body. At least for a time, therefore, the *spiritual flesh* became synonymous with the *mystical body* of Rabanus Maurus or of Paschasius Radbertus. Already, if the teaching of what appears to be the better established of his texts is to be believed, the latter had used it in more or less that way in the fifth chapter of the *Liber de corpore.*[26] Algerius of Liège would also write, after quoting Jerome:

> *He is not to be believed to have said this with reference to a double substance but in reference to the double form of the same substance, whereby he is understood to be now in human form and now in the form of bread and wine . . . This duality Christ himself pointed out at the supper, when, present in human form, he showed himself in the sacrament to the disciples. This duality, not of substance but of form, was noted by the saints . . . Since therefore the body of Christ is spoken of in three ways – the human body of Christ, the body of Christ in the sacrament, and the body of Christ as the Church . . .*[27]

Without being taken in absolutely the opposite sense, Jerome's text was thus distorted from its authentic meaning. The accent was shifted. The material flesh, to which he gave a pejorative nuance, became the historical body of Christ, considered in the full extent of its states, that is to say as much the glorious body, seated at the right hand of the Father, as the body that was born of the Virgin, suffered and died: there is nothing here that any longer recalls that flesh and blood 'which

---

24 John of Fécamp, *Confessio fidei* (PL, 101, 1092 A). cf. Wilmart, 'Distiques d'Hincmar sur l'Eucharistie?', *Revue bénédictine* (1928), pp. 87–96.

25 V. Leroquais, *Sacramentaires et Missels des Bibliothèques publiques de France*, passim.

26 PL, 120, 1261 C.

27 *De sacramentis*, 1, c. 17 (PL, 180, 790–791).

cannot possess the kingdom of God'. As for the 'spiritual flesh', from then on it was only used to define the *'body in the sacrament'*, that is to say to designate the Eucharist in its completely objective sense, which is no longer exactly that of Jerome, and which is more or less the opposite of the concepts of the real Augustine.[28]

* * *

This fatal inversion of perspectives, together with the necessity of maintaining the support of tradition, even with regard to wording, is certainly not the only culprit. One influence was certainly no stranger here, that of St. Ambrose. This is because not everyone understood this 'spirituality', in which the distinctive mark of the 'second body' could be detected, uniquely as the result of its sacramental state, a state that was still being called *'invisible'*, or *'intelligible'*, *'rational'*, *'intellectual'* or *'mystical'*.[29] Even when this Eucharistic body was being distinguished from the body seated at the right hand of the Father, it was possible to see further, in its 'spirituality', the result of the *'change of the flesh into spirit'*[30] operated by the resurrection. Now, this was a particularly Ambrosian notion.

The whole of tradition from Saint Paul onwards knew it and affirmed it: *'It is sown an animal body, it will rise a spiritual body'*,[31] and there was certainly not going to be an exception in the case of the Lord's body! Τοῦτο, οὐ τοιοῦτο. *'Same in nature, different in glory.'*[32] But the assertion could be understood in a more or less radical sense. What exactly was this 'spiritual glory' into which the body that emerged from the tomb was transformed?[33] What was this absorption of the mortal flesh 'into the majesty of divinity'?[34] The Greek here offered resources that were lacking in the Latin language. Think, for example, of the richness of thought that can serve to express such an opposition

---

28 cf. Geoffrey of Vendôme (PL, 157, 213 C).

29 A classical formula of Lanfranc: 'from the flesh of Christ and the blood, each invisible, spiritual . . .'. See *infra*, Chapter 7. cf. the Latin translation of Chrysostom, *Homily 60 to the people of Antioch*.

30 cf. John Scotus, *In Joannem*, frag. 2 (PL, 122, 317 A); *De divisione naturae* 5, c. 987.

31 1 Cor. 15:44.

32 Gregory the Great, *Homilia 26 in evangelia*, n. 1 (PL, 76, 1198 A).

33 Hilary, *In psalmum 118* (Zingerle, p. 492); *De Trinitate* 11, n. 40, 49 (PL, 10, 425, 426). cf. Rufinus, *In Apol. Pamphili, praef. Ad Macarium* (PG, 17, 542).

34 Jerome, *In Jeremiam* (PL, 24, 787 D); *In Marcam* (if these homilies on Mark are of Jerome, according to the attribution of Dom Morin; *Anecdota Maredsolana*, vol. 3, p. 2, p. 356).

as that between μορφή (form) and σχῆμα (likeness).[35] Now the Latin translations of the Bible render these two words haphazardly, together with the other two words εἶδος (idea) and τύπος (type), using the vaguely synonymous words *form* and *figure*.[36] Nevertheless Saint Ambrose, whom it was possible to call 'the last of the Greek Fathers before Saint Augustine',[37] had inherited from them, even more than Saint Hilary, a notion of the transfiguration of the body and of the whole being[38] that the genius of his great disciple, ripened in another climate, could only exploit imperfectly. When, in the ninth century, this matter began to be discussed again, theologians would find themselves quite naturally divided into two camps, according to the Fathers in whose school they had been formed. The Augustinian Florus would take a stand against the spiritualism of the Hellenist John Scotus,[39] and, as the latter would affirm in his own terms, it was in the name of St. Augustine that a resistance movement would be organized against the doctrine 'of Gregory the Theologian, Maximus and Ambrose'.[40] John Scotus could have added: against the doctrine of Athanasius.[41] He himself certainly made several efforts to bring Augustine back into their camp, but in this case objectivity is on Florus's side.

For Augustine, a body is always an individual organism of flesh and bones, made up of distinct and strictly localized organs. Like everyone, he certainly accepted the idea of a spiritual flesh, a body that would no longer be 'flesh and blood'.[42] In speaking of the body of the inhabit-

---

35 Zorell, N.T. *Lexicon graecum.* Moulton-Milligan, *The Vocabulary of the Greek Testament.* Lightfoot, *In Philip.*, II, 6–8, p. 133. cf. Origen, *Periarchon,* 2, c. 10, 2 (Koetschau, p. 174).

36 cf. Dom Wilmart, *Auteurs spirituals et texts dévots du moyen âge,* p. 398, note.

37 M. Lot-Borodine, *Revue de l'histoire des religions,* 1933, vol. 1, p. 49.

38 Origen, *In Lucam,* hom. 29 (Rauer, p. 182); *In Rom.*, (PG, 14, 852); *Contra Celsum* (Koetschau, vol. 1, p. 237). [For the English, see the *Ante-Nicene Christian Library* series, vol. 23 (2 Parts), (Edinburgh, 1872).] Didymus, *Fragmenta in Actus* (PG, 39, 1660 B). Gregory of Nyssa, *Contra Eunomium* (45, 697, 706–8, 836–7) [for the English, see NPNF vol. 5]; *Adversus Apollinarem* (45, 1276–7); *De anima et resurrectione* (46, 148 C), etc.

39 Florus, *Adversus Joannem Scotum,* c. 8 (PL, 119, 153 C–D). Braulio of Saragossa, *Ep.* 42 (80, 688 A; Madoz, pp. 179–180). *Liber sive definition ecclesiasticorum dogmatum,* c. 43 (Turner, *Journal of Theological Studies,* vol. 7, p. 97). Amalarius (PL, 105, 1236–7), etc. With Rabanus Maurus, *De videndo Deum,* one assumes hesitations (PL, 112, 1277 B–C).

40 *De divisione naturae* 5 (PL, 122, 880 B–C, 987, 990–991, 995, 1015 C). cf. Gratieux, *Khomiakov,* vol. 2, p. 81; Rosenberg, *Le Mythe du XXe siècle.*

41 *Fourth letter to Serapion,* n. 19 (PG, 26, 655–668). [For selected letters and works of Athanasius, see A. Robertson, NPNF, vol. 4.]

42 *De fide et symbolo,* n. 24 (PL, 40, 195). *De agone christiano,* c. 32 (40, 309).

ants of the heavenly Jerusalem, he did not hesitate to say '*a body that is now heavenly and spiritual, an angelic body in the society of angels*'.[43] It would be wrong, however, to take such expressions too literally. Their author is manifesting a tendency to transpose them onto the moral plane. This tendency became more and more pronounced as the years went by, and by the end of his life, was usually accompanied by some polemical point.[44] What he anticipates in the city of the blessed is a perfect '*concord of flesh and spirit*'. It is a spiritual flesh, he explains repeatedly, that is to say above all a flesh that is obedient to the spirit in a spirit obedient to God;[45] it is a flesh that no longer disturbs the soul in any way and no longer distracts it from contemplation.[46] He certainly also made a very clear distinction between a corruptible state and an incorruptible state. He still made a distinction between the state of Adam's body before the Fall and that of the risen body, and would only permit talk of a 'spiritual body', without distinction, with regard to the latter.[47] And in the final analysis, there appears to be no very great difference between the one and the other: it is only a matter of a somewhat greater degree of miraculous effects produced by the power of God. The contrast that he was anxious to maintain between the two cases did not prevent him from keeping the same principles as his guide for both of them. If he set the risen body free from *the need to be eaten*, he still recognized its *power to feed*.[48] He was struck with admiration at the 'marvellous means' by which God eternally protected from corruption this mass of flesh and blood, as he once suspended the destructive effects of the fire in the furnace of Babylon.[49] According to him, though they were in fact incorruptible, the members of this glorious body remained no less *mortal members* while gifted with 'every facility', they remained no less circumscribed in space than during the time of their natural solidity: *the outlines of form remaining*,[50] and just as the apostles had been able to touch Christ's body in

---

43   *In psalmum 145*, n. 3 (PL, 37, 1805).

44   *De civitate Dei*, 13, c. 20 (PL, 41, 393). *Retract.*, 17 (32, 613).

45   *Enchiridion*, c. 91 (PL, 40, 274). *De civitate Dei* 13, c. 20 (41, 393). *Contra Adimantum*, c. 12, n. 4 (42, 145). *Contra duas epistolas Pelagianorum* 1, c. 10, n. 17 (44, 559). *Ep. 43*, n. 6 (33, 588), etc.

46   *In psalmum 75*, n. 5 (PL, 36, 96).

47   *De Genesi ad litteram* 6, c. 19, n. 30 (PL, 34, 351–352). *De civitate Dei*, 13, c. 20 (41, 393–4). *Florus*, c. 8 (119, 153–4). cf. Giles of Rome, *In Sententias* 2, d. 22, q. 1, a. 1.

48   *Ep. 205*, n. 4 (PL, 33, 943). *De civitate Dei* 13, c. 22 (41, 395).

49   *Ep. 205*, n .4 (PL, 33, 943). cf. *In psalmum 62*, n. 10 (36, 753–4).

50   *ibid. De Genesi ad litteram*, 12, c. 7, n. 18 (PL, 34, 459–460), etc. See again *De civitate Dei*, 22, c. 15–16, and *Enchiridion*.

the upper room on the night of the resurrection, it would be possible to do so in Heaven, and when he returned at the end of time . . .⁵¹ How different was the notion that Ambrose put forward! No more in the 'Hellenist' camp than in the other was there any question of doubting the substantial permanence of the risen body. It was no longer carnal, but it had been enfleshed. It still was in one sense: it was *transfigured* flesh. *Not other, but the same, changed from animal to spiritual* as was specified by John Scotus,⁵² who liked to quote the bishop of Milan in order to show that he was not simply following the line of Greek authors.⁵³ Ambrose's belief, which came down to him from Origen,⁵⁴ had nothing in common with the musings that were often attributed to the school of Origen on the abandonment of the gross body of this earth for another, more subtle body, made up of some heavenly matter,⁵⁵ such as Christ's body might have been, according to certain Docetists, even during his life on earth.⁵⁶ *The truth of the body remaining*, He had himself declared,⁵⁷ and John Scotus went on to comment: '*true and spiritual bodies . . . though not material, which appear not in phantasm but in truth*'.⁵⁸ There was no contradiction apparent in such an expression. After all, did people not talk, in the tradition of St. Paul and with the Augustinians themselves, of the 'spiritual construction of the body of Christ',⁵⁹ and say that Christians, through their spiritual union with Christ, became 'co-enfleshed' with him?⁶⁰

* * *

51 *Ep. 205*, n. 2 (PL, 33, 942–943). *Roman Catechism* (p. 1, a. 1, n. 15).

52 John Scotus, *De divisione naturae*, 5 (PL, 122, 993–4).

53 PL, 122, 830 C, 880 B, etc.

54 cf. Periarchon, 2, c. 2, 3 (Koteschau, pp. 112–13, 116), on Paul, I Cor. 15.44 ff.: G. Verbeke, *L'Évolution de la doctrine du Pneuma du Stoïcisme à saint Augustin*, p. 465.

55 Gregory the Great, *Moralia in Job*, 14, c. 55, n. 71 (PL, 75, 1077 B). Eleventh council of Toledo (Mansi, vol. 11, 136 E). Julian of Toledo, *Prognosticon future saeculi*, 3, c. 17 (PL, 96, 504 B–C).

56 Amphilochius, frag. 10 (PG, 39, 105–108). Didymus, *In epistulam primam Joannis* (Zoepfl, p. 66).

57 *In psalmum 1*, n. 51 (PL, 14, 949 C). cf. Gregory Nazianzen, *Discourse 40*, c. 45 (PG, 36, 421 C). [For the works of St. Gregory in English, see C. G. Browne and J. E. Swallow, NPNF vol. 7; M. Vinson, *The Fathers of the Church* series, vol. 107 (Washington, 2003).] John Scotus, *De divisione naturae*, 1, c. 10 (122, 451 B); c. 40 (483 B); 5, c. 8 (876, 881). F. Prat, *Origène*, p. 94.

58 *De divisione naturae*, 5 (PL, 122, 993 D).

59 Fulgentius, *Ad Monimum* (PL, 65, 109 B).

60 Pseudo-Primasius, *In epistulam ad Hebraeos* (PL, 68, 708 B). Algerius (180, 795 D). Albert the Great, *De sacrificio missae*, tract. 3, c. 21 (Vivès, vol. 38, p. 157).

Now, this double manner of perceiving the risen body could not fail to have profound resonances in Eucharistic doctrines. For centuries, among many Augustinians, the localization of the body of Christ would constitute the principal obstacle to sacramental realism:[61] '*The body of the Lord in which he rose can be in one place.*'[62] For Ambrose, on the other hand, and for those who took their inspiration from him, there was no difficulty. Nevertheless, there would remain a long-term underlying opposition, and on each side, while vehement argument continued on other points, there was agreement, or there was thought to be agreement on a common 'spiritualist' vocabulary, which other considerations contributed to endorsing.

Saint Ambrose held firmly to the Pauline assertion that 'the Lord is Spirit'. In the very chapter of *De mysteriis* where he had enumerated the works of the divine power that cause us to believe in the *sacrament of flesh*, passing immediately from the Incarnation to the Eucharist, he urgently called to mind the spiritual state that was Christ's from Easter morning onwards:

> *Christ is in this sacrament because the body is Christ's. It is there-*
> *fore not bodily but spiritual food. This is why the Apostle says of*
> *its type, 'Because our fathers ate spiritual food' . . . For the body of*
> *God is a spiritual body; the body of Christ is the body of the divine*
> *Spirit, because the Spirit is Christ, as we read, 'The Spirit before our*
> *face is Christ the Lord'.*[63]

In this short but important passage, which would often be quoted,[64] Ambrose in some sense accumulated the different agreements – each one in continuity with the others – by which the Eucharistic body can and must be said to be spiritual: because it is invisible, hidden within the sacrament; because it is spiritual food, thanks to the Spirit who

---

61 Again, for example, Wycliffe, *Sermonum*, p. 3, s. 51 (Loserth, p. 445).

62 Augustine, *In Joannem*, tract 30, n. 1 (PL, 35). cf. *Berengarian writing* (Matronola, p. 112). Yves of Chartres, *Decretum*, p. 2, c. 8 (161, 150–1); Gratian, *De consecratione*, d. 2, c. 44 (Friedberg, 1330), etc.

63 *De mysteriis*, n. 58 (PL, 16, 408–9). cf. *De Spiritu sancto*, 1, c. 9, n. 105 (16, 729 D). Compare the *res caelestis* (οὐρανίον) of Irenaeus, *Adv. Haer*, 4, c. 18, n. 5 (PG, 7, 1029 A); cf. H.-D. Simonin, 'Note à propos d'un texte eucharistique de saint Irénée', *Revue des Sciences philosophiques et théologiques* (1934), pp. 281–92) and the *celestial flesh* in Hippolytus, *In cantica* (Bonwetsch, *Hippolyt's Kommentar zum Hohenlied*, p. 66; in TU, NF, 8, 2).

64 Durandus of Troarn (PL, 149, 1385 D). Gratian, *De consecratione*, 2.85 (Fr. 1349–1350), etc.

operates within it;[65] because it is the spiritual fulfilment of the Old Testament figures; and finally because it is the body of Him who rose *totus Spiritus*, rising *per omnia Deus*.[66] This last characteristic is the one on which Ambrose is most insistent, the one to which he relates all the others. It is also the one that bears his strongest personal hallmark.[67] Thanks to this, the Ambrosian doctrine of the Eucharist was able to establish a greater equilibrium than the Augustinian doctrine, despite its being the more profound of the two. It was a true forerunner of the doctrine of transubstantiation, to the extent that it scandalized Godescalc,[68] and brought together the simple affirmations of faith without any difficulty. But at the same time it united with no less difficulty the most consistent realism with the most intrepid spiritualism, in such a way that both Paschasius Radbertus and Ratramnus were able to claim it each for his own. It has to be said that Paschasius only ever attributes it to Ambrose once, in the little anthology that he attaches to his letter to Frudegard.[69] He quotes it, nevertheless, in his own rather free and easy manner, and he quite evidently takes his inspiration from it.[70] As for Ratramnus, he announced from the rooftops, so to speak, the end of the text that has just been quoted, and in opposition to his antagonist he drew from it an argument in favour of the particular distinction that he wanted to place between the historical body and the sacramental body:

> *We are taught on the authority of this most learned man that there is a great difference between the body in which Christ suffered and the body which in the mystery of the passion of Christ is daily celebrated by the faithful.*[71]

It could perhaps be argued that there is a danger in the path that Ratramnus chooses here, by saying that it is too Augustinian to adopt the Eucharistic spiritualism of Ambrose (and that from the standpoint that he occupies, it is already too Paschasian), to attach itself without

---

65 See Cyril of Alexandria (PG, 73, 481 B and 561 C).

66 *De fide resurrectionis*, n. 91 (PL, 16, 1341). cf. Jerome, *In Jeremiam* (24, 787 D). Bede, *In Leviticum* (91, 335 B). John Scotus (122, 993 B). Rupert, *In Cantica*, 4 (168, 904 C). Bessarion, *De sacramento Eucharistiae* (PG, 161, 498 C).

67 Tixeront, *Histoire des dogmes*, vol. 2, 9th edn., pp. 319, 344–345. See Ambrose, *In Lucam*, 10 (PL, 15, 1845–1846).

68 Lambot, pp. 325–326.

69 PL, 120, 1360 B.

70 Compare *Liber de corpore*, c. 1, 4 (PL, 120, 1267–1272, 1279 B–C), and Ambrose, *De mysteriis* (16, 406–407).

71 PL, 121, 154–155.

risk to the ecclesial symbolism of Augustine. The Augustinian understanding of the body renders particularly delicate the application to the
Eucharist of the Ambrosian understanding of the spiritual body, and
on the other hand, the primacy given by Paschasius and before him by
Ambrose to the problem of objective presence entailed considerable
difficulties for those wishing to reserve the pride of place given it by
Augustinian Eucharistic doctrine to the notion of the ecclesial body.
It was a question of two traditions, either one of which it would have
been harmful to sacrifice, but which could not, as such, be accepted at
the same time. A total and simultaneous fidelity to both Doctors could
only result in the creation of something new. This was too much to ask
of a ninth-century mind. And indeed no synthesis was ever achieved.
Later on, when Ambrose's text was being quoted in favour of realism and identity, care would be taken to end the quotation before
the words where spiritualism would find expression in its own turn.[72]
Ratramnus himself wanted on the contrary to put the spotlight on
the '*spiritual Christ*' whom Ambrose had borrowed from Saint Paul;
but unconsciously influenced by the rather curtailed Augustinianism
that he shared with nearly all his contemporaries concerning the state
of risen bodies, he translated it as: '*Spirit of Christ*'.[73] It is a revealing
detail.

This Ambrosian Christology, which in following the Greeks puts
such a strong accent on the difference between the conditions of life
on earth and those in glory, would nevertheless continue to bear fruit
in the field of Eucharistic doctrine long after Ratramnus. For example,
it is what is presupposed in the explanations of Rupert that we have
already met. For him as for Ratramnus, it is still more or less allied to
an Augustinian strain, which in some ways compromises his efforts.
In the second half of the twelfth century, it can be rediscovered, in
fully conscious mode, in the two brothers Gerhoh and Arno of
Reichersberg. In their long and ardent controversy with the disciples
of Peter Lombard and Gilbert de la Porrée, the two of them would
never cease appealing to the twin authorities of Hilary and Ambrose.
But, being more logical – or simply by coming later on – they disen-
gaged themselves more from Saint Augustine, in such a way that their
realism would appear more solid, and the doctrine of these tradition-
alists would be anything but archaic: '*In the truth of the sacraments
of Christ God is adored, who is also received in the body taken from*

---

72 Gregory of Bergamo, c. 27 (H., p. 104).
73 PL, 121, 153 A.

the Virgin and assumed into heaven.'[74] Not, of course, that they were
throwing off the mantle of such a great name: but their position with
regard to it was comparable to that of John Scotus in his opposition
to Florus. How many distinctions were they not forced to think up in
order to give what they considered to be an acceptable meaning to the
texts that were quoted in opposition to them![75] They had the lively
impression that if, as Augustine seemed to be saying, the risen body
were to be assigned a particular place in a material heaven, it would be
the end of the reality that is hidden by the mystery. Was it not precisely
this, they wondered, that provoked the likes of Folmar into renewing
Berengar's blasphemy?[76] It was therefore not only for the heavenly
glory of the Son of Man, a glory whose champions they claimed to be,
but it was also for the salvation of their faith in the sacraments that
they distanced from the risen body all limitations due to '*the time of
bodily and providential lowliness*'.[77] Only in this way could the presence at the right hand of the Father be affirmed '*without prejudice to
the presence of the body of Christ in the sacrament of the altar, which
the Church offers daily in the many places at the same time and so
participates in the truth*'.[78] Only in this way could the believer say
in all truth, repeating the Augustinian formulations, that: '*Wholly in
heaven, wholly on the altar; wholly in the mouth of the communicant,
. . . wholly in the heart of the believer.*'[79] Reality of presence, identity
of the body: if our two adversaries held both to one and to the other,
like Ambrose, it has to be added that for them, as for him, the body
in question is and can only be the spiritual body: '*In the sacrament of
that altar he offers the truth of his body and blood as food and drink of
everlasting salvation, while, certainly, his now spiritual body is hidden
in its essence in the sacramental species.*'[80] We can see that everything
is driven by the Ambrosian principle, which Gerhoh repeats once again
when he says: '*He died as man, he lives as Lord.*'[81]

＊ ＊ ＊

---

74 Gerhoh, *Ad Adamum abbatem Eberacensem* (PL, 193, 497 B). cf. *supra*,
p. 97.

75 Arno, *Liber apologeticus contra Folmarum* (Weichert, pp. 202-5).

76 Gerhoh, *De Gloria et honore Filii hominis*, c. 13, n. 2 (PL, 194, 1117 D).
cf. J. de Ghellinck, DTC, vol. 5 c. 1266.

77 Arno, *op. cit.*, p. 230; cf. pp. 196, 228, 198.

78 Arno, *op. cit.*, p. 202.

79 Gerhoh, (PL, 193, 497 B). cf. Augustine, cited by Gratian, *De consecratione*, 2.70, 75 (Friedberg, 1341, 1345).

80 *ibid.* cf. Arno, *op. cit.*, p. 223; Hugh of St. Victor, *De sacramentis*, 2, p. 8,
c. 11 (PL, 176, 469 C–D).

81 Gerhoh, *In psalmum* 17 (PL, 193, 889 B).

After this incursion into a later age, which was necessitated by the particular position of Gerhoh and Arno of Reichersberg, we need to step backwards for a time.

In very varying degrees, the theology and even the language of Saint Ambrose were actually in competition with the texts of Saint Jerome and Saint Augustine[82] in order to get a 'spiritualist' vocabulary adopted in Eucharistic matters. But this vocabulary was not in any way of itself going to undermine faith in the bodily reality of Christ *in sacramento* – had not Saint John Chrysostom himself at one point spoken of 'spiritual blood'?[83] It was simply a means of repudiating any materialism in the way of understanding this bodily reality. Besides, it was in conformity with John's Gospel. There was equal encouragement to this effect to be found in the expressions used by Saint Paul with regard to the manna and the water that sprang from the rock in the desert: if the Apostle had called them 'spiritual', could one not say that it was primarily because they had been produced 'spiritually', like the Eucharist itself?[84] They owed this to the divine power, which had been exercised through the ministry of angels, without recourse to any natural agents. Was this not principally because, according to a 'spiritual' understanding, they signified something 'spiritual', which is the Eucharist?[85] Abelard's commentary on the Pauline Epistles, recently published by M. Landgraf, would say of the manna, in a latter-day link with a tradition going back at least as far as the *Ambrosiaster*:[86] '*It is called spiritual food, because it means food for the soul, which is to say, the body of Christ.*'[87] From the ninth century to the eleventh century, we also find widespread use of such language, notwithstanding divergences of doctrine that do not need to be uncovered here. Up till then, it evoked no misgivings. It is true that Ratramnus made particularly abundant use of it:

---

82 Ratramnus cites Jerome right after having commented on Ambrose, and speaks of the second as the first (PL, 121, 156 A).

83 *In Hebr.*, hom 16, n. 2 (PG, 63, 125). The Latin version of Mutianus (col. 343–344) omits 'spiritual blood'. cf. the *Responsio cujusdam* (d'Achery, vol. 1, p. 150).

84 Chrysostom, *In I Cor.*, x, 4 (PG, 51, 249).

85 See the commentaries of 1 Cor. 10. Sedulius Scotus (PL, 103, 147 C–D). Rabanus Maurus (112, 88 C; 117, 558–559). Lanfranc (150, 188 A). Pseudo-Strabo (114, 535 A). cf. Pseudo-Bede, *In psalmos* (93, 899 D). St. Bruno, *In psalmum* 77 (152, 1037, 1038 A), etc. Wycliffe, *Sermonum*, p. 3, sermo 16 (Loserth, p. 125). See *infra*, note 122.

86 *In I Cor.*, 3 (PL, 17, 234 A).

87 *Commentarius cantabrigiensis in Epistulas Pauli e Schola Petri Abaelardi*, *In I Cor.*, x (vol. 2, 1939, p. 255).

Is tasting the Lord a discerning of something bodily? [Spirit] invites us to experience the savour of a spiritual taste, and to think of nothing in the drink or bread in a bodily way, but to discern the whole spiritually, since the Lord is spirit.[88]

But it is not only in Ratramnus that we can read such assertions as this: *'The body which is so named through the mystery of God is not bodily but spiritual'*,[89] or again this one:

So nothing here is to be discerned in a bodily way but in a spiritual one: it is the body of Christ, but not in a bodily way; and it is the blood of Christ, but not in a bodily way . . . Under the veil of bodily bread and bodily wine, there is spiritual body and spiritual blood.[90]

Ratramnus was not the one who invented these formulations. They were traditional both in Augustinianism[91] and in 'Hellenism', where they were not only used in a Eucharistic context.[92] Many more of exactly the same kind can be found in Paschasius Radbertus himself, and that in his letter to Frudegard, in which he defends and reinforces his realism, as well as in his preceding works: *'The body of Christ is not subject to corruption, since it is spiritual.'*[93] He had already said, in the first edition of the *Liber de Corpore*: *'Understand that these things are spiritual'*, *'they are spiritual'*, *'completely spiritual and divine'*.[94] Similarly in his commentary on Saint Matthew he would say: *'All the things that are administered in the sacrament are to be received spiritually . . . Let it be understood that everything takes place in the Spirit.'*[95] It is true that today we can read, in the ninth chapter of the *Liber de Corpore*:

Just us they are clothed in Christ through baptism, so may Christ remain in them in a bodily way through this sacrament.[96]

---

88 *De corpore et sanguine Domini*, c. 58 (PL, 121, 151 B). c. 16 (134 B).
89 c. 62 (PL, 121, 152 C), etc.
90 c. 60 (PL, 121, 152 A); c. 16 (134-135); c. 65 (153-154), etc.
91 For example, Cassiodorus, *In psalmum 103* (PL, 70, 733-4).
92 cf. John Scotus, *De divisione naturae*, 5, c. 38 (PL, 122, 1015 C).
93 PL, 120, 1356 B. Compare Ratramnus, c. 63 (121, 153 A).
94 c. 8 (PL, 120, 1287 C); c. 2 (1274 B); c. 8 (1280 C). See also c. 1277 B, 1281, 1327 B–C, 1328 D, etc.
95 Bk. 12 (PL, 120, 895 A).
96 PL, 120, 1296 A.

But on this point we would probably be better advised to give preference to the variant *'spiritually'*, which is in greater conformity with
the language that was customary to Paschasius himself, as well as to
his era,[97] and more in harmony with the context: because in this chapter we are dealing with the presence of the Christ who dwells in the
faithful soul as the Father dwells in the Son; it is certainly a 'natural'
presence, according to the word that Saint Hilary insisted on, but no
less certainly 'spiritual'. If Paschasius demonstrates within this presence an effect of communion, he nevertheless does not confuse it with
the sacramental presence, beyond which it endures. And does he not
in any case say further on, in another chapter: *'will the blood of Christ
flow over us spiritually from the altar of the body of Christ?'*[98] In the
ninth chapter, it seems as if the adverb must have been changed later
by a scrupulous copyist – just as it was apparently suppressed in an
analogous text by Christian of Stavelot.[99] Given what we know of
later controversies, and of the evolution in Eucharistic language, a
correction in the inverse sense would be far harder to understand.[100]

Knowing his tendencies, it is no surprise to read from the pen of
Florus:

> The bread of the sacred offering is the body of Christ, not in matter
> or visible form but in power and spiritual potency.[101]

But Hincmar of Rheims, who was certainly closer to Paschasius
Radbertus than to Florus, and was just as hard on Scotus Erigena as
Paschasius could be on Ratramnus, also recalled, with regard to the
Eucharist, that 'the letter kills', and that recourse needed to be had
to 'spiritual understanding'.[102] In the following century, Hériger of
Lobbes not only called the body of Christ spiritual nourishment, after

---

97 No other example with Paschasius of 'corporaliter' (except in a different
sense: 1278 C, 1325 A, B). Applied to the sacramental bodies, the word remains
at least rare up to Guitmond of Aversa. See, however, the Auxerre Commentary
In Hebr. (PL, 117, 730 A–B).

98 c. 21, n. 2 (PL, 120, 1334 B).

99 *In Matthaeum* (PL, 106, 1476 D).

100 M.-H. Peltier, *Pascase Radbert*, p. 216, n. 1, is nevertheless of an opposite
opinion.

101 *Adversus Amalarium* 1, n. 9 (PL, 119, 77 C-D; cf. 77 D; 78 A). cf. Paschasius, PL, 120, 890, 1625. Hesychius, *In Leviticum* (PG, 93, 1071 B). Faustus of
Riez, c. 5 (PL, 30, 273 C). John Scotus (122, 92 C). Ratramnus (121, 150 A, cf.
153 A). Note the parallel (160 C). Also Gerard of Cambrai (142, 1280 A–B). On
the contrary in the continuation: thus Durandus of Troarn (149, 1387 C), etc.

102 *De cavendis vitiis* (PL, 125, 920–1). Hincmar cites Ambrose (927C).

the universally widespread custom, but he also said: '*Nor does the spirit lose what he received spiritually in the bodily reality with complete faith.*'[103] The phrase is copied in a tract whose author is unknown to us, and who also says: '*it was done spiritually*', '*the sacrament of spiritual nourishment*', '*is received purely in the spirit*'.[104] It is obvious that no one tendency really has a monopoly over such formulations. Aelfric of Canterbury († c. 1020), who inherited Ratramnus's thought, would repeat that the bread and wine of the sacrifice are changed '*into a spiritual body, into spiritual blood*', and that this change is itself of a spiritual order: '*thus it becomes his body and blood spiritually*', and that on the altar, '*in the spiritual mystery*', contrary to how it was on the cross, '*it is not the body of Christ in the flesh but in the spirit*'.[105] He would insist on the distance that separates the body in which Christ suffered from his spiritual body 'which we call the Eucharist'.[106] But a century earlier, Adrevald of Fleury, who can so strongly be considered as representing the opposite view that for a long time his anthology was taken to be a piece of polemical writing against Scotus Erigena,[107] did not hesitate, in his slim collection, to quote the Fathers in speaking of spiritual flesh, spiritual nourishment, a spiritual understanding of the mystery and of being spiritually filled.[108] Odo of Cluny, who was a pupil of Remigius of Auxerre, would not baulk either at repeating Saint Jerome's two adjectives: '*it is divine and spiritual*',[109] and John of Fécamp, speaking of the 'saving victim' whom the liturgy celebrates '*according to a spiritual conception*', would also exclaim: '*May nothing there be understood other than divinely and spiritually!*'[110]

In short, for several centuries in turn, with no distinction between schools of thought, if the noun 'body' was accepted by everyone, the adjective *bodily* was no less rejected by everyone, since 'bodily'

---

103 c. 9 and 10 (PL, 139, 188 D).

104 *Respondio cujusdam de corpore et sanguine Domini* (d'Achery, vol. 1, p. 149).

105 *Ex epistulis ad Wulfstanum et ad Wulfsinum* (J.-M. Routh, *Scriptorum ecclesiasticorum opuscula*, 3rd edn., vol. 2, pp. 166–77).

106 In the notes of Bede's *Ecclesiastical History* by Abraham Whelocus (1644), 5, c. 22, and 4, c. 24.

107 Chardon, *Histoire des sacrements*. The idea has been fought by Dom Cappuyns, *Jean Scot Érigène*, pp. 90–1.

108 PL, 124, 949, 950. Adrevald cites the text of Jerome (949 C).

109 *Collectiones*, 2 (PL, 133, 575 B).

110 *Confessio Fidei*, p. 4, c. 1 (PL, 101, 1087 B), and c. 2 (1088 A–B). cf. Florus (*infra*, note 118).

appeared to them all to be inextricably linked to 'sensible',[111] '*spiritual*', which was set in opposition to it, was, like '*mystical*', part of general sacramental vocabulary.[112] In the case of the Eucharist, it became predominant for a number of reasons. First of all, it naturally qualifies food: *banquet, food, nourishment, sustenance, victuals, bread*,[113] this food by which Christ spiritually nourishes his Church.[114] Then it determines a manner of presence: the '*spiritual body*' is the body that can be found '*in the spiritual sacraments*',[115] it is the one that is celebrated '*in the spiritual mysteries*',[116] which is offered '*in the spiritual sacrifice*'.[117] It is at one and the same time the body which, unlike the victims of the ancient sacrifices, '*is not celebrated through a bodily slaughter but according to a spiritual conception*'[118] and the body of him who was not only conceived through the Spirit, but who gave himself up and is still giving himself through the Spirit.[119] Following a very ancient tradition, 'spiritual' is still the equivalent of 'supernatural' or 'miraculous',[120] therefore what adjective could better serve for this miraculous change that takes place in the consecrated bread and wine?[121] How

---

111 Again in the twelfth century, Gilbert of Nogent, *Epistula de buccella Judae data* (PL, 156, 534 C).

112 cf. Pseudo-Bede, *In psalmum* 44 (PL, 93, 721 A), etc.

113 Numerous examples. One often finds also the explicit opposition of *corporalis*: thus in Ambrose, *supra*, and all those whom he cites. cf. Robert Paululus (PL, 177, 431 C).

114 Hervé of Bourg-Dieu, *In. Ephes.*, v (PL, 181, 1268 B), etc. cf. Athanasius, *Fourth Letter to Serapion* (Lebon, p. 203).

115 Cyprian, *Ep.* 63 (Bayard, vol. 2, p. 208). Chrysostom (PG, 61, 191). Ambrose (PL, 15, 1711 B; 16, 408–409). Caesarius of Arles (Morin, pp. 297–298). *Liber mozarabicus ordinum* (F., 165). Faustus of Riez, c. 2 (PL, 30, 272 B). Amalarius (105, 1131 B). Paschasius (120, 1534 B). Pseudo-Bede, *In psalmos* (93, 905 D, 915 A). Aelfric (*loc. cit.*). Fulbert of Chartres (PL, 141, 203 C). Ivo of Chartres (161, 140 A, 1073 D). Honorius of Autun (172, 842 B), etc. Cyril of Jerusalem, *Fifth Mystagogical Lecture* (Quasten, p. 102). Pseudo-Primasius (PL, 68, 734 D). Paschasius, *In Matthaeum* (120, 886 B).

116 Amphilochius (PG, 39, 36 A), etc.

117 Eusebius (PG, 22, 365 D). Cyril of Jerusalem (*loc. cit.*). Chrysostom (PG, 63, 111). Pseudo-Germain (98, 449 D). Celtic Mass (DTC, vol. 10, 1384). *Liber mozarabicus ordinum* (F., 310, 317, 328, 427). *Missale gothicum* (Bannister, vol. 1, p. 62). Raoul of St. Germer (B.M.P., vol. 17, p. 90 D), etc. (cf. Rom. 12.1).

118 Florus, *Expositio missae*, c. 59, n. 6 (Duc, p. 131), etc. cf. Didymus, *De Trinitate*, 1, c. 25; 2, c. 8 (PG, 39, 380 A, 589 C), and in la Chaîne de Cordier, *In psalmos*, 7, 39, 106, 22. Cyril of Jerusalem, *Catechesis* 23, n. 8 (Rupp, vol. 2, p. 384), etc.

119 Pseudo-Primasius, *In Hebr.* (PL, 68, 742 D). cf. Hebr. 9.

120 e.g. Chrysostom, *In I Cor.*, hom.7,23 and 29 (PG 61, 59, 191, 241) etc.

121 Christian Druthmar, *loc. cit.* Cabasilas, *Explanation of the Divine Liturgy*, c. 51 (Salaville, p. 283).

could this mysterious confection of the Bread of Life, which is the very body of Christ, be better described: '*In a marvellous and ineffable manner that which is by nature bread and wine from an earthly stem becomes spiritually the body of Christ*'?[122] Finally, in more than one case, over and above the reasons drawn directly from the Eucharistic mystery, it is in itself, and in some sense in its substance that the body is said to be spiritual. Such even is the sense that can be discerned more or less everywhere, in this first period, in the background of the others. It should be no surprise to readers of Saints Paul, Ambrose and Jerome.

Thus the Eucharist is a *spiritual body*, as it is a *mystical body*. The first expression would survive almost as long as the second.[123] At the beginning of the twelfth century, in his *Explanation of the Canon of the Mass*, Blessed Odo of Cambrai would still say, in his commentary on the words '*pure victim*':

> *This victim is pure since, although it is true flesh and blood, it is yet spiritual and incorrupt . . . This victim is flesh, and yet not fleshly, but is untainted light . . . It is body, and yet not bodily, but is spiritual light.*[124]

---

122 Florus, *Adversus Amalarium* 1, n. 9. (PL, 119, 77 D). Rupert (167, 659 C–D; cf. 169, 464 C). Peter Lombard (191, 1617 C–D), etc. See *supra*, n. 85.

123 *Philothei Achillini Somnium Viridarii*, c. 360 (Goldast, vol. 1, p. 219).

124 *Expositio in canonem missae*, distinctio 3 (PL, 160, 1064). cf. *Versus de mysterio missae* (PL, 171, 1194 D).

7

Interchangeable Expressions

Odo of Cambrai does not figure in this story as an antiquarian. This disciple of Saint Anselm 'liked applying the dialectical method' established by his master 'to the study of dogma'.[1] The language that we have just heard him using would nevertheless not be long in developing an archaic flavour. When he was editing his *Explanation of the Canon of the Mass*, the Berengarian controversy, which had echoed throughout the second half of the eleventh century, had just brought about yet another modification in theological language by necessitating a new caution with regard to form, at the same time as a new precision with regard to doctrine.

Leaning on 'Scotus' Erigena – who was in fact Ratramnus – quoting Augustine, Ambrose and Jerome,[2] protesting loudly that no one could contradict him without thereby condemning the whole of tradition, affecting to blame Paschasius as much for his innovations as for his 'foolishness',[3] Berengar repeated the old spiritualist themes, in a completely different intellectual context, with a worrying insistence and exclusivity. In the opposition that he placed between bodily reception and spiritual reception, the former referred only to 'external things', that is to say the bread and the wine, to such an extent that, notwithstanding some apparently clear affirmations,[4] there was some fear that his Eucharistic doctrine left no place for the actual body of Christ, since he also said that 'the sacrament of refection' was 'in everything comparable with the sacrament of regeneration'.[5] The *'mystical bread'* which the faithful received was certainly, according to him, *'the body*

---

1 D.-L. de Clerck, *Recherches de théologie ancienne at médiévale*, vol. 13 (1946), p. 160.

2 Letters to Lanfranc and Ascelin (PL, 150, 63, 66). D*e sacra cena adversus Lanfrancum liber posterior* (Vischer, pp. 36, 42, 50). He also quotes Cyprian, Hilary, Leo, Gregory . . . (pp. 269–75, etc.).

3 'Foolish Paschasius, astray and leading others astray.'

4 *De sacra cena*, p. 51 or p. 57.

5 *op. cit.*, p. 128.

of Christ', but, he added, '*the body of Christ in its spiritual nature*'.[6] And if he specified that, through the effects of the consecration, the bread and wine became the true body and blood of Christ, a suspect dative – suspect, although it also originated from traditional and liturgical expressions[7] – immediately qualified his formulation: '*after the consecration the bread and wine become in faith and understanding the true body and blood of Christ*'.[8] Combining these two glosses, which it was difficult not to see as deliberate reservations, Berengar also said: '*the body of Christ, true spiritually for the inner person*'.[9] Or else he professed that in the 'consecrated bread', in the 'bread of sacrifice', the communicant receives the body of Christ; and that after the consecration the bread offered on the altar can no longer be considered ordinary bread; but again it was only in order to specify: '*In respect of nature, what you see with the eyes of the body is bread; in respect of the divine blessing, the bread is the body of Christ, which you should contemplate with the eyes of the heart, the eyes of faith*', and this too could not fail to arouse anxiety, although it would be wrong of us to take the word '*nature*' as the equivalent of our '*substance*'.[10]

Moreover, we do not have to decide whether or not Berengar was fundamentally denying or admitting of a 'real presence', or exactly in what sense. To this day opinion is still strongly divided.[11] One of his most competent and least merciful adversaries, Guitmond of Aversa, does not appear to have considered him a pure symbolist: he did not resolve the question of whether it was the *umbratici* or the *impanatores* who were his authentic disciples.[12] Impanation itself, if he did profess it, would not have been for him exactly what it became for later theoreticians: because if he is unwilling to agree with Paschasius Radbertus 'that the substance of the bread is completely absent in the sacrament of the body of the Lord', he explains his thought by saying that the 'matter of the sacrament' does not do away with the sacrament itself, that the consecrated bread retains both its nutritive value

---

6 *op. cit.*, p. 194; cf. pp. 223, 246.

7 See Dom Bernard Capelle, *Pour une meilleure intelligence de la messe*, p. 71; *Sermo de excellentia*, n. 15 (PL, 184, 990 B).

8 *Purgatoria epistula contra Almannum* (Martène and Durandus, *Thesaurus novus anecdotarum*, vol. 4, c. 110). *De sacra cena*, pp. 255, 278; cf. p. 177.

9 *Purgatoria epistula, loc. cit.*

10 *De sacra cena*, pp. 164, 177, 178–9. cf. Algerius (*infra*, p. 147, n. 21).

11 Contrast, for example, Dom Cappuyns and M. Amann (*L'Église au pouvoir des laïques*, p. 529, n. 6).

12 *De corporis ... veritate*, 1 (PL, 149, 1430 D); 3 (1488 B and C, 1494 C–D). But Lanfranc, c. 8: (150, 237). Compare Durandus of Troarn, *De corpore ...*, I (PL, 149, 1377 B).

and all that we would nowadays call its 'species or appearances', all that is subject 'to the eye, the hand or the tooth':[13] and how could we do anything but agree? On the other hand it is not impossible that by means of the meandering line of his daring, his retractions and his successive explanations, his thought genuinely did evolve. At any rate what is certain is that where his Augustinianism was already truncated with regard to the localisation of the glorious body, it would come to grief more than anyone's when confronted with the difficulty that we have already seen facing the likes of Florus or Ratramanus, and, later on, Folmar.[14] Above all, his dialectician's temperament rendered him particularly badly suited to understand a doctrine in which the difference of period and problem alone was enough to obscure the original sense. It would seem that he thought himself in all good faith to have been slandered.[15] He was certainly perfectly sincere when he declared that he was confining himself to the traditional belief, developed by the Fathers and, according to him, faithfully reproduced by 'John Scotus'.[16] But the fact is nonetheless this: while under Charles the Bald Paschasius Radbertus appeared to be the great innovator, now Berengar was scandalizing the entire Church. 'You are crowning a universal error with the title of universal truth', he wrote to Lanfranc; and again: 'You give the name of Church to a group of simpletons.'[17] These contemptuous judgements are also admissions. Now, if the situation had become reversed in this way, the cause is not only to be found on one side. It is certain that over two centuries, the angle of vision had slowly shifted at the centre of orthodoxy; but it seems no less certain that, whatever he thought, Berengar's own no longer entirely coincided with that of Ratramnus, and even less with that of the ancient Fathers. It is the eternal story of all antiquarianism! The more Berengar held to the ancient formulations, the more in his apparent rigidity he subjected the thought behind them to subtle distortions. Therefore the anxiety that he aroused from the outset, followed by the condemnations that befell him, could not fail to provoke a reaction in theological discourse. Yet again (and it would not be the

---

13 Letter to Ascelin (PL, 150, 66). Explanations of the profession of faith of Lateran in 1050 (Mansi, vol. 19, 763 B–C, 764 B–765 A). *De sacra cena*, pp. 98–9. Matrolona Text, pp. 109–10, 116, 118. cf. Ratramnus, *De corpore . . .* , c. 15 (PL, 121, 134 A). Rupert, *In Exodum*, 2, c. 10 (167, 617 C–618 A).

14 cf. *De sacra cena*, pp. 266, 200.

15 *De sacra cena*, p. 50, p. 100, etc.

16 To Lanfranc and to Ascelin (PL, 150, 66). To the monk Richard (Sudendorf, pp. 211–12). *De sacra cena*, pp. 42, 50. Dom Cappuyns (DHGE, vol. 8, c. 405).

17 *De sacra cena*, pp. 36, 39; cf. p. 49, 74.

last time), under the guise of literal fidelity, a dangerous innovation could be detected insinuating itself, while traditional faith, in order to safeguard itself, had to transform its outlook and partly renew its articulation.

In this regard the attitude of Hildebert of Lavardin is highly significant. Hildebert was a former disciple of Berengar, if not, as has long been the belief, his pupil. Without following him into error, he remained faithful to his memory, as the eulogistic poem that he dedicated to him bears witness.[18] He therefore retained a profoundly spiritualist viewpoint. But he took pains to correct, by supplementing them, his master's questionable formulations. Taking up, for example, a word from the spiritualising tradition: '*not in fantasy, but in truth*', he added: '*not only in the sacrament, but in its very self*'.[19] Above all, he made what might seem a rather laboured attempt – he was more a man of letters than a theologian – to achieve clarification on the manner in which Christ is present on the altar *perceptibly* or *imperceptibly, bodily* or *non-bodily*:

> *It can be said to be there both perceptibly and imperceptibly. Perceptibly, because of the true perceptibility of the body and because of the sacramental form subject to the senses; imperceptibly, however, as regards the species and our sensory perception . . . It is there in a bodily way in one respect, because of the true nature of the body and the form, as has been said, of the sacrament, and because of a certain mode of existence; but (it is there) in a non-bodily way in another respect, that is, as regards the act of perceiving and a certain mode of existing.*[20]

*　*　*

But perhaps no author captures better for us the reaction, with its hesitations and its inevitable awkwardness, with those small inconsistencies that are part of any thought in the evolving, than Algerius of Liège. For the essentials, Algerius does little besides repeating the vacillations of his predecessors, particularly Lanfranc. Like so many before him, he begins by declaring that the body of Christ is not food for the body but food for the soul; that in the sacrament he is himself a

---

18　Martène and Durandus, *loc. cit.*, c. 102. cf. PL, 171, 1396–7.

19　*Brevis tractatus de sacramento altaris* (PL, 171, 1150 C, 1151 A). cf. Hériger of Lobbes on the Incarnation (139, 187 A).

20　*op. cit.* (PL, 171, 1151–1152, cf. 1151 B).

spiritual, invisible, incorruptible body; that this spiritual state is in any case natural to him after the resurrection:

> *That the body of Christ is spiritual, incorruptible and invisible . . .*
> *in the sacrament is affirmed by the saints . . . We have said the body*
> *of Christ is spiritual and invisible . . . All bodies are visible and palp-*
> *able; it is uniquely the body of Christ after the resurrection, after a*
> *change not of substance but nature, that is not bodily but spiritual*
> *and invisible.*[21]

He even adds expressly, in the note of concordance that we have seen, that this 'spiritual flesh' of which Saint Jerome spoke is none other than the body of Christ in its sacramental form.[22] Just as, according to Berengar, the changing of the bread and wine into the body and blood of Christ is an 'intelligible conversion',[23] so he deemed that the body of the Lord should be understood '*invisibly*'.[24] In all of this, and especial-ly in this habitual equivalence of the adjectives 'spiritual', 'intelligible' and 'invisible', he is following the language that had been common to the Latin translator of Hesychius,[25] to Paschasius Radbertus,[26] as well as to Ratramnus,[27] before it was adopted by Berengar.[28] It was just as much that of the first enemies of Berengar, such as Hugh of Breteuil,[29] and of his principal antagonist, Lanfranc.[30]

But Algerius alone also recalls the insistent terms of the profession of faith to which Berengar had to subscribe in Rome, at the Council of 1059: '*It is sensually that (the body of Christ) is handled and broken by the priests and chewed by the faithful.*'[31] There is no doubt that, despite certain attempts at apologetics, such as the one made by Guitmond,[32] and despite the more conservative bid made by Abbaud,[33]

---

21 *De sacramentis corporis et sanguinis Domini*, 1, c. 12, 18 (PL, 180, 775 A, 793 B–C). cf. c. 11 (772 A–C); 2, c. 1 (810 B).
22 See *supra*, Chapter 4.
23 cf. *De sacra cena*, p. 186.
24 PL, 180, 772 C and 814 C.
25 *In Leviticum* (PG, 93, 891 B), etc.
26 PL, 120, 1274 B, 1355 A.
27 PL, 121, 137 A, 138 B, 139 A, 161 A–B.
28 *Purgatoria epistula* (c. 110).
29 *De corp. et sang. Christi contra Berengarium* (PL, 142, 1330 D).
30 PL, 150, 424 A, 438 D.
31 Algerius (PL, 180, 797 B). cf. Lanfranc, c. 11 (150, 422 A–B).
32 Bk. 1 (PL, 149, 1432 A).
33 *Tractatus de fractione corporis Christi* (PL, 166, 1344 C–D).

which Walter of Saint-Victor would renew shortly afterwards,[34] the 'unhappy formulation' edited by Cardinal Humbert in such untraditional terms[35] had not succeeded in imposing itself. It was quoted in order to banish error – the adverb *'sensually'* was like a challenge to Berengar, who had defined his doctrine by aiming to reject it,[36] – but it was already being corrected or 'explained'. Some smoothed it over with a prudent 'as if'. Others used it indeterminately, without making clear if it referred to 'bread' or 'body'.[37] Still others, such as Saint Bruno (?), did not hesitate to say that the body of Christ was only 'broken' as if in appearance,[38] etc. Therefore Algerius avoided commenting on the official formulation in a sense that could very quickly become exaggerated. But nor was it enough for him, in order to stress the realism being disputed, to repeat the word that had recently enjoyed a new success in the discussions about sacraments received or conferred by the unworthy or the schismatic: *'essence'*, *'essentially'*.[39] He would not be any more satisfied with specifying repeatedly that, however spiritual and invisible it might be, the Eucharistic body is nonetheless substantial,[40] and substantially present, nor with interpreting in a somewhat tendentious fashion the Augustinian definition of the sacrament as *visible Word* in order to arrive from there at the presence of Christ *'in truth of substance'*.[41] To curb a formidable novelty sufficiently, these words were too antique, too worn-out.

We can certainly not consider as authentic antecedents *'substance of eternal life'*, or the *'vital substance'* or *'substance of power'* of St.

---

34 *Contra quatuor labyrinthos* (PL, 199, 1153–4).

35 Cappuyns, *Bérenger de Tours*, in *D.H.G.E.*, vol. 8, c. 393, and *Bulletin de théologie ancienne et médiévale*, vol. 1, p. 391. cf. Dom Paul Renaudin, *Questiones théologiques et canoniques*, vol. 1, p. 52 (PL, 141, 203 B).

36 *Purgatoria epistula* (c. 111), etc.

37 Odo of Cambrai (PL, 160, 1068 A).

38 *In psalmum 77* (PL, 152, 1038 D). Abelard (Gautier of St. Victor, *loc. cit.*). Hugh of St. Victor (176, 865). Robert Puyllen (186, 774 A, 964 C–D). Peter Lombard (191, 1640 C; 192, 865). Peter Comestor (Martin, p. 54). Gandulph of Bologna (W., p. 454). Peter of Poitiers (PL, 211, 1249–50, 1254 A). Innocent III (217, 862–863), etc. cf. St. Thomas, *Summa theologiæ*, IIIa, q. 77, a. 7; *Lauda Sion*. John of Fécamp, *Confessio fidei*, p. 4, c. 3 (PL, 101, 1088).

39 Lanfranc (PL, 150, 430 C, 436 D). Guitmond (149, 1430, 1448 B). Bernold, *De sacramentis excommunicatorum* (*Libelli de lite*, vol. 2, p. 91). *Epistula de sacramentis haereticorum* (vol. 3, p. 17). Bruno of Segni (PL, 165, 499 C). Gregory of Bergamo, c. 2, 4, 12, 21 (H., pp. 8, 18, 49, 85).

40 *De sacramentis . . .* , 1, c. 11 (PL, 180, 772 A).

41 Bk. 1, c. 21 (PL, 180, 802 A). Augustine (see *infra*, Chapter 10). cf. Berengar; Algerius (801 A). *Contra Faustum* (PL, 42, 356–7; *Panormia*, 161, 148 B).

Ambrose,[42] any more than the *'life-giving substance'* of Cassiodorus[43] and of Atto of Vercelli:[44] the accent is rather placed on 'life' or 'power' than on 'substance'. Similarly in these verses by Juvencus:

> *The vital substance of the holy bread comes today to us* . . .[45]

or in the prayers from sacramentaries where there is mention of *'the substance of eternity'*, of *'the substance of the heavenly table'*, of *'the substance of eternal life'*, of *'the substance of renewal and life'*, etc.:[46] it would be pointless to look for the type of precision conveyed by the modern sense of our word 'substance'.[47] Firmicus Maternus expressed himself in no less vague a way when he spoke of Christ handing over the substance of his majesty to believers.[48] Nor should we any more strongly rely on the numerous texts in which, alluding to the Our Father, the Eucharist is described as the 'substantial bread' *par excellence*, after Saint Cyril of Jerusalem[49] and Saint Jerome.[50] As for Saint Ambrose's *De Sacramentis*, he only explicitly mentioned the divine substance, not that of the flesh and blood.[51] The decree of Gelasius only succeeded in repeating the expression from *De sacramentis*[52] and there is no point in attributing any particularly pregnant significance to the Gregorian prayer that asks *'that we may live with his life, into whose substance you have changed us by means of these paschal remedies'*.[53] No truly innovative nuance is brought to bear, either by St. Avitus, addressing his flock on the 'heavenly substance' that the Redeemer

---

42 *In psalmum 118*, sermo 18, n. 28 (PL, 15, 1462 D). *De mysteriis*, n. 47 (16, 404 C). *De fide*, 3, c. 15, n. 127 (16, 614 C). Yves of Chartres, *Decretum* (161, 144 C, 145 C). Durandus of Troarn (149, 1384 D). Lanfranc, *Liber de corpore*, c. 6 (150, 416 C).

43 *In psalmos*.

44 *In Hebr.* (PL, 134, 755 A). Renallo of Barcelona (147, 602 A).

45 *Evangelica historia* (PL, 19, 133).

46 *Leoniarum* (F., pp. 5, 61, 117). *Gelasianum* (Thomazi, p. 123). Gallican Sacramentary, Mass of Lent (PL, 72, 479 A). *Missale gothicum* (567, Muratori; Bannister, vol. 1, p. 51).

47 C. L. Feltoe, *Journal of Theological Studies* 10, p. 578. St. Gregory (PL, 75, 551 A; cf. 563 B; 76, 122 D; 77, 1106 A); cf. Augustine (37, 1645). Luke 15.12.

48 *De errore profanarum religionum*, c. 18, n. 7 (Heuten, p. 89).

49 *Fifth Mystagogical Lecture*, c. 15 (PG, 33, 1119).

50 *In Matthaeum* (PL, 26, 43), etc. cf. Gregory of Nyssa, *On the Lord's Prayer*, c. 4 (PG, 44, 1169). John Damascene, *De fide orthodoxa*, 4, c. 13 (94, 1152), etc.

51 Bk. 6, c. 1, n. 4 (PL, 16, 455). cf. Gratian, *De consecratione*, 2.84 (Fr., 1349).

52 Routh, *Scriptorum ecclesiasticorum opuscula*, vol. 2, 3rd edn., p. 139.

53 Lietzmann, p. 72. *Missale gothicum* (PL, 72, 283 A).

wanted to leave to his followers after his death,[54] nor by Hériger of
Lobbes, explaining that the substance of Christ joins with our flesh as
once our flesh was assumed by his divinity.[55] Ratramnus, who twice
quotes one of Saint Ambrose's words,[56] also frequently spoke of substance in the context of the sacrament, but it was principally in order
to underline its invisible and mysterious character.[57] As for Paschasius
himself, while he affirms in the *Liber de Corpore* the 'conversion' of
the substance of the bread and wine into the body of Christ,[58] he is
hardly offering a precedent when he writes his letter to Frudegard:
'*nevertheless truly substance, irrespective of how the evidence might
be recounted*', since this is nothing more than a contorted quotation
from Scripture.[59] The two examples that we can find in Hincmar of
Rheims are open to similar comment,[60] as is a still later example, in
Anastasius the Librarian's note on Nicholas the First.[61]

But besides these texts, there were several others. There was the tradition of 'Eusebius of Emesus', who, as we know, was in fact Faustus
of Riez: '*He changed . . . visible creatures into the substance of his
body and blood*', '*earthly and mortal substance are transformed into
the substance of Christ*'.[62] In Faustus's language, the word '*substance*'
certainly did not yet have the precise meaning that it would have
later, when it would be contrasted with '*species*' or with '*accidents*'.
But already, as a synonym of '*nature*', describing the reality itself as
opposed to its '*name*',[63] applied to the body and blood of Christ and no
longer only to his divinity, it was preparing the way for a technical language whose elaboration would develop out of these formulations.[64]
Paschasius had quoted 'Eusebius'.[65] Alcuin had taken inspiration from
him.[66] Still others would take inspiration from him, such as the author

---

54 *Ex sermone die natali calicis*, n. 4 (Peiper, p. 104).
55 c. 9 (PL, 139, 188 A). cf. c. 3, taken with Godescalc (Lambot, pp. 326,
327).
56 c. 51, 69 (PL, 121, 147 C, 155 A, 156 A).
57 c. 30, 49 (PL, 121, 140 B, 147 A).
58 c. 8, n. 2; c. 21, n. 9 (PL, 120, 1287 C, 1340 C).
59 PL, 120, 1361 B–C. cf. Heb. 11.1 (Ratramnus, PL, 121, 132 A).
60 *De cavendis vitiis*, c. 9, 10 (PL, 125, 917 D, 926 B).
61 PL, 128, 1359.
62 *Homilia de corpore et sanguine Christi*, c. 2 (PL, 30, 272 B and C).
63 *Ep.* 3 (Engelbrecht, pp. 168–9). cf. Luc Richard, *Recherches sur la doctrine
de l'Eucharistie en Gaule du Ve au VIIe siècle* (thesis, Lyon, 1948), pp. 164–76.
64 Faustus also knows the other meaning of 'substantia': *Sermones* 2, 3 (Eng.,
pp. 232, 235).
65 *Ad Frudegardum* (PL, 120, 1354 B).
66 *Ep.* 41 (PL, 100, 203 A).

of the *Life of Saint Odo of Canterbury*,[67] and Faustus's text, in a collection by Ivo of Chartres,[68] would finally be included in Gratian's 'Decree'.[69] The formulation '[to change by] *consecrating into the substance of the body*' took up its place alongside similar formulations which only said either '*in the sacrament*', '*in the mystery*',[70] '*in the dignity*',[71] or '*in flesh*',[72] '*in body*'. At the beginning of the eleventh century, Fulbert of Chartres, who was Berengar's master, had three times used the term 'substance', with all its emphasis (but the authenticity as such of these passages is possibly not beyond question).[73] The word caught on immediately among Berengar's opponents.[74] Maurillus of Rouen († 1067), who had already presided over a council against the new heresy[75] in his own see in 1063 (and perhaps even in 1055), had made a point of using it as a testimony of faith on his deathbed.[76] Since then, the word had become current among all those who were writing about the Eucharist.[77] The adverbial form '*substantially*', which Durandus of Troarn seems to have been one of the first to use,[78] and

---

67 n. 10; PL, 133, 939 B–C.

68 *Decretum*, p. 2, c. 4 (PL, 161, 140 A).

69 *De consecratione*, c. 35 (Fr., 1325). Also cited by Peter Comestor (Martin, p. 41)

70 Isidore (PL, 83, 755 B). Etherius and Beatus (96, 941 B). Bede (94, 75 A). Rabanus Maurus (107, 319 A; 109, 992). Paschasius (120, 1294 C). *Gelasianum* (W., pp. 30, 220), etc. Honorius of Autun (PL, 172, 579 B, 1251). Gerhoh, *In psalmum 3* (193, 676 B).

71 Theodulphus of Orléans (PL, 105, 240 A).

72 Rabanus Maurus, *Liber de sacris ordinibus*, c. 19 (PL, 112, 1185 D). Paschasius, *Liber de corpore*, c. 8, n. 2 (120, 1287 C). cf. Hildebert, *Versus de mysterio missae* (PL, 171, 1193 C, 1194 D; cf. 1202 A). Cardinal Humbert, *Fragm. disputationis contra Graecos* (143, 1216 D). Ivo of Chartres (161, 158 D). Algerius (180, 755 B, 825 D), etc.

73 PL, 141, 195 A, 203 C, 204 D.

74 Durandus of Troarn (PL, 149, 1377 D, 1393 C, 1409 D, 1412 A, 1413 B). Lanfranc (150, 419 A, 756 D). Guitmond (149, 1450 B, 1477 D, 1478, 1490 A). Roman Council of 1079 (148, 809). Lanfranc, PL, 150, 430 C.

75 Mansi, vol. 19, 1028–30.

76 PL, 143, 1383 A. This kind of profession is a sign of these times. cf. St. Bruno (152, 554 A–B).

77 Anselm of Laon (PL, 159, 256 B). Odo of Cambrai (160, 1059 A, 1062 A–B, 1063 B). Werner of St. Blaise (157, 910 D). Ivo of Chartres, *Decretum*, p. 2, c. 9 (161, 159 B–C). Ernulf of Rochester (d'Achery, *Spicilegium*, vol. 3, pp. 473, 474). Osbern, *Life of Saint Dunstan* (PL, 137, 451). Bruno of Segni (165, 290 C). Rupert (167, 662 A–B, 770 C, 1665 B; 169, 462 A). Honorius of Autun (172, 1252 D). Hugh of St. Victor (176, 468 B). Algerius (180, 786 B). Hervé (181, 918 B). Hugh of Rouen (192, 209 C), etc. Bonaventure attributes the formula at one time to Ambrose, at another time to Eusebius of Emesa (Quaracchi, vol. 9, p. 248; vol. 4).

78 *Liber de corpore* . . . (PL, 149, 1405 A). cf. 1393 D, 1398 A.

which Guitmond had adopted in his turn,[79] together with its twin 'substantive',[80] had also spread quickly.[81] It appears in the profession of faith imposed on Berengar by the Lateran Council of 1079. That adverb had cost him particularly dear. He wanted to substitute the terms *'having its substance intact'* in its stead. He later explained that he had only said it under duress, and with the example of his Saviour in mind, who frequently did not intend his own words in the sense that was understood by the vulgar crowd; furthermore, he repented of it as a weakness, for which he asked pardon of God for the salvation of his soul.[82] These details demonstrate clearly the doctrinal interest that was attached to *'substantially'*. However, the adjective was less objectionable, and certain disciples of Berengar had not scrupled to adopt it, in a formulation of apparently considerable precision, without having to deny their master's doctrine. Guitmond of Aversa wrote of them: 'They proclaim that the Eucharist of the Lord is not truly and substantially the body of the Lord.'[83] This does not prevent us from reading in the words of one of them, who had to edit his manuscript under the very eyes of his master, and who was possibly his authorised mouthpiece: *'be changed into the substance of the body of Christ'*.[84]

Thus just as *'spiritual'* had until recently been the hallmark of the 'realists', *'substance'* became equally the hallmark of the 'spiritualists'. Given this, it is hardly surprising that Algerius of Liège went in search of a more rigorous precision. Lanfranc and Guitmond furnished him with it. By a distinction that was still subtle, though sufficiently clear, he explains, in accordance with them, that the body of Christ, which

---

79 *De corporis . . . veritate* (PL, 149, 1467 B, 1472 B, 1478 A, B, C, 1481 A, 1488 B, 1494 D, 1500 D).

80 *op. cit.* (PL, 149, 1469 D, 1478 A, D).

81 Pseudo-Haimon (PL, 118, 815 C–D). Bruno of Segni (165, 500 A). cf. Anselm of Laon (159, 256 C). Honorius (172, 1255 A). Hugh (176, 466 D). Algerius of Liége, *De sacramentis* (180, 761 A, 762 B). Pseudo-Bernard, *Instructio sacerdotis* (184, 785 C). Gregory of Bergamo (H., p. 116, etc.) Thus completed the preparation for the appearance of *'transubstantiation'*. The verb is read for the first time in Stephen of Baugé († 1139 or 1140), *Tractatus de sacramento altaris*, c. 13, 14 (PL, 172, 1291 C, 1293 C).

82 Mansi, vol. 10. 524 D–E. Martène, *Thesaurus*, vol. 4, pp. 108, 115–16, etc. cf. Cappuyns, Bérenger de Tours, in *DHGE*, vol. 8, c. 395–6. He had already blamed himself for its submission to the Roman Council of 1059, comparing his behaviour to that of Peter and Aaron (*De sacra cena*, pp. 61–5).

83 *De corporis . . . veritate*, 1 (PL, 149, 1430 A).

84 Text published by M. Matronola, O.S.B., in *Orbis Romanus*, 1936, and edited by R. Geiselmann, *Theol. Quartalschrift*, 1937. It is true that the author adds: 'according to a certain method' (M., pp. 116–17). cf. *Bulletin de théologie ancienne et médiévale*, vol. 3, pp. 240–2. cf. *De sacra cena*, p. 134.

he has just said is not bodily food, is nevertheless the object of a truly bodily consumption:

> ... *The sacrifice of the Church is confected of two thing and accords with two things – the visible form of the elements and the invisible flesh and blood of Christ* ... *Corresponding to these two there are also two ways of consuming Christ in the Church, one bodily and the other spiritual. One takes place with the mouth, the other with the heart* ... *We eat and drink bodily with our bodily mouth whenever from the altar of the Lord in the sacrament of bread and wine we receive by the hand of the priest the Lord's body substantially; we eat and drink spiritually with the heart whenever, as St Augustine says, we recall in memory that the Son of God hung on the cross for our salvation* ... *Of the bodily consuming the Lord said, 'Take and eat ... ;' of the spiritual consuming Augustine says, 'Eat spiritually the heavenly bread.'*[85]

Here Algerius is following Guitmond, who said both: '*spiritual food*' and '*we receive in a bodily way*'.[86] He is above all following Lanfranc, or rather, he is copying him.[87] But from one end of his work to the other, Guitmond had avoided speaking of 'spiritual flesh' or 'spiritual body', he only said '*incorruptible flesh*',[88] thus guarding against any possible verbal misunderstanding. As for Lanfranc, he had not opened up the way to his successors without some initial hesitation: he had first of all spoken of a double reception, '*both are necessary, both are fruitful*', without using with regard to either of them the word '*spiritual*' or '*bodily*'.[89] Although he was more decided on the matter, Algerius himself, in order to avoid too forceful a paradox, had to monitor his language. In passages such as the one we have just read, it is to be noted that there is no longer any question of '*spiritual flesh*', or of '*spiritual body*'. This is because Algerius could no longer use such a term in either one of these two permitted phrases without contradicting himself *in verbis*: either it would have conveyed the opposite sense from the one that he had just given it himself, or else he would have made it correspond in the most incoherent fashion to the '*bodily*

---

85 *De sacramentis* ... , I, c. 20 (PL, 180, 797–8; cf. 775 A, 806 A, 807 B). Compare Albert the Great, *In Matthaeum* (Vivès, vol. 21, p. 163).
86 PL, 149, 1439 A, 1500 C. Bruno of Segni (165, 290–291).
87 Lanfranc, *Liber de corpore* ... , c. 17 (PL, 150, 429 B–D).
88 PL, 149, 1494 B, cf. 1451 A.
89 PL, 150, 425 C–D.

eating'. There needed to be a smoother transition from the terminology of yesteryear to the one that was in the process of establishing itself. On the one hand the Eucharistic body, which was still 'invisible', was no longer, as before, 'spiritual':[90] the adjective was given an interpretation closer to the ancient rendering of Augustine and Jerome. But on the other hand, through this new usage that restricted it to the effect produced by the sacrament, people would for a while longer avoid connecting *'spiritual'* directly with *'flesh'*, or *'body'*, and they would restrict themselves to formulations such as: *'in the truth of substance – in the truth of spiritual grace'*. [91]

* * *

Nevertheless the separation was definitive. From now on, a series of words such as *'essential, substantial, bodily'* would on the one hand join the more ancient series *'invisible, intelligible, sacramental'* as adjectives qualifying the same body by supplanting *'mystical'*. On the other hand, there was the former equivalent of these words: *'spiritual'*, which the now-liberated *'mystical'* would sometimes replace.

We could take as an illustration of this newly established usage the little treatise *De corpore et sanguine Domini*, which was certainly not written by Haymon, the bishop of Halberstadt, to whom its editions attribute it on the strength of a manuscript, nor of his namesake the scholar of Auxerre. It is a much later work. It postdates the work of the first anti-Berengarian generation, and must very shortly pre-date Algerius of Liège:[92]

---

90 A phrase of book 1, chapter 11, made a sort of transition 'which is therefore spiritually the body and blood of Christ, food not of the flesh but of the spirit, by which spiritually Christ himself, as body to the head, unites and incorporates the Church to himself' (PL, 180, 774 A). The context shows that it concerns, at the beginning, the body objectively considered in its sacramental state: *'spiritual'* was at that time synonymous with *'invisible'*. But soon, through the intermediary of the idea of *'spiritual food'*, attention would fall upon the spiritual effect of communion, in such a way that the *'spiritual Christ'* modified or at least completed retrospectively the sense of the *'spiritual body'*. Such an elision or extension of the meaning, analogous with the one we find for example in Jerome or Ambrose (above, ch. 6), was made all the easier here because the communicant, being the church itself, could only be understood to receive Christ *'bodily'*.

91 PL, 180, 801 C; cf. 799 A, 773 C–D. *Liber de misericordia et justitia* (180, 885 B–C). Stephen of Baugé (172, 1298 D).

92 According to Geiselmann, it may be by another Haymon: Haymond of Hirschau, or Haymon of Telleia; at any rate, by a writer from the end of the eleventh century.

The bodily and temporal consuming and incorporation of the flesh and blood of Christ signify the spiritual and everlasting vision of the eternal fellowship and refreshment by which in the age to come we shall be incorporated in him and united to him.[93]

Here, as in Algerius and already in Lanfranc, as also in the preacher Herbert Losinga,[94] Saint Bruno of Segni[95] or Gregory of Bergamo,[96] the *bodily–spiritual* juxtaposition, while it already concerns the flesh and blood of Christ, is still only directly applied to reception by the communicant: *consuming, eating, incorporation.* It allows for the proper distinctions within the Augustinian formulation: '*There is no doubt that he who does not remain in Christ, and Christ in him, neither eats his flesh nor drinks his blood.*'[97] But the breach opened up by this would waste no time in opening wider. Soon double reception – *double eating* – would be explicitly presented as a consequence of the 'double flesh'. Hear, for example, the words of Otho of Luques:

Here we call the sacrament the very body . . . of the Lord – the reality of the sacrament, its efficacy, which Jerome calls the spiritual flesh of Christ . . . Therefore, as the flesh of Christ is understood in two ways . . . so the receiving of the body and blood of Christ is said to be twofold, that is, sacramental and spiritual.[98]

From the affirmation of bodily reception, we are led by implication to the affirmation of a bodily presence. This word was not unheard-of either. It even figured in the liturgy. The preface for the Easter octave, in the Gelasian sacramentary, contains the following:

. . . We implore your clemency, so that your Son our Lord Jesus Christ, who promised to be with his faithful until the end of the age, may by the mysteries of his bodily presence neither forsake those he redeemed nor deprive them of the benefits of his glory.[99]

---

93 PL, 118, 617 B.

94 *Sermo* 7 (Goulburn-Symonds, pp. 191, 196).

95 PL, 165, 290–1, 500 A. *Gloss on John* 6.57 (114, 384 B). Roland Bandinelli, *Sententiae* (Gietl, p. 229).

96 Hürter, pp. 117, 119.

97 *In Joannem*, tract. 26 (PL, 35, 1614). cf. *Sentences*, n. 341 (45, 1890). cf. Baldwin (204, 695).

98 Otho of Lucques, *Summa sententiarum* (PL, 176, 144). *Speculum Ecclesiae* (177, 366 A). Peter Lombard (192, 858–9; 191, 1006 B, 1647 C). *Breviarium sententiarum* (Landgraf, *Recherches de théologie ancienne et médiévale* (1931) p. 345). School of Laon, *Deus de cujus principio* (Weisweiler, *ibid.*, 1933, p. 269). Raoul Ardent (PL, 155, 1850 D). Gandulph (W., p. 443).

99 Wilson, pp. 96–7. Sacramentaries of St. Gall (Mohlberg, n. 1281) and of Angoulême (Cagin). *Missale Francorum* (PL, 72, 337 C).

This was something of an exception. But it might not even be appropriate to accept it simply in this sense, since the '*mysteries of the bodily presence*' could well be analogous to the '*mysteries of the passion*', which do not suppose a literal re-enactment of the Passion itself, but only its symbolic commemoration and the application in the present time of its fruit.[100]

At any rate, the theology was normally articulated in another way, and even among those who insisted particularly on the Eucharistic presence, the '*bodily presence*', assimilated to the presence in form of flesh, and to the sensible and localised presence,[101] was considered, following the teaching of Saints Augustine[102] and Leo,[103] as having ended on the day of the Ascension.[104] From that day onwards, there was only a '*spiritual presence*', although it was no less truly real. It was again through Saint Augustine that we came to understand the promise of the Gospels as referring to the Church, the body of Christ: 'Know that I am with you always; yes, to the end of time.'[105] *The Church of Christ, that is the body of Christ on earth*.[106] This way of speaking, which had been established without any initial particular intention of referring to the Eucharist, had naturally encapsulated it. '*Being absent in the body*', wrote Rupert in imitation of Saint Augustine;[107] and, comparing the Church with the widow of Nain, he justified the word 'widow' by explaining that her spouse, although risen and living, was no longer present in bodily form.[108] However, his language was already less consistent, and when he came to comment on Jesus's promise to remain forever with his followers, he expressed himself somewhat differently

---

100 *Supra*, Chapter 3, nn. 56–8, 71. Rupert, *De Spiritu sancto* (PL, 167, 1663).

101 Rupert (PL, 170, 40 C). John of Paris, *De potestate regia et papali*, c. 2 (Goldast, vol. 2, p. 110).

102 *In Joannem*, tract. 50, 92 (PL, 35, 1760, 1763, 1862). *In epistulam Joannis ad Parthos*, tract. 10, n. 9 (35, 2060–2061). *Sermo 235* (PL, 38, 119). However, see *In Joannem*, tr. 50 (35, 1759).

103 *Second Sermon for the Ascension*, c. 2 (PL, 54, 398 A). cf. Cyril of Jerusalem, *Catechesis* 14, c. 30 (PG, 33, 865 A). Bernard (PL, 183, 302 D).

104 Bede (PL, 94, 129 B). *Glose in Marcum* (114, 229 D). Gilbert of Nogent (156, 631 D. 649 C, cf. 534 C). Raoul of St. Germer, *In Leviticum* (B.M.P., vol. 17, pp. 88 A, 216 D). Bruno of Segni (B.M.P. vol. 6, p. 697 C). Amalarius, *De ecclesiasticis officiis*, 1, c. 12 (PL, 105, 1017 D). Yves of Chartres (162, 591 D). See again St. Thomas, *In Joannem*, c. 13, l. 7, n. 1; c. 14, l. 1, n .4.

105 *In psalmum 56*, n. 1 (PL, 36, 662).

106 Augustine, *In psalmum 71*, n. 8 (PL, 36, 906).

107 PL, 167, 1459 A. cf. Augustine, *In psalmum 44*, n. 23; *In psalmum 46*, n. 7 (PL, 36, 508, 528).

108 *De spiritu sancto*, 8, c. 13 (PL, 167, 1796 D). cf. *supra*, p. 138.

from his master. Jesus, he said, does indeed return after his ascension, *'by a return or invisible presence, but in reality, or by a visible sacrament'*.[109] Others would soon be bolder than Rupert. The same formulations that were used to define the presence of Christ on earth among his followers during his mortal life would also be used to define his sacramental presence:

> *... He showed you for a time his bodily presence in order to draw you to his spiritual one. He came to you in bodily form and showed you for a time his bodily presence in order that this might reveal his spiritual presence, which was not taken away ...*[110]

Not content with twice repeating that *'showed'* – yet another word arrived at by bringing together the Eucharist and the Incarnation,[111] and which could already be found in Algerius of Liège,[112] – Hugh of Saint Victor instituted an explicit parallel with the historical presence:

> *And so by assuming flesh he once came into the world, and according to his bodily presence lived with mankind for a time, in order to stir them to seek and find his spiritual presence. Afterwards, when the dispensation had been accomplished, he departed according to his bodily presence, while according to his spiritual presence he remained ...*
>
> *In the same way in the sacrament he comes to you for a time in his own way and is with us in bodily form, in order that you may be stirred by his bodily presence to seek his spiritual one and be helped to find it. When you hold his sacrament in your hands, he is with you in bodily form. When you take him in your mouth, he is with you in bodily form. Finally in sight, in touch, in taste he is again with you in a bodily form. When the bodily senses are affected, his bodily presence is not removed. But after the bodily senses cease to perceive him, then his bodily presence is not to be sought after, but his spiritual presence is to be retained. The dispensation has been*

109 *In Ezech.*, 1, c. 10 (PL, 167, 1431 C). Nevertheless, *In Cantica 5*, the commentary of the same text contains no allusion to the Eucharist (168, 930 D; cf. 932 A).

110 Hugh of St. Victor, *De sacramentis*, 2, p. 8, c. 13 (PL, 176, 470 C). cf. Pseudo-Bernard, *Tractatus de corpore Domini* (182, 1150 B–C).

111 Pseudo-Primasius, *In Hebr.* (PL, 68, 733 B).

112 *Supra*, Chapter 6, note 27.

accomplished, the sacrament has been performed, but the power remains. Christ passes from the mouth to the heart . . .[113]

Hugh's many disciples would reproduce this passage, and several of them would go further than their master, by neglecting the discreet reserve that he still maintained through his hesitant *'in his own way'*: we find this in the author of the *Speculum Ecclesiae*,[114] and also in Peter Comestor.[115] We encounter an analogous development both in Peter Comestor again,[116] and in the treatise of Baldwin of Canterbury, where it possibly constitutes an interpolation.[117] From then on, *'visible'* and *'bodily'* no longer appear together.[118] Even the likes of Gerhoh and Arno of Reichersberg bear witness to this evolution. They would certainly not have followed Hugh in setting up a parallel between the Eucharistic presence and the earthly presence of Jesus. In conformity with their general doctrine, which we met in the preceding chapter, they took more care than others did to avoid separating 'bodily' and 'spiritual'. Nevertheless, they too banished the expression 'spiritual presence' from their vocabulary, as being suspect from now on. They not only spoke of a 'presence of the body', and of a 'presence of Christ in his body', but they did not hesitate either to say that Christ is 'bodily present' in the Eucharist. They even thought that they could and should proclaim it vigorously. For them less than for anyone else was the reality of the body linked to its visibility.[119]

In speaking not of 'species' but rather of the reality that they hide, it would therefore be common to say: *'bodily'* or *'in a bodily sense'*; or else, if *'sacramental'*, or *'sacramentally'* were used, it would commonly be assumed that these words were meant.[120] *'Intellectual'* was already banished, on suspicion of insinuating *'incorporeal'*:

---

113 *loc. cit.* (PL, 176, 470–1).

114 PL, 177, 364–5; 363 D.

115 *Sententiae de sacramentis* (Martin, p. 56).

116 *op. cit.* (pp. 55–6).

117 PL, 204, 695 D. Raoul Ardent (155, 1856 D). Alan of Lille, *Contra haereticos*, 1, c. 62 (210, 365 C).

118 Hugh (PL, 176, 467 A; 467–8).

119 Gerhoh, *De Gloria et honore Filii hominis*, c. 13, n. 1 (PL, 194, 1117 C; cf. A B). Arno, *Liber apologeticus contra Folmarum*, pp. 102, 223. And the texts cited *supra*, p. 136.

120 See the *Testament* of Francis of Assisi. [For the testament and further works of St. Francis in English, see H. Backhouse, *The Writings of* St. *Francis of Assisi* (London, 1994); B. Fahy, *The Writings of* St. *Francis of Assisi* (Dublin, 1963).]

The body which you said was crucified you make intellectual. It is manifest that you think it incorporeal.[121]

Even *'invisible'* and *'invisibly'* would tend to come under the second phase of this disjunction in company with *'spiritual'* and *'spiritually'*.[122] Of course, these progressive slippages would not appear to have happened overnight. They were not the result of any deliberate decision. Once they had been established, it would seem that, far from being innovations, they were a harking back directly to the outlook of the early Fathers. To all outward appearances, it looked purely and simply like a return to Saint Augustine.[123] – But this would only be in appearance. *'Bodily'* (or *'sacramental'*) and *'spiritual'* formerly related to one another, as did *'sacrament'* and *'power of the sacrament'*:[124] this is how we find it in liturgical texts that speak of a *'bodily reception'*.[125] Now each of them is placed beyond the pure *'sacrament'*, and they correspond respectively to the two *'matters'* that can be distinguished beneath the sign: *'two ways of eating, two realities in the sacrament'*.[126] The history of ideas never quite goes back to the beginning. In the course of its journey, *'sacramental'* became laden with new values, while *'spiritual'* had become rather worn out.[127]

*   *   *

Thus we find, enshrined in words, one of the principal results of the extensive efforts to avoid the innovatory archaism of Berengar. For a long time the antithesis of the flesh with the spirit had dominated speculation over the Eucharist as it dominated speculation over Scripture. *'These mysteries are not fleshly but spiritual'* – *'Everything is to be understood spiritually, for there is nothing fleshly here to be*

---

121 Hugh of Langres, *De corp. et sang. Christi contra Berengarium* (PL, 142, 1327 A).

122 *Speculum Ecclesiae* (PL, 177, 365 C).

123 Augustine, *Sermo* 71 (PL, 38, 453). *In Joannem*, tract. 26 (35, 1614). *De civitate Dei*, 21, c. 25 (41, 741), etc.

124 Bruno of Wurzburg, *In psalmum* 22 (PL, 142, 112 B, after Augustine and Pseudo-Jerome). *Glose in Joannem* (114, 384 B). Rupert, *In Joannem*, 6 (169, 469 D). Honorius, *Gemma animae*, c. 111 (172, 521 A), etc. Later Wycliffe, *Sermonum*, p. 2, s. 61 (Loserth, p. 455).

125 *Leonianum* (Feltoe, pp. 4, 72).

126 *Brevarium sententiarum* (Landgraf, *loc. cit.*, p. 345). Peter Lombard, *In I Cor.* (PL, 191, 1640 D). Peter Comestor (Martin, p. 36). Gandulph (Walter, p. 443). Peter of Poitiers (PL, 211, 1252–3). Master Simon (W., p. 34).

127 Later we will have the formula: *manducatio saltem spiritualis*. Thus St. Thomas, *Summa theologiæ*, IIIa, q. 80, a. 11.

perceived',[128] '*nothing fleshly and earthly is to be thought of as regards holy things, but they are to be received in a divine and spiritual way*'.[129] In the tradition of St. John, the Fathers had exploited this antithesis, as they had with the tradition of St. Paul regarding Scripture. Bede had received it from St. Augustine and handed it down.[130] Paschasius Radbertus was no stranger to it, despite the accusations of crude realism heaped on him by his opponents,[131] for which it must be admitted he had given some cause with his history of miracles.[132] This is also true of Hincmar, despite his extreme severity against any Erigenist tendencies.[133] The *Responsio cujusdam* rendered him supreme in this tradition with his attack on the Jews who refused the gift of the Lord '*because they closed the gates of perfidy and would not allow the truth to come in, and preferred to grasp the fleshly rather than the spiritual and cruelty rather than innocence*'.[134] Gerard of Cambrai had recourse to it, at the council of Arras in 1025, in order to sweep away the objections of the 'new Manichaeans'.[135] His position is made eminently clear in Samuel's controversy about the coming of the Messiah.[136] Its foundations were too solid to be swift in disappearing. This is how it comes to reappear in Hildebert's *Brevis Tractatus*[137] or when St. Hildegard has God the eternal Father say: '*My son remains with me in Heaven, and remains with humanity on earth; but this he does spiritually and not in the flesh.*'[138] Above all, Rupert remains faithful to it.[139] In a synthesis that, if it is not to be interpreted according to the spirit of the 'dialecticians' of his age, is nevertheless highly systematized, and with all the precautions dictated to him by his sincere concern for orthodoxy, he continues the spiritualizing tradition with great originality. For him the sacramental body, being the risen body, is

---

128 Paschasius Radbertus (PL, 120, 1330 C, 1305 C).

129 Hesychius, *In Leviticum*, 6 (PL, 93, 1071 C). cf. Athanasius, *Fourth Letter to Serapion*, n. 19 (Lebon, pp. 203–4; see the translator's note), etc.

130 cf. *In Joannem*, c. 6 (PL, 92, 718 C, 720 A, 721 D).

131 *In Matthaeum*, 12, c. 26 (PL, 125, 895 A). *Liber de corpore* (1287 C; cf. 1310, 1327–32, 1357 D).

132 *Liber de corpore*.

133 *De cavendis vitiis*, c. 10 (PL, 125, 920–1).

134 D'Achery, *Spicilegium*, vol. 1, p. 149.

135 Mansi, vol. 19, pp. 431–2.

136 Samuelis Marochani, *Liber de Messiae adventu praeterito*, c. 21 (PL, 149, 360 C).

137 PL, 171, 1150 C.

138 *Scivias*, 2, visio 6 (PL, 197, 529–30).

139 *In Joannem*, 6 (PL, 169, 463); *In Exodum*, 3, c. 11 (167, 662 A–B), etc. cf. St. Bernard, *In festo sancti* Martini, n. 10 (183, 495 A).

essentially invisible, intangible and free from all carnal elements.[140] But although he gave no evidence of agreeing with the doctrines of Berengar and his emulators, this great contemplator of truths arrived too late in the story to have a chance of being heard and followed. There was no longer any room for such exclamations as: '*O priests of the flesh, enemies of the Spirit*',[141] however apt it was within its own context. When the abbot of Tuy was composing his commentaries on the Liturgy and on Scripture, Eucharistic theology had already committed itself irrevocably to quite other paths. The fact is that a completely other antithesis, using the same words, had attempted to replace the traditional antithesis of flesh and spirit: that of reality and symbol. Having set itself in opposition to '*bodily*', and '*spiritually*', it had come to oppose not only '*sensually*' but '*naturally*' and '*substantially*'. It tended to become confused with the vague '*figuratively*'. Now, the whole of faith depended on this. '*To understand spiritually*' had for a long time described a condition of rectitude, but now, on the contrary, had come to describe a form of deviance. So as not to lose all sense of the mystery, and in order for the sacrament to preserve its power,[142] a way of speaking and, up to a certain point, of thinking, had reluctantly but generally been abandoned, since it lent itself to such potential corruption. One concern therefore came to dominate: that of defending the '*substantial, not ghostly body*',[143] the '*proper substantial body*'.[144] In this cause the champions of Eucharistic realism took up once more some indications from Paschasius Radbertus, reinforcing them and generalizing them. Among some of them, an understanding of the Eucharist in bodily terms no longer principally meant, as it did in the Gospel, a false way of understanding the mystery: all they saw was the fact that heretics, judging in their own sense, in that '*carnal sense*' condemned by Saint Paul, had brought the entire sacramental economy to ruin by denying the real and bodily presence.[145] Among nearly all of them, despite the Augustinian texts handed down through canonical collections, 'spiritualist' vocabulary gradually

---

140 *In Joannem* (PL, 169, 467, 806); *In Malachiam* (168, 821 A).

141 *In Malachiam* (PL, 168, 831 B, 829 D).

142 Hugh of Langres, *De corpore* . . . (PL, 142, 1327 C).

143 Guitmond (PL, 149, 1164 D). See also Durandus of Troarn 149, 1377 C; 1411 A–B; 1392). cf. Gilbert of Nogent, *Epistula de bucella Judae data* (156, 591 A–C).

144 Honorius, *Eucharistion*, c. 5 (PL, 172, 1252 D).

145 Guitmond (PL, 149, 1439 D); see nevertheless 1456–7. cf. Pseudo-Haimon (118, 816 C). cf. Paschasius (120, 1306 A). The ancient perspective is conserved by St. Thomas commenting on chapter 6 of St. John: 5, n. 1; 8, n. 3, 4, 5; cf. c. 7, l. 4, n. 1.

became, if not suppressed, at least rare or translated. Once *'corporeal'* had been banned as being a synonym of *'corruptible'*: now *'incorporeal'* was being banned as the equivalent of *'ghostly'*.[146] After controversies and attempts at systemisation stretching the length of a century, towards the middle of the twelfth century, Peter Lombard, in his usual way, noted this result in a matter of words.[147]

Nevertheless some traces still remained of the terminology that was prevalent up to Berengar. In a passage of his *Sentences* that depends on the *Summa* of Otho of Lucques, our friend Lombard was still using a formulation that had been repeated unchanged since Lanfranc, because it was attributed to Saint Augustine, and thought to have been extracted from the collection of 'sentences' made by Prosper of Aquitaine. In it the sacramental flesh is said to be 'invisible, intelligible and spiritual',[148] as opposed to the *'visible and palpable body'* of which it is the *'sacrament'*. This is a ready made expression, passed on as a matter of routine or copied down out of veneration for its author, but in fact it does no more than bear witness to a bygone age. Once our two writers of sentences begin to talk again in their own name, they revert back spontaneously to the new language, each of them changing terminology twice over in the course of the same chapter or even of the same *'distinction'*, and they no longer describe that same sacramental flesh as anything but *'invisible and intelligible'*.[149]

* * *

The reaction against Berengar had only served to strengthen a movement that had been initiated in the time of Paschasius Radbertus, and that was increasingly identifying the first two of the three 'bodies' and detaching from them the third. This has been alluded to previously.[150] The Paschasian theory, even when it was still preserving its earlier form, to all extents and purposes became increasingly a theory of the twofold body: the historico-sacramental body and the ecclesial body. Honorius of Autun was one of the last to give witness to the theological framework bequeathed by the ninth century. In the first chapter of his *Eucharistion*, he wrote:

---

146 See John Chrysostom, *In Hebr.*, hom. 8, n. 1 (PG, 63, 67).

147 *Supra*, Chapter 4.

148 Lanfranc (PL, 150, 424 A). Ivo of Chartres (161, 153 D, 1076 A). Algerius (180, 772 A, 793 B–C). Gregory of Bergamo (H., p. 81). Gratian, *De consecratione* 2.48 (Friedberg, 1332). Otho of Lucques (PL, 176, 144 B). Peter Lombard (192, 860). Peter of Poitiers (211, 1250 B), etc.

149 *loc. cit.* Gerhoh, *Liber de simoniacis* (*Libelli de lite*, vol. 3, p. 267).

150 Chapter 4.

The body of Christ is spoken of in three ways. First we speak of the
body incarnate from the Virgin which was offered up for us on the
altar of the cross . . . Secondly, we speak of the body of the Lord
which, because of the pledge given to the Church, is confected daily
from the substance of bread and wine through consecration by the
Holy Spirit . . . Thirdly, the body of the Lord is the title of the whole
Church, which from all the elect as from many members is joined
together into one.[151]

Honorius also had a liking for subtle phrases, after the manner of
Godescalc or Hériger, where the different 'bodies' are now distinguished from one another, now reunited.[152] But it would be vain searching in his treatise for the ancient expressions of '*mystical body*' or
'*body in the mystery*' as a description of the second body; and it would
be vain searching for something equivalent to Rupert's '*body of sacri-*
fice', or the '*vicarious body*' of Gilbert of Nogent. On the contrary, he
piles up explanations whose purpose is to demonstrate unequivocally
the identity of substance between the first two bodies.[153] Furthermore,
with him, the triple division comes to its natural end, despite the effort
that it makes to survive by attaching itself to the rite of fraction and
thus by becoming fused with Amalarius's theory of the '*triple body*'.[154]
A day would come when there would actually be talk only of a '*double*
body of Christ',[155] whose dedicated terms would be respectively '*true*
body' and '*mystical body*'. William of Saint Thierry would already
have done away with the three terms, as we will see, without any
major transformation.[156] The *Sententiae Florianenses* would already
be announcing: '*The Body of Christ is spoken of in two ways*',[157] and
in the same way Gregory of Bergamo would say:

The body which is the sacrament is one thing, and the body of which
it is the sacrament is another. We understand the Lord's body in
the Scriptures in a twofold sense, and recognize that Christ's body
which is himself is one thing and the body of which he is the head
is another.[158]

---

151 PL, 172, 1250 A. cf. c. 3 (1252 A–B).
152 c. 1 (1250 B); c. 2 (1250 C); c. 3 (1251 C), etc.
153 PL, 1250 A, 1252 A
154 Honorius, c. 1 (1250 B–C).
155 William of Auxerre, *Summa aurea* (fol. 116 v).
156 *Infra*, Chapter 8, note 25.
157 n. 66 (Ostlender, p. 30).
158 c. 18 (H., pp. 75–6).

The fact is that, to the extent that attention was concentrated on Eucharistic realism, and that the problem of presence was substituting itself for the problem of the sacred action, the very foundation of the distinction that was once made between the '*body which hung on the wood*' and the '*Body which is immolated in the mystery*' for the large part disappeared. From then onwards, notwithstanding the duality of the 'human' or 'personal' form and 'sacramental'[159] form, or of the 'visible' and 'invisible' state,[160] any gap between the historical body and the Eucharistic body became increasingly narrowed to the point of the words *Christ is in substance always the same.*[161] Were both sides not saying '*the same body*'?[162] Were not Hériger of Lobbes's *media caro*,[163] and the *medium corpus* that Paschasius himself had spoken of[164] the '*body itself*', '*the flesh itself*', as St. Augustine had said once or twice, in fact precisely in a passage where he was explaining the two ways in which it is possible to eat the flesh of Christ?[165] At the dawn of the Berengarian controversy, it was still possible, without giving scandal, to join Fulbert of Chartres in distinguishing the first two bodies of the ancient triptych as '*in a sense one thing and another*':

> . . . *The Lord's body . . . located in heaven dies no more; the body in the sacrament dies for us daily . . . The former was taken from the Virgin, while the latter is consecrated from the material and virginal creation.*[166]

Even at the height of the controversy, some thinkers who had no truck whatsoever with error nevertheless still remained attached to the earlier categories. But however 'prudent and religious' they might be, they still fell into disfavour. Durandus of Troarn was especially sharp in his criticism of these over-conservative theologians.[167] Without confusing them with Berengar, they nevertheless came under similar

---

159 Algerius, *De sacramentis* . . . , 1, c. 9, 17, 17 (PL, 180, 768 C–D, 790).

160 *Sententiae Anselmi* (Bliemetzrieder, p. 117), etc.

161 Guitmond (PL, 149, 1461 C). Bruno of Segni (165, 499 C). Manegold (155, 165 D). Geoffrey of Vendôme (157, 213 A–B), etc.

162 *Supra*, Chapter 4.

163 PL, 139, 186 A. cf. 186 C.

164 PL, 120, 896 C.

165 *Sermo 71* (PL, 38, 453). cf. *In psalmum 98* (37, 1265). Hériger (139, 180 C–D). Hugh of Langres (142, 1330 D). Théodwin of Liége (146, 1441 B). Hugo Metellus (188, 1274 A), etc.

166 *Epist. 3, Einardo* (PL, 141, 194–5).

167 Durandus of Troarn (PL, 149, 1387 B).

censure, and the 'metabolic' texts of Saint Ambrose were particularly used against them.

On the other hand, this increasingly pronounced rallying under the first point of Ambrose's Eucharistic doctrine was generally accompanied by an equally pronounced abandonment of the second point, that of his concept of the 'spiritual body'. So Durandus of Troarn, who quotes and comments on Ambrose at length, and who continues to use the phrase from the *De mysteriis* about the *spiritual body*, nevertheless avoids alluding to it in his commentary: on the contrary, he insists on the use that Ambrose makes of the word *flesh* in order to cut short any attempt at interpreting the Eucharistic body in a way that was too 'celestial' or too spiritual for his taste.[168] Augustinian spiritualism was also in retreat. What remained of it in Gilbert of Nogent or Rupert of Tuy was already little more than a surviving remnant, which, as we have seen, was poorly received by their circle, and would soon disappear. Finally – and it is a sign of the times – William of Saint-Thierry, whose thought was nevertheless so subtle and so open to the influence of Greek mysticism,[169] was no longer satisfied even with accepting, along with his contemporaries, the idea of a bodily reception: '*It is received bodily*'; but he goes as far as to speak, in reference to the Eucharistic body as well as to the historical body, of the '*material flesh*'.[170] No doubt the expression is less 'scandalous' than might first appear: indeed it is quite clear that William would never have chosen it to describe the Eucharist; the adjective only refers directly to the historical body. But the mere identification of one with the other gave this impression.

Double flesh, double body. The first of Jerome's two 'fleshes' could now correspond not only just to the historical body, but at the same time to the first two of Paschasius's three bodies, that is to say to the historico-sacramental body. For this it was enough to remove the pejorative inference that it had in Jerome, in order to use it in a completely objective sense solely to express the truth of the bodily presence, and to turn its sensible aspect into an abstract concept, so that it only referred to the simple reality of the 'essence'. In this way a second concordance could be obtained, that was completely different from

---

168 *De corpore et sanguine Christi*, p. 4a, c. 7, 7 (PL, 149, 1385–1386).

169 J.-M. Déchanet, 'De l'Apologie à la Lettre d'or' (*Revue d'ascétique et de mystique*, 1939, pp. 16–21), and *Aux Sources de la doctrine spirituelle de Guillaume de Saint-Thierry*, Collectanea Ordinis Cisterciensium Reformatorum, 1938–9. cf. Adam, *Guillaume de Saint-Thierry*, pp. 54, 98–9.

170 PL, 180, 355, 356.

the one that had been conceived by the ninth century. The spiritual flesh, dislodged from its central position, was now only the effect of the sacrament, not the reality itself. In addition to the witnesses quoted in the preceding pages, we hear Stephen of Baugé:

> *The flesh of Christ is double: that which was born of the Virgin and is received in the sacrament, and that which is eaten through faithful believing, without which the sacramental body is of no avail, for God said, 'The flesh is of no avail, it is the spirit that gives life' . . . So to eat the flesh of Christ is to receive it in spirit and truth.*[171]

This text, like many other similar ones, uses both Jerome and Augustine at the same time. The system of concordance has changed, but the two great doctors remain associated in the framework of the second system as they were in that of the first. Everything evolves in their name. Even more ingeniously, William of Saint Thierry, against a background of Augustinian resonances, makes use of a whole series of quotations from Saint Jerome. This can be found in the sixth chapter of his treatise *De corpore et sanguine Domini*,[172] a chapter which precisely he entitles: '*On the twofold body of Christ*'. After quoting that text from the commentary on the Letter to the Ephesians that we know, he continues:

> *From that earlier flesh that was crucified proceeds this second flesh (spiritual and divine). According to the psalmist God takes bread from the earth, when from the field of the earthly body which he took from us, he produces the mystery of the bread of heaven and the cup of salvation by which the Church is refreshed.*[173] *And just as the Lord's body that had died is called in the gospel a grain of wheat that falls into the earth, so in the psalm the 'fat of the wheat' is a name given to that mystical flesh to which the Lord exhorted the disciples when he said, 'Unless you eat . . '.*[174]
>
> *In the sacraments the body of the Lord is brought into being by the faith of holy Church, to whom in general terms the sacrifice belongs, whatever degree of merit is possessed by the one through*

---

171 PL, 172, 1296. Otho of Lucques, *Summa sententiarum*, tract. 6, c. 3 (176, 140 C, D). Hugo Metellus (188, 1273 C). Peter Lombard (192, 857, 859). *Speculum Ecclesiae* (177, 365 D). William of Auxerre, *Summa aurea* (fol. 258–9).

172 We cite this work more generally under a second title: *De sacramento altaris.*

173 Jerome, *In psalmum 103*, cited in the appendix (PL, 180, 363 B).

174 Jerome, *In Isaiam*, cited also, 363 B.

whom it comes into being; but the spiritual flesh is brought into being through the grace of God by the lives of those who administer or receive. This is why we say, 'so that it may become for us the body and blood of your Son'. 'May it become for us' is what is said. Now undoubtedly the body of the Lord always becomes present on the table of the altar when the solemn mystery is celebrated properly, but it does not always become present to those through whom it becomes present.[175]

---

175 PL, 180, 353, cf. 358. Letter to the Brothers of Mont-Dieu (184, 327–8, after Augustine; Davy, n. 55, p. 104). The interpretation of *to us* was classic: Paschasius (PL, 120, 1312 B, 1344 A). Bernold (*Libelli de lite*, vol. 2, p. 91, etc). Imitated from Augustine (PL, 35, 1618). Berenger, *supra*, n. 8.

8

'One Body', 'One Flesh'

The completion of this new concordance must have been even more laborious, given that it involved the perfect combining of the two final terms of each series: the *spiritual flesh* – which in the meantime had become for some writers *mystical flesh* – and the *body-Church* – itself in the process of becoming for several others the *mystical body*. If the former *spiritual flesh* had at one time become fairly painlessly fused with the *mystical body* of Rabanus Maurus and Paschasius Radbertus, before it gave way to *material flesh*, now it no longer applied in the same way: the new understanding of *spiritual flesh* no longer coincided so neatly with *mystical body* in its own new understanding. Given that it no longer simply referred to the Eucharist, the 'spiritual flesh' of Christ no longer *ipso facto* denoted the Church.

The attempt at unification was nevertheless made. It would tentatively take place in the context of the sacramental theory that distinguished three elements within the Eucharistic mystery: *sacrament only, reality and sacrament, reality only (sacramentum-tantum, res-et-sacramentum, res-tantum)*. The theory took its inspiration from Augustine, although it did not correspond exactly to St. Augustine's established way of speaking.[1] If the somewhat scholastic flavour of its conceptualism contrasted strongly with the fluidity of Augustine's own thought, at least it gave rise to the considerable advantage of dissipating the ambiguity etched into the two words *sacrament* and *matter of the sacrament (sacramentum, res sacramenti)*, thus avoiding contradictory interpretations, in both cases, of texts where the great Doctor used these words. Thus above all it served to bring about some much-needed order and clarity, as witnessed by a remark of Algerius of Liège, one of the first to have employed it.[2] Such a need was deeply

---

1 cf. *De Civitate Dei*, 10, c. 20 (PL, 41, 298); *Contra Faustum*, 19, c. 13–14 (42, 355); *Sermo* 22 (38, 1246); *Ep. 55*, n. 1 (33, 305); *Enchiridion*, c. 42 (33, 253), etc. Nevertheless, *In Joannem*, tract. 26 (35, 1614); *Sermo* 227 (37, 1100), etc. cf. Pseudo-Bede, *In Joannem* (PL, 72, 719 A). See *supra*, ch. ii.

2 *De sacramentis*, I, c. 4, 5, with the citation of a text of Lanfranc attributed to

felt at the time. Thus, among the theologians of the generation following Algerius, it already appeared as a classical theory.[3] All the
Sententiaries expounded it, and they handed it down to the Summists.
We know how St. Thomas turned it to good account.[4] There is no
need for us here to follow its evolution, nor to study its details, variants and vicissitudes.[5] There is only one particularity that interests
us directly: it is that two currents can be distinguished within it. And
although the vocabulary on this point is far from uniformly rigorous,
we could symbolize them by the two words that normally share the
task of describing the third term: on the one hand, *reality* (*res*); and on
the other *power* (*virtus*).[6]

Reality or *power*: each of them appears equally as the completion,
the perfection of the mystery: '*What is performed in appearance is
secured by the truth of the realities*', – '*what is performed in mystery is accomplished in power*'.[7] Broadly speaking, each can be taken
for the other. Nevertheless, in concrete terms they need to be defined
fairly differently. The *reality* is essentially the unity of the Church,
it is the unique body formed by the gathering together of a multi-
tude of members. The *power* is the spiritual efficacy of the sacrament,
considered above all under its aspect of food. The first is symbolized
both by the *sacrament* and by the *reality-and-sacrament*, that is to
say, by the Eucharistic species and by the individual body of Christ,
who is concealed within these species.[8] The ecclesial body is composed of members who are united and utterly purified, like members
of the body born of the pure Virgin, like the grains of pure wheat or
the drops of grape juice from which the bread and wine are made:[9]

Augustine; PL, 180, 752 B). cf. c. 3 (747–50), and *Liber de misericordia et justitia*,
p. 1, c. 62 (884 D).

3 For example, Gregory of Bergamo, c. 14, 17 (Hürter, pp. 59, 71). Stephen of
Baugé, c. 17 (PL, 172, 1295–6). William of St. Thierry, *Ep. ad Fratres de Monte
Dei*, n. 55 (Davy, pp. 103–4). Hugh of St. Victor, *De sacramento corporis Christi*
(Wilmart, 'Opuscules choisis de Hughes de St. Victor', in *Revue bénédictine*, 1933,
p. 243). Clear formulae in the *Summa sentarum* of Othon of Lucques, tract. 6, c. 3
(PL, 176, 140). Later, Innocent III, *Ep. ad Joannem lugdunensem* (214, 1120–1);
De sacro altaris mysterio, 4, c. 35–6 (217, 878–880).

4 cf. St. Thomas, *Summa theologiæ*, IIIa, q. 83, a. 3 and *IV Sent.*, d. 9, a. 1, 3°
(Moos, pp. 363, 365).

5 See *La 'res sacramenti' chez Gerhoh de Reichersberg*, *Études de critique et
d'histoire religieuses*. Lyon, Catholic Faculties, 1948.

6 cf. Eberhard of Bamberg, *Letter to Eberhard of Saltzburg* (PL, 193, 503 C).
cf. Adam Scotus, *De tripertito tabernaculo*, p. 2, c. 10 (PL, 198, 705).

7 Roman Missal. cf. Amalarius, *Liber officialis*, l. 1, c. 24 (PL, 105, 1044).

8 cf. William of Auxerre, *De officiis*, fol. 11.

9 The symbolism of purity, which makes use of an expression of John

'*confected from many grains and many grapes, from many grains of purest wheat*'.[10] The second comes from the flesh and the blood of Christ, which respectively symbolize the eternal life of the body and the soul,[11] the assumption and the liberation of each one by our Saviour:

> *so that it might feel the whole human being in his twofold substance.*

And this flesh and blood are in their turn symbolized by the two species, considered now no longer simply in themselves, or in what they are made of, but in their role as nourishment: *before all other forms of food or drink the body is refreshed by them*.[12] The bread that fortifies, the wine that gives joy, what better symbols could there be of this life-giving flesh and blood?[13]

In greater or lesser detail, this double symbolism is everywhere. But almost everywhere it also remains double in fact, without any real link and without any organizing principle. Thus on the one hand, we have the *food and drink*, in relation to *everlasting life*; on the other, we have the *bread and wine*, signs of the *unity of the body of the Church*.[14] On one side, according to the line of thought that originates with St. Paul and that subsequently exploits the figure of the sacrifice of wheat flour prescribed by Leviticus,[15] we end up with the ultimate

---

Damascene, *De fide orthodoxa*, 3, c. 2; 4, c. 14 (PG, 94, 985 B, 1160 C). cf. Anselm of Havelberg (PL, 188, 1245 B). Gandulph of Bologna (Walter, pp. 442–3). William of Auxerre (fol. 116 v°). Albert the Great, etc. See also *Summa* of Alexander, IVa, q. 10, m. 3, 4.

10 Numerous examples. We note a particular application in Anselm of Havelberg (*loc. cit.*).

11 After Ambrosiaster, *In I Cor.* (PL, 17, 243 B). Thus Amalarius (105, 1010 D). Gezonius of Tortona (137, 388 B). Anselm of Laon (159, 255 B; cf. 162, 1470–1). Atto of Vercelli (134, 379 B, 380 A). *Sententiae Florianenses* (O., p. 41). Florilegia of St. Amand (*Recherches de théologie ancienne et médiévale*, 1939, p. 320). Gilbert the Universal, *In psalmum 21* (*ibid.*, 1936, p. 58; cf. *Glose in Lucam*, PL, 114, 539 B). Honorius of Autun, *Eucharistion*, c. 12 (172, 1257–8). Peter Lombard, *In I Cor.* (191, 1642 D). Master Simon (W., p. 28). *Summa* of Prévonstin (Geiselmann, *Die Abendmahlslehre . . .*, p. 151), etc.

12 Numerous examples. *Remissio peccatorum* (Matt. 26.28); Ambrose *De sacramentis*, 4, c. 5, n. 24; c. 6, n. 28 (PL, 16, 444 B, 446 A); cited by Burchard (140, 756 B) and Gratian, *De consecratione*, p. 2, c. 14, 40 (Fr., 1319, 1328). Gerhoh, cf. Peter Comestor (Martin, p. 49).

13 Alcuin, *Ep. 137* (MGH, *Epistularum*, vol. 4, p. 212). Abelard's commentary on 1 Cor. 11 (L., vol. 2, p. 264).

14 Algerius, *De sacramentis* (PL, 180, 7994 C, 823 A–B). Peter of Poitiers (211, 1242). Peter of Celle (202, 768). cf. Bonaventure, *Breviloquium*, p. 6, c. 9 (Quar., vol. 5, p. 274).

15 Bede, *In Leviticum* (PL, 91, 334 A). Rabanus Maurus, *In Leviticum* (108, 257 A). Yves of Chartres, *De convenientia* (162, 543 C, 544 C) etc.

'reality' of the mystery. On the other side, according to the Johannine tradition in which, as in St. John himself, the figure of the manna is of first importance, the emphasis is on the fruit of this communion. On one side we have an objective and social reality, although there is also an equal inner reality: the unity of the Christian community: *this bread indicates unity*;[16] the whole Church is prepared and brought to fulfilment in this Bread.[17] On the other side, there is a 'subjective' reality, inherent to each communicant: the life, or rather the vivification, the nourishment of the spiritual person: *the power and fullness of spiritual nourishment*,[18] – *the inner being is filled by the power of the sacrament*.[19] Note a still further difference towards which these last words point: while depending on the sacrament that brings it about, as an effect depends on its cause, the *matter of the sacrament* (*res sacramenti*) can consequently be considered separately, as a given reality, while the *power of the sacrament* (*virtus sacramenti*) remains far more narrowly attached to the sacrament of which it is the power: it is a dynamic and no longer a substantial term. If the *matter* is the *effect*,[20] the *power* is rather *effectiveness*[21] or better still, *efficacy*.[22]

* * *

Now, it is clear that if *mystical body*, as we find it in Master Simon, tallied perfectly with the *sacramental matter*, *mystical flesh* for its part corresponded more naturally with *power*. Even in this last sense, it was less the already produced effect and, so to speak, objectivity of the sacrament than the sacrament itself, insofar as it produced its effect according to the dispositions of those who came to draw life from it. It was more or less the *'life-giving and saving substance'* of which

---

16 Rabanus Maurus, *In I Cor.*, x (PL, 112, 95 A, 103 A). *Madrid Treatise* (W., p. 92). Roman Catechism, part II, n. 19, 4°.

17 This idea is developed in the numerous texts that exploit the symbolism of the making of bread: the mill of the two Testaments, the water of baptism, the fire of the Spirit . . .

18 Hugh of St. Victor, *De sacramentis*, 2, p. 8, c. 8 (PL, 176, 467 D).

19 Rabanus Maurus, *De clericorum institutione* (PL, 107, 318). Honorius of Autun, *Gemma animae*, c. 111 (172, 581 A).

20 cf. William of Méliton, *Opuscule sur la messe* (Dansend, Mélanges Grabmann, vol. 1, p. 574).

21 Augustine (PL, 43, 255). *Speculum Ecclesiae* (177, 365–6). Otho of Lucques (176, 140 D). Nevertheless, Otho identifies successively *res* and *virtus*, *virtus* and *efficacia*, *res* and *efficacia*, and each of these three words with *spiritualis caro* (140 C, 140 D, 143 C).

22 *Speculum Ecclesiae* (PL, 177, 366 C).

Cassiodorus[23] had spoken. The 'power' with which the flesh of Christ was graced ought certainly to take possession of the faithful, but if the communicant should prove to be unworthy, instead of entering into them to dwell there, it would remain in Christ.[24] In this way we find a better explanation for how the same expression *spiritual flesh* could have been used successively for the two concordances we have been discussing. Now it was made to lean, so to speak, in the direction of the sacrament (the direction of the Eucharist), now in the direction of its effect (the direction of the Church), but its true place – since there was much insistence on placing it in a framework that was not made for it – fell more accurately somewhere between the two. At least one of our authors was fully aware of this. In his original way of interpreting the traditional formulation of the 'threefold body', William of St. Thierry, after having combined the first two bodies of earlier times, as we saw in the last chapter, inserted Jerome's *spiritual flesh* between the Eucharist and the Church:

> One must think in one way of that flesh or body which hung on the tree and is sacrificed on the altar, and in another way of that flesh or body whose eaters have life abiding in them, and in yet another way of his flesh or body which is the Church.[25]

Furthermore, before appearing as the unifying principle of souls, this second flesh, which was called spiritual or mystical, was for each soul the living and life-giving flesh, and its very name of *flesh* prevented it from evoking the idea of an organism, which was essential to the *matter of the sacrament*. In identifying it with *power* and separating it from the *reality*, this seemed a double reason for discouraging any attempt at confusing it with the *mystical body*. This was the origin of a sort of rivalry between the two expressions, between *flesh* and *body*, according to whether in the general theory the accent was put on the *power* or on the *reality*, on the *spiritual life* or on the *unity of the Church*. But as both were equally traditional, and equally essential, even those who could not succeed in organizing them or combining them for all that could often not decide to sacrifice one or the other. Therefore this rivalry nearly always ended up by sharing or juxtaposing them.

---

23 *In psalmum* 109 (PL, 177, 366 C).

24 Thus for the communion of Judas: Honorius of Autun (PL, 172, 1131–2). cf. Hugh of St. Victor.

25 c. 12 (PL, 180, 361–2).

Such, for instance, is the case for Pseudo-Haimon. After having developed Pauline symbolism, he passed by an *alternative way* to Johannine symbolism:

> *The body and blood of Christ . . . are truly called signs with refer-*
> *ence to the likeness of those who receive them; for just as the bread*
> *which when consecrated becomes the body of Christ becomes from*
> *many grains one bread, and the drink which when sanctified is*
> *made the blood of Christ becomes from many grapes one drink, so*
> *all who worthily receive this sacrament are made from many one*
> *body in Christ.*
>
> *The body and blood of Christ can be called signs in another way:*
> *what we eat and transfer into our body of Christ seems in a certain*
> *way to be embodied in us and united to us . . .*[26]

In the same way we get Honorius of Autun, in his *Elucidarium* saying:

> *Just as the body is fed with bread, so the soul is refreshed by the food*
> *of Christ; – and just as bread is confected from many grains, so the*
> *body of Christ is gathered together from many elect . . .*[27]

'*In another respect*', the author of the *Speculum Ecclesiae*[28] would say, he too passing from one symbolism to the other. The *Sententiae Divinitatis* distinguish two reasons for which Christ chose bread and wine, and these two reasons, which still have no other link than *or*, are our two symbolisms.[29] It is still a dualist formulation, if a little different, and we can take as representing it the *Liber de Canone Mystici Libaminis*[30] or the Abelardian collection of the *Sententiae Parisiensis*:[31] received under form of bread, the body of Christ is a figure for the unity of the Church and the communion of saints, whereas the blood obtains the remission of sins and signifies the life of the soul that proceeds from it, since, according to the 'physicians', as also according to Scripture, 'the life of the soul lies in the blood'.[32] The *Epitome*

---

26 *De corpore et sanguine Domini* (PL, 118, 817).

27 Bk. 1, c. 28 (PL, 172, 1129 A–B).

28 c. 7, *De celebratione missae* (PL, 177, 363 A, 365–6).

29 *Tractatus 5* (Geyer, p. 130). Odo of Ourscamp (Pitra, pp. 37–8). Algerius (PL, 180, 823 A–B).

30 PL, 177, 462 B.

31 Landgraf, p. 41.

32 After Deut. 12.23. Cyril of Alexandria, *Second Paschal Homily* (PG, 77,

theologiae christianae of Master Herman offers another variant, without further reducing the fundamental duality.[33] For William of St. Thierry, the Eucharist is equally a sacrament of two matters, which he is careful to distinguish – contrary to his custom – by the respective use of *flesh* and *body*: one of these two matters is the *spiritual flesh*, understood in the way that he explained above; the other is the '*body of Christ, which is the Church*'.[34]

The author (once again an Abelardian) of the *Ysagoge in theologiam*[35] and Otho of Luques[36] adopt a rather more complicated device. Even before arriving at the central element of the mystery, that is to say at the *matter-and-sacrament*, they already introduce the Church as body of Christ, in the context of the symbolism of the species, and only then do they refer to the *power* or *efficacy of the sacrament*, which they confuse with the spiritual flesh of Christ.[37] Now, while they see above all in the *body-Church* the unity of the members of Christ among themselves, the *spiritual flesh* is, in their eyes, the unity of each communicant – of each member of Christ – with the Head.

In these last two examples – and there are many others that could be quoted – the Johannine tradition has already been brought closer into line with the Pauline tradition, thanks to the explanation of the doctrine contained in the Bread of Life discourse by the doctrine contained in the discourse after the Last Supper. The union of Christ and his faithful, becoming '*the union of the head and the members*',[38] includes at least one allusion to the idea of '*the body made up of many members*'. The allusion becomes reinforced by the large quantity of texts where the subject who receives the sacrament is no longer the individual soul, even envisaged as a member, but the Church itself:[39] the *Sacrifices with which the Church is marvellously nourished and*

---

441 D). Augustine (PL, 34, 702–4; 42, 143–5). Pseudo-Primasius, *In Hebr.* (68, 790 B). Algerius (180, 826 C–D). Werner of St. Blaise (?) (157, 910 B). Peter Lombard (19, 1642 D), etc.

33 c. 29 (PL, 179, 1741).

34 *Liber de sacramento altaris*, c. 9 (PL, 180, 356–7).

35 Landgraf, p. 205.

36 *Summa sententiarum*, tract. 6, c. 3 (PL, 176, 140).

37 *ibid.*

38 Stephen of Baugé (PL, 172, 1295–6). *Speculum Ecclesiae* (177, 365 B–C). Baldwin (204, 716–18), etc. cf. the Gelasian Sacramentaries (W., p. 18) and the Gregorian (L., p. 36).

39 Algerius (PL, 180, 749), Hervé (181, 1268 B). *Epistula de sacramentis haereticorum* (*Libelli de lite*, vol. 3, p. 17), etc.

fed,[40] – *the life of the Church, the flesh of the Saviour*.[41] Since the moment the Church becomes a social reality, there is a manifest link between its life and its unity: is it not the union of its members, a union made closer by the sacrament, that measures the intensity of its life? – Nevertheless, the two Pauline metaphors of the union of Christ and his Church in one single flesh and the union of the members of Christ in one single body did not overlap. The double symbolism of the species, together with the natural opposition of meaning between *flesh* and *body*, maintained a separation between the Eucharistic tradition of St. Paul and that of St. John. Although there had been some reconciliation of the two, they remained rather parallel than convergent. As Gandulf of Bologna would say a short time later, the effect of the Eucharist was a *twinned reality*.[42]

Now, with Peter Lombard, who would soon be followed by Peter of Troyes,[43] any separation was suddenly suppressed. The effect of the mystery was presented as unique, the *power* identified with the *reality*. Like everyone, Peter Lombard juxtaposed the two symbolisms of species: the nourishment of the inner person, the confection of the unity of the Church.[44] But, in the unity of the members of the Church united in one single body, or *unity of the faithful*, he had no hesitation in perceiving the *mystical flesh of Christ*, in which consists the final 'reality' of the sacrament. *Reality-and-not-sacrament, its mystical flesh*. In this way the terminology was unified. The *mystical flesh* and the *mystical body* would become interchangeable. The first expression would have effectively paved the way for the second.

* * *

Such an amalgamation would certainly seem artificial. And it undoubtedly is, if one only considers the vocabulary. But if an effort is made to penetrate beneath the words, one realizes that it is principally caused by a more faithful attachment to the Eucharistic doctrine of St. Augustine. It appears as a deliberate exegesis of this doctrine,

---

40 *Gregorianum* (L., p. 58). Augustine, *Sermo 90*, n. 6 (PL, 38, 563). Fredegis of Tours, *Epistola de nihilio et tenebris* (105, 753 A), etc.

41 Guitmond, I (PL, 149, 1435–6). Renallo of Barcelona (147, 601 A), etc.

42 *Sententiae*, 4, n. 101–4 (W., pp. 442–3). Peter of Poitiers, *Sentences*, 5, c. 10 (PL, 211, 1241–2), William of Auxerre, *Summa aurea* (fol. 257 v 5°). And *Perpetuité* (Migne, vol. 2, 785).

43 *Sententiae de sacramentis* (Martin, pp. 35–6).

44 *Sentences*, 4, d. 8, n. 4 (Quaracchi, p. 792). D. 9, c. 3 (p. 796); *In I Cor.*, (191, 1643).

aimed at reproducing it in its rich unity.[45] If there is a desire to discern, beyond the visible artifice, the complexity of thoughts of which it is the sign and so to speak the knot, in the Lombardian formulation, it is also important to forget for a few moments the shrill personality of Lombard and enter into dialogue with St. Augustine himself.

The latter never created anything from the start. Not only are all his doctrinal principles contained in Scripture, but the essential elements can also be found ready-made among his predecessors, and chiefly St. Cyprian,[46] St. Hilary,[47] St. Gregory of Nyssa,[48] St. John Chrysostom,[49] or in a contemporary like St. Cyril of Alexandria.[50] Nevertheless, they are still only elements. They do not constitute one single current of thought. Augustine takes hold of them, brings them together, recreates them and takes them deeper by organizing them around one unique intuition. The admirable twenty-sixth treatise on the Gospel of St. John considers how the spiritual life drawn from this food which is the flesh of Christ results from being incorporated into the unity of his body, and should consequently be defined as a participation in the 'society of saints':

'For my flesh, he says, is truly food and my blood is truly drink.' Although human beings seek through food and drink to allay hunger and thirst, this is not really granted except by that food and drink which makes those who receive it immortal and incorruptible; that is, the fellowship of the saints itself, where there will be peace and full and perfect unity. Therefore, as was already understood before us by the men of God, our Lord Jesus Christ entrusted his body and blood to things which are assembled from many to make one entity; for the former from many grains becomes one, while the latter from many grapes flows into one.[51]

Note the nominative: *'the fellowship of the saints itself'*. These words are not the complement but the subject. It is this holy fellowship itself, a blessed state and the object of our desires, which is at the same time

---

45 PL, 192, 859. *Supra*, Chapter 7, n. 41.
46 *Epistulae* 63, 69, c. 5 (Bayard, vol. 2, pp. 199–213, 242–3). cf. J. Turmel, *Histoire des dogmes*, vol. 5, p. 274.
47 *De Trinitate*, 3, c. 24; 8, c. 15–16 (PL, 10, 66, 247–8).
48 *Catechetical Discourse*, c. 37, n. 3 (Méridier, p. 174).
49 *In Joannem*, hom. 46 (PG, 59, 260). *In I Cor.*, hom. 24 (61, 200). *In Hebr.*, hom. 6, n. 2 (63, 56).
50 *Adversus Nestorium*, 4 (PG, 76, 189–97). *In Joannem*, 11 (74, 560).
51 *In Joannem*, tract. 26, c. 6, n. 17 (PL, 35, 1614). Cited Pseudo-Bede (92, 718–19), Alcuin (100, 845 C). Rabanus Maurus (110, 494 A), Haimon, *Homilia* 62 (118, 349 A–B), Rupert (169, 482), Algerius (180, 794–5).

our food and our drink: '*He wishes this food and drink to be under-stood as the fellowship of the body and its members, which is the holy Church in the predestined.*'[52]

The last term coincides with the source, the Church is joined to Christ in perfection. The two *matters of the sacrament* are now only one, and in this double and unique participation, each one finds eternal life . . . '*the body is perfected in us, we are perfected in the body*'.[53] The underlying sense of this doctrine, and even its importance, were unknown to apologists whose concerns were too short-term. This is how Cardinal du Perron, exaggerating the significance of a remark that was nevertheless exact, could only see in it an expedient to which, in his view, Augustine had recourse in order to disguise the mystery of the real presence while addressing an uninitiated audience.[54] There would be strong grounds for criticizing it for being insufficiently analytical. But it would be creating a hardly less serious misunderstanding to believe that this constitutes a confusion, or even an exclusion, when, according to an habitual thought process of St. Augustine's, what we are dealing with is a fluid continuity.[55] There would certainly be no point in demanding conceptual precision from this astonishing mixture – so perfectly achieved if it is one, so little of a 'mixture', in fact – of doctrinal exegesis, familiar preaching and elevated lyricism.[56] Texts of this sort will always be difficult to defend on their own terms, against the distorting interpretations of those who Rupert, in talking of this same passage, called '*over-hasty readers and immature teachers*',[57] in the same way that they will never satisfy the needs of didactic explanation. And we might ask ourselves if these deficiencies are not in fact the price that has to be paid for a richness of thought that is not in the same order as a discourse, and whose meaning can only be conveyed by an elliptical and paradoxical turn of phrase.[58]

---

52 *In Joannem*, tract. 26, c. 6, n. 15 (PL, 35, 1614). Augustine, cited by Abelard (178, 1532), and *Glose* (114, 384 A). cf. Fulgentius, *Ep.* 12, n. 24–6 (PL, 65, 390–2).

53 *In psalmum* 39, n. 12, on the words *corpus autem perfecisti mihi* (PL, 36, 442). Adrevald of Fleury (124, 952 A).

54 *Examen du livre du sieur du Plessis* (*Les diverses œvres . . .* , 3ʳᵈ edn., 1663, p. 1100).

55 Augustine, *Sermo* 227, 272 (PL, 38, 1100; 38, 1247).

56 Fénelon, *Lettre sur les occupations de l'Académie*, ch. iv (Œuvres, Paris, vol. 6, p. 624).

57 *In Joannem*, 6 (PL, 169, 482). Hugo Metellus, *Ad Gerlandum* (188, 1273–4).

58 cf. P.-Th. Camelot, 'Réalisme et symbolisme dans la doctrine eucharistique de saint Augustin' (*Revue des Sciences philosophiques at théologiques*, 1947, pp. 394–410).

The return to St. Augustine, which marks Lombard's formulation, therefore did not only have the extrinsic merit of a stricter fidelity to tradition. In a few words, whose connection remains questionable, he condensed by means of allusion the whole of a profound and harmonious doctrine in which the two viewpoints of 'mystery' and 'communion' are organically brought together. Here St. Paul and St. John are commenting on each other, and so to speak fused into one another. St. John leads to St. Paul, St. Paul is given greater depth by St. John. The two apostles are not made to agree from the outside, as too often happens, by means of some superficial arrangement, but on the contrary are mutually enriched. The term that mediates this operation, and which owes its existence to the genius of St. Augustine, is the idea that is expressed in the famous formulation: '*You will not change me into you, as you do with the food of your body. Instead you will be changed into me.*'[59] The natural symbolism of food is reversed: '*Those eating are transformed into the nature of the food they eat.*'[60] This is because the Eucharistic bread is no ordinary bread: it is the Life in which all living beings participate. '*When Christ is eaten, Life is eaten.*'[61] He transforms into himself those whom he nourishes with his substance. He himself is the body whose food those who eat it become:

---

59 *Confessions*, 7, c. 10, n. 16 (PL, 32, 742); *In Joannem* (35, 1353), etc. [For more recent translations of the Confessions, see G. Clark, *Confessions* (Cambridge, 1995) and F. J. Sheed, *Confessions*, 2 vols. (Indianapolis, 1993).] Etherius and Beatus, *Ad Elipandum* (PL, 96, 943 A). Rabanus Maurus (107, 318 A). Paschasius (120, 1306 B). Honorius (172, 1129 C). *Ep. IIIa contra Folmarum* (B.M.P., vol. 25, p. 313 H). Hugh of St. Victor (PL, 176, 465, 471 A–B). *Speculum Ecclesiae* (177, 365 A). Gerhoh (193, 883 A, 1054 D, 1051 B–C). Richard of St. Victor (196, 262 C–D). Innocent III (217, 866 D). William of Auxerre, *Summa aurea* (f° 259 r°). Bonaventure: *In cena Domini* (Q., vol. 9, p. 249); *Sermo de sanctissimo corpore* (vol. 5, p. 555); *Breviloq.* (p. 275). Albert the Great, *In IV Sent.*, d. 9, a. 2, 4. St. Thomas, *In IV Sent.*, d. 8, q. 1, a. 3; d. 9, a. 1; d. 12, q. 2, a. 1, sol. 1 (Moos, pp. 318, 364, 524; In Jo., c. 6, p. 3, n. 5; 7, n. 3. Urban IV, bull *Transiturus*. The *Summa* of Alexander, IVa, q. 10, m. 9, a. 1. Gerson, *De septem sacramentis* (Opera, 1706, vol. 1, p. 270). Erasmus in his commentary on John (Basle, 1535, pp. 76–7). The text of Augustine cited in the Roman Catechism, part II, *Liber de natura et dignante amoris*, c. 13, n. 38 (PL, 184, 403).

60 William of St. Thierry, *Liber de natura et dignitate amoris*, c. 13, n. 38 (PL, 184, 403).

61 Augustine, *Sermo 131* (PL, 38, 729); *De peccatorum meritis*, 1, c. 24, n. 34 (44, 128). Ambrose, *In psalmum 118*, sermo 18, n. 28 (15, 1462 B–C; cf. n. 14, 1457 D). Caesarius of Arles, *Sermo 187*, n. 1 (Morin, p. 723). Florus, *Expositio missae*, c. 73, n. 6, 7 (Duc, p. 148). Hincmar (PL, 125, 923 D). John of Fécamp (101, 1088 D, 1091 C). Ivo of Chartres (161, 151 A). *Glose in I Cor.* (114, 536 B). Algerius (180, 783 C). Gratian, *De consecratione*, d.2, c. 70 (Fr. 1341). Peter Lombard (191, 1623 D). Gerhoh (194, 1122 D). PL, 150, 421 D.

Our Lord Jesus Christ, who wishes to be fed by the ministry of his servants, that is, to transfer believers into his body as if they were sacrificed and eaten . . .[62]

There has been considerable scholastic development of this great theme, which is not without its analogies in patristic tradition,[63] and to which it would perhaps not be difficult to assign a Platonic origin,[64] but which adapted itself so marvellously to the facts of revelation. William of Auxerre was already commenting on Augustine with the applied distinctions of a method that feels as if it is in full possession of its means. He separates out the act of eating into four operations, of which some, in communion, should be attributed to Christ, and others to the communicant.[65] Let us leave these impoverished notions aside, in order to stay with what is essential in all its profound simplicity, and to contemplate it for another few moments. In the same way that, according to the traditional outline, the Word of God took on our mortal condition in order to make us participants in his divine condition, so too, in fulfilling his work, he becomes our food in order to absorb us into his body.[66] *When they eat, they are eaten, and when they are eaten, they eat . . . , I myself am their food.*[67] So that humanity should be able to eat the bread of angels, the King of the angels made himself human,[68] and as he had assumed our fragile body, now he

---

62　Augustine, *Quaestiones evangeliorum* (PL, 35, 1353). Paulinus of Nola, *Ep.* 23, n. 16, commenting on Judges 14.14 (61, 268 A–B). St. Leo, *Sermo* 63, c. 7 (54, 357), etc. cf. a different application of the same idea in Augustine, *In psalmum* 34, s. 2, n. 15 (PL, 36, 341).

63　Gregory of Nyssa, *In Cantica*, hom. 2 (PG, 44, 801 B). Jerome, *In psalmum* 182 (Morin, p. 248), and Augustine, *In psalmum* 122, n. 1 (PL, 37, 1630).

64　The soul which nourishes itself on what is Beautiful is assimilated by the Beautiful.

65　*Summa aurea*, 4 (f° 258 v°). cf. Bonaventure, d.12 p. 1, a. 3, q. 1 (Q., vol. 4, p. 284).

66　*In psalmum* 87, n. 3 (PL, 37, 1111). Etherius and Beatus (96, 938 C). Pseudo-Bede. *In Psalmum* 103 (93, 1010 D). Alcuin (MGH, *Epistularum*, vol. 4, p. 215). Ermenrich of Ellwangen (vol. 5, p. 539). Jesse, *Epistula de baptismo* (PL, 105, 791 B–C). Durandus of Troarn (149, 1398 C). *Glose in Joannem* (114, 384 D). Raoul of St. Germer, *In Leviticum* (B.M.P., vol. 17, p. 187 F), etc. cf. Gezonius of Tortona, after Hilary (PL, 137, 382–3). *Vitis mystica*, c. 4, n. 16 (184, 646 C). Pseudo-Bernard, *In feria 2a Pasch. sermo*, n. 22 (184, 978 C).

67　St. Bernard, *In Cantica*, sermo 71, n. 5 (PL, 183, 1123 B). Bruno of Segni (B.M.P., vol. 6, p. 676 C). Peter of Poitiers, *Allegoriae super Tabernaculum Moysi* (Moore-Corbett, p. 84). Wycliffe, *Sermonum*, p. 2, s. 61 (Loserth, pp. 455–7).

68　Augustine, *Sermo* 194, n. 2 (PL, 38, 1016). Prosper, *In psalmum* 110 (51, 322 A). Ceasarius, *Sermo* 202, n. 2 (Morin, p. 772). Pseudo-Bede, *In psalmum* 40 (PL, 93, 699 A). Remigius of Auxerre, *Enarrationes in psalmos* (131, 155 A–B,

assumes us into his immortal body.[69] Now, since he is the head of this unique body in which the communicants are also members, the incorporation of these members brings about at the same time the union of each one with the head and their union among themselves. In a word, it is '*the union of the body in the head*'.[70] Gerhoh of Reichersberg is therefore not betraying Augustine's thought, nor dogmatic truth itself, when he writes:

> *The entire Christ is eaten in the mystery of the altar. The eater does not change him into himself, that is, into food for his flesh; but he himself will be changed into him, so as to become a member of his body which is the one Church, redeemed and fed by the one body of Christ.*[71]

And the same truth is no less faithfully handed down by these words of Arnold of Bonneval:

> *We ourselves, when we become his body, are by the sacrament and the reality of the sacrament joined and united to our head, each one of us being members of one another . . .*[72]

* * *

Such, indissolubly, is the *reality and power of the sacrament*. We are not dealing here with a collage of concepts. The *reality* is *life* as it is *unity*, the *power* is *unity* as it is *life*. '*Let them be incorporated, that they might live*.'[73] In a phrase that once again comes from Augustine, Pseudo-Bede calls the Bread of Life '*the sweet food of unity*'.[74] Thanks to this Bread of Life, promised in chapter six of St. John's Gospel,

---

312 C). cf. Hériger (139, 188 A–B). Bonaventure, *In cena Domini*, sermo 1 (Q., vol. 9, p. 248).

69 Faustus of Riez, hom. *Magnitudo* (PL, 30, 276 A). Pseudo-Primasius, *In Hebr.* (68, 702 C).

70 Werner of St. Blaise (?), *Sermo in cena Domini* (PL, 157, 911 B). cf. *Sermo de ressurectione* (929 A).

71 *Epistola ad Adamum* (PL, 193, 497 C). cf. 504 A–B, with the observations of Eberhard of Bamberg.

72 *Liber de cardinalibus operibus Christi* (PL, 189, 1649 D). William of Auvergne, *De sacramento eucharistiae*, c. 4 (*Opera*, 1574, vol. 1, pp. 441–2).

73 Augustine, *In joannem*, tract. 26, n. 13 (PL, 35, 1613); *In psalmum 26*, sermo 2, n. 2 (36, 200). *Ad Monimum*, l. 2, c. 10 (65, 188–90).

74 Pseudo-Bede, *In psalmum 68* (PL, 93, 848 D). Augustine, *In psalmum 68*, n. 6 (36, 859).

the '*one bread, one body*' from the First Letter of the Corinthians is brought into effect. This is because spiritual life is a social unity:

> *That power which is understood to be referred to here is unity, so that, gathered into his body and made his members, we are what we receive.*[75]

The principle of this life is none other than the Spirit of Christ, which is a Spirit of unity, in such a way that to live in the body of Christ is to be nourished by his Spirit.[76] Is this not once again the teaching contained in the farewell discourse of Saint John?[77] Starting with the allegory of the vine and finishing with the priestly prayer, nothing could better suggest that the intimacy of the communicant with Christ is a broadening of the dimensions of the Church. – There is no inter-changeability of expression here. Developed by St. Paul, St. John's doctrine is no less developed by himself, if it is true that the allegory of the vine and the whole narrative of that last night are no less Eucharistic than the foretelling of the Bread of Life. Had not St. Paul, for his part, also recalled the manna, the 'spiritual food' of the Hebrews in the desert? And was he not once again offering another means of bringing together the two viewpoints when, in speaking of another 'great mystery', he evoked the union of Christ and the Church, a union so intimate that the two now formed only one flesh?[78] *One bread, one flesh* . . .

This last characteristic must have been all the more striking because St. John himself, in his own way – demonstrated at Calvary, and at the site of the first paradise – the marriage of Christ and his Church, the new Adam and the new Eve . . . It could be further observed, by exploiting the Pauline symbolism of the *one bread*, that in the making of the dough, water plays the indispensable role of binding: *stuck together with water.*[79] Now, was this water not that of baptism,[80] which in fact

---

75 Augustine, *Sermo* 57 (PL, 38, 389); *Epistula* 185 (33, 815). Honorius of Autun, *Eucharistion*, c. 4 (172, 1252 B).

76 Augustine, *In Joannem*, tract. 27, n. 11 (PL, 35, 1621); cf. n. 6 (1618). Rabanus Maurus (107, 318 B). Algerius (180, 885 D).

77 The bond between the Last Supper of the Synoptics and the last discourse of John is noted, for example, in Manegold, *Contra Wolfelmum* (PL, 155, 166 B).

78 Augustine, *Sermo Denis* 3, n. 4 (Morin, p. 20); *In psalmum 127* (37, 1679), etc. Chrysostom, *In Matthaeum*, hom. 82, n. 5 (PG, 58, 743–4). Paschasius (PL, 120, 1286 A, 1304 B). Hériger (139, 186 A). *Glose in Ephes.* (114, 599 B).

79 Walafrid Strabo, *De rebus ecclesiasticis*, c. 16 (PL, 114, 936).

80 Augustine, *Sermo* 229 (PL, 38, 1103). Maximus of Turin, *Homilia 111* (57, 513–14). Caesarius of Arles (67, 1055–6). Faustus of Riez (30, 275). Isidore (83, 321 C, 323 D). Etherius and Beatus (96, 938 B). *Liber mozarabicus sacra-*

begins the work of unity that the Eucharist is meant to deepen?[81] From the time of St. Irenaeus,[82] the teaching of St. Paul had begun to receive this commentary, an image, it is true, but an authentic one, and St. Augustine enjoyed imprinting it on the minds of his neophytes. *We are all made into one bread, the Lord's bread.*[83] The correspondence of the symbols did not stop there. For was it not again St. John who showed this baptismal water flowing with the blood – a symbol of the Eucharist – from the side of Jesus pierced with the lance?[84] *What is drunk is what flowed from the side of Christ.*[85] The liturgies did not fail to recall it, at the moment when the priest mingles the water with the wine in the chalice.[86] Now, was not this mystical mingling at the same time a figure, as St. Cyprian had for a long time explained,[87] of

---

mentorum (F., p. 638). Bede (PL, 91, 334 A; 92, 595). Amalarius (105, 1131 B). Rabanus Maurus (107, 320 B; 108, 257 A; 111, 131–2; 112, 94–5). Walafrid Strabo (114, 936 C). Paschasius (120, 830–1, 1332). Remigius of Auxerre (131, 260 A). Peter Damian, Sermo 38 (144, 709 A–B). Durandus of Troarn (149, 1414 C–D). Guitmond (149, 1460). Ivo of Chartres (161, 135; 162, 543 C). Anselm of Laon (162, 1471 A). Franco (166, 777). Algerius (180, 794 D). Honorius (172, 554 C), 790 D, 1256 C, etc.). Gilbert the Universal (Smalley, *Recherches* . . . , 1936, p. 57). Commentary of Abelard on 1 Cor., x (L., vol. 2, p. 259). Hervé (PL, 181, 917 C). Gratian, *De consecratione*, d. 2, c. 36 (Fr., 1326). Master Simon (W., pp. 27–8). *Madrid Treatise* (W., p. 91). School of Laon, *De corpore Domini* (W., p. cxxxviii). Sicard of Cremona (PL, 213, 117), etc.

81 Fulgentius, *Ep. 12*, n. 24 (PL, 65, 390–1).

82 *Adv. Haer.*, 3, c. 17, n. 2 (PG, 7, 930). cf. I Cor., 12.13.

83 Augustine, *Sermo 6* (PL, 46, 835). *Sermones 227, 272* (38, 1110, 1247), etc.

84 Augustine, *In Joannem*, tract. 11, n. 4 (PL, 35, 1477); tract. 45, n. 9 (1723); *Sermo Wilmart 5* (Morin, p. 687). Hesychius (Pseudo-Athanasius), *In psalmum 136* (PG, 27, 1272 B). Jerome, *In psalmum 105* (M., p. 174). Pseudo-Primasius, *In Hebr.* (PL, 68, 769 B). Remigius of Auxerre (131, 225 C, 715 A). Atto of Vercelli, *In Hebr.* (134, 809 D), etc. cf. Chrysostom, *In Hebr.* (PG, 63, 124).

85 Ambrose, *In Lucam*, 10, n. 135 (PL, 15, 1838 C). Pseudo-Ambrose, *De sacramentis* (16, 447 A–B). Augustine, *Contra Faustum* (42, 265). Cyril of Alexandria, *In I Cor.*, x, fragm. (PG, 74, 880 B–C). Hesychius, In psalmum 35 (93, 1189 C). *Historia mystagogica* (*Journal of Theological Studies* 9, p. 264). *Liber sive definitio ecclesiasticorum dogmatum*, c. 41 (*ibid.*, vol. 7, p. 97). Faustus of Riez (PL, 30, 274 B–C). Rabanus Maurus (107, 320 A). Florus, *Expositio missae* (Duc, p. 136). Pseudo-Augustine, *Ad neophytos*, cited by Paschasius (120, 1352 C, 1354 A, 1355 A). Hincmar (125, 927–8). John of Fécamp (101, 1091 A). Rupert (169, 520 D). Werner of St. Blaise (157, 910 D). Honorius (172, 555 A). Hugh of St. Victor, *De sacramentis* (176, 425 D). Herman, *Epitome* (178, 1742 A). *Speculum Ecclesiae* (177, 367 C–D). Hervé (181, 935 C). Anselm of Havelberg (188, 1243 B–C). Peter of Blois (207, 1145 B–C). Sicard of Crémone (213, 117, 146). Stephen Langton (Geiselmann, *Die Abendmahlslehre* . . . , p. 85), etc.

86 Ambrosian, Gallican, Mozarabic liturgies.

87 *Ep. 63* (Bayard, vol. 2, pp. 205–8). The two explanations are given by Pseudo-Germain of Paris (PL, 72, 93 B). Also by Theodulphus of Orléans, *Liber de ordine baptismi*, c. 18 (105, 240), by the Council of Tribur in 895, canon 19 (Mansi, vol. 8, 131) etc.

the necessary union of Christ and the Christian people ransomed by the Passion of Christ in the sacrifice of the Church?[88] *Whoever separates the water, denies the union of Christ and the Church.*[89] Since each was necessary, on Calvary, to found the Church, the blood and the water each remain equally necessary in order to bring about our salvation.[90] This is the origin of the necessity of the water and the wine for the sacrament,[91] a necessity underlined in its own turn by the most recent liturgical prayers.[92]

Another text of St. John, this time taken from the Apocalypse, established by uniting it the double symbolism attached to the sacramental water. '*Many waters, many peoples*', the Apostle had written,[93] and so also seemed to be the complex meaning of the prophecy of the Psalmist: '*He drew me out of many waters.*'[94] Anselm of Laon could therefore write, in his commentary on St. Matthew:

Because we ought to remain in Christ and Christ in us, the wine of the Lord's chalice is to be mixed with water. For as John testifies, the waters are the peoples, and therefore no one may offer water

---

88 Faustus of Riez (PL, 30, 274–5). Fourth council of Braga, canon 2 (Mansi, vol. 9, 155–6). Etherius and Beatus (96, 941 B–D). Alcuin (MGH, *Epistularum*, vol. 4, p. 212). Rabanus Maurus (107, 320 A–B). Amalarius (105, 1131 A). Paschasius (120, 1308, 1353). Christian of Stavelot (106, 1477 A). Strabo (114, 903 C, 936 D). *Expositio 'Spiritus sancti'* (147, 202 B). Haimon, *Homilia 64* (118, 363–4). Réginon de Prüm (132, 204–5). Burchard (140, 752). Ivo of Chartres (161, 163 A–D), 1079 A–B). Anselm of Laon (159, 255 C). *Sententiae Anselmi* (Bl., p. 116). Gilbert the Universal (Smalley, p. 58). Commentary of Abelard, *In I Cor.*, x (Landgraf, vol. 2, p. 258). Humbert, *Contra Nicetam*, c. 19 (PL, 143, 991 B). Honorius (PL, 172, 556 A, 557–8, 1256 D). Stephen of Baugé (172, 1285 A). Otho of Lucques (176, 145). *Sermo de excellentia* (184, 988). Robert Puyllen (186, 963 B). Gratian, *De consecratione*, 2.7 (Fr., 1316). Anselm of Hevelberg (188, 1242 B). Peter Lombard (191, 1642–3). Master Simon (W., p. 29). *Madrid Treatise* (W., p. 91). Peter Comestor (M., pp. 38–9). Peter of Blois (PL, 207, 1144–5), etc. cf. St. Thomas, *In IV Sent.*, d. 8, q. 1, a. 2 (Moos, p. 314).

89 *Speculum Ecclesiae* (PL, 177, 367 C). Algerius (180, 795–6, 820).

90 Pseudo-Haimon, *In Isaiam* (PL, 116, 1034 A); *Homilia 64* (118, 363–4). cf. Vincent of Beauvais, *Miroir historique*, 8, c. 29.

91 Burchard (PL, 140, 753). cf. Pseudo-Isidore (83, 1227, 1242 B).

92 cf. Grancolas, *Les anciennes liturgies*, vol. 1 (1697), p. 553, following *Notes sur la liturgie de saint Pierre de Lindanus*.

93 Rev., 17.15. Hilary, *In psalmum 123*, m. 5, 124, n. 1, etc. (Zingerle, pp. 593, 596); and *Treatise on the Mysteries*, 1, 34 (Ps. 76, 17; 46, 2; 97, 8) (Brisson, p. 131).

94 *Brevarium in psalmos* (PL, 26, 867 A–B). Cassiodore, *In psalmum 17* (PL, 70, 129 A). Haimon (116, 249 A). Remigius of Auxerre (131, 225 C). Bruno of Wurzburg (142, 94 B). Bruno of Chartreux (152, 701 C–D). Peter Lombard (191, 194 D).

alone nor wine alone, just as one cannot offer a grain of wheat on its own without mixing water and making it into bread, lest such an offering should signify that the head could be separated from the members.[95]

Note the force of this last formulation, which shows us again the sacrifice of the Church – of each one of us – inseparable from now on, in right as in fact, from the sacrifice of Christ. Thus the consideration of the water in its double relationship to the Eucharistic mystery – the mystery of the Passion and the mystery of the Church, the mystery of the body torn apart and the mystery of the unified body – opened one more route by which it was possible to see rejoined the idea of *power* and the idea of *matter*, the idea of the most intimate union to the Saviour and the idea of the social building up of the Church, the idea of the union of the Church with Christ and the idea of the union of the members of Christ among themselves: *one flesh, one body . . .*

One bread, one body. One flesh, one body. It is all of this, in the end, it is all these facts of the tradition, it is all this mystical interlinking, which is condensed in the brief formulation: '*mystical flesh, unity of the Church*'. Through an artificial alliance, it heals an amputation that was no less artificial. Was Peter Lombard not aware of it? That seems to be implied by the way in which he so abundantly quotes, in his commentary on St. Paul, texts in which St. Augustine unites the two words *body* and *flesh*, and passes from the metaphor of the body and of the head to that of the husband and his wife.[96] Not everyone followed him in this. Soon Robert of Melun, commenting himself on St. Paul, would raise a protest against his eclecticism.[97] Representing what could be called (we understand in which sense) strict Pauline orthodoxy, without the mixture of any Johannine elements, Robert only wants to see in the *matter of the sacrament* the unity of the Church. As for the mingling of the water and wine in the chalice, he refuses to recognize, despite the ancient tradition, any allusion to the scene described by St. John: if it is to be believed, that mingling symbolizes nothing other than the uniting of the Gentiles to the Jews in the founding of the

---

95 *In Matthaeum*, c. 26 (PL, 162, 1471 A). cf. Peter Cantor, *Suma de sacramentis, de eucharistia*, q.21 (Dumoutet, *Archives d'histoire literature et doctrinale du moyen âge*, vol. 14, p. 249).

96 *In Ephes.* (PL, 192, 215–16). See Augustine, *In psalmum 138*. Ambrose, *In Lucam*, 5, n. 92 (PL, 15, 1661 A); 8, n. 26 (1773 A).

97 *Quaestiones de epistulis Pauli* (Martin, p. 211). cf. J. de Ghellinck, *Mélanges Baeumker*, vol. 1, p. 79.

Church.[98] Our Lombard saw it more accurately. But let us not exaggerate his merit in the case. Before him, others had known how to use the same shortcut in order to unite the two viewpoints that have been mentioned; thus Odo of Cluny, in this short poem that Gezon of Tortona inserts in the preface to his *Liber de Corpore*:

> . . . *And so we rejoice in this rite by which from the many there comes one, and whence the body cleaves to this head, and the head to the body . . .*[99]

Like him, many authors had quoted and commented on the principal texts of the tradition, above all those of St. Augustine. Better than he, many had taken close inspiration from the great Doctor. With a minimal care for harmonization of the words, they had sometimes reproduced more felicitously something of his rhythm. For thought, William of St. Thierry, Algerius of Liège,[100] Hugh of St. Victor[101] are superior to him, and it is for them above all that, in a history of doctrine, a place must be made. Peter the Venerable, Gerhoh of Reichersberg should also claim our attention. The master of the Sentences is above all an 'intelligent compiler'. He resumes, he co-ordinates, and his work appears rather like marquetry. But in this task of modest order, that led to such great success, 'he is not lacking in clairvoyance; in more than one point, a detailed study of his text allows us to discover in a tiny addition, in the changing of a word, or in the substitution of a preposition, a genuine originality of thought or of formulation, where an initial reading might only have led us to see a copyist'.[102] This judgement of Father de Ghellinck would appear to confirm the case that we have just examined.

The language of Lombard nevertheless only represents a transition. This is because the unity of the Church was, despite everything, more naturally expressed by the metaphor of the body than by the metaphor of the flesh. Thus it is that Master Simon's formulation was the one with a future. And this was all the more so because, by its origins,

---

98 cf. Baldwin of Canterbury (PL, 204, 772 B), etc.

99 PL, 137, 376 A.

100 See *De sacramentis*, 1, c. 3, 15, 19, 22 (PL, 180, 749–51, 783, 794–5, 806; 794 C, 823 A–B).

101 *De sacramentis*, 2, p. 8 (PL, 176, 465); 1, p. 10, c. 9 (342 D), etc.

102 J. de Ghellinck, 'L'histoire de la définition des sacraments au XIIe siècle', in *Mélanges Mandonnet*, vol. 2, p. 96; see also *L'essoir de la littérature latine au XIIe siècle*, vol. 1, pp. 70–3. cf. H. Weisweiler, *Recherches de théologie ancienne et médiévale*, 1934, pp. 161–80.

which made it strictly connected to the '*power of the sacrament*', *mystical flesh* would remain linked to the context of the Eucharist, while *mystical body*, now describing a '*reality signified and not contained*',[103] would easily detach itself from it.

---

103 See *infra*, Chapter 10, n. 124–8.

9

'Truth and Truth'

[210]

From the *mystical body* of Hesychius or Paschasius Radbertus to the *mystical body* of Boniface VIII, the distance is so great that the two expressions seem to bear no relationship whatsoever. Historically, the second is nevertheless derived from the first. Each of these two 'bodies', the ecclesial and the sacramental, successively acquired the same adjective in relation and in opposition to the other. – But how, ultimately, can such a '*total conversion*' be explained?

However widespread it was for a period of time, *mystical body* seems never to have been used in the liturgy, at least in the West.[1] Despite the prolonged success of Hesychius's translation, in which it appeared, and despite the prestige bestowed on it by the usurped authority of St. Augustine, this constituted a serious weakness. Consequently it gave way by degrees before a rival expression: *true body*, that the natural development of doctrine and the after-effects of controversies were making increasingly dominant.

* * *

Of course it had been well known for a long time, in fact since the beginning, and if necessary it was remembered in explicit terms, that the sacramental body was the *true body*,[2] the *true flesh*,[3] the *true flesh and blood*.[4] The *true body and blood of the Lord*[5] were confessions

---

1 For the East, one can cite the Syriac liturgy of James of Sarug (start of the fourth century). Renaudot explains, *Liturgiarum orientalium collectio*, 2nd edn., vol. 2, pp. 360, 370.

2 Faustus of Riez (PL, 30, 273 B). Braulio of Saragossa (80, 690 A). Pseudo-Bede, *In psalmos* (93, 597 D). Hincmar, *De praedestinatione*, c. 31 (125, 296 D). Bruno of Angers (147, 1203 A), etc. cf. Ambrose, *De sacramentis* (16, 445 A).

3 Ambrose, *De sacramentis* (PL, 16, 453–4; cf. Ivo of Chartres, 161, 147 A, B). *De 42 mansionibus filiorum Israel* (17, 20 C). *Brevarium in psalmos* (32, 1250–1). cf. Ambrose, *De mysteriis* (16, 407 A).

4 Hilary, *De Trinitate*, 8, c. 13 (PL, 10, 246). Jerome, *In psalmum 145* (Morin, *Analecta Maredsolana*, vol. 3, p. 3, p. 290). Coptic, Ethiopian, Armenian liturgies.

5 Hilary, *loc. cit.*, c. 14 (PL, 10, 247 A); cited again by Eberhard of Bamberg

of faith. It was claimed that in the holy mysteries Christ himself was present *in truth*,[6] and that his body and blood were received there *according to the truth*.[7] Already these declarations were becoming more insistent, in the ninth century, under the authorship of Paschasius Radbertus[8] and of Hincmar.[9] Nevertheless, in the language inherited from ancient Christianity, a fusion of the Hebrew Bible and of Platonism,[10] the words *true* and *truth* evoked spontaneously, in a number of cases, something quite other than the simple 'truth' of our current speech: a plenitude, a perfection of being, a spiritual completion which, in the case of the Eucharist, could in fact denote nothing other than the third and final of the 'bodies' distinguished in common usage.

Body, spirit, truth: on the other hand there was an intimate connection between these three words. What the body was to the shadow, the spirit was to the letter, the truth was to the figure.[11] *Bodily, spiritually, truly*: three adverbs that a whole series of texts shows us to belong in the one equation.[12] Sometimes other equivalents are added to them, which help us to a better understanding of their sense, such as the bar-

(PL, 193, 503 C). Muratorian Canon. Jerome, *In Matthaeum*, (PL, 26, 195 B). Leo, *Sermo 91*, c. 3; *Ep. 39*, c. 2 (54, 452 B). Ivo of Chartres, *Decretum*, p. 2, c. 4 (161, 139 B), and c. 9 (156 C). cf. St. Bernard, *Life of Saint Malachi*, c. 26, n. 57 (182, 1105 D).

6 *Libri Carolini*, 4, c. 14 (PL, 98, 1214 C–D). Nicholas I, *Ep.* 4 (119, 778 D). Remigius of Auxerre, *De celebratione missae* (101, 1260 D and 1261 B). *In I Cor.* and *In Hebr.* (117, 564 B, 572 D, 874 D, 886 C). cf. Isaac of Antioch, *Sermo de fide* (Assemani, vol. 1, p. 222). Coptic Liturgy (cf. Le Brun, *Explication des ceremonies de la messe*, new edn., vol. 2, 1860, p. 435).

7 Macarius Magnes, 3, c. 23 (Blondel, p. 106, cf. p. 103). Hesychius, *In Leviticum*, 6, c. 22 (PG, 93, 1071 B).

8 *Liber de corpore*, passim (PL, 120, 1274, 1277–81, 1356–7, etc.). *In Matthaeum* (890 C and D). Florus (119, 85 A).

9 *De praedestinatione dissertation posterior*, c. 31 (PL, 125, 296); *Vita Remigii* (MGH, *Script. rerum meroving.*, vol. 3, p. 334), etc.

10 Already the Johannine notion of ἀλήθεία, which is a translation of the Hebrew concept of 'eMeT (= α and ω, containing the double idea of solidity and plenitude). cf. St. Thomas, *In Joannem*, c. 6, l.4, n. 1.

11 Jerome, *Ep. 149*, n. 1 (Hilberg, vol. 3, p. 357). John Scotus, *In Joannem*, frag. 2 (PL, 122, 320 A–B); frag. 1 (310 B). Paschasius Radbertus (120, 1280 B). Auxerre Commentary, *In Coloss.* (117, 757 B). Atto of Vercelli (134, 623 A–B and 823 C). *Glose in Coloss.* (114, 613 A). Hervé (181, 1335 D). School of Abelard, *In Rom.* (Landgraf, p. 90), etc.

12 Augustine, *De Genesi ad litteram*, 12, c. 7, n. 17 (PL, 34, 459). Prosper, *Liber sententiarum*, s. 295 (51, 471 C). John Scotus, *In prologum Joannis* and *In Joannem*, frag 1 (122, 296 D and 299 C). *Libri Carolini*, 1, c. 19 (98, 1048 B). Hervé (181, 1331 A, C–D).

barous *completely*[13] and *fully.*[14] *The body, that is, the fullness.*[15] *The body, that is, the solid truth.*[16] *Not a shadow but the truth, not a figure but the fullness.*[17] *The body, that is, the truth of the thing . . .*[18] Given that the Eucharistic mystery was thought of as a spiritual meal destined to bring about the fulfilment of that body or of that 'plenitude of Christ', which constitutes the Church, it was doubly natural that the effect of such a mystery should be equally thought of as its 'truth', at the same time as its 'matter': *truth and matter, of matters, the truth.* We recall how Origen had already opposed, in a contrast that would often be poorly understood, the *body as a type* (σῶμα τυπικόν) and the *true body* (σῶμα ἀληθινόν),[19] for which the Christian would continue to hunger until the *fulfillment of the Passover.*[20] St. Ambrose had gone on to speak of the sacrifice of the altar as an offering 'in image' whose 'true nature' dwelt in the heavens.[21] Commenting on Pseudo-Dionysius's *Ecclesiastic Hierarchy*, St. Maximus had in the same way noted: 'Throughout he speaks of the divine liturgy and of the holy gifts as symbols of heavenly things whose true nature dwells above.'[22] St. Augustine had said: '*What is visibly received in the sacrament, should be eaten and drunk spiritually in truth*',[23] and again: '*They originally*

---

13 Pseudo-Primasius, *In Coloss.* (PL, 68, 653 C, cf. 655 B).

14 Auxerre Commentary, *In Coloss.* (PL, 117, 755 C–D).

15 Auxerre Commentary, *In Ephes.* (PL, 117, 707 B cf. 716 D, 720 D). Rupert, *In Joannem* (169, 483 A). William of St. Thierry (180, 357 D). Hervé (181, 1219 B), after Augustine, *In psalmum* 67, n. 23 (36, 828).

16 Hervé, *In Coloss.* (PL, 181, 1335 D). cf. Etherius and Beatus, *Ad Elipandum*, 2, c. 53 (96, 1008), following Augustine, *In psalmum 67* (36, 828).

17 Gregory of Elvira (Tractatus Origenis, tract. 8; Batiffol Wilmart, p. 95). Ambrose, *In Lucam*, 7, n. 96 (PL, 15, 1724 B). Jerome, *Ep.* 121, n. 10 (Hilberg, vol. 3, p. 44). Amalarius, *De ecclesiasticis officiis*, 3, c. 11 (PL, 105, 1119 A; cf. c. 19, 1128 A–B). Again Bossuet, *Second écrit sur le livre des Maximes*, n. 17; Lachat, vol. 19, p. 387.

18 Sedulius Scottus, *In Coloss.*, II (PL, 103, 227 C).

19 *In Matthaeum*, vol. 9, n. 14 (Klostermann, p. 58). The two epithets of Origen would be often taken again in a very different direction. Therefore, Alexander Natalis, *Dissertatio de fide christianorum decimi saeculi circa eucharistiam* (Zaccaria, *Thesaurus theologicus*, vol. 10, p. 947). cf. *Perpetuity* (Migne, vol. 2. 851).

20 *In Matthaeum series*, n. 86 (Klostermann, p. 198). cf. Luke 22.15–16.

21 *In psalmum 38*, n. 25 (PL, 14, 1051 1052). *De officiis ministrorum*, 1, c. 48, n. 238 (16, 97 A).

22 *Scholia in eccl. Hiérarch.*, c. 3, 3, 12 (PG, 4, 149 C).

23 *Sermo 131*, n. 1 (PL, 37, 729 = *De verbis apostoli*, s.2); cited by Algerius (180, 798 C), Gratian, *De consecratione*, 2.58 (Friedberg, 1336), etc. The same distinction and use of *verum* regarding miracle; thus *Sermo 98* (PL, 38, 592: *de verbis Domini*, s. 44).

received the sacrament of Christ's body in the true body of Christ.'[24]
A faithful imitator of the great African Doctor in language as in
thought, St. Fulgentius of Ruspe, writing against Fabian, had in his
own turn said: '*By the gift of charity there is conferred on us to be in
truth that which we celebrate mystically in the sacrifice*',[25] and also,
more subtly: '*Not only according to the mysteries of the truth, but
according to the truth of the mystery.'*[26]

Now, this was not some more or less esoteric language among
learned theologians. It was the language of the liturgy itself. A prayer
from the Leonine sacramentary runs as follows:

> *By receiving the pledge of the heavenly secret, and being while yet
> on earth filled with the bread from above, we pray you, Lord, in
> response to the prayers of your servants, that what is mystically
> performed in us may be truly accomplished.*[27]

Notice that opposition of *mystical–true*, which is identical to the one
found in Fulgentius's *Fragment against Fabian*. In what was originally
envisaged as the order of the Eucharistic action, it corresponds to
the opposition between the *mystical* (sacramental) *body* and the *true*
(ecclesial) *body*. The Gelasian[28] and Gregorian[29] sacramentaries contain a similar prayer, which used to be attributed to St. Gregory the
Great, and still figures today in the Roman Missal:[30]

> *May your sacraments, Lord, accomplish in us what they contain,
> so that which we now perform in appearance we may obtain in the
> truth of the realities.*

Those final words would frequently be quoted, commented on and
debated throughout the Middle Ages, starting with Ratramnus, who
thought he had found within them a proof for his doctrine.[31] Gregory
of Bergamo would give this formal definition of them: '*What is called
the truth of the realities is the accomplishment of the realities to be*

---

24 *De civitate Dei*, 21, c. 25, n. 3 (PL, 41, 742).
25 *Contra Fabianum*, frag. 28 (PL, 65, 790 A).
26 *Ep. 12*, n. 24 (PL, 65, 390 C).
27 Feltoe, p. 3.
28 Wilson, p. 202.
29 Lietzmann, p. 95.
30 Saturday of the Ember Days of September, postcommunion [From the
Missale Romanum that pre-dates the revisions of 1970 and later.] Note the
resemblance with Origen, *In Jesu Nave*, hom. 8, n. 4 (trans. of Rufinus: Baehrens,
p. 339).
31 *De corpore et sanguine Domini*, c. 85-8 (PL, 121, 160-5).

effected', in order then to go on and specify their concrete content: '*the mystery of our peace and indissoluble union*'.[32] With equal prudence, Guitmond of Aversa had explained: '*Let us obtain it in the truth of the realities, that is, let us in true reality be the one body of Christ and the one Church.*'[33] St. Peter Damian prayed in similar terms:

> *O God, who deigned to give us a pledge of eternal salvation, grant to us . . . to attain to the fullness of the same truth.*[34]

Despite the numerous and profound modifications that will need stating further on, it is still possible to collect examples of this ancient language throughout the whole of the twelfth century, which would only gradually disappear. Hugh of St. Victor,[35] soon followed, as usual, by the author of the *Speculum Ecclesiae*,[36] speaks of the grace of the sacrament as the *truth* of which the species are the sign, at the same time as of the *power* of which the flesh and the blood of Christ are the source. As we saw in the last chapter, Peter Lombard identifies in two passages the *unity of the faithful* or the *unity of the Church* with the *spiritual flesh* or the *mystical flesh* in which, according to him, the *matter of the sacrament* consists. He immediately adds that this is what tradition, along with the liturgy itself, calls *truth*:

> *(Augustine) says here that the sacrament is the proper body of Christ, taken from the Virgin, and that the reality is the spiritual flesh of Christ . . . They who eat spiritually, are said to receive the truth of the flesh and blood . . .*[37]
>
> *A good person . . . receives the sacrament, that is, the proper flesh and blood of Christ, and the reality, that is, the union of the faithful and the increase of grace. But a wicked person receives the sacrament, that is, the body of Christ under the sacrament, but not the reality, that is, the unity of the Church. In other words: the good person eats spiritually and sacramentally, but a bad person only sacramentally . . . A collect seems to relate to this: 'May they accomplish, etc.', that is, just as we receive the flesh of Christ under the sacramental appearance, so may we receive the flesh of Christ in the truth of the reality, that is, spiritually.*[38]

---

32 *De veritate corporis*, c. 10 and 11 (H., pp. 42, 44).
33 Bk. 2 (PL, 149, 1468 B).
34 PL, 145, 953 D. *Gelasianum* (W., p. 252).
35 *De sacramentis*, 2, p. 8, c. 8 (PL, 176, 467).
36 c. 7 (PL, 177, 365).
37 *Sentences*, 4, d. 9, c. 3 (PL, 192, 859).
38 *In I Cor.* (PL, 191, 1643).

Some years later, Master Simon would again write: '*to proceed to the truth of this body*'.[39] Following on as they do, in the same paragraph, from the sentence where the Eucharist and the Church are respectively named *true body* and *mystical body*, these words from then on assumed something of a paradoxical significance. In Peter Lombard we have a mixture of ancient terminology and new explanations: here it is the two terminologies, both the old and the new, that are placed in juxtaposition. But the formulation was not Master Simon's invention. We can read it as well in Arnold of Bonneval:

> *Just as in the person of Christ the humanity was seen and the divinity was hidden; so the divine essence poured itself ineffably into the visible sacrament, so that religion should include devotion round the sacraments, and also that there should be a more full access to the truth whose body and blood the sacraments are.*[40]

Lastly, in a sermon addressed to the clergy, Peter Comestor says:

> *Be cleansed, you who offer the victim of the Lord. Be cleansed, you who administer to others the body of the Lord; so that, having been cleansed, what you now perform in likeness you may one day obtain in the truth of the realities.*[41]

In all of these texts we can recognize the vocabulary of our 'scriptural sphere', where, according to the Christian understanding of allegory sketched out in St. Paul and the Epistle to the Hebrews, events and things, acts and persons, in their very reality, whether historical or substantial, are the figures of spiritual realities which alone participate in the pure and definitive Truth of the Logos by integrating the fullness of his Body.[42] The words in which the relationship of Israel to Christ or of Christ himself, in his earthly state, to his eternal 'Pleroma' were traditionally expressed, serve here to define the relationship of the sacrament to its end.

Now, there is one initial observation that needs to be made about

---

39 *Tractatus de sacramentis* (W., p. 28).

40 *Liber de cardinalibus operibus Christi* (PL, 189, 1643-4).

41 Pseudo-Hildebert, *Sermo 93* (PL, 171, 776 A).

42 cf. Cyril of Alexandria, *Contra Julianum*, 10 (PG, 76, 1029 C, 1044 C, 1048 A–B); see also *In Joannem*, 4, c. 2 (73, 561 A). cf. Epiphanius, *Haeresis 8*, c. 7 (41, 216 A–B). [For the work of Epiphanius against the heresies in English, see the translation of F. Wiliams, *The Panarion of Epiphanius of Salamis* (Leiden, 1987–94) in the *Nag Hammadi Studies* series, vols. 35–6.] Hilary, *De Trinitate* (PL, 10, 139). Ambrose, *In Lucam* (15, 1542 C), etc.

this parallel. Although he is the true Isaac and the true Moses, Christ does not for all that make the historical Moses or Isaac unreal. In saying of him that he is David 'in substance',[43] there is no suggestion that the founder of the Judaean monarchy was nothing but a ghost. Nor, when she claims to be the true Israel according to the spirit, is the Church attempting to persuade us that the Israel according to the flesh was nothing but a myth. The earthly Jerusalem *'was type, not truth'*:[44] but this does not mean that it was not a real city . . .[45] And when St. Augustine[46] and St. Jerome[47] teach us that the acts of our Saviour, his life, death and resurrection are the 'sacraments of the inner person', when they tell us that all his actions were 'mystical' and that it is within us that they must find their truth, these Fathers are obviously not denying either their historicity or their eminent spiritual value. In the same way, therefore, the claim that the 'true body' is the Church does not permit us to doubt the reality of the body 'as a type' or the 'mystical' body that is its figure or its sacrament. Hugh of St. Victor, following Guitmond of Aversa, observed of this that:

> *What then? Is the sacrament of the altar not truth because it is figure? Then neither is the death of Christ truth; and the resurrection of Christ is not truth, because it is figure. For the Apostle openly declares that both the death of Christ and his resurrection are figure, image, likeness, sacrament, and model . . .*[48]

* * *

But there is often more, in our texts, than an implicit parallel or a transposition. There is more than the borrowing of language initially formed with another object in view. The Eucharist *in itself*, and not only in its effects, is very often described by words that normally serve to designate the New Testament. This is because it is considered explicitly as

---

43 Pseudo-Bede, *In psalmum 27* (PL, 93, 619 C). cf. Severus of Antioch, *Contra impium grammaticum* (Tr. Lebon, p. 208), etc.

44 Jerome, *In Jeremiam* (PL, 24, 874 B). Augustine (36, 959), etc.

45 Nothing is more current than this turn of language. Some more examples. Irenaeus, *Adv. Haer.* (PG, 7, 1057 B, 1064 C). Pseudo-Chrysostom (55, 602). Rabanus Maurus, *De clericorum institutione* (PL, 107). Pseudo-Bede, *In psalmum 33* (93, 655 B). Ivo of Chartres, *Sermon for Epiphanius* (162, 575). Herbert Losinga, *Sermo 2* (G.-S., p. 56). Joachim of Flora, *In Jo.*, iv (Fournier, p. 10, n. 4).

46 *De Trinitate*, 4, c. 3, n. 6 (PL, 42, 891–2). *Enchiridion*, c. 53 (40, 257). *De spiritu et littera*, c. 6, n. 10 (44, 206). cf. Braulio of Saragossa (80, 661 D). Amalarius (105, 1022 D). Remigius of Auxerre (101, 1253 C).

47 *Tractatus in Marcum* (Morin, p. 355).

48 *De sacramentis*, 2, p. 8, c. 6 (PL, 176, 466). Guitmond, 2 (149, 1457). cf. Bessarion, *De sacramento eucharistiae* (PG, 161, 498 A–B).

forming part of the New Testament, or even as constituting its very heart. *The blood of Christ, the new covenant.*[49] The Eucharist is *par excellence* the *mystery of Christ*, the *mystery of Christians*, in which the entire 'fullness of the Gospels' is contained. In its riches it sums up everything that St. Paul, in the Letter to the Ephesians, encapsulated in the single word 'mystery', that is to say the totality of God's plans for the world revealed and realised in Christ.[50]

Now, according to the whole of tradition, there were two ways of envisaging the revelation of the New Testament: either as the definitive truth succeeding the preparations and figures of the Old Testament, or as the intermediate state between the shadows of long ago and the full light of eternity. We can expect, therefore, to meet two further new series of texts, in which the Eucharist will be envisaged according to each of these points of view in turn.

When Ambrose, for example, tells us that today, in the Church, Christ is offered 'in representation',[51] let us not imagine that he is only alluding to the rites of the Mass which symbolically recall the real sacrifice of Calvary; and even less, that he is in some sense denying the sacrificial value of these rites or the hidden completion of which they are the forerunners. His intention is not focused on the commemoration of the cross, but in the opposite sense, at the anticipation or the reflection of heaven.[52] The mystery of the altar is accomplished 'in representation', as are all the mysteries of our salvation, as they develop over time, and as we can know them while this salvation remains incomplete. In its currently accepted sense, the expression derives from the Epistle to the Hebrews.[53] It is not specifically liturgical. Far from restricting itself to describing a ceremony, or a figurative or commemorative act, it reaches out to cover the whole order of the Incarnation – unless we prefer to say, which would be completely in conformity with the characteristic ideas of the Epistle to the Hebrews, that this whole order of the redemptive Incarnation should itself be considered as a vast liturgy, the earthly and temporal image of the eternal Liturgy which is taking place in Heaven: '*The Passion, that Christ will* celebrate *once and for all.*'

Representation: the word therefore defines that intermediate place

---

49 Florus, *Expositio missae*, c. 61 (Duc, p. 134). See *supra*, c. 111. Erasmus on Luke (Basle, 1535, p. 218). cf. Luke 22.20.

50 Cyril of Alexandria, *Adversus Nestorium*, 4, c. 5 (PG, 76, 193–7).

51 *De officiis ministrorum, loc. cit.*; cited by Ivo of Chartres (PL, 161, 142 D) and Abelard (178, 1520 A). See also c. 49, n. 239 (16, 94 B).

52 cf. *Apologia David altera*, c. 7, n. 36 (PL, 14, 901 B).

53 Hebrews 8.5 and 10.1.

which I said is occupied by the New Testament in its present form: between shadow and truth, nearer the shadow because of the form of knowledge with which we are left – *through a mirror and in enigmas* – ,[54] but how much nearer the truth because of its profound substance! *Shadow in the law, image in the gospel, truth in the heaven.*[55] Thus it is with the sacrifice of the Church, compared on the one hand with figurative sacrifices and on the other hand with what can be called the heavenly sacrifice. It has a reality in representation, as does Christ himself, in his whole indivisible being. Here we must set aside our watered-down concepts,[56] and reflect that, for the ancients, affirming that the Son of God is the perfect image of the Father was to affirm the total communication between the one and the other, a true identity of nature.[57] *'This image'*, as Pseudo-Primasius's commentary on the Epistle to the Colossians would say, *'is true: not weak, but strong; not empty, but full of life'.*[58] Once more these are Ambrosian formulations. *Christ is not the shadow but the image of God,*[59] *whoever follows the Gospel walks in Christ the image.*[60] Our mystery is no empty image, but it is still or rather already the truth: *not an empty image, but the truth.*[61] As Algerius of Liège would say, this is no longer the era of truth promised, but that of truth given, although not yet of truth revealed.[62] Here, then, the Eucharist is no more treated as an image in a sort of opposition to a realist concept of the mystery, than

---

54 Ambrose, *In Lucam*, 7, n. 39 (PL, 15, 1709 B).

55 Ambrose, *In psalmum 38*, n. 25 (PL, 14, 1051–2). *De excessu fratris sui Satyri*, 2 (=De fide resurrectionis), n. 109 (16, 1347). Origen, *In psalm. 38*, h. 2, n. 2 (PG, 12, 1402–3). Maximus, *Scholia in eccl. Hierarch.*, c. 3, 3, 2 (4, 137 D). cf. Ivo of Chartres, *Decretum*, p. 2, c. 6 (PL, 161, 142 D). cf. John Damascene citing Chrysostom, with a slightly different terminology; *Sur les images*, discourse 1 and 3: σκία – ἀλήθεια – τὰ πράγματα (PG, 94, 1269–72 and 1361–4).

    No more than *shadow*, *image* is not here simply synonymous with *type* or *figure*, as it is elsewhere. (For example, Chrysostom, PG, 63, 55; Cyril of Alexandria, PG, 74, 629 B). cf. Bruno of Segni; Pascal (Chevalier, 673).

56 For the force of the word in the New Testament: Kleinknecht, in *Theologisches Wörterbuch zum N.T.*, vol. 2, p. 386.

57 cf. Athanasius, *Letters to Serapion*, 1 (Lebon, p. 127). Hilary, *De Trinitate*, 11, c. 5 (PL, 10, 400 B). The same for the Incarnation; cf. Faustus of Riez, *Sermo 2, de Nativitate* (Eng., p. 227).

58 PL, 68, 652 B.

59 *De excessu, loc. cit. In psalmum 38*, n. 24 (PL, 14, 1051 A). Paschasius Radbertus, *Ad Frudegardum* (120, 1353 A–B). cf. G. Kittel, *Theologisches Wörterbuch zum N.T.*, vol. 2, p. 386.

60 *In psalmum 38*, n. 24 (PL, 14, 1051 A).

61 PL, 16, 1347 c. cf. Athanasius, *Epistulae heortasticae*, 14, n. 3 (PG, 26, 1420 C).

62 *De sacramentis*, 1, c. 8; 2, c. 3 (PL, 180, 763, 815). cf. Du Perron, *République à la Response du Serenissme Roy de la Grand Bretagne* (Paris, 1620), pp. 871–2.

it is treated in relation to the historic past. We must not impose such a self-contradiction on St. Ambrose. His Eucharistic formulations are sufficiently clear in other respects, and when he compares the provisional sacrifices of Judaism with the permanent sacrifice of Christ, he is careful enough to oppose them as *type* and *truth*.[63] Nevertheless he warns us that it is still part of the great *sacrament of Christ*, and that by participating in it we must still anticipate and petition for this future good '*in which is found perfection and truth*'.[64]

While adding that dynamic tone that his ardent soul communicated to all his writings, St. Augustine took up a point of view close to that of Ambrose, when, in the twelfth book of the *Contra Faustum*, he compared our present rites to the rites of eternity:

> . . . It signifies the end of the age, when there will be the repose of the saints, no longer in the sacrament of hope, by which the Church is bound together in this age, as long as she drinks what flowed from Christ's side; but then in the perfection of eternal salvation, when the kingdom will be handed over to God the Father, so that, (wrapped) in the clear contemplation of immutable truth, we shall need no bodily mysteries.[65]

---

63 *In Lucam*, 1, n. 22 (PL, 15, 1542 C).

64 *De officiis, loc. cit.* cf. *Gregorianum* (L., p. 15). *Gelasianum* (M., p. 12), etc. Pseudo-Bede, *In psalmum 26* (PL, 93, 613 C). Paschasius, *In Matthaeum* (120, 896 B).

If *image* is understood in its ordinary, material sense, as in the iconoclast controversy, then we know that we must reject it as totally inadequate: witness the *Livres carolins*, l. 4, c. 14 (PL, 98, 1093–6); cf. above, c. 1, note 16. On the other hand, the categories of biblical exemplarism imposed themselves by virtue of such constant usage that the author of this diatribe remains entirely dominated by them. It is what would permit Pastor Claude to write, regarding the same passage, in his *Réponse au premier traité* . . . , pp. 30–1: 'It is therefore clearer than daylight that the Council (of Frankfurt) disapproves of the word Image, not in the sense that we understand it as a sacred sign of Jesus Christ who died for our salvation . . . ; but that as an Image we take it for a legal shadow, or for a prefiguration of the Christ who is to come' (1667). The letter of Hadrian I to Patriarch Taraisius (787) offers another rather curious mixture of two points of view: in order to justify the cult of painted images, the pope takes as an example the image of a lamb, which is a figure of the true Lamb, and he adds, '*therefore formerly figures and shadows, as indications and harbingers of the truth, now things cherished having been entrusted to the Church*' (Mansi, vol. XII, 1080). Even when, in contrast, in order to forbid the cult of images, the latter were likened to the Eucharist, the precisions of language would still be insufficient to preclude all misunderstanding. Nicholas I, *Epistula 4, ad Michaelem imperatorem*, in 860 (PL 119, 778 B–D).

65 Bk. 12, c. 20 (PL, 42, 265). And 19, c. 2. cf. *In psalmum 64*, n. 1 (36, 773).

How, indeed, can we speak of the Eucharist other than as of the Lord himself? Does he not exercise here, as in his life on earth, the office of Mediator? Is he not here still our way to the Father? Now, all that touches on the way is destined to pass: '*Nor did the Lord himself, in so far as he deigned to be our way, want us to hold on* [to him] *but to pass over . . .*'[66] This *hope of the sacrament* and these *bodily myster-ies* thus come together with Ambrose's image. They come together with Gregory Nazianzen's *perfected type* (τυπικῶς ἔτι).[67] They are that '*great type and hope of life*' found in one Syriac liturgy.[68] But formulations of this sort – or like the formulations '*truth in mystery*' or '*image of the sacrament*' of the ancient sacramentaries[69] – do not refer so specifically to the Eucharist that they cannot just as well apply to the whole '*sacrament of the incarnation of the Lord*', or '*sacrament of the risen body*'.[70] In reality they embrace, as does the Eucharist itself, the whole order of the '*sacraments of the holy faith*',[71] that is to say the whole Christian economy. As long as this world lasts, we are still living '*in the sacraments*', that is to say, explains St. Gregory the Great, not yet in our permanent home, but hovering on the thresh-old, '*between doors*'.[72] Our Passover from now on is Christ, but it is always taking us further. And in the providential diversity of their forms, without it ever being possible to separate their 'spiritual' and the 'bodily' aspects, are not all the means of salvation at the same time, according to whether we see them from within or from outside, and in relation to a sterile past or to good anticipated, an image, that is to say simultaneously both figure and truth?[73]

This was a point of view familiar to the Middle Ages. It was what lay behind Hugh of St. Victor placing the same difference between 'sacrament' or 'image' and 'matter' or 'power' as between faith and contemplation.[74] It was what caused a disciple of Hugh to be given this symbolic explanation of the three tents that Peter wanted to erect on Mount Tabor:

---

66 *De doctrina Christiana*, 1, c. 34, n. 38 (PL, 34, 33).

67 *Discourse on Easter*, 45, c. 23 (PG, 36, 653–6); c. 21 (652 D).

68 *Liturgia Gregorii catholici orientis* (Renaudot, vol. 2, p. 458).

69 *Gelasianum* (W., p. 186). cf. Ratramnus (PL, 121, 162). Honorius of Autun, *Speculum Ecclesiae* (PL, 172, 939 C).

70 Ambrose, *De fide*, 3, c. 7, n. 50 (PL, 16, 600 A), etc. *Apologia David altera*, c. 7, n. 39 (14, 902 B).

71 Gregory the Great, *In Ezechielem*, 2, hom. 10, n. 8 (PL, 76, 1063 A).

72 Gregory, *In Ezechielem*, 2, hom. 1, n. 16 (PL, 76, 945–7).

73 Good commentary on this point in *Perpétuité* (Migne, vol. 2, 715).

74 *De sacramentis*, 1, p. 10, c. 8 (PL, 176, 342 B–D).

There are three tabernacles – the synagogue, the Church, heaven . . .
The first was in shadow and figure, the second in figure and truth,
the third in truth alone. Life is exhibited in the first, given in the
second, and possessed in the third.[75]

It was what made William of St. Thierry write: '*As long as we are in*
transit in the image, we are bound by the bodily sacraments, lest we
depart from God.'[76] It was what inspired this same William to write
his beautiful commentary on the verse of the Canticle: '*until day dawn*
and the shadows lengthen'. The Bridegroom and the Bride are already
united, but in the darkness of faith. We are still in the era of '*mirrors*
and enigmas', not in that of the '*vision face to face and the fullness of*
all good'. We are therefore living '*in the flower of hope*', not '*in the*
enjoyment of reality, in the full richness of the fruits of the spirit'. Vain
shadows surround us. But they will die away one day, yielding to the
triumphant light of truth:

> *Then, just as once the new sacraments of grace put an end on the old*
> *sacraments, the reality itself of all the sacraments will put an end to*
> *all sacraments completely. In the sacraments of the New Testament*
> *the day of new grace began to dawn; at the end of all consumption*
> *(of sacraments) it will be midday . . .*[77]

In his own turn, St. Thomas Aquinas would enter the same stream of
thought, in the article of the *Summa* where he would ask himself if
the ceremonies of the ancient law ended with the coming of Christ.
In answer, he would distinguish a threefold state of interior worship;
only the third, that of the blessed itself, would no longer entail anything 'figurative'.[78]

As it continued in this way throughout the Middle Ages, the chain
of tradition has not been so interrupted in modern times that today
such expressions should seem foreign or suspect to us. Our greatest
orator was not afraid to repeat them.[79] Indeed, brought up on the
Fathers, Bossuet not only borrowed from their doctrine, but he seemed
to speak spontaneously in their language:

---

75 *Miscellanea*, 7, tit. 55 (PL, 177, 896 C–D).

76 *Liber de natura et dignitate amoris* (PL, 184, 406 C).

77 *Expositio in Cantica*, c. 2 (PL, 180, 536). Hugh of St. Victor (PL, 176, 346
C–D).

78 St. Thomas, *Summa theologiæ*, Ia IIae, q. 103, a. 3. cf. a. 2. *In IV Sent.*, d. 8,
q. 1, a. 3 (Moos, pp. 318–19). cf. *In Joannem*, c. 3, l. 1, n. 2.

79 Also Pascal (Br., 670).

We must recognize that everything that is most true, as it were, in the Christian faith, is altogether a mystery and sacred sign. The Incarnation of Jesus Christ is for us a figure of the perfect union that we should have with the Godhead in the state of grace and in glory. His birth and death are the figure of our spiritual birth and death. If, in the mystery of the Eucharist, he deigns to draw near our bodies in his own flesh and in his own blood, then through it he invites us to the unity of the spirit that he prefigures. Finally, until we come to the fully revealed truth that will make us happy for all eternity, all truth will only be for us a figure of a more intimate truth: we will only taste Jesus Christ in all purity in his true form, and freed from all figures, when we see him in the fullness of his glory at the right hand of the Father.[80]

Finally, we can see in the word *pledge*, that occurs so frequently in liturgical prayers and that the Council of Trent would consecrate,[81] a sort of condensed form of the Ambrosian *image* and the Augustinian *hope* or other analogous words. There is no point in insisting on its original sense, which proves a poor preparation for the translation of the Greek *deposit* (ἀρραβών).[82] A deposit is something other, and much more than a pledge. But is not this new sense, midway between a simple promise and the totality of the gift, that the choice of a clumsy translator ended up by imposing, a happy expression for the sacrament of the new economy? An *image*, like Christ, the Eucharist is also, like the Spirit, a *pledge*. *He gave himself as a pledge.*[83] And just as the Spirit, at baptism, was the *pledge of our inheritance*,[84] Christ, in the Eucharist, is the *pledge of the body*. Objectively, the *pledge* is therefore not less than the *matter*: it is already, at least partially, that *matter* itself, although not yet in all its fullness,[85] that is to say not yet possessed in depth nor fully revealed for our contemplation. '*It*

---

80 *Histoire des Variations*, 4, c. 12 (Lachat, vol. 14, p. 151). Also Fénelon, *Entretiens affectifs pour les principales fêtes de l'année*, XIV, for the day of the Ascension (*Œuvres*, Paris, vol. 1, p. 484). Pascal (Chevalier, 671).

81 *Sessio 13*, c. 2. cf. Leo XIII, encyclical *Mirae caritatis* (*Acta Leonis XIII*, vol. 22, p. 124).

82 Eph. 1.4; 2 Cor. 1.22. Jerome (PL, 30, 457 B). cf. Tertullian, *De carnis resurrectione*, c. 51 (Kroymann, p. 105). Auxerre Commentary, *In Ephes.* (117, 705–6). Hervé (181, 1214–15).

83 Atton of Vercelli, *In Ephes.* (PL, 134, 549 C). cf. Cyril of Alexandria, *Homiliae diversae*, hom. 10 (PG, 77, 1028 B).

84 Eph. 1.14; 2 Cor. 1.22; Rom. 8.23. cf. Augustine (PL, 37, 1723). Gerhoh (PL, 193, 1062 B and 1658 D). William of St. Thierry (180, 323 A).

85 Gaudentius of Brescia, *Tract.* 2 (Glueck, pp. 30–1). Augustine (PL, 35, 1877).

possesses a general pledge of substance', said Gregory of Elvira.[86] '*May the* sacraments *accomplish what they contain*', said our Gregorian prayer. It is an ambiguous concept, as is Christian reality itself, under the conditions of this present life. In order to grasp the exact meaning in its application to the Eucharist, we only need remember once again that the habitual thought of the Ancients, in its reflection on this mystery, was not concerned with defining or measuring explicitly, and as one might say abstractly, the manner of an objective presence, but it concentrated above all on the double question of sacrificial action and communion:

> *When the Son of God says; 'My flesh is truly food and my blood is truly drink', this is to be understood as saying that the mysteries of our redemption are truly the body and blood of the Lord. We must believe the pledges of that perfect unity which we now enjoy with our Head in hope and will then possess in reality.*[87]

This helps us to understand how Paschasius Radbertus brought the word *pledge* itself into his definition of the sacrament[88] and the Eucharist came commonly to be called '*the pledge of salvation*',[89] '*the pledge of immortality*',[90] '*the pledge of future glory*' . . .[91] For the *pledge* is to the *reality* or the *effect*[92] what the *image* is to the *truth* – or, from a more subjective viewpoint, what *hope* is to *eternal life*.[93] Like *image* and *hope*, it is defined in relation to the *fullness of the truth*,[94] or to the *truth of things*.[95]

* * *

---

86 *Tractatus 17* (B.W., p. 187).

87 Walafrid Strabo, *De rebus ecclesiasticis*, c. 17 (PL, 114, 937 D). Gezonius of Tortona, c. 38 (137, 389 C). cf. Fulbert of Chartres, *Ep. 5* (141, 202 A).

88 PL, 120, 1275 A. Compare Augustine, *Ep. 55*, n. 2 (33, 205), *Sermo 334*, n. 2 (38, 1469), and Isidore, *Etymologiae* (82, 255 C).

89 *Gelasianum* (W., pp. 182, 186). *Vetus missale gallicanum* (PL, 72, 379 C). *Gregorianum* (L., p. 33). Fulbert of Chartres (PL, 141, 202 A). Peter Damian (*supra*, note 34), etc.

90 *Gelasianum* (W., p. 349). *Gregorianum* (L., p. 87). *Leonianum* (*supra*, n. 25), etc. cf. Athanasius, *Epistulae heortasticae*, 2, n. 10 (PG, 26, 1366 A–B).

91 cf. Theodoret, concerning baptism (PG, 83, 512 B), etc.

92 *Gregorianum* (L., pp. 28, 82, 96). Similar opposition between *gustus* and *effectus* (L., pp. 28, 105). *Epistula de sacramentis haereticorum* (*libelli de lite*, vol. 3, p. 17). The two metaphors are already brought closer, concerning the Holy Spirit, by Augustine, *Sermo Wilmart 11*, n. 9 (Morin, p. 701).

93 We will note the varying orations cited *supra*, note 28. Thus Peter of Poitiers, *Sentences* (PL, 211, 1253 B).

94 cf. Peter Damian, *Carmina et preces* (PL, 145, 953 D).

95 One sees the internal contradiction of the Calvinist position of a Claude, *Réponse aux deux traités*, Charenton, 1667, p. 300.

There remains a last series of texts, in truth the most important one, where the New Testament, summed up as the sacrifice of Christ, is quite simply presented as the spiritual fulfilment of the Old Testament and, as it were, the truth of all that it prefigured.[96] *'Departing now from the shadow, let us come to the truth.'*[97] Now, in the movement from the *paschal type* to the *true Pasch*[98] the object of perpetual meditation in the Christian consciousness, the Lamb that was sacrificed and eaten evoked the Eucharist just as much as it did Calvary, according to whether attention was focused primarily on the sacred meal or on the sacrifice. But around this central figure other figures divided into two groups, according to whether they applied more directly to the sacrifice on the cross, such as the holocaust of Isaac prepared by his father,[99] or to the sacrament of the altar, such as the offering of Melchizedek[100] or the gift of the manna in the desert. One of the most perfect formulations that Christian antiquity has left us of the fulfilment of the Old Testament by the New, is precisely relative to Melchizedek and to the Eucharist. It comes from St. Cyprian:

> *First there came the image of sacrifice, contained in bread and wine. The Lord, to perform and accomplish this reality, offered bread and a cup mixed with wine; he who is fullness accomplished the truth of the prefigured image.*[101]

In the same way, it was about the manna that Paschasius Radbertus wrote: *'Then was adumbrated the image of the truth; but now, (there is) the mystery of accomplished truth.'*[102] Christ, said Hesychius, desired to eat the Passover with his disciples before he died: not only 'the Passover', but 'this Passover', a Passover in which, all figures having passed away, the truth was fulfilled.[103] This is an essential contrast that can never be too strongly emphasised. The era of Melchizedek,

---

96 Cyril of Alexandria, *Glaphyra in Leviticum* (PG, 69, 581 A).

97 Athanasius, *Epistulae heortasticae*, 1, n. 3 (PG, 26, 1361–2). Jerome, *In Isaiam* (PL, 24, 275 B).

98 Jerome, *In Matthaeum* (PL, 26, 195). Hesychius (PG, 93, 1078–82), etc. Berengar of Venouse (Morin, *Recherches de théologie ancienne et médiévale*, 1932, p. 120).

99 cf. Rupert, *In Joannem*, 7 (PL, 169, 491 B).

100 See nevertheless Amalarius, *Eclogae de officio missae* (PL, 105, 1324 A).

101 *Ep. 63*, c. 4 (Hartel, p. 704). Cyril of Alexandria, *Homiliae diversae*, hom. 10 (PG, 77, 1024 A). *Gelasianum*, n. 27 (M., pp. 4–5). Rabanus Maurus (PL, 1–7, 320 D). John of Avranches, *Confessio fidei*, 4, c. 2 (101, 1087 C).

102 *Liber de corpore*, c. 5, n. 1 (PL, 120, 1280 B–C). Ambrosiaster, *In I Cor.*, xi (PL, 17, 243 B). Gregory Nazianzen, *Discourse 45* (PG, 36, 652 D), etc.

103 *In psalmum 37*, 10. Devresse, *Revue biblique*, 1924, p. 515.

Abraham and Moses was '*the era of figures*': today the '*day of truth*' is shining.[104] The ancient sacrifices were offered '*in shadow*', '*in figures*', '*in types*', '*in mystery*', '*in prefiguring*': the new Sacrifice is celebrated each day '*in truth*'.[105] We hear echoes of all the Fathers in the words of a late liturgist, who makes no attempt at originality:

> *What in the Old Testament is promised, prefigured and greeted from afar is in the New, however, given, revealed and openly achieved; here it is manifested by its presence, not in shadow but in truth, not in figure but in reality . . . All these things are daily performed through Christ in the Church in the presence of the spiritual ark of the Lord.*[106]

Thus only the sacrifice of the new Law is '*a true sacrifice*'.[107] It is also still a sacrament, but a spiritual sacrament,[108] the heavenly mystery and sacrament,[109] the sacrament of salvation.[110] It is the only divine

---

104 Rupert, *In Genesim*, 4, c. 4 (PL, 167, 329 B). Hildegard, *Ep.* 47 (197, 223 C). Fulgentius, *Ep. 14*, n. 46 (65, 433–5). cf. Zeno of Verona, 2, *Tract 56* and *59* (11, 511 B and 515 A).

105 Ambrose, *De mysteriis*, c. 8, n. 48, 49 (PL, 16, 405 A); *De fide*, 3, n. 89 (607 D). Pseudo-Ambrose, *De sacramentis* (16, 423 B, 427 C). Epiphanius, *Haeresis 8* (PG, 41, 213 C). Jerome, *In Matthaeum* (PL, 26, 195 B). Pseudo-Haimon, *In Hebr.* (117, 874 D, 886 C). Abelard, *Sic et Non*, c. 117 (178, 1522 D). Rupert, *In Joannem* (169, 391 D), *De Spiritu sancto* (167, 1662 B), etc.

106 Robert Paululus, *De officiis ecclesiasticis*, 2, c. 13 (PL, 177, 418 B–D).

107 Florus, *Expositio missae*, c. 65 (Duc, p. 140). Remigius of Auxerre, *Homilia 8* (PL, 131, 909 D). Rupert, *In Matth.* (168, 1548 D), etc.

108 *Apostolic Constitutions*, 8, c. 8, n. 5 (Funk, p. 485). Chrysostom, *In I Cor.*, hom. 23 (PG, 61, 191). Caesarius of Arles (Morin, pp. 297–8). Honorius of Autun, *Speculum Ecclesiae* (PL, 172, 842 B), etc. Pseudo-Ambrose (17, 650 C). cf. Remigius of Auxerre (131, 535 C). See *supra*, Chapter 4, n. 115.

109 Tertullian, *De baptismo*, c. 10: the ancient rite (PL, 1, 1211 A). Chrysostom, *In Hebr.*, hom. 14, n. 1 and 2 (PG, 63, 111, 112). Ambrose, *In Lucam* (PL, 15, 1711 B, 1721 B); *In psalmum 118*, sermo 18 (15, 1461 C); *De paenitentia*, 2, n. 89 (16, 518 A); *De sacramentis* (16, 419 C, 427 B, 437 C, 442 B, 447 C, 448 A, 449 A, 452 C; cf. 427 B, 443 A). Pseudo-Ambrose, *Precatio* (17, 754 C). Gregory of Elvira (B.W., p. 180). Cassian, *Collatio 23* (49, 1279). *Gelasianum* (M., pp. 2, 11, etc.). *Gregorianum* (L., pp. 9, 23, 24, etc.). Fourth Council of Braga, canon 3 (Mansi, vol. 11, 156 C). Bede, *Ep.* 2 (PL, 94, 666 A–B). Alcuin (101, 459 A). Amalarius (105, 1151 B). Florus (Duc, p. 132). Pseudo-Primasius, *In Hebr.* (68, 734 D, cf. 745 C). *Vetus missale gallicanum* (72, 373 A). Paschasius Radbertus (120, 81 D, 668 B, 719 B, 86 B). Gerard of Cambrai (Mansi, vol. 19, 438 D). John of Fécamp (101, 1086 C). Peter Damian (144, 627 D, 727 D; 145, 712 D). *Missale gothicum* (72, 261 D, 300 D). Gozechin, *Ep. ad Valcher*, c. 30 (143, 900 D). Lanfranc (150, 427 A). Gerhoh (194, 785 C), etc. cf. Cyprian (Hartel, pp. 215, 712, 802, 808; Ivo of Chartres, *Decretum* (PL, 161, 155 B); Gratian, *De consecratione* 2.35 (Fr., 1325), etc.

110 cf. Paschasius Radbertus, *In Matthaeum* (PL, 120, 726 C), etc.

sacrament,[111] the only sacrament in eternity.[112] It is no longer 'a figure of a figure' or a 'sacrament of a sacrament',[113] as were the Mosaic rites; it is no longer '*a sacrament of shadows*'[114] or '*a sacrament in figures*',[115] no longer '*a sacrament pointing to the future*',[116] but '*the true sacrament*',[117] '*the true mystery*'.[118] The children of Israel received 'mystical bread' from heaven: we receive the true Bread.[119] Their whole existence passed by '*in the shadow of the sacraments*':[120] today we celebrate their sacrifices *mystically* by participating *in truth* in the sacrificed body of our Saviour. What they possessed only '*in carnal prefigurations*', we have today '*in spiritual truth*'.[121] *We are dealing with the reality itself.*[122] At the heart of our worship dwells *the very Truth of the reality.*[123] Consequently, between the two economies,

> *There is a great difference . . . between shadow and bodies, between image and truth, between copies of future things and the things themselves that were prefigured in the copies.*[124]

---

111 cf. Council of Rome of 1074, c. 13, 18 (Mansi, vol. 20, 316 B, 424 C). Paschasius Radbertus, *In Matthaeum* (PL, 120, 719 D), etc.

112 Pseudo-Clement, *Epistolae decretales*, *Ep.* 2 (PG, 1, 485 A). Cyprian, *De catholicae Ecclesiae unitate* (Hartel, p. 215). Didymus, *De Trinitate*, 3, c. 21 (PG, 39, 905 C). Hilary, *In Matthaeum*, c. 30, n. 2, on Judas (PL, 10, 1065 B). Hesychius (Pseudo-Athanasius), *In psalmum* 22 (PG, 27, 729 D, cf. 660 C). *Gelasianum* (W., pp. 34, 92, 93). *Gregorianum* (L., p. 41). Pseudo-Primasius, *In Hebr.* (PL, 68, 735 B). *Vetus missale gallicanum* (72, 372 D). Paschasius Radbertus (120, 741 B), etc.

113 Baldwin (PL, 204, 650 A). Gregory Nazianzen (PG, 36, 653). Chrysostom, *In Hebr.* (cited by John Damascene, *Sur les Images*, discourse 1 and 3, PG, 94, 1272, 1364; cf. Chrysostom, hom. 12). Rabanus Maurus, *In I Cor.*, x (PL, 112, 88 B). Hugh of St. Victor, *De sacramentis*, 1, p. 11, c. 1 and 2 (176, 343 B, C).

114 Augustine, *De spiritu et littera*, c. 14, n. 25 (PL, 216).

115 St. Thomas, *Summa theologiæ*, IIIa, q. 66, a. 2; q. 70, a. 1, ad 2.

116 cf. Augustine, *Contra Faustum*, 19, c. 13, 14 (PL, 42, 355).

117 Jerome, *In Matthaeum* (PL, 26, 195 B). Etherius and Beatus (96, 941 A). Paschasius (120, 1360 A). Adrevald of Fleury (124, 948 D). Berengar of Venouse (Morin, p. 20). Bruno of Segni, *Sententiae*, 4, c. 9 (PL, 165, 1004 D), etc. cf. John of Paris, *De potestate regia et papali*, c. 4 (Goldast, p. 112).

118 Hesychius, *In Leviticum* (PG, 93, 1078 B), etc.

119 Jerome, *In psalmum 109* (Morin, p. 201). Francon, *De gratia Dei*, 10 (PL, 166, 775 B).

120 Ivo of Chartres, *Sermo 1* (PL, 162, 508 A).

121 *Libri Carolini*, 1, c. 19 (PL98, 1048 B). Atto of Vercelli, *In Hebr.* (134, 828 B). cf. Fulgentius, *Epistula 14*, n. 46 (65, 434). Remigius of Auxerre, *In psalmum* 74 (131, 535 C).

122 Rabanus Maurus, *In I Cor.*, x (PL, 112, 90–1, cf. 94 B).

123 Rabanus Maurus, *In Numeros* (PL, 108, 678 B–C); *In Josue*, 3, c. 17 (108, 1107–8). Pseudo-Haimon, *In Hebr.* (117, 889 B). Rupert, *In Matthaeum*, 10 (168, 1548 D). cf. Cyril of Alexandria (PG, 74, 612 D). Chrysostom (63, 97–8).

124 Jerome, *In Tit.*, c. 1 (PL, 26, 569 A). Isidore of Seville, *De ecclesiasticis*

It is certainly pointless to pile up quotations. Let us simply establish that there were two vocabularies in competition with one another. Earlier on, what was 'a type' or 'a mystery' was the Eucharist itself – *we are celebrating mystically, the mystical body* – while the 'truth' revealed within the rite to our spiritual understanding was its effect, its ultimate 'thing', that is to say in particular the ecclesial body, still to come to fulfilment. In the final analysis the truth was to be found beyond the sacrament. Now the sacrament itself has become the 'thing' and the 'truth' of the ancient rites, which receive within it both their 'spirit' and their 'body', that is to say their understanding and their ful-filment.[125] Earlier on it was a matter for us of passing from the present image to the full daylight of truth: '*We see blessings now in image, and we possess blessings in image . . . We strive to attain to the truth.*'[126] Now we are asked to believe that, despite the enduring darkness, the passage has already been made, as from the shadow to the body, from the figure to the truth.[127] The *New and everlasting Covenant.*

> *May the new drive out the old,*
> *and truth the shadow . . .*

However different they might be, the two viewpoints nevertheless do not involve any doctrinal contradiction. First of all, this is precisely because they are successive points of view. The consideration of the sacrament, in the effect that it is intended to produce in the one receiv-ing it, is replaced by the consideration of the mystery that from now on is enveloped within the sacrament. The central perspective shifts from being communion to being sacrifice. A concrete example of this shift in viewpoint can be given by observing that the formulations most characteristic of the first series were borrowed from post-communion prayers, whereas we derive most of the second series from prefaces or from secrets. We can also see the vocabulary changing in the same author as his viewpoint changes. Thus St. Augustine, who, as we have

---

officiis, 1, c. 18, n. 10 (83, 756 C). Etherius ad Beatus (96, 942 C). *Libri Carolini*, 4, c. 14 (98, 1214 B–C); cf. 1, c. 19 (1048 B). Gregory of Bergamo, c. 12 (H., p. 51). Basil, *De Spiritu sancto*, c. 14, n. 32 (PG, 32, 125 A).

125 Florus, *Expositio missae*, c. 60 (Duc, p. 132). Rabanus Maurus, *In Mat-thaeum*, 8 (PL, 107, 1107 B). *Glose in Lucam* (114, 337 D). Peter Damian, *Dialo-gus inter Judaeum et Christianum* (145, 60 B). Hervé, *In Coloss.* (181, 1335 D).

126 Ambrose, *In psalmum 38* (PL, 14, 1052); *De fide resurrectionis* (16, 1347 C). Compare, for example, with Pseudo-Haimon, *In Hebr.* (117, 890 C).

127 See again Cyril, *In Joannem*, 3 (PG, 73, 512 s.); *Adversus Nestorium*, 4, c. 5 (76, 196 B, 197 A–B). Paschasius, *Ad Frudegardum* (PL, 120, 1359–60), etc.

seen, speaks of the sacrament and of the fruit that can be expected from it, discovers in the '*Christian celebration*' no less of the fullness of light and truth, possessed only in '*so to speak nocturnal figures*'[128] by the Jews in the flesh.

We must admit, in the second instance, that just as the words *type, pledge, hope* or *image* did not then imply any sort of reservation about faith in a 'real presence' – all that can be conceded is that they sometimes fell short of that explicit truth – no more now does the word *truth* constitute of itself a direct witness in its favour. A good many texts in which it appears fall short of the analysis that would clearly distinguish the Eucharist from Calvary. Like *spirituality* and *fullness*, the *truth* that they exalt primarily characterizes the whole Christian economy in contrast to the ancient economy:

> . . . *The flesh and blood of a spotless lamb are offered daily on the sacred altars, and is received beneficially in the mouths of the faithful as food for their souls, in order that, when the shadow of the law recedes, the truth of the gospel may be revealed.*[129]

'*The true sacrament*' is therefore, above all, '*the full sacrament*', the '*accomplished sacrament*'.[130] The ancient sacraments only promised a Saviour: today's sacraments actually bring us salvation.[131] They are '*sacraments of Christian perfection*',[132] '*true sacraments of the Passover*',[133] '*sacraments in the fullness of truth*',[134] '*potency and the potently salvific sacraments of Christ*'.[135] The truth we are dealing with here is thus the common attribute of all the essential rites of

---

128 *Sermo de sancta Pascha* (=Wilmart 8; Morin, p. 691).

129 Rabanus Maurus, *In Josue* (PL, 108, 1108 A). cf. Pseudo-Primasius, *In Hebr.* (68, 782 B). For Ambrose, the 'spiritual mystery' is the whole of the Christian mystery: *In Lucam*, 9, n. 19 (PL, 15, 1797 A–B). See also Augustine, *In Joannem*, tract. 11, n. 8 (35, 1479). Ambrosiaster, *In I Cor.* (17, 233 D). Gaudentius, *Tractatus 2 in Exodum* (Glueck, pp. 25–6). Fulgentius, *Ep. 14*, n. 44 (PL, 65, 432).

130 *Glose in 4m Librum Sententiarum*, ms. of Bamberg (Weisweiler, *Mélanges Grabmann*, vol. 1, p. 378). Hugh of St. Victor, *De sacramentis* (PL, 176, 447 A, 448 C). cf. the Sacramentary of Serapion of Thmuis, consecration of the baptismal waters (Brightmann, *Journal of Theological Studies* 1, p. 263). *Supra*, note 58.

131 Augustine, *In psalmum 73*, n. 2 (PL, 36, 931). Fulgentius, *Ep. 14*, n. 44 (65, 432). cf. Bessarion, *De sacramento Eucharistiae* (PG, 161, 498 D).

132 Walafrid Strabo (PL, 114, 939 A).

133 Rabanus Maurus, *In Matthaeum*, 8 (PL, 107, 1106 D). Florus, *Expositio missae*, c. 4, n. 7 (Duc, p. 90). Jerome, *Ep. 78*, n. 43 (Hilberg, vol. 2, p. 86).

134 Pseudo-Primasius, *In Hebr.* (PL, 68, 747 B).

135 Gerhoh, *In psalmos* (PL, 194, 294 C; 357 D).

Christianity. It is the reality of baptism, for example, as well as of the Eucharist:

> *If baptisms in the figure were of such effect, how much more effective is baptism in truth.*[136]
>
> *If then the figure of the sea was of such effect, how great will be the effect of the visible form of baptism? If what was done in figure brought the people who had been led across to receive manna, what will Christ reveal in the truth of his baptism, when he leads his people across?*[137]

The truth of these rites certainly presupposes that Christ is present within them, but it is a presence that is still understood in a broad and indeterminate fashion. As does its equivalent *the thing itself*,[138] it more directly signifies that they have their own power in themselves:[139] *'true sacrifices, by which we can be perfectly cleansed . . .';*[140] and that they are fully efficacious in themselves. From the figure to the truth, says St. John Chrysostom, stretches the whole distance between weakness and strength.[141] As Rupert was to say, the sacrament of the altar is, for those of us who are alive, what the descent of Christ into Hell after his death was for the dead: '*To us . . . is sent the sacrament in which under the appearance of bread and wine there is hidden the benefits of his death and resurrection.*'[142] And as his contemporary Gilbert of Nogent was to say, what the chalice contains after the words of the consecration is nothing less than the whole grace of the New Testament, '*effective of great good, and not empty and shadowy . . .*' This, continues Gilbert, is how the words '*mystery of faith*' that the priest pronounces are to be understood:

---

136 Ambrose, *De sacramentis*, 2, c. 4, n. 13 (PL, 16 427 C).

137 Augustine, *In Joannem*, tract. 11, n. 4 (PL, 35, 1477). Like the Eucharist, baptism is called 'a sacrament of Christ': Augustine, *Letter to Jerome* (Hilberg, vol. 3, pp. 210, 211), or 'a sacrament pertaining to things spiritual': Ambrose, *In Lucam* (PL, 15, 1627 C), etc. cf. Basil, *On the Holy Spirit*, c. 14, n. 31–3 (PG, 32, 121–8). Chrysostom, *In I Cor.*, hom. 23 (PG, 61, 191).

138 cf. Hildebert, *Poem on the end of the Jewish rites* (Hauréau, 'Notice sur les mélanges poétiques d'Hildebert de Lavardin', in *Notices et extraits des manuscripts de la Bibliothèque nationale . . .* , vol. 28, 1878, p. 358).

139 Atto of Vercelli, *In Hebr.* (PL, 134, 778 C).

140 Pseudo-Primasius, *In Hebr.* (PL, 68, 745 C, 748 B).

141 *In Hebr.*, hom. 17, n. 3 (PG, 63, 131).

142 *De Victoria Verbi Dei*, 12, c. 12 (PL, 169, 1472 C).

It is as if he were to say: The secret of the entire faith, in which lies hid the glory of all our ability to believe. Because of this, as the following words say, the cup of the blood contains nothing but divine fruit, namely, the forgiveness of sins.

May they say what the shadow is, which produced so great a truth![143]

Despite the tendency of St. Augustine to inject into his formulations a sort of equivalence between faith in the Christ who is to come and faith in the Christ who is already here,[144] it is already remarkable that the memorial should nevertheless never be treated as a simple parallel for the figure. They do not, as it were, form the two panels of a triptych, equally exterior to the central picture. The *'new shadow'* is much more than a shadow or reflection; it prevails incomparably over the *'old shadows'*.[145] It would not be possible to confuse what regards either the dignity or the value of the *prefiguring* of the body offered in the sacrifice of Melchizedek with its *transformation* in the sacrifice of the Church.[146] The antitype cannot be distinguished from the truth as the type can, but it is understood within it: one and the same word is often used to describe them, and once again that word is 'truth'. However, in itself, this still does not imply the clear affirmation of the 'real presence'.

The same reasoning covers the word *body*. It also embraces, in certain cases, the whole sacramental reality of the new economy, without for all that containing any precise allusion to a 'bodily' presence. Like *truth*, it must therefore be understood by its contrast to the words *shadow* and *figure*, opposing the emptiness of the Jewish ceremonies, whose entire value was figurative, with the evangelical fullness, which is the fullness of Christ itself: *it was the shadow of law, it is now the body of Christ*.[147] In distinguishing the sacraments of the ancient law and those of the new law, the Church, says St. Fulgentius, divides the

---

143 *Epistula de buccella Judae data* (PL, 156, 527–8).

144 For example, *In Joannem*, tract. 26, n. 12 (PL, 35, 1612); tract. 45, n. 9 (1722–3); and parallelism between 'prophecy' and 'memory' of the unique Sacrifice: *Contra Faustum*, 20, c. 18, 21 (42, 382–3, 385); *De catechizandis rudibus*, n. 6, 27 (40, 313, 332). *In psalmum 77*, n. 2 (36, 983). Fulgentius, *Ep.* 14, n. 47 (65, 485). But cf. *supra*, n. 131, and c. 3, n. 77, etc.

145 Algerius of Liége (PL, 180, 815 B).

146 See *supra*, Chapter 3, n. 76. *Sacramentarium gallicanum vetus* (PL, 72, 375 B).

147 Pseudo-Primasius, *In Coloss.* (PL, 68, 656 B). Hugh of Rouen, *Tractatus de memoria*, 2, n. 8 (PL, 192, 1313 B). St. Thomas, *Summa theologiæ*, Ia IIae, q.107, a.2. See *supra*, pp. 189–90.

figures from the truth, the shadows from the body.[148] In one sense *body* is therefore a metaphor, and even as far as the wording of the Eucharistic mystery, where this fullness achieves so to speak its extreme point of condensation, our theologians still use it, in imitation of St. Augustine and in the tradition of several Pauline texts, *'because of the analogy of shadows'.*[149]

* * *

Nevertheless, this highly natural and well-grounded use of the most classical language was not without its influence on the development of Eucharistic theology, in helping to articulate realist claims. Applied solely to the mystery of the *body of Christ*, the two words *truth* and *body*, originally used in parallel fashion would be fatally brought together, in what we might almost be permitted to call word-play, to form no longer just the *body of the truth* but also the *true body.* Already Novatian,[150] and then St. Hilary[151] had made use of an analogous process to express the Church's faith in the reality of the Incarnation. St. Ambrose imitates them with regard to the Eucharist, and this is no surprise, given the particular clarity of his realism. His *De mysteriis* offers us the first example of the subtle mental manoeuvre that we are looking to find in operation. It occurs during a comparison with the manna:

> *More potent is light than shadow, truth than figure, and the body of the creator than manna from heaven.*[152]

That *body of authority*, as we can see, is no longer in any way the simple correlative of *shadow*. There has been a leap of thought that takes us to another level altogether.[153] It will be the same with Paschasius Radbertus, commenting on the words of institution:

---

148 *Ep.* 14, n. 45 (PL, 65, 432–3).

149 Augustine, *De Genesi ad litteram*, 12, c. 7, n. 17 (PL, 34, 459). Prosper, *Liber sententiarum* (51, 471 C). Pseudo-Primasius (68, 653). Sedulius Scottus (103, 226 D). Atto of Vercelli (134, 623 A–B).

150 *De Trinitate*, c. 9 (PL, 3, 900 C).

151 *De Trinitate*, 5, c. 17 (PL, 10, 139 A–B).

152 c. 8, n. 49 on 1 Cor. 10 (PL, 16, 405 B); cited by Ivo, *Decretum*, p. 2, c. 7 (161, 145 D), Abelard, *Sic et Non* (178, 1522 D), etc. Du Perron, *Traité de l'Eucharistie.* cf. De sacramentis, 4, c. 3, n. 10 (PL, 16, 438 B).

153 Analogous example in Gregory of Nyssa, *Life of Moses* (PG, 44, 368 B–C).

I wonder why some people now wish to say that the truth of the flesh and blood of Christ is not in reality . . . that it is figure and not truth, shadow and not body: when in fact this appearance takes on truth and figure, as the body of the ancient sacrifices.[154]

St. Jerome can furnish us with another example:

After the Passover had been accomplished in type, and he had eaten the flesh of the lamb with the apostles, he took bread, which strengthens the heart of man, and proceeded to the true sacrament of the Passover, in order that, just as Melchizedek, priest of the most high God, by offering bread and wine acted in such a way as to pre-figure him, he also might manifest himself in the truth of his own body and blood.[155]

The same slippage of sense, ending up with the same vital precision, can be found in the fifth letter of Fulbert of Chartres and in Algerius of Liège:

What the manna of the law signified under a shadow is revealed and opened up by the truth of the Lord's body.[156]
   He ordained one sacrament that was more worthy than all the sacraments of the law, so that by this sacrament . . . through the truth of his body he might, by completing them, dispel as superflu-ous the shadows of the ancient sacrifices.[157]

The case of Cardinal Humbert is possibly more curious. He had to give a response to one of the complaints raised by the Greeks against the use of unleavened bread in the Latin rite.[158] Did this not charac-terize the Jewish Passover, which was abolished by Christ? Humbert spends long chapters striving to demonstrate that the Old Testament is not cancelled or destroyed by the New, but fulfilled and brought to perfection. The traditional vocabulary comes naturally to his pen: he speaks of the passage *'from the shadows to the truth, from the sign to the thing itself'*; we ourselves, he observes, must pass, by means of our

---

154 *In Matthaeum*, 12, c. 26 (PL, 120, 890 D).
155 *In Matthaeum*, 4, c. 26 (PL, 26, 195); cited by Adrevald of Fleury (124, 948–9), Gratian, *De consecratione*, 2.88 (Fr., 1350) etc.
156 PL, 141, 203 B.
157 *De sacramentis*, l.2, c. 3 (PL, 180, 818 C–D). See also Augustine, *In Joannem*, tract. 26, n. 12 (35, 1614), and the commentary of Algerius, *Liber de misericordia et justitia*, p. 1, c. 62 (180, 884–5).
158 cf. *Nicetae libellus contra Latinos*, c. 2 (PL, 143, 973 C).

exegesis, *'from the letter that kills to the life-giving spirit'*, etc. And it is in this context that he writes:

> *According to the rite, venerating and retaining the Body of truth from the unleavened bread, and in the unleavened bread, by mouth and heart we taste in advance how sweet is the Lord.*[159]

Thus he did not even need to invert the words or to transform the *'body of truth'* into the *'true body'*, in order to make use of a word normally consecrated to scriptural interpretation to describe the Eucharistic presence.

A short time later, in the parallel that Rupert establishes between Isaac and Jesus, we find the classic antithesis: *'in figures–in truth'*. But here again, instead of directly qualifying the sacrifice of Christ, as *in figures* qualified the sacrifice of Isaac, the formulation *in truth*, thanks to the surreptitious addition of the complement *'of flesh and blood'*, finds itself qualifying the presence of Christ itself in the bread transformed into his body. Thus, to the traditional opposition of the figurative sacrifice with the 'true' sacrifice, is added another, the opposition of the sacrifice which only takes place figuratively because of the persistent duality of Isaac and the ram that is substituted for him, and of the sacrifice which is accomplished in truth as a result of the unity realized between the matter offered, bread and wine, and the body and blood of Christ. All this is contained in two lines:

> *There in figure Isaac was sacrificed in the ram, here in bread and wine the Son of God is sacrificed in the truth of his flesh and blood.*[160]

And in a similar parallel between the Jewish supper and the Christian Supper, Rupert again says: 'The figure was then to be accomplished in the reality of the truth of the presences, in the truth of the present reality.'[161]

Through a more daring procedure, coupled with an interpolation, a liturgical prayer transforms a text from St. Paul:

> . . . *Christ has been sacrificed as our pasch; that now not with the old leaven, nor with the blood of fleshly victims, but now in the unleavened bread of sincerity and of the truth of the body are we to sacrifice.*[162]

---

159 *Adversus Graecorum calumnias*, c. 43 (PL, 143, 961 C). cf. c. 42 (958 D).

160 *In Joannem*, 7 (PL, 169, 491 B).

161 *De Spiritu sancto*, 3, c. 21 (PL, 36, 441–2).

162 *Missale gothicum*, missa paschalis, feria 4ᵃ, contestatio (Bannister, vol. 1, p. 86; cf. vol. 2, p. 69). *idem*: *Vetus missale gallicanum* (72, 374 B).

It was partly via an analogous route that the Eucharistic words '*substance*' and '*substantially*' came into general use, as we realize when reading Durandus of Troarn, who several times uses these words in explicit contrast to '*shadow*' and '*figure*' when they are describing the manna.[163] In the same way as with *truth, body* is coupled with *substance* in order to offer a new expression for triumphant realism under the aegis of biblical exemplarism:

> *Everything . . . occurred in the figure, which indeed has no effect compared to the reality itself which it prefigures, just as a shadow is not the same as the substance of a thing or a body.*[164]

Thus the same words and the same formulations are preserved from century to century, but their signification changes, becomes enriched, or sometimes impoverished, because the problems, the concerns and the focus of interest also change, or supersede or interfere with one another. Take the formulation *truth of the mystery* again as an example. In the first centuries of the Middle Ages, it still normally operates in the general context of the relationship between the two Testaments. Thus in Rabanus Maurus we find: '*the mystery, of which we possess the truth*',[165] or in Walafrid Strabo: '*to consecrate offerings to the Lord, which . . . contain the truth of the mystery*'.[166] It was with a same meaning that St. Cyprian had once written: '*let us celebrate the truth of the sacrament*'[167] and that St. John Chrysostom, commenting on the Epistle to the Hebrews, spoke '*of the figure and the mystery whose truth we possess*'.[168] But then we have Guitmond of Aversa undertaking a refutation of Berengar's symbolism. The traditional formulation comes naturally to his mind. Only, he borrows it from St. Ambrose, with the sense that favours his new purpose: '*Let us show the truth of the mystery.*'[169] Shortly afterwards, in the course of another controversy, but with the identical aim, Bernold of Constance would use the same idea: '*the truth of the sacraments . . . which are believed to be present in the same completeness for both the good and the wicked*'.[170]

*   *   *

163 p. 5, c. 13, 15 (PL, 149, 1393–8).
164 Rupert, *In Joannem*, 6 (PL, 169, 461 C).
165 PL, 112, 802 C.
166 *De rebus ecclesiasticis*, c. 16 (PL, 114, 937 C).
167 *Ep. 63*, c. 16, n. 1 (Hartel, vol. 3, p. 714); c. 14, n. 4.
168 *Homilia 27*, n. 1 (PG, 63, 185).
169 Bk. 3 (PL, 149, 1472 D). Ambrose, *De mysteriis*, c. 3, n. 53 (16, 407 A); cited by Ivo, *Decretum* (161, 146 D).
170 *De sacramentis haereticorum* (MGH, *Libelli de lite*, vol. 2, p. 90). Honorius of Autun, *De offendiculo*, c. 41 (*ibid.*, vol. 3, p. 51).

In the evolution that has been roughly sketched out above, faith in the body present in the sacrament, a faith actively present in the consciousness of the faithful was guiding them even without their always realizing. But, as the last case quoted already shows us, this evolution was precipitated, from the ninth century and above all the eleventh century onwards, by well-known controversies.

Rightly or wrongly, Hincmar of Rheims took issue with opponents who, he said, were claiming '*that the sacraments of the altar are not the true body and true blood of the Lord*'.[171] In equivalent terms, Paschasius Radbertus wrote of them to Frudegard: '*They want to minimize the word body, claiming that what is now celebrated in the sacrament is not the true flesh of Christ.*'[172] The same basic accusation is made against Berengar: '*You are denying the truth of the flesh and blood*', Durandus of Troarn says to him straight out, and again: '*(the heretics say) that nothing in the sacraments of the Lord becomes truth*'.[173] Adelmann of Liège writes to his straying correspondent in exactly the same terms.[174] St. Bernard was to write in the *Life of Saint Malachy*[175] – and this text is very apt for demonstrating the reversal of meaning that the traditional formulations suffered under pressure from their abuse by heretics: '*A certain cleric . . . had the presumption to say that in the Eucharist there is only the sacrament but not the reality of the sacrament, that is, only sanctification but not the truth of the body.*' Hence the origin of the multiplication, outside any historical connotation and any biblical reference that we have seen up to now, of simple formulations such as *true body, true flesh, true blood*, etc.[176] Treatises *De veritate corporis* succeeded or added to treatises *De corpore* or *De sacramentis corporis*.[177]

This is true flesh, the flesh of the true lamb on which we are fed!

sang Hildebert.[178] Soon Peter the Venerable, in a famous sentence,

---

171 *De praedestinatione dissertation posterior*, c. 31 (PL, 125, 296).

172 PL, 120, 1356 D. Gezonius of Tortona, c. 41 (137, 392–3).

173 *De corpore et sanguine Christi*, p. 1 (PL, 149, 1377 A).

174 *De eucharistiae sacramento ad Berengarium epistula* (Heurtevent, p. 288. cf. Osbern, *Life of Saint Odo of Canterbury*, c. 10 (PL, 133, 939–40). Peter the Venerable (189, 788 C), etc.

175 c. 26, n. 57 (PL, 182, 1105 C–D).

176 Numerous examples. See *supra*, Chapter 4; *Sententiae Florianenses*, n. 74 (Ostlender, p. 35).

177 Treatises of Guitmond, of Bernold (Weisweiler, in *Scholastik*, 1937, pp. 80–93), of Gregory of Bergamo . . .

178 *Liber de sacra eucharistia* (PL, 171, 1200 B).

would praise Lanfranc, Guitmond and Algerius for having argued well on behalf of '*on the truth of the body and blood of Christ, which is disguised by the veil of the sacraments*'.[179] Innumerable priests would prepare to celebrate the sacrifice by saying to the Lord, following the prayer of John of Fécamp: '*Your flesh is received in truth, your blood is drunk in truth.*'[180] In theological thought, the viewpoint of action quite decidedly yields before the viewpoint of presence, and the consideration of different states equally gives way to that of essence or of identical substance: '*true and substantive body*', '*the true nature of flesh and blood*'.[181] Following on from Lanfranc, and before reproducing the profession of faith that Berengar had to sign, Ivo of Chartres collected in a long chapter of his *Decrees* all the evidence from St. Augustine that permitted him to conclude: '*Therefore his true flesh is what we receive, and his true blood what we drink.*'[182] Between the altar and the cross, if there is any difference in the manner of sacrifice, in the immolation and in the offering, there is none at all in the reality of the priest and of the victim: '*There is no variation in the truth of Christ himself*', as Algerius of Liège declares.[183] And again William of St. Thierry says: '*There is in the mysteries the true substance of the Lord's body.*'[184] And soon Gerhoh of Reichersberg, in one of his letters against Folmar, who in his eyes was another Berengar, would write: '*In the truth of the sacraments of Christ God is worshipped, who is received in the body taken from the Virgin and taken up into heaven.*'[185] They all insisted on the '*essential truth*',[186] or on the '*truth of the essence*'.[187] In 1079, Berengar had been made to confess the '*truth of the substance*',[188] and the terms of this profession of faith were repeated over and over again.[189] '*No one of sound mind doubts the truth of the substance*', we read in a theological fragment from

---

179 *Tractatus contra Petrobrusianos* (PL, 189, 788 D).

180 Oration *Summe sacerdos*, attributed to Ambrose by the Roman Missal. cf. Wilmart, *Auteurs spirituals et texts dévots du moyen âge latin*, p. 117.

181 Durandus of Troarn (PL, 149, 1393 C, 1405 A; 1412 A), etc.

182 *Decretum*, p. 2, c. 9 (PL, 161, 160 D).

183 *De sacramentis*, 1, c. 16 (PL, 180, 787 C); c. 18 (792 C), etc.

184 *Epistula ad quemdam monachum* (PL, 180, 343 B–C).

185 *Ep. 7, ad Adamum* (PL, 193, 497 B).

186 Algerius (PL, 180, 787 C).

187 Guitmond (PL, 149, 1448 B). Gregory of Bergamo, c. 13 (H., p. 53).

188 'Not only by the sign and power of a sacrament, but in the character of a nature and truth of a substance.'

189 Odo of Cambrai (PL, 160, 1062). Algerius (180, 884 D, 786 D). Abelard, *Theologia Christiana*, 4 (178, 1286), etc.

the School of Laon.[190] Durandus of Troarn makes clear that in the sacrament, Christ exists *'in truth naturally'*.[191] Whereas once upon a time it could have been said of the Mass, in an allusion to the Mosaic sacrifices: *'Nothing is to be thought empty in the sacrifice of truth'*, now it is more a question of preferring a quotation attributed to St. Ambrose: *'nothing false'*.[192] This truth with respect to the sacrament is still undoubtedly a fullness, but it is primarily a 'sincerity':[193] *'there exists the true flesh and true blood of Christ, by which Christ himself is proved to be truthful'*.[194] It is a 'simple truth': *'He gave his body and blood without any ambiguity, in simple truth.'*[195] *'To receive in truth, truly . . .'* has simply become a parallel term for *'to consecrate in truth, truly'* etc. This is no longer a matter, as it was for St. Augustine,[196] of feeding on Christ in spirit and in truth: it is, whether worthily or not, to receive the true body of Christ.[197] On this last point, however, the ancient turn of phrase is open to change, and concessions would need to be made to it for some time; but then care would be taken to avoid any ambiguity, and the phrase used would be, for example: *'to feed on the holy and true body'*.[198] Algerius of Liège, in whom an earlier witness is found to the hesitations around the 'bodily eating', can again here give witness to similar hesitations around the 'true eating':

Even though in his sacrament he is truly present and is truly received as regards the substance, nevertheless he is more truly and more perfectly received by faith and devotion as regards the grace of salvation.[199]

---

190 Lottin, *Recherches de théologie ancienne et médiévale*, 1939, p. 253; cf. p. 252.

191 *Liber de corpore* (PL, 149, 1392).

192 Peter Lombard, *In I Cor.*, xi (PL, 191, 1644 D). Peter Comestor, *Sententiae de sacramentis* (M., p. 54). Peter of Poitiers, *Sententiae*, 5, c. 12 (PL, 211, 1250 A). William of St. Thierry, *Ep. ad quemdam monachum* (180, 343 C). cf. Fulbert of Chartres (141, 202 A). Durandus of Troarn (149, 1412 A).

193 Durandus of Troarn (PL, 149, 1413 B).

194 *ibid.*, col. 1378.

195 Hugh of Rouen, *Contra haereticos* (PL, 192, 1281 D; cf. 1271 D, 1276 D).

196 *De civitate Dei*, 21, c. 25, n. 2 (PL, 41, 741). Rabanus Maurus, *De clericorum institutione*, 1, c. 31 (107, 318 B).

197 John of Fécamp, *Confessio Fidei* (PL, 101, 1089 B). Manegold, *Contra Wolfelmum* (155, 166 A). Peter of Blois (207, 1140 A). Innocent III (217, 860 C, cf. 862 A), etc. cf. Lanfranc (PL, 150, 414 B). Algerius (180, 779 A, 886 A). Gregory of Bergamo (H., p. 11). *Florilegia of Saint-Amand* (Lottin, 1939, p. 320), etc.

198 William of St. Thierry, *De sacramento altaris*, c. 4 (PL, 180, 351 B).

199 *De sacramentis*, 1, c. 11 (PL, 180, 773 C).

There is therefore truth and truth. These two sorts of truth certainly do not contradict one another, but they each concern a quite different object. One of them was felt to be more directly under threat, and so in reaction, impinged more distinctly on the general consciousness, so that a need was felt to establish its claims more forcefully by the increasingly exclusive reservation of the name. Hence, in Hugh of St. Victor, who distinguishes carefully between one and the other,[200] the slight transformation of vocabulary in his account of the classic theory: after the *sacrament* comes the *truth*, which is itself already the *reality of the sacrament*, then, in third place, the *reality of the sacrament* which is at the same time the *reality of truth*.[201] Hence also, through a phenomenon analogous to others that we have already encountered, and in which in some sense the whole evolution described in this chapter is summed up, the change of meaning, in terms of the words themselves, of the old *type-truth* opposition.

In the Gregorian prayer – *what we do in appearance* . . . – the *appearance* had to be understood in a broader sense. It embraced the entire holy action, with emphasis on its human, sensible and temporal side – *what we perform for a time, what we celebrate in our temporal action*,[202] – but without in any way rejecting the interiority or 'mystery' implied or presupposed by that action,[203] any more than the mention of the temporal death of the Saviour, in prayers that came from the same mould, was a negation of his eternal fruitfulness.[204] Unlike *theology*, is not the whole *economy* concerned, by its very essence, with matter and time? Is not the pilgrim Church the *temporal Church*,[205] without for all that ceasing to be the Bride and the very Body of Christ? This Eucharistic *type* was therefore the approximate equivalent, certainly not of the 'carnal' sacraments of the old Law in opposition to which those of Christianity are said to be spiritual,[206] nor of what

---

200 *De sacramentis*, 2, p. 11, c. 13 (PL, 176, 505).

201 *De sacramento corporis Christi* (Wilmart, p. 243).

202 *Gelasianum* (W., pp. 164, 184, 209). *Gregorianum* (L., pp. 67, 73, 78, 85). cf. Gregory the Great, *In Ezechielem*, 2, hom. 1, n. 16 (PL, 76, 947 A). Roman Missal, postcommunion of *Corpus Christi*. Formulae where the human part of the sacrifice is particularly underlined in *Gregorianum*, (L., p. 90) and the Sacramentary of Alcuin (PL, 101, 449 D), etc.

203 cf. Postcommunion of an Anglo-Saxon Sacramentary, for the anniversary of a martyr (Bannister, *Journal of Theological Studies* 9, p. 402); Roman Missal [prior to 1970], 19th January.

204 *Gregorianum* (L., p. 44; Roman Missal, postcommunion of Wednesday in Holy Week [prior to 1970]).

205 Remigius of Auxerre, *In psalmos* (PL, 131, 368 D, 466 D, 583 D).

206 *idem*. (131, 535 C), etc.

St. Augustine calls in a restrictive sense, whose context permits of no misinterpretation, '*the visible sacrament*' or '*external sacrament*',[207] but of what he calls '*corporal sacraments*' or '*corporal mysteries*',[208] or again '*temporal sacraments*', that is to say, as he himself explains, '*whatever is performed in the Church in time*'.[209] Others would also say: '*visible mysteries*',[210] '*visible mysteries of the new law*'.[211] Within it, although from a particular angle, the whole cultic mystery of the Church was envisaged. It was that '*visible Eucharist*' of which John Scotus spoke, a figure and pledge of the completely spiritual union with Christ of which salvation consists.[212] The action that it defined was the action '*in mysterio*' or '*in sacramento*' of so many other texts.[213] – As for the *truth* that corresponds to it – *let us grasp things in their truth* – we have previously seen its equally broad and profound meaning, identical to that of the *reality of the sacrament*: its understanding was linked to that of eternity, in which alone, like the Body of Christ itself, it came to fulfilment.[214]

Now, in the theology that followed Berengar's era, and precisely through the effect of his use of the Gregorian formulation following 'John Scotus',[215] the opposition of the two words, which remained frequent, was no longer understood except in a completely different sense that was much simpler and more obvious. The positive relationship between pre-figuration and anticipation of the mystery and its fruit was therefore abandoned, and it was retained as no more than a banal antithesis. In its second meaning, the *type* became the *sacrament as such* of the threefold theory that was being elaborated, minus its particular character as a sign. These are already our 'types', although the rites could be specifically understood here, but only in their exterior

---

207 *Ad Bonifacium*, n. 2 (PL, 33, 360), etc. *De Civitate Dei*, 21, c. 25, n. 2 (41, 741).

208 *Contra Faustum* (PL, 42, 265); *Confessions*, 13, c. 20, n. 28 (Labriolle, p. 387); *De peccato originali*, n. 35 (PL, 44, 402). In a more general sense: PL, 36, 376. cf. *De mendacio*, n. 40 (40, 514). Florus (Duc, p. 136). John of Fécamp (PL, 101, 1091 A). Ivo of Chartres, *Decretum* (161, 148 B). Algerius (180, 764 A). Hervé (181, 935 C), etc. *Gelasianum* (W., p. 206).

209 *In psalmum 146*, n. 8 (PL, 37, 1903).

210 *Gregorianum* (L., p. 68). Ivo of Chartres, *Sermo 1* (PL, 162, 505 C), etc.

211 John Scotus, *Super Hierarchiam caelestem* (PL, 122, 142 D). Or *ecclesiastica novi testamenti mysteria* (182 B).

212 *Super Hierarchiam caelestem* (PL, 122, 140 C–D). Gregory Nazianzen, *Discourse 17*, c. 12 (PG, 35, 980). *Liturgy of Saint Basil*.

213 *Gregorianum* (L., pp. 39, 40, 64, 75).

214 Pseudo-Alcuin (John of Fécamp), *Confessio fidei*, p. 3, c. 12 (PL, 101, 1061 C–D, 1062 A; after Augustine).

215 cf. Ascelin, *Letter to Berengar* (PL, 150, 67–8).

sense. They are principally the appearances of bread and wine: deceptive, 'specious' appearances, as opposed to the 'truth', that is to say the reality of the body and the blood whose substance there, on the altar, is really present. It is the *type of the sacrament*,[216] the *shadow of the sacrament*[217] beneath which Christ is truly hidden:[218] *'the body veiled by the appearances of bread'*.[219]

Ratramnus, as well as Paschasius Radbertus,[220] already knew the antithesis, and he allowed himself to use it.[221] Thus the novelty does not lie in the use that we make of it now, but in its extreme generalization and in the subsequent ignorance of its earlier use. '*It is the true flesh of the Lord and yet the appearances remain*', wrote Renallo of Barcelona.[222] So we also find it in Lanfranc,[223] and Guitmond of Aversa, distinguishing on the one hand *'the visible species and the visible mysteries'*, and on the other hand *'the truth of the substance of the body'*.[224] And in Peter Damian,[225] Rudolph of St. Tron,[226] Gilbert of Hoyland,[227] Algerius of Liège,[228] Hugh of St. Victor,[229] with his whole host of satellites,[230] Geoffrey of Vendôme,[231] Gerhoh of Reichersberg,[232] etc. And also in Roland's *Sentences*,[233] or the *Tractatus de schismaticis* (between 1164 and 1168): '*sacrament in appearance, reality in the truth of the body*',[234] or the treatise on the Eucharist of Peter Comestor.[235] And again in Peter of Celle,[236] or Pseudo-Damian, who it must be remembered was not earlier than the end of the twelfth century: '*the

---

216　Hugh of St. Victor (PL, 176, 467 A).
217　Adam of St. Victor, *Sequence* (PL, 196, 1434).
218　First state of the *Adoro te* (Wilmart, *Auteurs spirituals* . . . , p. 393).
219　*Ep. 3a contra Folmarum* (B.M.P., vol. 25, p. 314 F).
220　PL, 120, 1269, 890 D.
221　c. 16 (PL, 121, 135 A); c. 49 (147 A; 150 A).
222　About 1080 (PL, 147, 606 A).
223　PL, 150, 423 C.
224　PL, 149, 1461 C.
225　*Opusculum 47*, c. 2 (PL, 145, 712 B). cf. Werner of St. Blaise (157, 910 D).
226　cf. Mansi, vol. 20, 845 A.
227　*In Cantica sermo 7*, n. 8 (PL, 184, 46–7).
228　*De sacramentis* (PL, 180, 753 C, 755 C–D).
229　PL, 176, 466, 467.
230　*Speculum Ecclesiae* (PL, 177, 365). Richard of Wedinghausen (177, 361 A). *Sermo de excellentia* (184, 989–90). Innocent III, a. 1202, *Letter 121*, to John, Archbishop of Lyon (214, 1121 A–B).
231　PL, 157, 212 D, 213 C. Werner of St. Blaise ? (157, 910 D), etc.
232　*Tractatus adversus simoniacos*, n. 29 (PL, 194, 1367 A).
233　Gietl, p. 216.
234　MGH, *Libelli de lite*, vol. 3, p. 127.
235　M., p. 56
236　*Liber de panibus*, c. 1 (PL, 202, 934 A).

appearance is chewed, but the truth is never injured'.[237] To the appearance of bread, all of them oppose the truth of the body as the invisible to the visible, as what is believed to what can be touched and seen. Theology would never look back.

Nevertheless, there will have to be at least some backward glances, in order to be able to continue reading the traditional texts: texts from the Scriptures, from the Fathers or the liturgy. Only some of them would now transfer to the side of 'objections'. They were hardly ever used any longer in the positive presentation of dogma, but they had to be snatched away from innovators who were claiming them in favour of their denials. This is how, in one of his letters, Lanfranc claimed that Augustine, in speaking of 'figures', appeared, and still very much appears, to deny the 'truth'.[238] These venerable texts, in which faith had found its expression, and on which the spiritual life had nourished itself for centuries, thus became primarily sources of difficulty, and it is because of this that they became a matter of concern: *'In order to put a stop to blasphemy, we are obliged to show that the words that are adduced against us are no objection at all to our assertion'*, Gregory of Bergamo, to whom we owe this declaration,[239] undertook the programme methodically. In order to realise the extent of this, one has only to run through the titles of his chapters: a series of little dissertations sets at a distance one after the other these witnesses to an age that was soon to pass, thanks to 'explanations' that extracted from them all the poison that had entered into them through heresy, but also, too often, all the virtue that had been bequeathed to them by the past. One after the other St. John, St. Paul, St. Ambrose, St. Augustine . . . thus found themselves more or less neutralized.[240] And our Gregory was not the only one. We have met similar examples previously[241] and we will have the opportunity of quoting one or two of them again in the following chapter. But for the moment let me confine myself, in conclusion, to the Gregorian prayer, which was still the object of numerous commentaries in the course of the twelfth century. Here is what the *Liber septem partium*, possibly the work of Anselm of Laon, has to say:

---

237 *Expositio canonis* (PL, 145, 883 C).
238 *Ep. 10, ad Domnaldum* (Mansi, vol. 20, 32 E).
239 c. 10 (H., p. 39).
240 c. 5 to 10.
241 cf. ch. iv. And the fragment of the School of Laon, published by Dom Lottin (*Recherches de théologie ancienne et médiévale*, 1946, p. 280).

> *It is to be believed to be the true body of Christ, etc. Even though*
> St. Gregory *in a post-communion prayer permits himself to call it*
> *appearance,* he does not mean *that the bread that is consecrated*
> *merely represents the body of Christ, because it is that body. What*
> *he means is that there is something else we have to do.*[242]

We can see the intention and the thought behind it. They are the same
in Robert of Melun:

> *It is asked whether it is* in reality or only in appearance *that in the*
> *present age the body of Christ is received by the Church. That it*
> *is in appearance only and not in reality seems to be intended by*
> *Gregory, who at the end of a communion prayer says, 'so that what*
> *we receive (sic) in appearance we may obtain in the truth of the*
> *realities'. This is to be explained as follows, etc.*[243]

'Explanations' of this sort are certainly not made up of assertions
in formal contradiction to the original sense of the texts. They cannot normally be treated as contradictions, or even always accused of
inexactitude. They are sometimes pertinent. Such is the case of the
one given by Robert of Melun.[244] But they also often derive from other
sources and clear the way for a reflection from other perspectives than
those of the texts themselves. At the very least, what constituted their
essence became an accessory. Thought neither stopped nor derived
any nourishment there. The interest in recovering the true sense lay
above all in the fact that, in this way, a dangerous interpretation was
avoided. That is why, instead of adopting a firm exegesis, the reader
was willingly given the choice between two explanations: satisfied
with getting out of an awkward spot, the author did not feel the need
to choose for himself. This was the case with Lanfranc,[245] who would
soon be quoted, under the name of Pope Gregory himself, by Ivo of
Chartres[246] and by Gratian,[247] and whom Peter Lombard would copy
for posterity:

---

242 Cited by R.-M. Martin, edn. of Robert of Melun, *Quaestiones de divina*
pagiana, p. 22, n.

243 *Quaestiones de divina pagiana* (between 1143 and 1147), q. 38 (Martin,
pp. 22-3). cf. Peter of Poitiers (PL, 211, 1253 A-B).

244 *loc. cit.*

245 *Liber de corpore*, c. 20 (PL, 150, 436 B, C).

246 *Decretum*, p. 2, c. 9; *Panormia*, 1, c. 132 (PL, 161, 157 B, 1745 A).

247 *Decretum, De consecratione*, 2.34 (Friedberg, 1324-5).

The priest is asking that the body of Christ which is exhibited in the appearance of bread and wine may one day be attained in a direct vision of what it truly is. The word 'truth' is often found in sacred literature in place of 'manifestation' . . . However, some people offer the not improbable interpretation that in this passage the 'truth' of the flesh and blood is their efficacy, that is, the forgiveness of sins. For in every way the true flesh and blood of Christ are present for those who receive them worthily . . .[248]

Speaking roughly, and looking less at the letter than at the spirit, it is therefore true to say that the ancient texts are no longer understood, because the spirit in which they were composed has partly been lost.[249] The fact is that Eucharistic theology became more and more a form of apologetic and organized itself increasingly round a defence of the 'real presence'. Apology for dogma succeeded the understanding of faith. This evolution, this contrast, the misunderstandings and the awkward problems of interpretation that resulted from them, the incomprehension that is the price paid for new insights, all that is summed up symbolically in the two successive meanings of *truth*.

---

248 *Sentences*, 4, d. 9, n. 3 (PL, 192, 859). *In I Cor.* (191, 1643–4). St. Thomas, *In IV Sent.*, d. 8, q. 1, a. 3; q. 2, a. 1 (Moos, pp. 319, 333; cf. *supra*, p. 223).

249 On this subject, see Mabillon, *Praefationes in Acta sanctorum ordinis sancti Benedicti*, in saec. 4m, n. 96 to 100 (Trent, 1724, pp. 337–8).

10

From Symbolism to Dialectic

[248]

The 'second body' was therefore as much a *true body* as the other two, and for exactly the same reason as the first. From now on, this would be its explicit and, in some sense, official title. There was no logical incompatibility between this title and that of *mystical body*. Consider the phrases of Paschasius and Algerius, '*true and mystical body*', '*true and mystical flesh*',[1] or again, in the tradition of St. Hilary, '*true, under the mystery*', '*true in the mystery*'.[2] Had not Hériger of Lobbes declared that in the Eucharist things had to be understood at one and the same time *in figures* and *in truth*?[3] Nevertheless, the fact is that the invasion of *true* caused *mystical* to give way.

Fixated on the truth of presence, it was undoubtedly fatal for theological attention in some sense to neglect the 'mystical' meaning of the sacramental body. We can distinguish in outline what appear to be four attitudes with regard to this. For some, truth had to be assured, more explicitly than hitherto, as the condition without which the whole economy of the mystery would perish, but for all that we must not ignore the fact that, within its very truth, the Eucharist is a figure: its mystical link to the Church is essential to it. – For others, the two claims were maintained equally, but their relationship became inverted: if the figure was conceded, it was only in order to add immediately that what is a figure is first and foremost the truth: '*Therefore these things are signs, so that they might also be what is signified*'[4] – '*Not only mystically, but also in truth.*'[5] Besides, these two first

---

1 Algerius of Liège (PL, 180, 748), etc. Cf. Paschasius, *Liber de corpore*, c. 4 (120, 1277–8); *Ad Frudegardum* (1353 A).

2 Hilary, *De Trinitate*, 8, n. 13 (PL, 10, 246 B). Gezonius of Tortona (137, 833 A). Otho of Lucques (176, 143). St. Bernard, *In Cantica*, sermo 33 (183, 952).

3 4 (PL, 139, 182 B).

4 Cardinal Humbert, *Adversus simoniacos*, 2, c. 39 (MGH, *Libelli de lite*, vol. I, p. 188). Hugh of St. Victor (*supra*, ch. ix, note 48), etc.

5 Gregory of Bergamo, (Hürter, pp. 8, 18). Cf. Deodwin of Liège (PL, 146, 1439). Council of Plaisance (1095), canon 6 (Mansi, vol. 20. 803 C); *Bernoldi Chronicon*, (MGH, *Script.*, vol. 5, p. 462). Cf. *Hugonis Chronicon*, 2 (*Script.*, vol. 8, p. 443).

attitudes were not mutually exclusive. Many would adopt now one, now the other, according to the stage they had reached in their articulation. Witness this double assertion by Durandus of Troarn:

> *We do not have to deny that the Lord's sacrament is a figure and likeness in regard to something in order to profess that the body and blood of Christ exist naturally in truth . . .*
>   *The perception of the body and blood of Christ . . . is agreed to be true as regards the authenticity of the realities, and yet is not lacking in the grace of signification.*[6]

In the same spirit of synthesis, Gregory of Bergamo praises St. Jerome[7] for having, on the one hand, given a good explanation, in the tradition of St. Matthew, of the '*true body and blood of the Lord*', without neglecting to show, on the other hand, in the tradition of St. Mark, that the Eucharist is nonetheless '*a figure of the body of Christ, which is the Church present*'; then he concludes:

> *We believe and profess the truth of the body and blood of Christ without hesitation, and we gratefully admit that the preserved appearance of bread and wine is a figure of the body which is the Church.*[8]

The flow of the controversy went in the opposite direction, in certain cases, to the extent of making people forget the ecclesial symbolism altogether. Thus everything was considered finalised once the *true body* had been duly established, and that was one more reason for not speaking of the *mystical body*. The declaration that Berengar had to sign: '*the bread and wine after the consecration are not only the sacrament but also the true body and blood*', was reasserted and commented on, apparently without remembering that this 'true body' is in its own turn itself a 'sacrament'. It is not surprising that short polemical treatises, which went to the heart of things, without aspiring to offer a complete doctrinal explanation, halted there. But in more important, more mature works, such as Guitmond of Aversa's treatise, this disappearance of the symbolic point of view indicated a new departure. We might add that neither in Guitmond, nor in those who would

---

6 *Liber de corpore et sanguine Christi* (PL, 149, 1392, 1414).
7 Pseudo-Jerome (PL, 30, 632).
8 c. 18 (H., p. 77) and c. 25 concerning a text of St. Gregory (pp. 99–100). Hugh of St. Victor, *De sacramentis*, 2, p. 8, c. 7 (PL, 176, 467 A–B).

continue his tendency, would the paralipsis be total.[9] Finally, to put it bluntly, a last group of theologians allowed itself to be manipulated by its adversary. While their aim was to contradict him more convincingly, they foolishly followed him into his own territory, without realizing the danger that awaited them there. We know that Berengar was making a great deal of a few sentences from 'John Scotus' (Ratramnus), whose significance he was in any case exaggerating. Following him, he quoted the famous Gregorian prayer in order to claim the authority not to accept in the Eucharistic mystery anything but a *type* without any objective fulfilment, and in the same way he interpreted Ambrose's *image* as a pure and simple *figure*, exterior to any truth that would follow on from it. This was a fatal dichotomy, whose hypothesis ought to have been refuted from the outset. Several authors were satisfied simply with inverting it, thus proving themselves as uncomprehending as Berengar, although heading in the opposite direction. Such was the case of the Roman deacon who was present at the Council of Vercelli. Hearing the passage being read, in which Ratramnus had defined the sacramental body as '*the pledge and image of a future thing*',[10] he cried out: '*If we are still in the figure, when will we grasp the reality?*' ...[11] This would also appear to be the case with Berengar of Venouse, in the letter against his namesake that he addressed to Gregory VII.[12] If we wanted to translate into conscious intentions what appear from the outset, as in so many other theological discussions, to have been nothing but a series of obscure misunderstandings, it could be said that the ultra-orthodox party fell into the trap that had been set for them by the heretic, or again that they allied with him in mutilating the traditional teaching: one group holding to symbolism, the other to the 'truth'. Against *mystically, not truly*,[13] was set, in no less exclusive a sense, *truly, not mystically*. Perhaps orthodoxy was safeguarded, but on the other hand, doctrine was certainly impoverished. In the past Paschasius Radbertus had been better inspired.

This last group remained a tiny minority. We should not automatically add into it all the theologians who at one point or another set aside 'figures' in order to make room for 'truth'. When someone like

---

9 Guitmond, *De corporis veritate*, 2 (PL, 149, 1468 A–C); *Confessio* (1500 B–D).

10 Ratramnus added his commentary (PL, 121, 164).

11 Berengar, *De sacra cena* (Vischer, p. 43).

12 Morin, *Recherches de Théologie ancienne et médiévale*, 1932, p. 120. Analogous mentality with Ascelin, *Letter to Berenger* (Harduin, *Concilia*, vol. 6, c. 1020) and with pretentious Gozechin, *Ep. ad Valcher*, c. 30 (PL, 143, 900).

13 Cf. Algerius of Liège, *De sacramentis* (PL, 180, 776). Cf. *supra*, note 5.

Baldwin of Canterbury, for example, wrote in line with so many others: '*therefore what Christ said, "This is my body", is expressed truth, not a figure*',[14] we can understand the precise purpose and meaning of his assertion, and the rest of his work shows sufficiently well that he was not abandoning traditional symbolism. And still for many who came after him, the Eucharist would remain explicitly *the figure and the matter*[15] *the truth and the figure.*[16] Only, that same word *figure* can be taken – the *truth* or the *matter* being equally safeguarded – as being understood in two quite different ways. Already, almost at the outset of the crisis opened up by Berengar, the author of that letter to Abbot Gerald that was quoted above was thus formulating his profession of faith:

> . . . *That so great a consecration is called bread and flesh, sacrament or figure, I not only do not reject, but embrace and approve, assembling all these affirmations generally in the exposition of the faith. Certainly no-one who shows good sense would doubt that it is orthodoxly spoken of as bread* . . . . *It is truly sacrament, because the visible appearance that is seen is consecrated secretly by divine power* . . . *It is also figure, because it is understood differently from how it is seen* . . .[17]

Thus he could well conclude in a formulation apparently similar to that of Gregory of Bergamo: '*Therefore after the consecration of so great a mystery, I believe that I receive the Eucharist of the Lord in such a sense that I in no way deny that the sacrament contains a figure.*'[18]

This figure is no longer that of the Church. Our author should in fact be counted among those whose reaction against heresy caused them to forget all ecclesial symbolism. All he means here is that the Lamb of God does not present himself in the Eucharist under the appearance of flesh. Many others would express themselves in the

---

14 PL, 204, 661. Manegold, *Contra Wolfelmum*, c. 18 (PL, 155, 166 A). Durandus of Troarn (149, 1377 D), etc. (Dom Morin, *Revue bénédictine*, 1908, p. 17; cf. *ibid.* p. 11, text similar to the *Exaggeratio*: Hériger?)

15 *Florilegia of Saint-Amand* (Lottin, *Recherches de Théologie ancienne et médiévale*, 1939, p. 309). Hugh of Rouen, *Dialogues*, 5, n. 14 (PL, 192, 1209 C).

16 Innocent III (PL, 214, 1120). Durandus of Mende, *Rationale divinorum officiorum*, 4, c. 42, n. 21 (p. 176). Bessarion, *De sacramento Eucharistiae* (PG, 161, 497 D). Cf. Pascal, *Thoughts* (Br. 862).

17 PL, 149, 433 D, 434 B. Cf. *Supra*, p. 95.

18 *loc. cit.*

same vein. Symbolism would continue to lose ground – although the reality behind it has never been lost in the tradition of the Church. Thus we can establish that those two words *truth and figure*, sometimes without even changing order, took on a new meaning, through a phenomenon of transference analogous to the one established in the previous chapter for the couplet *species–truth*. Even when it still seemed to be being treated as an attribute of *the body of Christ* (with a verbal illogicality that would be enough to reveal a departure from the authentic sense), the *figure* would still only be the 'species or appearance' of the bread:

> *The body of Christ is truth and figure: truth, because it is in reality flesh and blood; and figure, because in appearance and taste we see bread.*[19]

* * *

Just as, among our authors, there was more than one misunderstanding with regard to the words *mystery, image and figure* . . . , there was also more than one about the word 'symbolism', that I have just used to characterize traditional thought, whereas on the contrary it was often used to designate the doctrine of Berengar himself, and of his imitators, in opposition to the 'realism' of the orthodox tradition. In actual fact, if I were to seek to characterize this doctrine not so much by the arguments in which it ended, as by the spirit that animated it and by the methodology it used, it would be better to say that it presented itself as a form of rationalism and dialectic. Ultimately, there is no doubt that its adherents wanted to see in the Eucharist nothing but a symbol of Christ: but, far from developing traditional symbolism to excess, they were the first to withdraw from it. The fact is that the very nature of their understanding made them recoil from it, and its new techniques had no affinity with it. Their rationalism was in fact something quite other than an anxiety to make more space, alongside *authority*, for *reason*, and their dialectic did not entirely derive from the love of discussion for its own sake, the use of syllogism or the massive borrowing of terms from Boethius's logic.[20] All of this was mere outward appearance. It was further down, in the dark basements of the mind, in that mysterious zone where everything becomes entangled

---

19 St. Peter Celestine, *Opusculum*, 1, c. 49 (BMP, vol. 25, p. 784 F).

20 Sigbert of Gembloux, *De scriptoribus ecclesiasticis*, c. 154 (PL, 160, 582 B–C). Fr. de Ghellinck (DTC, vol. 5, col. 1242). See also his study *Dialectique et dogme aux Xe et XIIe siècles*, in *Mélanges Baeumker* (1913), vol. 1, pp. 79–99.

in advance, before seeing the light of day, that the major change took place whose symptoms manifested themselves virulently for the first time in the Berengarian crisis. Now our new dialecticians were only capable of dissociating a reality that was believed to have been united for ever by those geniuses of ontological symbolism, the Fathers of the Church. At the hands of Berengar, the sacramental synthesis disintegrated, as once the Trinitarian and Christological synthesis had done at the hands of the Arians and their successors.[21] On the one hand, there was a real body – whether earthly or heavenly – which could only be understood *sensibly*; on the other, there was a spiritual body, which no longer had real corporality nor, to be frank, any objective existence. On the one hand, there was the idea of a substantial presence, which came to an end for us when Christ returned to heaven;[22] on the other, a power bereft of the pregnant significance that it still had for the theologians of the previous age. Finally on the one hand, there was Christ himself in his personal reality or, within the sacrament, its power; on the other, ourselves, the Church . . . If others were tempted to an excessive confusion of Christ with his Church, the Head with the members of the Body, for his part Berengar, entirely on the other side, no longer had any sense at all of their mutual immanence. His dialectic prevented him from understanding Augustine's '*one Christ, full Christ, total Christ, whole Christ*'.[23] No one could have been more of a stranger to the mystery of the '*head in the body and body in the head*' than this copier of Augustinian formulations.[24] All the symbolic inclusions were transformed, in his understanding, into dialectical antitheses. Thus he constantly separated what tradition unified.[25] In the way in which they have just been formulated, several of these antitheses will perhaps appear, historically speaking, rather forced: I have said that Berengar's thought was elusive. Furthermore, it is difficult, in the mutilated state in which his articulation of them has reached us, to measure the exact extent of his margin of negation. At the very least it bears more than just their seeds, and we will see them blossom at the foot of the slope where they took root.

---

21 Cf. the essential reproach addressed by St. Hilary to the Arian dialectic, *De Trinitate*, 2, c. 5 (PL, 10, 54 A).

22 *De sacra cena* (Vischer, p. 266; cf. p. 200). Cf. *supra*, Chapters 6, 7.

23 Augustine, *De peccatorum meritis*, 1, c. 31, n. 60, citing 1 Cor. 12.12 (PL, 44, 145), *In Joannem*, tract. 28, n. 1 (35, 1622); *In Joannem*, tract 28, n. 1 (35, 1622); *In psalmum* 37 (36, 399), etc. Cf. Chrysostom, *In I Cor.*, hom. 30 (PG, 61, 250).

24 Prosper, *In psalmum* 142 (PL, 51, 406 B).

25 V., p. 223. Cf. Gerhoh of Reichersberg. *In psalmum* 67 (PL, 194, 192 B).

Now – and this is where the conflict of the eleventh century appears in all its tragic grandeur – what was indeed, from the orthodox point of view, a downward slope, appeared crowned with all the prestige of a life in the process of evolving from the point of view of thought. Berengarian rationalism was a landmark in the direction of progress. Historians of theology have no hesitation in recognizing it. They generally place Berengar at the head of the initiators of modern theology, before Anselm and Abelard.[26] Still quite recently M. Amann wrote: 'The Berengarian episode signifies that a new era is about to begin for Christian thought or, rather, for human thought'; he added that within it could be perceived 'the beginnings of the intellectual movement that would lead to the great renaissance of the twelfth century'.[27] With the intemperate daring of all precursors, he who was branded as a heresiarch marks the ideal from which, in the following centuries, the most notable works of theology would take their inspiration:

> *It is plainly characteristic of the heart in the highest degree to have recourse in everything to* dialectic, *because to have recourse to it is to have recourse to* reason, *and whoever does not have recourse to reason, despite being rational, as made in the image of God, forsakes his own honour, and cannot be renewed day by day in the image of God.*[28]

Thus when Berengar celebrated, even in his meditation on the mysteries of faith, 'the eminent role of reason'[29] his voice found an echo everywhere. In vain did his enemies, with greater or less skill, knock down the authorities with which he protected himself, others might well mock his dialectic, 'taken', they said, 'from Aristotle, from Chrysippus and from Cicero'[30] or else, on the contrary, borrow it from him in order to use it to refute one or other of his arguments,[31] and thus retrieve from him several disciples who had originally been

---

26 See Mandonnet, *Dante le Théologien* (1935), pp. 168–9.

27 *L'Église au pouvoir des laïques*, p. 530 (Fliche-Martin, *Histoire de l'Église*, vol. 7, 1940).

28 *De sacra cena* (V., p. 100). Cf. Hériger of Lobbes (PL, 139, 185 B). Cf. Augustine, *In psalmum* 42, n. 6 (PL, 36, 480); M. Gilson, *Introduction à l'étude de saint Augustin*, 2nd edn, 1943, p. 288, note 3; Berenger (p. 222, 221, 99).

29 *De sacra cena*, p. 53.

30 Anastasius of Angers, cited by J. de Ghellinck, *La Littérature latine au moyen âge*, vol. 2, p. 93.

31 See Lanfranc, c. 7, 8 (PL, 150, 416–18). See also his declaration of principles, *In I Cor* (150, 157 B).

seduced:[32] no one had the power to stop his influence. Because this was
no longer a matter of that direct and tangible influence which exercises
itself through the propagation of ideas or of precise formulations, nor
even of that more subtle influence that we saw earlier on at work
in the reactions that the new teaching was provoking. It was not, in
all honesty, a matter of one man's influence. More profoundly, more
universally, it was a new mentality that was spreading, a new order of
problem that was emerging and catching people's interest, a new way
of thinking, the formulation of new categories. Understanding was
entering into a new era, and Berengar of Tours, however mediocre his
genius might have been, was nevertheless one of its first examples and
most vigorous architects. At that time there was enough lively faith
around to eliminate his error on the spot; continually re-emerging,[33]
it would be vanquished on each occasion for some centuries to come.
But the symbolism in which that faith expressed itself and flourished
was mortally wounded. It would appear to survive for a long time, and
it was in the twelfth century that several of its sweetest fruits would
ripen. Already, however, it was showing numerous signs of decadence.
Its roots were being slowly gnawed away by the analysis with which it
necessarily had to collude to an ever-greater degree. Its sap was slowly
drying up. It continued to spread on the surface, but its deepest life
force was passing on elsewhere. It was becoming more and more, in
the modern sense of the word, an allegory, 'with its laws of interpretation, its "keys" of explanation and its theory of numbers, which
accentuated their rigidity'.[34] It was not this that would resolve the new
problems that had become impossible to avoid from now on. Lanfranc
could still say to his enemy: '*You take refuge in dialectic*';[35] but soon it
would be the opposite: those who avoided dialectic would be viewed
as counting for nothing. *But dialecticians ask*, said Algerius of Liége
towards the end of his great work, and a paragraph was still sufficient
for him to dispatch these importunate questions, whose exploration
could be of no interest for the understanding of mystery. Now, however, these questions were becoming urgent, they were developing and
constantly giving birth to one another. First of all relegated to some
appendix, now they were increasingly gaining the centre ground and
demanding the entire field. There had to be a response, or everything

---

32 Cf. Guitmond, 1 (PL, 149, 1428 B).

33 Abelard, *Theologia Christiana*, 4 (PL, 178, 1286). Zacharias Chrysopolita-
nus (186, 507–8). Hugh Metel, *Ep.* 4 (PL, 188, 1273–6).

34 J. de Ghellinck, *L'essor de la literature latine au XIIe siècle*, vol. 1, p. 97.

35 *Liber de corpore*, c. 7 (PL, 150, 416 D).

would be compromised. The *dialecticians ask* became an *it is usually asked*, which would continue to multiply. The beautiful considerations of the past, the symbols flowing with doctrinal richness were in their turn relegated to second place, though without in any way being formally repudiated. Only another dialectic could triumph over a dialectic whose aim was insidious negation, to which it was no longer enough to oppose simple recourse to the Almighty. After a series of tentative attempts, it would be ready, two centuries after Berengar. Its weapons would be forged. The dialectic of substance and accidents, and of the quantity of vice-substance . . .[36] would correspond to the dialectic of the sign and the reality. Sacramental realism would no longer be anything but that which symbolism augmented, and persistent faith in a real presence of Christ in the sacrament would be protected, for further centuries, by a sacramental theology with quite other appearances and implications.[37]

Such an evolution cannot be explained by tactical necessity alone. The proliferation of new questions would not always invade the field of theology as a fearful scourge. These questions became much loved, and even when there was no longer any fear of heresy, theological minds would commit themselves to their examination as to the finest part of their task. The rest was little more than a matter of memory, whose sense was gradually being lost or dulled because there was no longer any interest in it. From having been an enemy, dialectic thus developed into a temptation. There was danger without and within! The very words *they ask, it is asked, questions* which would from now on appear to rise up on all sides, were 'a sign of the times'; they 'proclaimed the passion for research within the religious sciences',[38] but it was a renewed and transformed passion, aiming in quite another direction from the religious contemplation of the mysteries. Then there happened what comes about in every era of change, or rather, of progress. How was it possible to discern at first sight between those seeds that carried fruit for the future and those in need of condemnation? At any

---

36 Cf. Bonaventure, *De decem praeceptis*, col. 3, n. 13 (Quar., vol. 5, p. 517). A day would come when, among certain theologians, the whole treatise *De sacramento altaris* would be barely more than the application of a preliminary treatise '*On the distinction of point, line, surface, quantity, body, quality and substance*': this is the title of a long treatise written by Ockham in 1349 (ed. Bruce Birch, 1930, p. 2).

37 Cf. F. Cavallera, *La théologie positive* (*Bulletin de literature ecclésiastique*, 1925, p. 42).

38 J. de Ghellinck, *Sacra Pagina* (Mélanges Pelzer, 1947, p. 40). Similar words punctuated the *Periarchon* of Origen, noted in R. P. Bonnefoy, *Origène théoricien de la méthode théologique*, in *Mélanges Cavallera* (1948), p. 141.

rate, are not the latter most often hidden within the former? Those zealous for orthodoxy became alarmed. Once more assuming the attitude that Florus in the ninth century showed towards Amalarius and John Scotus, they denounced the *'questions that were full of scruples and scandals'* of the new Doctors.[39] They mocked the 'subtleties' that they invented 'drunk on a wine that was more scholastic than theological'. They condemned their recourse to 'alien doctrines', to 'the reasonings of a worldly philosophy' and to arguments taken from 'physics'. They warned against the 'sacrilegious' desire to 'understand' mystery.[40] But while some among them attempted to prolong the great traditional current and sometimes still met with success, others satisfied themselves with multiplying appeals to the simplicity of faith. Obstinate in their refusal, they thought they were being faithful to the ancient Fathers because, like them, they repudiated with horror what one of them called *'the tortuous question of clever philosophizing'*.[41] But they came no nearer to that original spirit. Under the paradoxically combined action of these people and those they condemned, perspectives were transformed. A somewhat new concept of mystery was developing, which managed to quench symbolism while suppressing, even in the understanding of the believer, the momentum that had given birth to it. This is what we must investigate in greater detail.

* * *

St. Augustine – to whom we must return, as the great teacher of our early Middle Ages – certainly had no inclination to deny the obscurity essential to faith, or to contest the penitential submission that it demands of our understanding. If the Manichean mirage had seduced him momentarily, when the brilliant Faustus promised to teach him a doctrine that would address itself to his reason alone, he had swiftly come to recognize an insane pretension in this braggart's propositions, that was not only fallacious in its facts, but in all points contrary to the human condition. It would never be possible to explain all that is mysterious.[42] Nevertheless, the humble wisdom to which he had

---

39 William of St. Thierry, *Disputatio adversus Petrum Abaelardum* (PL, 180, 276 A). *ibid.* (281 A).

40 Gerhoh of Reichersberg, *De Gloria et honore Filii hominis* (PL, 194, 1074–6); *In psalmum 67* (194, 215 D). Arno, *Liber apologeticus* (Weichert, pp. 73–4, 113), etc.

41 St. Hilary, *De Trinitate*, 12, c. 19 (PL, 10, 444 B).

42 Augustine returns to his Manichean period, for example *Sermo 51*, n. 6 (PL, 38, 336–7).

already allied himself for ever was no mutilation. It did not comprise any renunciation of the exercise of intelligence. Augustine would only repudiate any premature impatience or perverse deviations that the thirst for understanding might entail.[43] He wanted those searching to begin by laying the foundations of faith, but it was only with a view to raising the building higher.[44] Any disciple of his must believe not *as a substitute* for understanding but *in order* to achieve it. *Faith, if it does not involve thought, is empty.*[45] Understanding is the obligatory result and usual reward of faith.[46] Faith assures the contact that allows us to be brought to life by understanding.[47] Revealed truth is therefore primarily a *dogma*, in the sense that the mind receives it without argument on the authority of the Church of Christ which here below is the very voice of God, in the same way that the will receives the commandments: but this dogma is also a *mystery*. Now, if the mystery is essentially obscure to our carnal faculties, it is in itself radiant with a secret intelligibility. If it constitutes a challenge to faith, it is at the same time a sign and an appeal. It invites us, and stimulates us to question. We can glimpse a deep luminosity in the background. It is an enigma to be solved; it is a truth whose expression takes us beyond itself. Beneath the letter, we can discern the spirit. Beyond the sign, we have to reach out to the thing itself, to the life-giving reality. *Let us nourish our inner self with spiritual understanding.*[48] Such is the object of that *inner way* in which each of us must exercise ourselves after having gathered the facts of revelation to the best of our ability.[49] – In short, if we could for a moment translate Augustine's thought into our own language, we would say that for him any mystery, that is to say any revealed truth, is a sacrament, that is to say a sign, and that on the other hand any sacrament, that is to say any sacred rite, is itself a mystery, that is to say broadly a truth to be understood.

The unity of the mystery and the sacrament thus defined is realized

---

43 *De Trinitate*, 1, c. 1 (PL, 42, 819).

44 *In Joannem*, tractatus 39, n. 3 (PL, 35, 1682). *Ep. ad Consensium* (PL, 33, 454, 456). Cf. Contra *academicos* (32, 257); *De Trinitate*, 15, c. 28, n. 51 (42, 1098), etc.

45 *De praedestinatione sanctorum*, n. 5 (PL, 44, 963).

46 *In Joannem*, tract. 22, n. 2 (PL, 35, 1574 and 100, 839 A). *Sermo 126* (38, 698). *In psalmum 8*, n. 6 (36, 111).

47 *Sermo 51 de verbis Domini*. Cf. *De peccatorum meritis*, 1, c. 21, n. 29 (PL, 44, 125). *De vera religione*, n. 45 (34, 141).

48 *De spiritu et littera*, c. 4 (PL, 44, 203). *In Epistulam Joanuis ad Parthos*, tract. 10, n. 5 (35, 2057).

49 *De Trinitate*, 8, procemium, n. 1 (PL, 42, 97).

to its fullest extent in the case of the Eucharist, the central point of Christian faith and worship. The Eucharist and Scripture: these are indeed the two privileged fields open to the exploration of the believer. Of the understanding of the Eucharist, as of the understanding of Scripture, we must say with St. Augustine: *Love the intellect great-ly.*[50] How could anyone possibly sustain that there is no reason to be found here? The more mystery there is, the more reason there is. *To understand the mystery, to grasp the sublimity of the mystery*, was already a saying of St. Ambrose,[51] who would hand on to the convert of Milan the essential features of the ideals of the Greek Fathers; he also liked comparing miracle with mystery, in order to underline by the contrast between them the intellectual fruitfulness of the latter.[52] The Augustinian concept of miracles as mysterious signs containing doctrine is equally well known: *Things done by miracle are like the words of the sacraments.* It was in this spirit of Ambrose and Augustine that Rupert would write, for example: *'with a miracle, we have at the same time a mystery'*,[53] or that Gerhoh of Reichersberg would seek the *'mystery of the miracle'.*[54] How, then, could anyone set mystery against reason, precisely where everything hangs on the perception of a 'mysterious reason', or *mystical reason?*[55] Our Augustinians would repeat it *ad nauseam.* For them, mystical facts are full of sense, full of divine intentions, as opposed to fortuitous events.[56] Like Rupert, they would exclaim in their amazement: *'All things are glorious, all things are full of divine reason.'*[57] In the Eucharist as in Scripture, they thought that everything was full of mystery, that is to say that every-

---

50 *Ep.* 120, n. 13 (PL, 33, 459).

51 *In Lucam* (PL, 15, 1675 C and 1676 B).

52 *In Lucam* (PL, 15, 1633 B; 1579 B; cf. 1689 A, etc.). However, with Ambrose we can note, as with St. Hilary, a more severe reserve perhaps against the mystery than with Augustine (De fide, 1, n. 65; PL, 16, 543 C).

53 *In Reg.*, 5, c. 25 (PL, 167, 1261 D; cf. 645 B). Cf. Faustus of Riez ('Eusebius of Emesa'), *Serm. de Epiphania* (Eng., pp. 247, 256); or Paschasius Radbertus, *In Matthaeum* (PL, 120, 359 C, 518 D, 524 B, 529 B).

54 *In psalmum* 77 (PL, 194, 450 B).

55 *Supra*, Chapter 11, n. 126. Cyril of Alexandria, *In Joannem* (PG, 73, 456 C). Gregory of Elvira (Tractatus Origenis, p. 58, 76). Ambrose, *In psalmum* 1, n. 41 (Petschenig, p. 35). Pachymer, *In eccl. Hierarchiam*, c. 3, n. 3 (PG, 3, 457 A), etc. Cf. Origen (Rufinus), *In Genesim*, hom. 12, n. 5; In Numeros, hom. 12, n. 1 (PG, 12, 229 D, 658 A), etc. Also Lanfranc (PL, 150, 425 C) or Stephen of Baugé (172, 1285 A–B).

56 Gilbert, *In Cantica*, sermo 4, n. 4 (PL, 184, 28 C). Rupert (167, 739 A, 1245 D), etc.

57 *In Exodum*, 2, c. 5 (PL, 167, 612 D).

thing is full of reason.[58] The two words were generally offered as synonyms.[59]

It is a great sacrament and is not lacking in reason.[60]

The mind needs to enter into this mysterious reason as one enters into a sanctuary, to penetrate it and press on ever further – *to enter more fully and more perfectly into the mysteries*[61] – that is to say, to seek and obtain an ever-greater understanding of them. 'As long as we live, we should never cease our searching.'[62] Shame on anyone who, like the sullen and fearful servant of the Gospel, buries the talent entrusted to him by his master, shrinks from these explorations and with false respect hides away the chest in whose depths the mystery shines uselessly, without even attempting to open it! The homage that the Lord has a right to expect of our faith is no such over-cautious gesture, but, on the contrary, an exploration carried out with avid fidelity.[63] Our weakness will finally succumb in the attempt, but we are not allowed to give up.[64] What wonderful vistas open up in this way before our understanding! What vast landscapes will it not be given us to travel through, in search of these mystical reasons! And what honing of our thought, what flights, what leaps of our whole being, launching itself up from the springboard of our faith *to an understanding of divine subtlety*![65] What ingenuity used to scrutinize so many reasons hidden beneath signs and figures! What richness in their discovery! What enchantment in establishing oneself '*in the system of mystical correspondences*'![66] What a delicious foretaste of the joys of eternity!

---

58 Florus, *Expositio missae*, c. 59, n. 6 (Duc, p. 131). John of Fécamp, *Confessio fidei*, 4, c. 2 (PL, 101, 1088 A–B). Gilbert the Universal, *Glosula in psalmos* (Smalley, 1936, p. 58). Cf. Origen, *In Exodum*, hom. 7, n. 3 (B., p. 207); *In Leviticum*, hom. 5, n. 3 (p. 340). Giles of Rome, *De ecclesiastica potestate*, 1, c. 3 (Scholtz, p. 9).

59 Eucher, *Instructiones* (PL, 50, 803 A). Amalarius (105, 1101 C, 1244 A). Pseudo-Primasius, *In Hebr.* (68, 739 D). Raoul of St. Germer, *In Leviticum* (BMP, vol. 17, pp. 68 G, 164 G).

60 Hildebert, *Versus de mysterio missae* (PL, 171m 1180 A).

61 Missal of Bobbio, *missa in cena Domini* (Lowe, p. 62). Gallican Sacramentary, *ibid.* (PL, 72, 493 B).

62 Hugh of St. Victor, *De sacramentis*, 2, 14, 9 (PL, 176, 570), etc.

63 Otho of St. Emmeran, *Dialogus de tribus quaestionibus*, c. 33 (PL, 146, 101–2).

64 St. Leo, *Sermo 11 de passione Domini*, c. 1 (PL, 54, 350 A), etc.

65 Gilbert of Nogent, *De pignoribus sanctorum*, 2, c. 6, n. 4 (PL, 156, 650).

66 Otho of St. Emmeran, *Dialogus de tribus quaestionibus*, c. 43 (PL, 146, 120 A).

Some may object that this is mere playing with words, or at least that such an idea presupposes an entirely mystical concept of understanding, little of which remains to us in this day and age. That remains to be seen. But we are only dealing with history here. Might it not perhaps be precisely this mystical concept that makes St. Augustine so original? Is it not in this – whether we take him on his own merits or we recognize in his work the summit of the patristic age – that he constitutes a memorable landmark in the history of the human mind? He stands precisely at the point where intellectual research and spiritual tension coincide, participating in the same impetus and sketching the same curve. There has been much discussion to establish whether Augustinian contemplation is simply 'intellectual' or truly 'mystical'.[67] The same discussion could be had over the subject of the inspiration of his entire theology. But perhaps the very posing of the problem in these terms, setting against one another concepts elaborated from an experience other than his own, condemns us never to understand the uniqueness of that experience. For it is not only in their solutions, it is primarily and far more profoundly in their problems that great minds and, through them, great eras differ from one another. No two great thinkers, no two great mystics approach essential problems in identical terms. Even at the heart of the same doctrinal or spiritual tradition, each one of them communicates to us, if we know how to ask the right questions, that sense of perpetual invention that necessarily constitutes the life of the mind, and, as it were, of the perpetual shifting of its frontiers. Not one of them passes without leaving his mark on the very regions where we think ourselves in the presence of eternal categories. More fortunate than the greatest captains and the greatest empire builders, they manage to make us entirely forget the previous state of the spiritual world that they succeeded in reforming. But also, in an inevitable revenge, as soon as their work becomes in its own turn 'out of date', it is immediately ignored. We lack the imagination, even if we still have the texts to hand, to reconstitute their mental universe. For that we would have to reach into our very depths, and lean on the support of what has just been newly reconstructed. The words may well have been preserved, and the whole paraphernalia of proofs: but we cannot do it for all that, above all we cannot resurrect within ourselves the mother-lode of concepts that this verbal and logical apparatus was aiming to express. This is why we struggle today, I not only say to

---

67 Fr. Cavallera, 'La contemplation d'Ostie', in *Revue d'ascétique et de mystique*, 1939, p. 183. See also M.-D. Chenu, *Revue des sciences philosophiques et théologiques*, vol. 19 (1930), pp. 572–3.

revive on our own account, or even to justify retrospectively, but simply to rediscover in thought that 'understanding of faith' that was the soul and the driving force behind the whole of Augustinianism. The idea of such a thing appears to me to be incurably ambiguous: there seems to be no middle ground that can be assigned between the mystical and utterly supernatural illumination capable of ravishing the soul of an otherwise profoundly ignorant saint, in order to bring him to an intellectually inexplicable participation in the most hidden secrets of God, and the work of rational elaboration of the facts of revelation to which either the theologian or the philosopher dedicates himself, each according to his own methods. What, then, is this 'understanding' which in our eyes is neither reason, nor mysticism but which aspires to being both one and the other at the same time?

This is, inevitably, how the mind, even the Christian mind reasons today. We can do nothing about the fact that it became laicised a long time ago. The atmosphere in which it moves spontaneously, the natural rhythm of its breathing, are utterly different from that of the patristic era. For the Fathers, the essential mainspring of thought was not identity, or analogy, but *anagogy*. With its roots still in the time original to it, it nevertheless looked forwards to the future. From creation, it reached up towards Christ, and through Christ had access as far as to the *invisible things of God*. Everything sensible was a sacrament, not so much requiring organization or justification, as open to being transcended. *Touching on everything, going through everything.*[68] In the broadest sense, and according to an interpretation by St. Jerome of an idea of Origen's, it was therefore *perspicacity in the contemplation of the sacraments*. Being 'rational' or 'contemplative' therefore meant fundamentally the same thing. The reason that defined humanity was its aptitude for contemplation: *it is proper to humanity to be rational and contemplative.*[69] Do we think there were no consequences for the whole of intellectual life that the same word should designate human reason and the Word of God? The uncreated image of the Father and the created creature 'in his image' shared an intimate relationship that the activity of reasoning had the aim of bringing to perfection. Starting from Nature, starting from History, or Scripture, or the Liturgy, starting from everything, the mind had the same orientation towards

---

68 Gilbert, *In Cantica*, sermo 4, n. 8 (PL, 184, 31 B). Augustine, *De diversis quaestionibus*, q. 43 (PL, 40, 28). Paschasius Radbertus, *In Matthaeum* (120, 59 A, 173 B, 719 B). Cf. F. van der Meer, *Sacramentum chez saint Augustin, loc. cit.*, p. 56.

69 Hesychius, *In Leviticum*, 6, preface (PG, 93, 1019 B-C).

spiritual understanding, always in the light of the Word and under the impulse of the Spirit.

In this sense the Augustinian doctrine of illumination is far more than the theory of a particular writer: it was the expression, and bears witness for us to a state of mind. Ought we simply to say that it represents an age that has effectively been superseded by the intellectual progress achieved since that time? Should we not rather fear that such a concept of 'progress', in its simplistic arrogance, might cut us off for ever from a kingdom for which we would no longer even have any nostalgia. Let us admit with Max Scheler that 'phases of evolution are not simply steps that lie one above the other, but that each one of them has its own nature and its own value'. Let us be capable of recognizing that 'development is not only progress, but it is always and at the same time decadence'.[70] Certainly there is nowhere that this law is confirmed more substantially than here. Besides, let me simply repeat that it would be pointless to try either to criticize or to justify an intellectual activity that all attempts at critique or at justification according to our present norms can only distort without succeeding in bringing it back to life. If we are still living – albeit only too feebly – off the benefits that it bequeathed to us, the unique thing in itself has long since died.[71] Since the end of the eleventh century, the balance that it presupposes has been broken. Anselm and Rupert, Abelard and Hugh of St. Victor were all the heirs of Augustine. They all sought this understanding with an ardent desire that he handed down to them. But between the 'rationalist' theology of an Anselm or an Abelard and the 'symbolist' or mystical theology of a Rupert or a Hugh, the chasm was already opening up.

The case of St. Anselm is particularly important, and consideration of it is particularly instructive. It marks a change of direction

---

70 *Nature et formes de la sympathie* (tr. fr., 1928), pp. 53-5 [E.T. by P. Heath, *The Nature of Sympathy* (London, Routledge and Kegan Paul, 1979 [1954]).]

71 Charles Journet, *Introduction à la théologie*, p. 113. 'We see', writes Mgr. Charles Journet (*Introduction à la théologie,* p. 113), 'that still today the expression "understanding of faith" should preserve for us the fullness of its dynamism and its virtue, because a process of differentiation which avoided constantly returning for nourishment to its own roots, its original implications, the idea from which it was born, cannot fail to veer off course, to shrivel up and become lost.' This could not be put more effectively and these words define the very effort that I am attempting here, for my part. But this effort will only bear fruit if my readers begin by acquiring as lively an awareness as possible of the diversity which has built up over time. If it claims to be a serious matter our 'understanding of faith' will never simply reproduce, in the concrete details of its way of proceeding, that of Augustine or of Anselm.

that seems to be unaware of itself, and gives little clear forewarning of the new direction towards which thought would tend from then on, but which was nonetheless already more than half way achieved. Following in Augustine's wake, Anselm was well aware of resuming an effort that those centuries less favourable to it had allowed to slacken off. Like his master, inner faith is what moves him. Without challenging it or setting it aside, he sought to understand it.[72] *Faith seeking understanding*: that was the programme mapped out by tradition. But since Augustine time had marched on, and the eleventh century could not simply fuse itself together with the fifth century. The renaissance that blossomed at that time followed the laws of all rebirths. It could not be a return to the past. Far more than it intended, far more than it was aware of, it constituted an innovation, we might almost say a revolution.

Thus we should not be surprised that historians of Anselm's thought find themselves divided between two contradictory interpretations, without either of them ever definitively triumphing over the other. There is right on both sides, because this thinking is ambiguous. It is 'neither a theology, properly speaking', in the modern sense of the term, 'nor a purely mystical doctrine'.[73] It is still Augustinian in its most fundamental intentions, as it is in its principal formulation, but it turns its back on Augustine in the new emphases that it presses into service and in the ideal of understanding that seduces it. Like Augustine, Anselm was working to 'transform raw truth into understood truth', but neither the process nor the goal was exactly the same any longer. For Anselm as for Augustine, it can be said that 'belief is simply a substitute for knowledge',[74] but Anselm's 'knowledge' is not the same as Augustine's 'knowledge'. Without relinquishing the desire to be contemplative, for Anselm understanding takes the form of a demonstration. If St. Anselm was not a rationalist in the modern understanding of the word, it does not mean that he hesitated to demonstrate rigorously the object of faith, satisfying himself with probabilities in order to understand it better: it is just that for him demonstration itself was the work of a reason whose guiding light is still divine. For him faith was not opposed to understanding, as for us

---

72 *Prologium* (PL, 158, 224): *De fides Trinitatis*, praefatio (158, 261 etc.).

73 Dom John Leclercq and J.-P. Bonnes, *John of Fécamp*, pp. 78-9.

74 Étienne Gilson, *L'esprit de la philosophie médiévale*, vol. 1, p. 37; cf. p. 43: 'Opaque faith suddenly yielded within them to transparent understanding.' These formulations define at one and the same time, according to Gilson, Augustine's theology and that of Anselm and of Thomas Aquinas.

the supernatural order is opposed to the natural order, or as the order of revelation is opposed to the order of simple reason. If faith presupposes a positive revelation, understanding presupposes a rational revelation, and, as the latter applies to the former, the former is normally destined to transform itself into the latter. Anselm's concept of reason had thus not yet been laicised. But, on the other hand, it was already no longer the understanding of Augustine; in its dialectical flavour, in its orientation towards proof, it was the herald of a new era.[75] Anselm was in no way a rationalist – any more than Abelard would be. Nevertheless, Anselm and Abelard were the founders of 'Christian rationalism'.

This Christian rationalism could no longer envisage the understanding of mysteries outside their demonstration. Such an ambition would naturally provoke a mystical reaction, in such a way that what were virtually the two tendencies in Augustinianism would grow more and more opposed to one another. It would also by contrast give rise to an ideal of pure and simple faith that was no less distant from the true Augustinian ideal. This was above all what happened in Eucharistic theology. It was the principal cause of this major turning point that can be observed in Christian thought, and for us it remains its best illustration.

* * *

Against an 'indiscreet understanding' which, by transforming its problems, also transformed its methods, the reaction operated first of all by means of a certain number of traditional axioms, on which an increasingly insistent and exclusive accent was being placed. On the subject of the Eucharist it was remembered what St. Hilary had said against rationalism, that it does not know how to respect mystery.[76] A brake was put on explorations inspired by mere curiosity – but there was also a risk of discouraging the traditional effort of 'understanding' through the repetition of the old formulation that in someone like

---

75 Paul Vignaux, overcoming the opposition which set at loggerheads Dom Cappuyns and Adolphe Kolping on the one hand and Dom Stolz on the other, insists on this ambivalence in the work of Anselm: *La pensée au moyen âge*, pp. 38 and 42. A further example can help us to grasp this. The Proslogion's *vere esse* comes, as Dom Stolz remarks, from Augustine and the neo-Platonists, for whom it is synonymous with *incommutabiliter esse*; but Dom Cappuyns also remarks that in Anselm *vere esse* undergoes 'a slight transposition or rather a restriction of sense' which leaves it hardly any stronger meaning than that of: existing as such, really, *in fact* (*Bulletin de théologie ancienne et médiévale*, 1938, pp. 288–9).

76 *De Trinitate*, 2, c. 2 (PL, 10, 51). Gezonius of Tortona (PL, 137, 376).

Gregory the Great marked the submission of the mind before the fact of the miraculous, or the refusal to allow reason to argue with the reality of the dogmas of faith,[77] a formulation that long since had found its place in the liturgy: *'the divine sacraments are not so much to be discussed as believed in'*[78] – *'more to be venerated than discussed'*.[79] To these opportune warnings the complementary advice was no longer added, as it was before. Moreover the mind was no longer invited to search out what is hidden beneath the enigma of the rites and words. No longer was it said, in line with Florus:

> *Do you recognize, I ask, the enigmas of your venerable mother, and do you grasp what my mysteries signify?*[80]

Convenient use was made of the instruction of Ecclesiasticus: *'Do not seek higher things.'*[81] This was said to be a profound and inscrutable mystery that no one should dare to attempt to fathom.[82] The author of the *Letter to Patrick*, who was not Ratherius of Verona but a considerably later author,[83] demanded a simple faith, unencumbered by any speculative effort: *'I beseech you not to concern yourselves over the rest.'*[84] Once upon a time, explains Hugh of Liége, Jacob could wrestle with the angel: but he had the limbs of a patriarch, and at the end of his night's struggle, he had hope of seeing the dawn; for us, whose understanding is weak, it would be folly to want in some sense to fight with God: not only would we gain nothing, but we would lose, and we have previous warning that the whole fight would be in the dark, right to its very end.[85] It is a pointless enterprise to seek the 'how' of the mystery! Lanfranc also affirmed this: *'If you ask how this can be, I give this brief reply at present: the mystery of faith can be beneficially believed but cannot be profitably investigated.'*[86] Even more, to

---

77 *Moralia in Job*, 6, n. 19 (PL, 75, 739 B–C). Cf. concerning the Incarnation, *Conc. Francof. Ep. synodica ad praesules Hispaniae missa* (101, 1331 B). Cf. St. Ambrose, *De fide*, 1, n. 78 (PL, 16, 547 A; cf. n. 42, 84, col. 537 A, 548 B).

78 Galican Sacramentary, *Missa in symboli traditione* (PL, 72, 488 C).

79 Florus, *Expositio missae*, c. 66, n. 1 (Duc, p. 140). Remigius of Auxerre, *De celebratione missae* (PL, 101, 1262). Innocent III (PL, 217, 863).

80 *De injusta vexatione Ecclesiae lugdunensis*, c. 57–8 (MGH, *Poetae aevi carolini*, vol. 2, p. 557).

81 Lanfranc (PL, 150, 427 A). Ernulf, *Ep. 2a* (d'Achery, *Spicilegium*, vol. 3, p. 473), etc. Augustine, *Ad Orosium*, c. 11, n. 14 (PL, 42, 678).

82 *Speculum Ecclesiae*, c. 7 (PL, 177, 367 B).

83 Cf. *Revue d'Histoire ecclésiastique*, 1927, p. 308.

84 PL, 136, 647–8.

85 Hugh of Liège, *De corpore et sanguine Christi* (PL, 142, 1328 C).

86 *Liber de corpore*, c. 10 (PL, 150, 421 D).

let oneself be carried along by such curiosity is already to lay oneself open to the suspicion of being lacking in faith: '*He who is known to raise questions about the faith seems to doubt his own salvation.*' It was Arnulf of Rochester, a pupil of Lanfranc, who proclaimed this, addressing those who were asking whether in the Eucharist we receive only the body of Christ, or the soul with the body.[87] He added that we should avoid those arrogant enough to desire, by raising questions of this sort, to appear wise, and rather than encouraging such pointless arguments, offer our humble and faithful obedience to the decrees of the Church and the sacred authorities,[88] and oppose the subtlety of reason by the purity and simplicity of faith.[89]

Thus the mystery to be understood gave way before the miracle to be believed, because the very idea of what 'understand' means had changed. Faith does not open up a path to contemplative understanding: it is an obstacle, set up by God himself, to cut across the appetite for rational speculation. There was therefore no longer any question of raising oneself from faith to understanding: from an *understanding* that had become *dialectic*, it was clear that on the contrary, we should say: '*understanding transcends faith*'.[90] If, despite everything, there was still some talk of 'understanding', only one thing was now understood by it: the development of a correct idea of the object to be believed. '*You see bread, understand flesh.*'[91] If the classic adage was retained: *faith seeking understanding*, it was only with a view to clarifying in some way, against those who denied it, the 'how' of the mystery. It was in order to respond to the objections that they raised against it. The end being pursued was no longer dogmatic or contemplative but purely apologetic. (Following the usual law, dogmatics would nevertheless end up by gaining some advantage from it.)[92] With greater or less enthusiasm and good grace, this task would be undertaken in order to obey the recommendation of the Apostle Peter, who wanted all believers to be ready to render an account of their faith.[93] The *giving of reasons* had taken the place of the *discerning with the*

---

87 *Epistula 2a* (d'Achery, vol. 3, p. 473).

88 Ænulf, *ibid.* Herbert Losinga, *Sermo 7* (Goulburn–Symonds, p. 190).

89 John of Fécamp, *Confessio Fidei*, 4, c. 3–6 (PL, 101, 1088–90). Hugh of Rouen, *Dialogorum*, 5, c. 15 (PL, 192, 1210).

90 *Speculum Ecclesiae*, c. 7 (PL, 177, 362).

91 Berengar of Venouse (Morin, *loc. cit.*, p. 119). Durandus of Troarn, p. 5, c. 16 (PL, 149, 1400 A).

92 Cf. 'Apologétique et théologie', in *Nouvelle Revue théologique*, vol. 52 (1930).

93 *Iᵃ Petri*, 3, 15.

mind.[94] But in the eyes of a good many, it still constituted a path built of concessions, along which they refused to travel.

Thus little by little a new mentality came into being. Perhaps the following detail will afford a clearer grasp of its development. It concerns the response to the classic question: why does Christ give himself to us under the form of bread? The basic purpose of the question consisted in asking oneself why God had established the sacramental order so as to communicate himself to us? To which the response was that such an 'economy' was in order to adapt to our human condition. We need sensible signs, because we are sensible beings. The sacraments – *visible sacraments, bodily mysteries* – are a continuation of the incarnation. They were instituted *for our instruction.*[95] Since, in order to reveal himself to us, God made himself one of us, so, in order to give us access to him, he presents himself primarily under these 'species', which bring the divine reality close to our being of flesh. And if then the precise question were to be asked: *'why under* those *species?'*, the response would be self-evident, furnished by the rich symbolism of bread and wine. Or else, if the emphasis were placed more specifically on the flesh and the blood present on the altar, the marvel was rather that they were hidden there, *'under* other *species'*, either because the body of Christ itself, in its glorious state, would remain inaccessible to us,[96] or above all in order to spare us a quite natural feeling of horror . . . Since the *De sacramentis*[97] and St. Gregory, this last consideration could be found repeated everywhere.[98]

To sum up, the purpose of all these responses was to say that God could not dispose of things otherwise if he wanted to take into account what we are. – But to the extent that the concept of mystery changed, as we have just seen, another response gained the upper hand: the veil of these 'species' no longer had any other aim than to exercise our faith. At least from now on, that was its essential role. *'So that*

---

94 Compare Augustine, *De Trinitate*, 1, c. 2, n. 4.

95 Hugh of St. Victor, *De sacramentis*, 1, p. 9, c. 3 (PL, 176, 320 A–B). Bonaventure, *Tractatus de Cantatione paradisi* (vol. 5, pp. 574–5). Gaudentius of Brescia, *Tract.* 2 (Glueck, pp. 31–2).

96 Cf. Geoffrey of Vendôme, *Tractatus de corpore et sanguine D.N.J.C.* (PL, 157, 212–13).

97 Bk. 4, c. 4, n. 20 (PL, 16, 443 A). Similarly, Cyril of Alexandria, Theophylactus, etc. Mozarabic liturgy (PL, 85, 249).

98 Werner of St. Blaise (PL, 157, 910 B–C, 910–11). Bruno of Segni (165, 502 B). Ivo of Chartres (161, 144 D, 147 B–C). Rupert, *De Spiritu sancto*, 3, c. 21 (167, 1662 D). Hildebert (171, 1194 A). Pseudo-Hugh, *Miscellanea* (177, 492 C). Fragment of the School of Laon (Lottin, *Rech. De th . . .*, 1946, p. 280). Gratian, *De consecratione*, d. 2, c. 43, 55, 73 (Fr., 1329, 1335, 1344), etc.

the concealment of the mystery may give scope for gaining merit by exercising faith', says Algerius of Liège,[99] following his compatriot Adelmann.[100] Paschasius Radbertus had already said it,[101] but for him this reason was merely subsidiary, it came last in consideration, whereas from the twelfth century onwards it was placed in the forefront and broadly developed. This is, for example, what Peter Comestor[102] did, and Innocent III[103] and Pseudo-Damian.[104] From the *species of bread* to the *flesh of Christ* there was no longer any focus except on otherness. The expressions that St. Thomas would use, in a passage in his seventh opuscule, demonstrate very aptly the change that had come about. Where formerly the similarity between the analogy of the sign and its reality had been emphasized, now they were satisfied with underlining the difference between them:

> . . . *Accidents without a subject subsist in it so that faith may have a role, while the visible is received invisibly, concealed by an alien appearance.*[105]

Of similar significance was the application to the Eucharist that began to be made, around the same period, of St. Gregory the Great's famous maxim: '*Faith is not meritorious when human reason furnishes a proof.*'[106] Gregory had pronounced it in his homily for the octave of Easter, referring to the miracle of the risen Jesus' entry into the Upper Room '*the doors being closed*'. It expressed an idea that was familiar to him,[107] and there can be no denying, moreover, that this holy pope gave little encouragement to intellectual adventurers. He nevertheless believed, as had his mentor St. Augustine, that, if unconditional submission to divine facts constitutes the necessary foundation for a life of

---

99 *De sacramentis*, 2, c. 3 (PL, 180, 821). Cf. *Prologus* (741). Gilbert of Nogent (156, 640 A–B).

100 Heurtevent, p. 294. Cf. *Liber de sacra eucharistia* (PL, 171, 1203 C).

101 c. 13, n. 1 (PL, 120, 1315 C). Hériger, c. 1 (139, 180 A–B).

102 *Sententiae de sacramentis*, *De corpore . . .* , n. 8 (Martin, p. 37).

103 *Ep.* 121, to John, Archbishop of Lyon (PL, 214, 1121 A).

104 *Expositio canonis* (PL, 145, 884 B). Peter Comestor. *Glose sur le IVe livre des Sentences*; R. P. Weisweiler, *Mélanges Grabmann*, vol. 1, p. 392. Cf. Bonaventure, *Sermo de sanctissimo corpore Christi* (vol. 5, p. 564).

105 Bossuet, *Exposition de la doctrine catholique*, ch. 10 (Vogt, pp. 151–2). Cf. Note G.

106 *In Evangelia*, 2, hom. 26, n. 1 (PL, 76, 1197 C). Cited in Ivo of Chartres, *Decretum*, p. 2, c. 9 (PL, 161, 159 A), Abelard, *Sic et Non*, 1 (178, 1349–50).

107 Cf. *Moralia in Job*, 6, c. 15, n. 19 (PL, 75, 439 B–C; 9, c. 15, n. 22 (871 C). *In Ezechielem*, 2, hom. 8, n. 10 (76, 1034 B). Cf. St. Thomas, *In Joannem*, c. 20, l. 4, n. 1.

faith, it should nonetheless be followed up by an effort to 'understand' the mystery hidden under the outer wrapping of these facts.[108] The novelty now consisted in saying of the Eucharist, that is to say of a mystery, what Gregory asserted with regard to a miracle,[109] and sometimes even in claiming the authority of his words, which were condemning a profane and rationalising enquiry, in order to stop short any effort at 'understanding'.[110]

Nevertheless, the 'miracle' of the Eucharist did not easily make sense. This was the origin, as an aid to faith, *to strengthen our carnal minds,* of recourse to other miracles. St. Ambrose had invoked the analogy of the two great miracles that were the creation and the Incarnation: if these must be reckoned to be possible, why should not the Eucharist, which resembles them?[111] Another tradition, going back, via Paschasius Radbertus[112] and Pseudo-Germanus of Paris,[113] to St. Gregory, added to all of this the testimony of 'Eucharistic miracles', a collection that would only go on growing.[114] Those who wanted to limit things to the simple exercise of faith willingly made use of these sorts of miracles. If the Eucharist appeared unbelievable, rather than undertaking an apology that was inevitably negative and, in their opinion, always dangerous, they had recourse to this extrinsic and positive apologetic. Instead of directly setting aside rational difficulties, they bowed their minds before the marvel that prevailed over sense itself: '*May marvels give credibility to marvels, and the incomprehensible to the*

---

108 Also, John Scotus, *Ad S. Joannem,* tractatus 2 (*In Boethium,* Rand, pp. 49–50).

109 Thus Lanfranc, Guitmond, Algerius (PL, 180, 885 B), Gregory of Bergamo (H., pp. 98, 123), Master Simon (W., p. 27), Peter Comestor (Martin, p. 7), Peter Lombard, *Sentences,* 4, d.11, c. 3; Pseudo-Thomas, *Opusculum 51,* c. 7 (Vivès, vol. 28, p. 195). Cf. Gerhoh (PL, 193, 576 A); Arno (Weichert, p. 6); Eberhard of Bamberg (PL, 193, 505 C). Otho of St. Emmeran, *Vita sancti Wolfkangi episcopi,* c. 28 (MGH, Script., vol. 4, p. 538). Cf. Bonaventure, *Sermo 3* (Quar., 5, p. 564).

110 Gregory is cited by William of Auxerre, *Summa aurea,* prologue (Pigonchet, fol. 22); *De officiis* (Douai, 65, fol. 11a: cf. Martineau, *Études d'histoire litt. et doctr. du XIIIe siècle,* vol. 2, p. 32). Gregory IX, bull of 7th July 1228.

111 Similarly, John Damascene, *De fides orthodoxa,* 4, c. 13 (PG, 92, 1140). Paschasius Radbertus (PL, 120, 1267–72, 1279 B–C), Ratherius of Verona (136, 646), Gezonius of Tortona (137, 376–7), Fulbert of Chartres (141, 204 A), Geoffrey of Vendôme (157, 213 D) . . .

112 *Liber de corpore,* c. 9, n. 8–12; c. 14 (PL, 120, 1298–1303, 1316–21).

113 PL, 72, 93 A–B.

114 Gezonius of Tortona, c. 41 (PL, 137, 393 A). Gerard of Cambrai (142, 1281–4). Peter Damian (144, 277; 145, 118, 573, 712). Lanfranc (150, 426 A–B, 435 C).

incomprehensible!'.[115] In such a way, established by God himself, the truth received its guarantee without the risk of violating the mystery. Historians have indicated[116] that 'the multiplication of Eucharistic miracles towards the eleventh century coincides remarkably with the controversies raised by Berengar, and the official definition of a real, substantial change of the bread and the wine at Mass'.[117]

No less worthy of remark is the fact of their more systematic use by those who, rejecting the old 'understanding', were also wary of the new 'dialectic'.

* * *

The clearest outcome of these varying transmutations was the devaluation of symbols. Augustinian theology consisted in the consideration of 'signs' and 'things':[118] the consideration of 'signs' would soon suffer an eclipse. This happened when, for example, in Trinitarian theology the doctrine of image and of vestiges began to be demolished. The school of Gilbert de la Porée denied it all noetic significance, already reducing it, as modern writers would, to simple comparisons. The critique that it instituted consisted in saying that these comparisons are without interest from the moment when it becomes impossible to extract any proof from them.[119] The Porretans were wary 'rationalists', younger brothers of those intemperate 'rationalists' whose dialectic went as far as challenging the Trinity. They formed, so to speak, the second wave of precursors of modern theology. Enthusiastic reason characterized the first, critical reason the second: both of them are far removed from the methods of Augustinian symbolism. This too was when the centre of gravity concerning sacramental matter shifted, while the standpoint of its meaning gradually disappeared. Nowhere was this evolution clearer than in Eucharistic doctrine. Even among those who still considered it of great importance, symbolism became something artificial and accessory. For example, this is how Berengar

---

115 John of Fécamp, (PL, 101, 1090 C–D). Cf. Gregory (76, 1197 C). Osbern, *Life of Saint Odo of Canterbury*, n. 10 (133, 939 B–C).

116 DHB, in *Bulletin de théologie ancienne et médiévale*, 1, n. 378, p. 206 (Report of Browe, *Die Eucharistischen Wunder des Mittelalters*, 1938).

117 Wycliffe will complain that these miracles were invented for the service of the 'new' doctrine. *De eucharistia*, prologue (Loserth, p. 1).

118 *De doctrina Christiana*, 1, n. 2 (PL, 34, 19). Cf. Bessarion (PG, 161, 494 C).

119 See Roland Bandinelli, *Sentences* (Gietl, pp. 25–6), and *Liber de vera philosophia*.

of Venouse was already explaining St. Augustine's doctrine on the grains of wheat that symbolize the fruit of the unity of the mystery:

> *What else does St Augustine urge us to understand, and indeed employs a certain force to make us see? – This, that by receiving the body and blood of Christ we should embrace unity and love . . . In affirming this statement he uses the neat simile of bread and wine, which are so united out of many parts that single elements can no longer be distinguished or separated from each other.*[120]

The doctrine was maintained, even in explicit terms. But it no longer had any backbone. We are no longer dealing with anything except a consequence in the practical order, a moral exhortation, applied to an 'elegant comparison' . . . The essential link that bonded the Eucharistic rite to the unity of the Church has disappeared. In the next century, if we search among the Eucharistic writings of the Abelardian school, it becomes clear that the very word *mystical* is missing:[121] this is an indication of the new direction of thought of which this school was one of the principal agents. Later, and for a long time afterwards, the ordinary themes of symbolism would continue to unfold: but it would only be a form of survival. Long-established custom kept them in place, but their 'power of evocation'[122] had worn out.

Here again a slight change in the classic formulations will signal to us the transformation that was operating unconsciously in thinking. We remember that, during an initial period, the 'reality' or the 'truth' of the sacrament was that unity of the ecclesial body upon which the gaze of faith would alight in a single leap. We remember, too, that from the time of Algerius of Liège onwards it had become customary to distinguish, in the categories of the threefold theory that was being worked out at the time, a double *reality of the sacrament*: the first was *reality and sacrament*, that is to say at the same time *the reality signified and the signifier*, while the second was *the reality and not the sacrament*, that is to say *the reality signified but not the signifier*: what was still being expressed in calling it *the reality signified as such*, or more briefly, *the reality as such*. Both 'realities' were thus distinguished and opposed within the sacrament, which, in its totality, contained them both. '*For this sacrament*', says the *Treatise of Madrid on the Seven Sacraments*, '*contains two realities in itself*:

---

120 *Ep. ad Gregorium VII adversus Berengarium* (Morin, 123).
121 The same for the *Sentences* of Roland.
122 Cf. E. Mersch, *Le Corps mystique du Christ*, vol. 2, p. 162.

most truly Christ and the union of charity.'[123] Now, from the middle
of the twelfth century onwards, the opposition to this began to be
translated in another formulation, the first of the two 'realities' being
called *the reality signified and contained* and the second *the reality
signified and not contained.* We find this already in Peter Lombard's
commentary on the First Letter to the Corinthians.[124] We find it also
in Peter Comestor's *De sacramentis*[125] and in a sermon by Peter of
Celle.[126] Soon *signified as such*, which originally meant: *and not signifying*, would imply: *and not contained*. The ultimate reality of the
sacrament, what was once upon a time its reality and truth *par excellence*, was thus expelled from the sacrament itself.[127] The symbolism
became extrinsic: from now on it could be ignored without damaging
the integrity of the sacrament. From the moment when it became the
mystical body, the ecclesial body was already detaching itself from
the Eucharist. Durandus of Mende would one day write, condensing
in one line the two terminologies that had prevailed: '*The form of
bread . . . both contains and signifies the true flesh, while it signifies
but does not contain the mystical flesh.*'[128] Once again, is this a minor
detail in wording? No doubt it is. But this minor detail is the sign of an
important fact. At the same time that it was being thrown out of the
true Body, the Church was beginning to be thrown out of the *mystery
of faith*.[129]

A conservative by instinct, St. Bonaventure adopted a somewhat different way of speaking. For him, the Eucharistic body was the *middle
reality*, and the ecclesial body was the *ultimate reality*.[130] It thus retained
all that it could of ancient symbolic thought. For him the Augustinian
concept of mystery remained very conscious.[131] But his synthesis only
constituted a pause in the course of a fatal evolution. It did not succeed
in staving off the rupture between mysticism and rational speculation.
Indeed time itself halts no more than thought does, and these sorts of
ruptures are the indispensable condition of new syntheses. The past
could not be born again; the whole weight of eternity that it carries

---

123 Weisweiler, p. 92.

124 PL, 191, 1642 A.

125 Martin, p. 35.

126 *Sermo 40, in cena Domini* 7 (PL, 202, 768).

127 A first step in this direction was taken when, from *veritas* or *res*, one distinguished *effectus*: see Bernald (PL, 148, 1064 or Algerius (180, 884).

128 *Rationale*, 4, c. 42 (p. 176). Cf. Innocent III (PL, 14, 1120-1).

129 However, Innocent III again: PL, 214, 1121 A.

130 *In IV Sent.*, d. 9, a. 2, q. 1 (vol. 4, p. 208); but p. 184. See also, Bonaventure, *In cena Domini*, sermo 2, c. 3 (vol. 9, p. 252).

131 *In Parasceve sermo* 2 (vol. 9, p. 262); *In Sententias*, q. 2, *ad objecta.*

passed on into other hands. The school of Bonaventure was a crowning point, that is to say, in many regards, an end. Thomism itself, although a long time in preparation and still weighed down by the same traditional elements,[132] was more of a starting point. From here onwards would flow the stream that would carry thinking humanity into new adventures.

---

132 For St. Thomas, *In Iv Sent.*, d. 8, q. 2, a. 1, as for St. Bonaventure, the Church, mystical body, is the *res ultima* of the Eucharistic mystery; similarly, if our interpretation is correct, *res contenta* (Moos, pp. 335–6). Nevertheless, *In Joannem*, c. 6, l. 7, n. 3. On the mystical body of the Church and on the Eucharist and Church in St. Thomas, cf. C.-M. Travers, *Valeur sociale de la liturgie d'après saint Thomas d'Aquin* ('Lex Orandi', 5), pp. 172–81 and 222–7. We note also that in the *Summa* Thomas chooses the Augustinian sign idea to introduce to the doctrine of the sacraments: cf. H.-F. Dondaine, 'La définition des sacrements dans la Somme théologique', in *Revue des sciences philosophiques et théologiques*, vol. 31 (1947), pp. 213–28. See also I.-H. Dalmais, *La Maison-Dieu*, 14, p. 73.

One has perhaps the indication of the fact that the sense of the ecclesial symbolism lost itself in the following, in a variant of *Summa theologiæ*, IIIa, q. 83, a. 5, ad 8.

Conclusion

More than anything, this study has shown us why the word *true* supplanted the word *mystical* as a description for the sacramental body. It remains to be seen more precisely why *mystical*, instead of disappearing, took the place of *true* as a description for the ecclesial body.

From the beginning of Christianity, the Eucharist had always been considered in relation to the Church. The 'communion of the body of Christ' of which St. Paul spoke to the faithful of Corinth[1] was their mysterious union with the community, by virtue of the sacrament: it was the mystery of one Body formed by all those who shared in the 'one Bread'. In the same way, from that time on the Church had never ceased to appear linked to the Eucharist. If, for example, we open the *Glossa* on St. Paul, it is not, as might be supposed, with reference to the account of the Last Supper, but with reference to the metaphor of the body, applied by the Apostle to the Christian community, that we read this sentence: 'This is the sacrifice of Christians, *so that the many might be one body in Christ.*'[2]

This mutual bond, long perceived as essential, explains the sense of *mystical body* applied to the Church. It is noticeable that it was with reference to the Eucharist that the Church was first given this description; so much so that, in order to study the expression, we have hardly had to leave the Eucharistic context. However, later theologians, who were able to base their teaching on one or two passages from St. Thomas Aquinas,[3] thought that in this case *mystical* was more aptly opposed to *natural*. According to them, it would be more correct to say that 'mystical body' was used in contrast to 'physical' or natural body. This would appear to be the explanation offered by the Roman Catechism.[4] In itself, this was no mistake; because once the expression was acquired, it is clear that this opposition immedi-

---

1 1 Cor. 10.17–18.
2 *In I Cor.*, xii, 3 (PL, 114, 510 D).
3 See *supra*, Chapter 5.
4 p. 1, a.9, n. 16.

ately presented itself, in the way that the *mystical sense* of Scripture is opposed to the *literal sense*. But a temptation developed here, in the case of the Church, precisely as in that of Scripture: the temptation of no longer seeing anything in this metaphor except the metaphor itself, and of considering 'mystical' as a watering-down of 'real' or of 'true'. To a greater or lesser extent, many fell victim to it. According to some, *'mystical body'* was merely the same as expressions such as *'the fellowship of Catholics'* or *'the congregation of the faithful'*.[5] From that time onwards there was no group that could not be given this description: that is how Antoine de Rosiers comes to distinguish five principal *mystical bodies*, because within the assembly of humankind he counts a hierarchy of five societies.[6] Some who remembered that St. Augustine[7] and St. Gregory[8] spoke of a *demonic body* had no difficulty in speaking in their own turn of a *demonic mystical body*.[9] It is true that other theologians resisted the temptation and protested against such an extensive use of the word, which they considered an abuse. This was the case, in the eighteenth century, with Noel Alexandre;[10] it is the case in our own day with Fr. Prat's interpretation of St. Paul.[11] They do not want the mystical body of Christ to be confused with any sort of 'moral entity'. There is no doubt that they are right, given that ancient tradition, the faithful interpreter of Scripture, offers us so many ultra-realist statements concerning the ecclesial body.[12] But the temptation itself would have had nowhere to take hold, had we been more careful to preserve the original sense of the word that gave rise to this quarrel.

When it was applied to the Eucharist, the *mystical body* meant the *body in mystery*, immediately connected to a *mystery of the body*.

---

5 Philothei Achillini, *Somnium Viridarii*, c. 360 (Goldast, pp. 218–19).

6 *Monarchia*, p. 2, c. 6 (Goldast, p. 312).

7 *De Genesi ad litteram*, 11, n. 31 (PL, 34, 441–2); *In psalmos* (36, 938; 37, 1807). St. Ambrose, *In psalmum 37*, n. 9 (Petschenig, p. 143), and St. Jerome, *In Ezechielem* (PL, 25, 279 D) speak of 'body of the dragon'.

8 *Moralia in Job*, passim (PL, 75). The expression 'demonic body' is frequent in the Middle Ages (for example: Godescalc, Lambot, pp. 189, 203; Paschasius Radbertus, *In Matthaeum*: PL, 120, 4690; *In Lamentationes* Jeremiae: 1155 A; Rupert, PL, 168, 530 B, 613 C, 665 B, 670 D), and we find it again in Luther, who also says 'corpus mysticum Judae' (cf. W.Wagner, Zeitschrift für katholische Theologie, 1937, p. 35).

9 Thus the author of the titles added to the chapters of *De Genesi ad litteram* (PL, 34, 441).

10 *Theologia dogmatica et moralis* (1703), vol. 1, p. 50.

11 *La théologie de saint Paul*, vol. 2, 14th edn, p. 344.

12 For example, Remigius of Auxerre (PL, 131, 276 A). Alger of Liége (180, 747). *Summa* of Alexander, IVa, q.10, m. 3, a.6.

From then on it can be understood that during a whole initial period, it seemed natural to distinguish the sacramental body from the historical body, the crucified body: that was to distinguish the sacrament of the Passion from the Passion itself; it did not mean denying the profound identity that it was the sacrament's purpose to affirm. When the author of the *Opus imperfectum in Matthaeum* wrote with reference to the vessels on the altar: '*in which not the true body of Christ, but the mystery of his body is contained*',[13] he was not, in his manner of underlining a contrast, giving an exact interpretation of traditional belief.[14] Through the stages that have been described, the expression *mystical body* passed from the Eucharist to the Church: and once again there was, in an analogous sense, a *mystery of the body*. The *mystical body* was the mystery that described this ecclesial body by means of the sacrament, and, in its radical meaning, it could strictly speaking be described as being 'contained' in the Eucharist. Then, from the *mystery of the body* it developed into being a *body in [the] mystery*; from the signification itself to the thing signified.

Thus the Church is the mystical body of Christ: that is to say, quite simply, that it is the body of Christ signified by means of the sacrament. *Mystical* is a contraction of *mystically signified, mystically designated*. That is the sense that clearly emerges from the first statement offered to us on the subject in the work of Master Simon: '*In the sacrament of the altar there are two (bodies): that is, the true body of Christ and also that which it signifies, his mystical body, which is the Church.*'[15]

Is this not a true definition of *mystical*? The generation that preceded Master Simon's had still not reached the definitive version, but there was a definition which heralded it and in some sense called it into being. This is what we find in Gregory of Bergamo. In chapter 18 of his *Treatise*, after quoting St. Paul on the one body formed by all those who share in the one Bread, Gregory writes:

> *That we, though many, are one body, through the life-giving power of the Holy Spirit,* is designated mystically by this sacrament, *and it was clearly expressed in these words by the Apostle.*[16]

---

13 PG, 56, 691. Cf. Dom Martin, 'Les homélies latines sur saint Matthieu attribuées à Origène', in *Revue bénédictine*, vol. 65 (1942).

14 Cf. Dom Morin, *op. cit.*

15 *Tractatus de sacramentis* (Weisweiler, p. 27). Cf. *Madrid Treatise* (W., p. 91). Gerson (*Opera*, Anvers, 1706, vol. 1, p. 257).

16 Hürter, p. 74.

Soon it would be altogether natural to call this body mystically signified by means of the Sacrament a 'mystical body'. Others were to say:
signified body,[17]and it would mean the same thing. By virtue of the law
operating in the transference of idioms, the adjective that described the
Eucharist as signifying could pass to the Church as signified – from the
sacred sign to the *sacred secret*.[18] If we wanted to interpret some intention of restrictive nuance within this new usage, it would only consist
in saying that while the particular body of Christ is present 'in truth'
in the sacrament, the ecclesial body is only present 'as a mystery'.[19]
But we are not dealing here with a restriction relating to the affirming of its reality. Moreover, even when all reference to the Eucharist
had disappeared, the expression would continue to be adapted to its
object because, as Cardinal du Perron expressed it, 'the word mystical is not always used by writers to exclude the reality of the thing,
but to exclude imputing to it evidence and comprehensibility'.[20] The
Church, the body of Christ, is a mystery and, against the flat notion of
it conceived in the Enlightenment and repeated by a few followers of
liberal Protestantism, it should be maintained that a mystery is what
continues to remain obscure, hidden and 'mystical', even once it has
been described, signified and 'revealed'.

*   *   *

Eucharistic realism and ecclesial realism: these two realisms support
one another, each is the guarantee of the other. Ecclesial realism safe-
guards Eucharistic realism and the latter confirms the former. The
same unity of the Word is reflected in both.[21] Today, it is above all our
faith in the 'real presence', made explicit thanks to centuries of controversy and analysis, that introduces us to faith in the ecclesial body:
effectively signified by the mystery of the Altar, the mystery of the
Church has to share the same nature and the same depth.[22] Among the
ancients, the perspective was often inverted. The accent was habitually

---

17 Sicard of Cremona (PL, 213, 132). Peter of Tarentaise (cited by Botte,
Recherches de théologie . . . , 1929, pp. 306–7). *Summa* of Alexander IVa,
q.10, m.5, a.2. Cf. Nicholas Cabasilas, *Explanation of the Divine Liturgy*, c. 37
(Salaville, *Sources chrétiennes*, 4, p. 208). Cf. St. Thomas, *In Joannem*, c. 6, l. 7,
n. 3, 5.
18 Odo of Ourscamp, *Quaestiones*, p. 2, q. 266 (Pitra, p. 92).
19 Gregory of Bergamo, c. 19 (Hürter, pp. 79–80).
20 *Traité de l'Eucharistie* (1622), p. 599. Cf. Wycliffe, *De Ecclesia*, c. 5; c. 6,
c. 18 (Loserth, pp. 102–3, 138, 440).
21 Rupert, *De devinis officiis*, 2, c. 2 (PL, 170, 35).
22 Paschasius, to Frudegard (PL, 120, 1361 C).

placed on the effect rather than on the cause. But the ecclesial realism to which they universally offer us the most explicit testimony is at the same time, and when necessary, the guarantee of their Eucharistic realism. This is because the cause has to be proportionate to its effect. The authors of *Perpétuité* put it most effectively when they said: one hundred passages from the Fathers

> Only contain the one doctrine, which is that the body of Jesus Christ, being received by the faithful, effects among them a sort of union, which is not only moral, but physical and natural, since it consists in the real union of our body with that of Jesus Christ; by virtue of which it can be said that all these bodies with which Jesus Christ is united by means of the Eucharist form only one body, because they only have one individual body, which is the body of Jesus Christ. Thus these passages are worlds away from contradicting the real presence, on which, on the contrary, they are founded, because the faithful are only united among themselves in one body because the Eucharist, which is the body of Jesus Christ, is united to them.[23]

By virtue of the same internal logic – and this counter-experience has its price – those in modern times who water down the traditional idea of the Church as the Body of Christ find themselves also watering down the reality of the Eucharistic presence. This is how Calvin made efforts to establish the same notion of a 'virtual presence' of Christ in his sacrament and among the faithful. The reason behind it is the same in both cases: 'because he is in heaven and we are here below on earth'.[24] And the pastor Claude, when wanting to set aside the testimony that apologists had extracted from the Fathers in favour of the Catholic doctrine of the Eucharist, found himself obliged to contest the implications of their texts concerning the Church.[25] – How, indeed, could the Church be truly built up, how could its members be gathered together in a truly united body by means of a sacrament that only symbolically contained the One whose body it was meant to become, and who alone could bring about its unity? St. Augustine himself becomes incomprehensible, and his entire mysticism, so full

---

23 Bk. 5, c. 9 (Migne, vol. 2, p. 427). Cf. Rupert, *In Joannem*, 6 (PL, 169, 482). Honorius of Autun, *Elucidarium*, 1, c. 27 (172, 1128 D). Algerius of Liège (180, 747). Erasmus, *In Matthaeum*, c. 26 (Basle, 1535, p. 162), etc.

24 Sermon 41, commenting on Eph. 5.30 (*Opera*, vol. 51, col. 770). Cf. Mersch, *Le Corps mystique du Christ*, vol. 2, 2nd edn., pp. 422–3.

25 Cf. *Perpétuité*, 4, c. 9 (Migne, vol. 2. 318–22).

of meaning as it is, evaporates into hollow formulations if, on analys-ing the implications of his doctrine, we refuse to recognise within it the faith of the common tradition. For him, the Eucharist is far more than a symbol, because it is most truly that sacrament *by which the Church is bound together in this age*,[26] since the water and the wine of the sacrifice, like the water and the blood that flowed down from the cross, are themselves the sacraments *from which the Church is built*.[27] It is a real presence because it makes real.

This link of causality and of reciprocal guarantee between the two mysteries of the Church and the Eucharist cannot therefore be too highly stressed, not only in order to understand the dogma in itself, but also to understand the Christian past. If our theologians sometimes have difficulty – as they loyally admit – in finding the 'real presence' in one or other Eucharistic doctrine from antiquity, it is perhaps because they are looking too hard. If they were more simply to ask themselves, without worrying about anything else, what this doctrine was, they would undoubtedly be more successful in seeing that the real presence was implicit in it. But while they are seeking it without finding it, they are failing to pay sufficient attention to certain other essential charac-teristics, which are precisely those that would reveal that presence to them. They even manage, through an unconscious tactical error, to minimise those characteristics, affecting to see in them only chance considerations, some sort of 'morality' without dogmatic significance, whose terms it would be inappropriate to insist on, and which are not even worth keeping. They make great efforts to find excuses for the great Doctors who were implicated in this, and seem not to notice that this flowering [of dogma] that they so disdain has its solid and vigor-ous roots in Scripture itself.

Negligence of ecclesial symbolism or minimisation of ecclesial real-ism: these are two faults that often go hand in hand. As has already been established, the general evolution of doctrine tended towards this. The consequences of the controversy with the protestants contrib-uted to making it worse. This is how Bellarmine comes to say nothing about the relationship with the Eucharist. This silence is in such stark contrast with his learning, that, in the numerous texts that he quotes, he would seem to be systematically avoiding the repetition of any sen-tences in which this relationship might be mentioned. At one point

---

26 *Contra Faustum*, 12, c. 20 (PL, 42, 265). M. Comeau, 'Les Prédications pascales de saint Augustin' (*Recherches de science religieuse*, 1933, p. 268).

27 *De Civ. Dei*, 22, c. 17 (PL, 41, 779). Cf. *In psalmum* 126 (37, 1672), etc. *Sermo Denis* 3, n. 3 (46, 828).

nevertheless forced to allude to it, in connection with several passages of St. Augustine put forward by his adversaries, he is only prepared to examine these passages in order to use them as objections, and he finally concludes that Augustine was only trying to conceal the truth in them: '*Let us reply . . . that Augustine with devoted labour disguised the question and proceeded to moral exhortation!*'[28] Du Perron argued in the same vein. In his view, the ecclesial doctrine developed by the Fathers in speaking of the Eucharist is only an 'oblique, secondary and accessory doctrine', that dwindles into 'hyperbolic and allegorical' language. All that they say about it can be compared to a shadow in relation to a body, an echo or 'counter-voice' in relation to a voice.[29] Its entire aim is to 'recreate the minds of those who read it through the pious cheerfulness and ingenious inventiveness of these allegorical allusions and applications'. And if anyone is surprised when the 'counter-voice' is sometimes the only one to be heard, or the shadow is so prominent that the body itself does not always appear, du Perron, like Bellarmine, finds an explanation for it in a fact analogous to what would soon come to be called the 'arcane discipline'. Someone addressing catechumens cannot yet reveal to them the heart of the mystery:

> . . . St. Augustine, out of concern for the Catechumens, interprets the words that our Lord uses in speaking of his body and blood, not as his true and real flesh and his true and real blood, . . . but as the moral and political body of Christ, which is understood as the society of his Church . . . This is a moral and secondary understanding, which St. Augustine uses and sustains in order to satisfy the curiosity of the Cathecumens, waiting until they are capable of coming definitively to the proper, direct and immediate understanding of these words . . .[30]

Once more according to du Perron, the same must also be said of works addressed to pagans: within them the Fathers 'disguised and masked what they were saying . . . with cloudy ambiguities, in order to keep their profane readers or audience in a state of suspense and

---

28 *De sacramento Eucharistiae.*

29 Comparing (with some accuracy) these two ways of speaking about the Eucharist with the two 'understandings' of Scripture that can be found in the Fathers, Du Perron does not see that, in his desire to give weight to literal understanding, he misinterprets the traditional terminology.

30 *Réplique à la Response du Serenissime Roy de la Grand Bretagne* (1620), pp. 879–80; *Traité de l'Eucharistie* (1622), pp. 55–9.

incertitude about the true purpose of the Church'.[31] However, there exist sermons addressed to the baptised that are not any more explicit. Would true doctrine still remain hidden from those who are already members of the Church? *Perpétuité* does not think so; but, in the sense given there, we are dealing with 'moral' discourses, not 'dogmatic' discourses. Supposing that his audience 'were well-informed about the substance of their faith', the preacher would attempt 'only to edify their devotion'.[32] Supposedly, therefore, the Fathers were almost always addressing an audience that they still had no right to instruct, or that they presumed were already well instructed! As we have already seen, there were parts of *Perpétuité* that were better inspired than this.

Several more recent historians follow a similar path. They cheerfully divide up the ancient texts relating to the Eucharist into two groups: the first group is made up of 'realist' texts, while all the 'allegorized' texts are lumped into a second group, which is abandoned. But the so-called 'realist' texts are not always as realist as these historians would have us believe, and by abandoning these 'allegorized' texts, they sometimes deprive us of the most effective testimony to authentic realism. The fear of 'symbolism' proves a poor counsellor here. For example, we find written: 'the allegorism of some of the Fathers, whereby the body of Christ is presented as his mystical body or the Church, or again its doctrine, or its teaching, does not permit us to consider those who taught it as partisans of Eucharistic symbolism'.[33] How true! In fact it is often quite the contrary. But it is therefore doubly deplorable that, through a desire to escape a negative 'symbolist' interpretation, we should deliberately be deprived of an *essential* part of the Eucharistic doctrine of our forebears. It is also deplorable that a theology that sets out to be strictly historical and 'positive'

---

31 *Examen du livre du Sieur Du Plessis* (*Les diverses œuvres* . . . , 3rd edn., 1633, p. 1100). We know that the protestant Daillé retained this 'discipline of the arcane' (his own phrase) in order to affirm the irremediable obscurity of the Fathers. From this derive both his acceptance of du Perron's principle and his criticism of the Cardinal's application of it, 'that great and curious observer of all the ways of antiquity': 'Such flexibility would be difficult to believe in these holy men, if we did not have such a great Cardinal as guarantor . . . This observation pleased him so much that he repeated it on every possible occasion; and it can be said that it is the source from which he draws most of the subtle and admirable solutions that he offers to patristic passages. Perhaps the curious will find something to remark on in some of the applications he makes. But it is sufficient for us to accept his assertion that the Fathers themselves often use this method . . .' (*Traité de l'emploi des saints Pères*, part I, c. 6, 1632, pp. 170–4).

32 Migne, vol. 2, col. 759; cf. 768–78. Cf. Comeau, art. Cit., pp. 263–5; Batiffol, *l'Eucharistie*, pp. 235–6.

33 G. Bareille, *Eucharistie* (DTC, vol. 12, col. 1123)

should sometimes commit the historical nonsense of lending its own state of mind to an age where a quite opposite state of mind pertains. Ontological symbolism holds in the history of Christian thought – and in Christian thought itself – too important a place to remain unknown or neglected with impunity – particularly in sacramental theology.

*　*　*

It now seems fairly clear how and why *mystical body* passed from Eucharistic usage to ecclesial usage, and what precise significance ought not be attributed to it in one and the other case. Nevertheless, the total significance of the change that ensued can only be fully understood by insisting on the following observations. Of the three terms: historical body, sacramental body and ecclesial body, that were in use, and that it was a case of putting into order amongst each other, that is to say simultaneously to oppose and unite them to one another, the caesura was originally placed between the first and the second, whereas it subsequently came to be placed between the second and the third. Such, in brief, is the fact that dominates the whole evolution of Eucharistic theories.

This evolution should not be imagined as a rupture or a sudden deviation, any more than as a rectilinear development or a simple explanation. It should rather be compared to a circular movement that was no more precipitate or more rigid at any one particular point of its life. Through the effect of this movement, viewpoints were continually but almost imperceptibly changing. Some new aspect would be discovered, which would continue being confused with the one that preceded it, until that one disappeared. New habits of thought came into being, to all extents and purposes without being noticed. The wheel carried on turning, as inexorably, if not as regularly as time itself, and under the influence of whatever mentality was then prevalent, it was the problems, far more than their solutions, that changed. Naturally there resulted a series of interferences, and also a series of misunderstandings between those minds that remained more attached to the past and those that looked more to the future. Discussions arose, that were often more lively than was warranted by any real distance that lay between the positions of those who were more attentive to new needs, and therefore eager to detect error in any form of antiquarianism, and those who, on the contrary, had a confused sense that in the abandonment of ancient viewpoints, great riches were in danger of being lost. This is the origin of the double phenomenon of traditional formulations that perpetuated themselves by changing, or mostly that changed gradually in spirit while remaining unchanged in the letter. Furthermore a real doctrinal continuity is maintained here.[34] It is very rare that an innovation, even a slight one, cannot claim authority from some earlier text, and the syntheses elaborated from it all have their roots in the furthest reaches of the past. Between one era and another, as between one Doctor and another, it is often no more than a question of a simple difference of emphasis – admittedly all the more irreducible because they escape the rules of logical discussion. It may be the evolutions, oppositions and awkwardnesses that I have tried to point out in the course of this study are therefore often rather forced; to those familiar with the entire collection of texts it may even seem that to comment on them is to be over-scrupulous, perhaps even arbitrary. It was difficult to avoid this trap altogether: but was it not necessary to emphasize somewhat fleeting characteristics in order to grasp them more clearly?

The most serious misunderstanding that arose from such an evolution was certainly, from an historical perspective, the one to which St. Augustine's thinking fell victim. As time went on, it proved fatal that it became more misunderstood, and we see as the centuries go by those who claim to be his partisans dividing into two opposite camps, representing two contradictory interpretations each of which is nearly always equally false. We have encountered various examples of this above. One of the most typical cases is found in Augustine's teaching on reception of communion by the unworthy. These approach the holy table and receive the sacrament. What does the Lord do meanwhile? Not what he did at the Last Supper, where he ate the Passover with his disciples with such delight. He does what he did on the Cross when, having tasted the bitter drink that was offered to him, he refused to drink it. *He does not admit them into his body.*[35] This should be translated as: 'he does not incorporate them into himself'. This is the habitual perspective of Augustine, who always sees the ecclesial body as an extension of the Eucharist. But once we have in some sense divided the ecclesial body from the sacramental body, by a shift in the caesura, the problem of the interpretation of texts of this sort becomes insoluble. The *to be received by Christ* and the *to receive Christ* being from now on separated, it would seem that Augustine, who distinguished them with the most subtle of nuances, by denying the first thus also denied

---

34 Cf. Gerberon, *Synopsis Apologiae pro Ruperto* (PL, 167, 42 A–B).

35 *In psalmum 68*, sermo 2, n. 6 (PL, 36, 859). Cf. *In Joannem*, tractatus 59, n. 1 (35, 1796), etc.

the second. The problem, for Augustine, was that of the fruitfulness of the sacrament, that of its spiritual fruit (*being transformed into the body of Christ*); what happens is that this is made into a problem of validity, a problem of sacramental presence. It was indeed a question of communion; but it would primarily become a question of the effect of the consecration.[36] According to these new perspectives, the reading of Augustinian texts became distorted. They were searched for a response that they could not provide. Do schismatics, heretics and the excommunicated truly receive the sacrament? Do they truly have the Body of our Lord on their altars? This is the question posed from the eleventh century onwards. No, replied a certain number of theologians, such as Gerhoh of Reichersberg: is the Catholic Church not indeed the only place of true sacrifice? 'Who could imagine that heretics, especially self-declared heretics and those under a ban of excommunication or interdict, could have Christ present in their liturgies?'[37] Yes, would reply partisans of the doctrine that was to emerge triumphant, while others thought they had found a solution through better distinguishing between the cases that Gerhoh was aiming at and the case of those who were simply unworthy . . .[38] The two extremist parties could claim Augustine for their own, as well as the third; but if the second is certainly much more justified in doing so, nevertheless it makes equally little sense in each case.[39]

We should not conclude, from all this, that evolution was a negative thing in itself. It was normal and therefore good. Furthermore, it was needed in order to remedy error and to offer a response to the questions inevitably raised by progress in understanding. Preserving the

---

36 Note equally the double sense of the distinction between *sacramentum* and *res sacramenti*: cf. Pseudo-Bernard (PL, 184, 954 A) and a fragment of the School of Laon (Lottin, 393, *Recherches de théologie ancienne et médiévale*, vol. 13, 1946, p. 280).

37 *In psalmum 23* (PL, 193, 1088 B–C). *Epistola ad Innocentium papum* (MGH, *Libelli de lite*, vol. 3, pp. 225–6). *Opusculum ad cardinales* (p. 408); *In psalmum 64* (p. 483), etc.

38 Honorius of Autun, *Elucidarium*, 1 (PL, 172, 1130–31); *Eucharistion*, c. 6–10 (172, 1253–5). Cf. Peter Lombard, *Sent.*, 4, d.9 (192, 858–9). Gerhoh, *Liber contra duas haereses*, c. 5 (PL, 194, 1181–2). Cf. Rupert, *De Spiritu sancto*, 3, c. 22 (167, 1663–4).

39 One of the last to untangle the ambiguities (before the historical work of the moderns) is Rupert, who still remains close to Augustinianism: *De Spiritu sancto*, 3, c. 22 (PL, 167, 1663–4; *De divinis officiis*, 2, p. 11, c. 13 (176, 505–6). See also Hugh of St. Victor, *De sacramentis*, 2, p. 11, c. 13 (176, 505–506) and fragment *De sacramento corporis Christi* (Wilmart, p. 243). Cf. L. Brigué, 'Le communicant mal disposé reçoit-il vraiment le corps du Christ? La question à la fin du XIe siècle', in *Science religieuse, travaux et recherches*, 1943, pp. 70–101.

status quo in theories and viewpoints has never been and can never be an adequate means of safeguarding the truth. In the present case, many misunderstandings that the ensuing changes brought about were the sorts of inconvenience that all good brings in its wake. But this cannot be said for the mutilations that actually accompanied it in many cases. Could Eucharistic realism not have been safeguarded without the virtually total abandonment of symbolism? What ruination heresy accomplishes here, even when it is vanquished! 'Woe to those', we could say, with apologies to Pascal, 'who have led the defenders of faith to turn from the foundation of religion', in order to direct speculation about the Eucharist towards external problems of apologetics! These should not have been set aside, but they ended up by absorbing the entire effort of reflection. More scientific than religious, the syntheses that ensued could in no way be definitive. However, rather than in their inevitable fragility, the damage lay in the abandonment that they appeared to sanction. The eighteenth century, as we have seen, had used the stones of our ancient inheritance to build new structures. But evolution was not slow in coming, and if some formulations lasted, they remained all too often nothing but formulations. The Magisterium, from far off, recalled the essence: theology, without contradicting it, did not always listen to it, or merely proved itself its feeble echo.

The damage equally affected the domain of the Eucharist and of the Church.

Indeed at one level the constant build-up of Eucharistic piety[40] became more easily oriented towards an overly individualistic devotion,[41] and sometimes proved poorly defended against certain sentimental excesses. This is how one of the most magnificent examples of progress afforded by the history of Christian life was prevented from bearing some of its finest fruit. As for the Church, insofar as, by defending itself against internal and external attack, it managed to give itself or to define for itself the characteristics of its exterior constitution, by that very fact a good many theologians developed an idea of it that was less and less realist, because less and less mystical. The Thomist

---

40 F. Baix and C. Lambot, *La devotion à l'Eucharistie et le septième centenaire de la Fête-Dieu* (1946); Axters O.P., etc.: *Studia eucharistica DCCi anni a condito Festo Sanctissimi Corporis Christi* (1946).

41 The historians often noted it. For example P. Batiffol, *L'Eucharistie*, 5th edn, p. iv. The traditional doctrine was recalled once again by Cardinal Maglione in his letter of 11th July 1939 to Eugène Duthoit (*Semaine sociale de Bordeaux*, 1939, pp. 7–8). More recently Pius XII, message of May 1942.

synthesis, still so nourished on tradition and so highly organised, was too quickly abandoned in favour of theories which were of quite different orientation and too dependent on controversy.[42] Except among a few isolated thinkers, such as Nicholas of Cusa in the fifteenth century,[43] this is how the 'mystery' of the Church disappeared from the horizons of thought, as if there necessarily had to be a conflict between the perfection of the 'visible society' and the intimate solidity of the 'Body of Christ'![44] It seems that it would therefore be of great interest, we might even say of pressing urgency, given the present state of what remains of 'Christendom', to return to the sacramental origins of the 'mystical body' in order to steep ourselves in it. It would be a return to the mystical sources of the Church. The Church and the Eucharist are formed by one another day by day: the idea of the Church and the idea of the Eucharist must promote one another mutually and each be rendered more profound by the other.[45] *By the food and blood of the Lord's body let all fellowship be bound together!*[46]

I am certainly not so naïve as to think that this living synthesis was never realised in its perfect state in the thinking of the Doctors or the practice of the people of any century. The periods from which I have to cull most of the material for my explorations were, as any other, troubled times, eras where disunity and hypocrisy ruled . . . If the tragic needs of our time plead for us in some sense to reinvent in its first vigour the doctrine whose loss is being the death of us, such an effort at reinvention no more consists in 'taking mental refuge in an idealised past' than in 'building for ourselves some imaginary refuge' in a future painted according to the whims of our imagination.[47] We must, however, recognise or rediscover the genuine riches bequeathed to us by the Christian past. We need to relearn from our Fathers, those of Christian antiquity and also those of the Middle Ages, to see present in the unique Sacrifice the unity of the 'three bodies' of Christ.[48] Such an assessment seems to impose itself all the more because without it

---

42 Cf. M.-J. Congar, *L'idée thomiste de l'Église*, in *Esquisses du mystère de l'Église*, pp. 51–91.

43 *De concordantia catholica*, 1, c. 6, and 3, c. 1 (Paris, 1514/Bonn, 1928, fol. ix, lii).

44 Nevertheless, the Roman Catechism (p. 1, a.9, n. 21).

45 Scheeben, *Dogmatik*. Pseudo-Haimon, *In psalmos* (PL, 116, 248 D). Cf St. Thomas; Bossuet, *Explication de quelques difficultés sur les priers de la messe*, n. 36.

46 Oration of the Mozarabic liturgy, Julian of Toledo (PL, 96, 759 B).

47 Cf. Romano Guardini, *Liturgische Bildung*, p. 52.

48 Nicholas Cabasilas, *Explanation of the Liturgy*, c. 38 (Salaville, p. 211). Cf. PG, 150, 452 D.

the very strength of the corporate aspirations which can currently be felt at the heart of the Church, and which are in particular driving the liturgical movement, cannot be without peril. Here or there, it could degenerate into a naturalist impulse. Indeed there is always a risk of forgetting: it is not the human fact of gathering for the communal celebration of the mysteries, it is not the collective exaltation that an appropriate pedagogy succeeds in extracting from it that will ever in the very least bring about the unity of the members of Christ. This cannot come about without the remission of sins, the first fruit of the blood that was poured out.[49] The memorial of the Passion, the offering to the heavenly Father, the conversion of the heart: these, therefore, are the totally interior realities without which we will never have anything but a caricature of the community that we seek. But the Eucharist does not offer us some human dream: it is a *mystery of faith*. In order to meditate on this mystery of faith, which also encapsulates the whole mystery of salvation, we can finish by borrowing once more one of the voices of antiquity that has spoken to us throughout this book:

> . . . To the one and only Son of God and Son of Man, as to their head, all the members of the body are joined, all those who are received in the faith of this mystery, in the fullness of this love. Thus it is one single body, it is one single person, one single Christ, the head with its members, who raises himself up to heaven, and in his gratitude cries out, presenting the Church in its glory to God: 'Here is bone of my bone and flesh of my flesh!' And, demonstrating that he and the Church are joined in a true unity of persons, he says again: 'and they will be two in one flesh'.
>
> Yes, this is indeed a great mystery. The flesh of Christ which, before his Passion, was the flesh of the only word of God, has so grown through the Passion, so expanded and so filled the universe, that all the elect who have been since the beginning of the world or who will live, to the very last one among them, through the action of this sacrament which makes a new dough of them, he reunites in one single Church, where God and humankind embrace one another for all eternity.
>
> This flesh was originally nothing but a grain of wheat, a unique grain, before it fell to the earth in order to die there. And now that it has died, here it is, growing on the altar, coming to fruition in our

---

49 Cf. Matthew 26.28.

hands and in our bodies, and, as the great and rich master of the harvest is rising up, he raises with him to the very barns of heaven this fertile earth at whose heart he has grown.[50]

---

50 Rupert, *De divinis officiis,* 2, c. 11 (PL, 170, 43). Cf. *In Joannem,* 6 (169, 482–3). Augustine, *In psalmum* 59, n. 9, 69, n. 1 (36, 720, 805–6). Gregory, *In evangelia,* 1, hom. 8 (PL, 76, 1104 B), cited by Florus (119, 89 D). Paschasius Radbertus (120, 1304). Etherius and Beatus (96, 936 D). Leonian Sacramentary (Feltoe, p. 35). Adelmann of Brescia (Heurtevent, p. 300). Franco (PL, 166, 777). Pseudo-Hildebert (171, 1208). Stephen of Baugé (172, 1285), etc. Cf. St. Thomas, *In Joannem,* c. 12, l. 4, n. 5.

II

AMALARIUS'S 'THREEFOLD BODY' AND WHAT BECAME OF IT

Introduction

Arian! Nestorian! False prophet! Man of unheard-of audacity, puffed up with carnal ideas, worse than Pelagius! Enemy of the faith, of Scripture and of the Church! Ridiculous and sacrilegious opinions! Confused and muddle-headed words! Perverse dogmas, foolish fables! Monsters of absurdity! Books full of stupidity, folly, delirium and profane novelties, full of pernicious errors, lies, blasphemies and heresies! Books inspired by demons, books that absolutely must be burned! . . .[1] – who is this heresiarch being denounced with such vigour? Amalarius of Metz, the bishop of Trèves and a considerable personage, confidant to Charlemagne and Louis the Pious, the disciple, collaborator and successor of Alcuin in the great liturgical reform of the ninth century. – And where does this denunciation come from? – From a small circle, a clan, as Dom Wilmart writes,[2] whose central figure is Florus, the archdeacon of Lyon, an equally considerable personage, a writer of merit and himself also a liturgist of the first order. In this 'furious offensive', 'all the batteries are firing at the same time'.[3] One circumstance should be noted immediately, which will explain the violence of the attack and dispense us from getting too upset over it. Agobard, the archbishop of Lyon, took the side of the sons of Louis the Pious in their revolt against their father in 833, and subsequently had to go into exile in Italy. Amalarius was imposed by the victorious emperor as administrator over the Church of Lyon, and, despite resistance from its conservative and particularist spirit[4] immediately undertook to make it bend under the yoke of the liturgical customs that he was

---

1 Florus, *Adversus Amalarium* (PL, 119, 76–87; MGH, *Concilia*, vol. 2, p. 770). Agobard, *Contra libros quatuor Amalarii* (PL, 104, 342–9); *De divina psalmodia* (104, 327–34).

2 'Un lecteur ennemi d'Amalaire', in *Revue bénédictine*, 1924, p. 326.

3 Cf. Wilmart, 'Une letter sans adresse écrite vers le milieu du IXe siècle', in *Revue bénédictine*, 1939, pp. 158–9; *Histoire littéraire de la France*, vol. 5, p. 136.

4 P. Chevallard, *Saint Agobard* (1869), p. 168.

promoting.[5] In this, he was continuing a task that he had only been able to initiate at the beginning of the century, during a first stay in Lyon as assistant bishop under the authority of Leidrade.[6] But Louis the Pious was easy-going. By 838 Agobard was back in his good graces. Fortune having changed camps, Lyon took its revenge. – What was, at least, the pretext for such an outburst? – There were many. Amalarius had particularly irritated our friends in Lyon by having '*popular canticles*'[7] sung during Mass. For those who would not permit any singing other than that of inspired words, this was a grave assault on the divine simplicity of the liturgy.[8] It was nevertheless difficult to find material of formal heresy in this, and furthermore, if there was any novelty, it lay rather in Agobard's intransigent purism.[9] But there was also, and primarily, the *threefold body*!

More than twenty years previously, Amalarius had composed a great and learned work on the Liturgies of the Church. In this *Liber Officialis*,[10] whose first edition appeared in 813,[11] he had introduced, among a good deal of erudite information and traditional explanation, some symbolism of his own devising. One example of this symbolism drew fire down upon his head. It was an exegesis of the rite of fraction. In the course of the Mass, between the Our Father and the Lamb of God, the priest – as still today in our Latin liturgies – divided the consecrated host into three parts. These three parts, according to Amalarius, symbolised the three parts of which Christ's Body is composed:

> *The body of Christ is threefold, that is, of those who have tasted death or are about to die: the first, holy and immaculate, taken from the Virgin Mary; the second, which walks on earth; and third, which lies in tombs. The particle of the host that is put in the chalice rep-*

---

5 Cf. Florus, *Adversus Amalarium I* (PL, 119, 73 B–C, 76 C).

6 This last detail is not entirely assured. The history of Amalarius remains obscure on many points.

7 Agobard, *Liber de divina psalmodia* (PL, 104, 327 A).

8 Florus, *Adversus Amalarium* (PL, 119, 80 C–D). Cf. *Mémoire du Chapitre primatial de Lyon, contenant ses motifs de ne point admettre la nouvelle Liturgie* (1776), pp. 37, 68, 115.

9 Cf. Mabillon, *Musaeum italicum*, vol. 2, p. 4. Dom Guéranger, *Institutions liturgiques*, 2nd edn, vol. 1, pp. 247–8.

10 Such is the true title of the *De ecclesiasticis officiis* (PL, 105, 985–1242). In a posterior work, *De ordine antiphonarii* (after 831: Bishop, *Liturgiica historica*, p.334), Amalarius makes many allusions to his *Libellus officialis* (105, 1280–1314). It was a current title there (1308 A).

11 Cf. J.-M. Hanssens, *Le texte du Liber officialis d'Amalaire*, in *Ephemerides liturgicae*, 1933 and 1934.

*resents the body of Christ which has already risen from the dead,
the particle that is consumed by the priest or people represents that
which still walks on earth, and the particle that is left on the altar
that which lies in tombs . . .*[12]

In this text, Florus discovered an Achilles' heel . . . He aimed at it
with dogged fury and finished by hitting it. He had already written
in 835 to the bishops gathered in Thionville to denounce Amalarius's
allegorism to them.[13] His strategy appears not to have been effective
on that occasion. But in September 838, at the Council of Quierzy,
following a feverish indictment,[14] he obtained the condemnation of
the *threefold body*. However, despite his indignation, despite the sentence of Quierzy and despite the subsequent interventions in the quarrel of Agobard himself, and then Remigius,[15] his second successor in
the see of Lyon, the authority of Amalarius, due both to the scientific
value of his work and to the taste for symbolism current at the time,
was not seriously undermined. The victory for Lyon's purism was a
one-day marvel. The *threefold body* would enjoy a long success. But,
as often happens in such cases, while the formulation went on being
repeated, its meaning was gradually to change. It may be of interest to
follow these vicissitudes, starting by pinpointing the original sense of
the expression, the one that Amalarius himself attached to it. This is
because several people have treated it as some sort of hieroglyph, and
not all the historians who have dealt with it have understood it in the
same way.

---

12 Bk. 3, c.35 (PL, 105, 1154–5).

13 PL, 119, 76 B–C.

14 MGH, *Concilia*, vol. 2, pp. 768–78. It is the start of this discourse which
forms in PL 119 the *Adversus Amalarium III* (col. 94–6). In fact we only know
the council's decision from Florus's account (MGH, *ibid.*, pp. 778–82; it is the
first part of the *Adversus Amalarium II* in PL, 119, 80–5). We would be within
our rights to think that his objectivity is not much more perfect than that of which
he boasts in his discourse (p. 770). Cf. 82 C: 'This doctrine has been judged to be
in every way damnable, and by all the those founded in the Catholic faith to be
thrown out.'

15 *Liber de tribus epistolis*, c. 40 (PL, 121, 1054). This treatise could well be by
the hand of Florus, who survived Amalarius and never laid down his arms.

I

Amalarius's Text

[301]

The different interpretations proposed for the *threefold body* are of two types, which I will call, for the sake of brevity, the 'individual' type and the 'collective' type. According to the individual type of interpretation, the three 'forms' of the Body of Christ that Amalarius distinguishes are three different aspects, or three successive states of Christ as an individual, that concern his 'natural' body, to the exclusion of what we today call his 'mystical body'. This is already how it was understood by a certain number of theologians of the twelfth century, whom Arnulf of Rochester qualified as '*men of outstanding competence*':

> *It seems to some men of outstanding competence that in the sacred solemnities of the Masses of the Lord's body there occurs a threefold division, in that there is a solemn remembrance with a number of parts corresponding to the fact that the same substance of flesh assumed by the Word of God in the form of a human body was displayed to men for the sake of men in threefold variety: to mortal eyes he appeared mortal, he lay dead in the tomb, he rose immortal . . .*[1]

The only problem was that such an explanation did not present itself at the time as an historical exegesis. As whimsical as much of their speculation may seem to us, the theologians of that era had more serious concerns than the reconstruction of the exact thought of the liturgist from Metz.[2] According to several modern historians, this was, however, the authentic sense of the *threefold body*. 'If it is to be understood correctly', writes M. R. Heurtevent, who touches on the question briefly in his work on *Durandus of Troarn and the Beginning*

---

1 *Epistola Secunda* (1115) in d'Achery, *Spicilegium*, vol. 3, p. 472. Cf. Durandus of Mende, *Rationale divinorum officiorum*, 4, c. 51, n. 21.

2 Arnulf had originally made reference to two other explanations, which we will find further on.

of the Berengarian Heresy,[3] 'Amalarius's thinking is not theologically wrong. The Body of Christ, similar as it is to *our* mortal bodies, when envisaged at three different points of its existence, really did have a threefold aspect, a threefold appearance.' Mgr. Gaudel, in his article entitled 'The Mass' in the *Dictionary of Catholic Theology*,[4] rallies to M. Heurtevent's opinion. In the course of the article entitled 'The Eucharist' in the same dictionary, Mgr. F. Vernet had opted for an explanation of the same sort, while endeavouring to cling more closely to the text:

> This is Amalarius's symbolism: the part of the host put into the chalice represents the Body of Christ, holy and sinless, born of the Virgin Mary, risen from the dead; the part that serves as communion for the priest and the Christian people represents the Body of Christ which, through communion, is among the living; the part that is reserved represents the Body of Christ which lies in the tomb, that is to say which is within those who have received and who have died.[5]

We find the same interpretation again in M. A. Michel.[6] As far as can be guessed from somewhat muddled editing, this is more or less how Abbé Mignon understood things.[7] But Dom Ceillier, long ago, understood them quite differently. Equally indulgent with the *three-fold body*, he had a different strategy for 'saving' it. He said that there is a way of giving it an acceptable sense, 'because, beside the natural body of Jesus Christ, it can also be said that the Church militant is his Body, but in another way, and that the Church of the dead, which includes those who are in heaven and those who are in purgatory, also makes up part of the Body of Jesus Christ'.[8] As we see, this is an explanation of the 'collective' sort. Dom Ceillier quite simply copied it in *Perpétuité*, but dropped the rest of the text. After having noted that, interpreted in this way, Amalarius's expression was 'innocent in itself',

---

3 In 1912, p. 174. Cf. 184, note 2, the analysis of the interpretation given by Florus.

4 Vol. 10, col. 999. [Paris: Editions Letouzey et Ané, 1899–1950].

5 *Eucharistie du Xe siècle à la fin du XIe siècle* (vol. 5, col. 1212). Vernet, *Eucharistia* (1934), p. 798, reproduced in Baix-Lambot, *La devotion à l'Eucharistie* . . . , pp. 42–3.

6 DTC, vol. 15, col. 2035, *Ubiquisme*.

7 *Les origins de la scholastique et Hugues de Saint-Victor*, vol. 2 (1895), p. 148.

8 *Histoire des auteurs ecclésiastiques* (Vivès, vol. 12, p. 350).

Perpétuité added that it 'was bad in the sense given to it by Amalarius, who seems to have thought that the Body of Jesus Christ was really in the tombs, as part of the body of the elect who have died, and really in the living faithful'.[9]

While Mgr. Vernet followed, as we have seen, this second exegesis, Mgr. E. Amann very recently took up the first, the one retained by Dom Ceillier. But, as a wary historian, he guards against repeating, with regard to the 'Church of the dead', the anachronistic precisions of his illustrious forebears. According to Amalarius, we read in the volume that he consecrates to *The Carolingian Era*, the three parts of the host 'represented the *threefold body*: the body born of the Virgin and resurrected being represented by the fragment mixed in the chalice; the mystical body of Christ, that is to say the Christian people living on earth, being represented by the fragment that is used for communion; the gathering of the faithful departed, themselves part of the mystical body, being signified by the piece reserved on the altar'.[10]

Revised in this way – and despite the verbal anachronism of the '*mystical body*' – I think that this second type of explanation is the best one, although the first more often finds favour with modern historians. Two groups of arguments seem to prove it. The first arguments are borrowed from the general context of the writings of the time. The second emerge for an attentive reading of the text itself.

First of all, in a completely general fashion, we know that all the theologians of the ninth century, when they treat of the Eucharist, put it in relation to the ecclesial body. This is so to such an extent that if the word *body* is found in one of them without any other precision, we usually have the right to presume that what is being dealt with there is that body in its entirety – although without excluding the head. Amalarius himself gives us an example of it in the page that precedes the one on the *threefold body*: by the crucified Body, he says, '*the human race in the four climates attained to the unity of the one body*', and again, in the immediate context, quoting Bede, he says: '*if he does not partake in his body, that is, the Church*'.[11] – The very attacks of

---

9 Migne, vol. 1 (1841), col. 881.

10 In 1938, p. 309. [*L'époque carolingienne* (Paris: Bloud & Gay).] We can once again see the incoherent interpretation of Héfélé-Leclercq, *Histoire des Conciles*, vol. IV (1911), p. 92. [All of the volumes of the work of Héfélé are available in English translation under the same title, *History of the Church Councils* (T. & T. Clark, Edinburgh, 1871–96).]

11 *De ecclesiasticis officiis*, 3, c. 31, 34 (PL, 105, 1152 B, 1153 D). Cf. 4, c. 29 (1216 C); c. 17 (1198 A); c. 23 (1203 B–C; cf. Augustine, *In Joannem*, tract. 99). Cf. col. 1022 D, 1226 B, etc.).

Florus are the guarantee that this was the case for our *threefold body* itself. It is quite clear that he systematically misunderstood the enemy he was intending to condemn,[12] since his 'bitter malevolence'[13] led him astray. The connection he makes between the *threefold body* of the unfortunate liturgist and the *twofold body* spoken of by Tychonius and criticised by St. Augustine is as ridiculous as it is false.[14] The same can be said for his insistence on claiming that his enemy would divide Christ 'into three bodies'.[15] Did not Amalarius himself say: *'The hosts that are many because of the prayers of those offering are one bread because of the oneness of the body of Christ'?*[16] But Florus's impassioned and unjust polemic against this continued despite being conducted within a framework whose essential outline he was powerless to deform. The two antagonists lived in the same period and so breathed the same atmosphere, and between them there existed the minimal understanding that pertains within the spontaneous use of common categories. For example, when Florus exclaims: *'How does he divide the bread of heaven into three, affirming one of these to be Christ, another the living faithful, and another the already departed?'*,[17] he is certainly wrong in emphasising that triple *'another'* and in drawing all sorts of horrible conclusions, in the teeth of Amalarius's most explicit statements:[18] but he starts from a valid point and correctly defines the three terms of the *threefold body*. When he speaks of the Church whose unity Christ wished to seal by his blood, or of the ineffable mystery of unity that was once prefigured in Adam and Eve, he is undoubtedly saying nothing that Amalarius is not equally prepared to admit, and in this sense his words are futile, but they are not off the point.[19] In no way is Amalarius, as he claims, destroying the unity of the ecclesial body, but he is indeed discussing the ecclesial body, and it cannot be said that the argument put forward by his implacable foe was simply based from start to finish on a clumsy conclusion following falsely from the argument claimed for it (*ignoratio elenchi*) that would have put it beyond consideration. Besides which we should note that Amalarius is less of an innovator than is sometimes claimed.

---

12 MGH, *loc. cit.*, p. 770.

13 M. Andrieu, *Immixtio et Consecratio*, p. 43.

14 Cf. *Adversus Amalarium I*, n.8 (PL, 119, 77 B; 74 B, 76–7, 81 A, 83 A).

15 *Adversus Amalarium II* (PL, 119, 87 D).

16 *Eclogae de officio missae* (PL, 105, 1328 C).

17 *Adversus Amalarium II* (PL, 119, 85 D).

18 *Eclogae de officio missae* (PL, 105, 1316 C, 1318 A, 1328 C).

19 *Adversus Amalarium II* (PL, 119, 87); cf. 86 A–B. *Adversus Amalarium I* (76–7).

He invented a new symbolism, in the sense that he interpreted the rite of the triple fraction and of the immersion by a threefold division of the body of Christ. But this threefold division is not of his inventing. It can be found more than a century earlier, in virtually the same terms, recorded in the work of Etherius and Beatus against Elipandus of Toledo (c. 685). The two Spaniards – whose most habitual sin is not an excess of originality – take issue with the opinion according to which the just who have been entirely purified are already in heaven, body and soul, with Christ. In this case, they ask, '*how, in the body of the Church whose head is in heaven, can we have part that ascended and part that suffers here, and part that already lies buried?*'[20] This is already an example of the *threefold body*. Now, it is explicitly designated as the *body of the Church*.

It is time we looked at the text of the *Liber Officialis* itself. In it the first of the three bodies is said to be raised: '*it has already risen*'. If the other two 'bodies' were two other states of the individual body, as M. Heurtevant thinks, the order followed by Amalarius would be strange: Christ would first of all be envisaged in his resurrection, then in his mortal life, then in the tomb. Furthermore, this is how the first body is presented: '*holy and sinless, flesh taken from the Virgin Mary*'. Is this a privilege of the risen body? Clearly the definition applies to the individual body of Christ in whatever moment of its existence is envisaged, in its state of death or of glory as much as in its earthly condition. It therefore seems clearly to contradict M. Heurtevant's interpretation. It might be less of a contradiction of Mgr. Vernet's interpretation, since he sees the Eucharist as being described by the second and third body: now we know that at that time, the '*body born of the virgin*' and the '*body in the mystery*' were generally distinguished, as witnessed by the doctrine of Paschasius Radbertus himself, and even more by that of Florus. Nevertheless, if the attribute '*born of the virgin*' naturally opposes the historical body with the sacramental body, the attribute '*holy and sinless*' is much better understood if what corresponds to the first body consists of these less holy 'bodies' made up of the various categories of the faithful.

But let us look at some further particularities of this text. At the very beginning, the introductory formulation is already enlightening: '*The body of Christ is threefold*, certainly that of those *who have tasted death and are about to die.*' However grammatically tortured the turn of phrase may be, that plural '*certainly that of those*' in conjunction

---

20 *Ad Elipandum*, 1, c. 90 (PL, 96, 949–50).

with '*the body of Christ*' seems to give sufficient indication that the body under discussion is comprised of a plurality of individuals. – Amalarius goes on to say, in order to define the second body: '*which walks upon the earth*', and to define the third: '*which lies in tombs*'. This applies far more naturally to the faithful, living and dead, than to the presence of Christ realised within them through communion; were that in fact to be the case, we would have had instead: '*the body in those who walk . . . the body in those who lie . . .*' Those who understand it differently sometimes refer to a practice of giving communion to the dying,[21] or to the dead,[22] or else to the parallel custom, still alluded to in the ninth century in a text from Godescalc,[23] of placing a piece of consecrated bread on the chest of the corpse at the moment of burial.[24] At the very least they refer to the belief, shared by our friend the liturgist, that the Eucharistic body in some sense remains present in communicants once they have received it. There is, in fact, a possibility that in one passage, Amalarius is referring to the burial rite that Godescalc recalls, while condemning it.[25] As for this last notion under consideration, as we are about to see, it is not totally incorrect, although there is no reason here to attribute a grossly materialist meaning to Amalarius. But none of these reasons obliges us to choose an interpretation of the *threefold body* that has so much evidence against it. – Consider, indeed, the commentary relating to the third body. It would appear to dissipate any remaining hesitation:

> . . . *The same body leads the host with itself to the tomb, and holy Church calls it the viaticum of the dying, to show that those who die in Christ should not be considered dead but sleeping . . . This particle remains on the altar until the end of the Mass because until the end of the age the bodies of the saints rest in tombs.*[26]

This third body is therefore not carried to the grave by those who die, as could be said of the Eucharist that these dead people have just

---

21　Cf. the *Life of Saint Melanie* (Rampolla, p. 39, 83). Cf. Paulinus, *Vita Ambrosii* (PL, 14, 43).

22　DACL, vol. 3, col. 2445–6. Cf. Pascal, letter of 17th October 1651.

23　*De corpore et sanguine Domini* (Lambot, p. 337).

24　Amphilochius, *Life of Saint Basil* (*Acta Sanctorum*, junii, vol. 2, p. 93 E). Gregory the Great, *Dialogues*, 2, c. 24 (PL, 66, 180–2). Burchard, 5, c. 31 (140, 758 C). Cf. Dom Martène, *De antiquis Ecclesiae ritibus* (edn of Venice, vol. 2, 1783, pp. 367–8).

25　*Liber officialis*, 4, c. 41 (PL, 105, 1236 B–C), after Bede (see the note in PL, 78, 473).

26　*loc. cit.* (PL, 105, 1155).

received as viaticum or, in a more general sense, in the course of their mortal life. On the contrary, it is the Eucharist that takes the body there with it: '*The same body leads the host with itself to the tomb.*' Elsewhere Amalarius speaks specifically about communion received as viaticum.[27] He also believed, in line with the whole of tradition, that communion received in this mortal life is a pledge not only of immortality for the soul, but also of the resurrection of the body.[28] The present text assumes both this custom and this belief. However, we should not be mistaken here: the subject of the sentence here is the person who receives the pledge, and not the pledge itself. Of necessity we must recognize in this not the Master but the disciple, or rather the faithful departed themselves. Is this not what is implied, furthermore, by the symbolic intention imagined by Amalarius: a fragment of the consecrated host, the very one that is destined for the dying, remains on the altar until the end of Mass, just as the bodies of the 'saints' must remain in the tomb until the end of time . . .

Perhaps finally we can be permitted to explain Amalarius in his own words, without abandoning the *Liber Officialis*. In Chapter Ten of the same Book Three, in slightly different words, does he not effectively

---

27 Second preface of *Liber officialis* (PL, 105, 989 B). The question of Viaticum had a vital importance at the time. Cf. the Capitulary of 810, c. 16 (PL, 97, 326 A), frequently reproduced in the collections (PL, 119, 707 A, 734–5, etc.).

28 The idea could be understood in a more or less material sense. Certain expressions would sometimes seem to indicate a belief in a miraculous 'physical remaining' of Christ's flesh within that of the communicant. But these are no doubt only figures of speech. The question is linked to that of 'stercoranism'. Indeed three opinions could be professed at the time, regarding what happens to the Eucharistic presence after communion: the first, summed up in the word 'stercoranism', was probably not held by anyone, although several people had to defend themselves against charges of doing so; the two others are mentioned by Amalarius as two hypotheses between which he does not choose: . . . *invisibly he is assumed into heaven inasmuch as he is reserved in our bodies up to the day of our burying* . . . (*Epist.*6, PL, 105, 1338). Mgr. Vernet (*ibid*, col. 1212) interprets this text as a modification of Amalarius's on his doctrine of the '*body which lies in tombs*': in the *Liber officialis*, he appeared to profess that Christ remains materially in a corpse until the end of time, and then, possibly daunted by the criticism he received, he thought that the presence came to an end on the day of burial . . . There is no reason for us to understand this ingenious explanation in any other way than as '*the body that lies*'. We should add that Amalarius seems to have understood the role of communion with regard to the resurrection in as spiritual a way as many others (cf. PL 105, 989 B), and notably as Hériger of Lobbes, as noted in Mgr. Vernet's excellent commentary (*ibid*, col. 1224–7).

Perpétuité, seeking to justify the Council of Quierzy, accuses Amalarius of stercoranism. However it is precisely this remaining of Christ's body in the faithful, affirmed by Amalarius, that the enemies of stercoranism would put forward. Thus Cardinal Humbert, in *Contra Nicetam*, c. 23, (PL, 143, 993 C).

offer us a first attempt at his *threefold body* as far as we understand it? He is talking about the bishop's throne in his church. Our liturgist's thoughts naturally rise from this earthly throne to the heavenly thrones mentioned in Scripture, then he asks himself why, among the disciples of Christ, some are seated and some stand; this leads him to distinguish two categories of members in the one body of Christ:

> *There sit with him (Christ) those to whom he promised: 'When the Son of Man will sit in his seat of glory, you too will sit . . .' Of them the Apostle Paul writes to the Ephesians, 'He raised them up with him and made them sit in the heavens in Christ Jesus.'*
> *Of those who have ascended with him, some sit and some stand. By those who sit are represented the members of Christ who rest in peace, by those who stand the members engaged in contest. The head and the members are one body. Just as Christ sits in some texts and stands in others, as Stephen saw him in his appointed place during his trial, some of those ascending sit while others stand.*[29]

In the face of such an array of arguments, the only analogy that, to my knowledge, could be invoked in favour of the 'individualist' interpretation will no doubt be judged of little weight, though it is an analogy worth noting, nevertheless. Thus a passage in the appendix given at the end of the first book of Rabanus Maurus's *De Clericorum Institutione* can be found to say:

> *. . . The particle of the host that is put in the chalice represents the body of Christ which has already risen from the dead; the particle consumed by the priest and people represents that which after the resurrection still walked with the disciples on earth and showed himself as food; and the particle left on the altar points to his lying in the tomb and desertion by the disciples at the time of the passion.*[30]

The author of this text – whether it is Rabanus Maurus himself or some other – was writing after Amalarius.[31] Despite fundamental differences, the similarity of form seems to make it clear that it is dependent on him. He no doubt has his reasons for preferring another symbol to the one found in the *Liber Officialis*. Nothing obliges us to make

---

29 PL, 105, 1117 B–C.

30 PL, 107, 326.

31 The *De clericorum institutione* is of about 813, contemporary with the *Liber officialis*.

them coincide. Perhaps we should only discern in his choice an indication of the late character of the addition made to Rabanus Maurus's
book.

It would appear that several years before the *Liber Officialis*,
Amalarius had already composed another liturgical work, the *Eclogae
de officio missae*,³² in which he gave a slightly different explanation
for the rite of fraction and the rite of mingling. This text, enigmatically
concise as it is, proves not to be without its difficulties. Nevertheless
I believe that it confirms the 'collective' interpretation that seems to be
required by the corresponding text in the *Liber Officialis*:

> ... *Just as there are many churches through the whole world because
> of the diversity of places, and yet there is one holy, Catholic Church
> because of the one faith, so too the hosts that are many because of
> the prayers of those offering are one bread because of the oneness of
> the body of Christ. If you ask why a complete host is not put in the
> chalice, even though it was clearly the complete body of the Lord
> that was raised, it is because it is partly about to be raised, partly so
> living as to die no more, and partly mortal and yet in heaven.*³³

Once again, there is therefore only one body in Christ, that is to say
only one Church, and it is that oneness which makes the Eucharistic
bread one within the multiplicity of its oblations. The link between
this first sentence and the second³⁴ assures us that, without excluding
the individual body, which is its head, the latter is dealing with the
ecclesial body.³⁵

I have no hesitation in discussing the value of this speculation. If
there is agreement today on washing its author clean from the taint
of heresy,³⁶ nevertheless several people still speak of his 'errors',³⁷ or
at least of his 'follies'.³⁸ The judgement brought to bear on him generally remains negative. He is blamed both for the novelty and for the
extremity of his symbolism, and thus his *threefold body* serves as the
statutory example. What can sometimes be the excessively negative

---

32 Cf. J.-M. Hanssens, *Ephemerides liturgicae*, 1927.
33 PL, 105, 1328 C–D.
34 It is through having considered only the second part of the text that Mgr.
Vernet thought he could cite it in favour of his 'individual' interpretation.
35 *Eclogae*, PL, 105, 1328-9. Cf. *De ordine antiphonarii*, c. 21 (col. 1276 C).
36 See Dom Morin, DTC, vol. I, col. 934.
37 See Dom Leclercq, in Héfélé-Leclercq, *Histoire des Conciles*, vol. IV,
p. 102.
38 J. P. Bock, *Le Pain quotidian du Pater* (tr. Villien), p. 289.

view of him, especially in historians of the Lyon school,[39] can be put
down to the remaining influence of Florus: the fulminating archdeacon
still influences even those who think themselves forewarned against
him. In others, this same negative view also derives from a sadly widespread lack of understanding of the mentality presupposed by the use
of symbolism,[40] and from the fact that people too often stop at the
external and entirely artificial details of the symbolic process brought
into play. Finally, the preventative measures against Amalarius were
upheld and aggravated by the general belief that everything an author
attributes to symbols in his thought, he detracts by that very fact from
realist beliefs: this is a prejudice of protestant origin, exploited by
rationalism, and by which apologists have sometimes allowed themselves to be intimidated.[41] – Besides, these remarks chiefly serve to
permit a more exact appreciation of the doctrine to which Amalarius
bore witness, more than of the author responsible for it, despite the
original form in which he was able to present it. He himself should
not be over-estimated either. He may well have been a person of great
standing and, for his time, a remarkable scholar, but his was not a
great mind. It is clear that, taking it on its own merits, his theory of the
threefold body can have no more than an historical interest for us. But
it is precisely the least 'theoretical' of theories possible. By means of a
symbolism that clearly was in no way objective, but which was at least
in conformity with the 'analogy of faith', and which certainly did not
in any way exceed either in 'childishness' or 'strangeness'[42] a hundred
other symbolisms that Amalarius did not invent,[43] it was simply a way
of expressing, with certain nuances which reflect the theology of that

---

39 P. Chavallard, study on the *Expositio missae* of Florus of Lyon p. 29.

40 The authors who demonstrated themselves more accesible to the assessment of the profound value of symbolism were all naturally more favourable to
Amalarius. Thus, Dom Guéranger, *Institutions liturgiques*, 2nd edn., I, p. 256.

41 Cf. Claude, *Réponse aux deux traits intitulés 'La Perpétuité de la foi de
l'Eglise catholique touchant l'Eucharistie'* (Charenton, 1667), Pt. 3, ch. II,
pp. 485–8. – Armand Dulac (J. Turmel), concerning Bernold of Constance cf.
Revue d'histoire et de littérature religieuses, 1911, p. 466. Cf. *La crise morale du
temps présent et l'éducation humaine*, 1937, pp. 247–8.

42 Dom Morin, *loc. cit.* Chevallard, *op. cit.*, pp. 175–6.

43 Like most authors of his era, Amalarius's work was above all that of a
compiler. Furthermore, to judge by his writing, he was a modest and conciliating
character. He 'sinned rather through too much candour and good-naturedness',
says Dom Morin (*Revue bénédictine*, 1899, p. 420). He does not impose his opinions, he is at pains to make clear what he asserts on no authority other than his
own, and does not condemn usage that he does not follow for his own part (cf. *De
ordine antiphonarii*, PL, 105, 1244 A, 1292 C–D, 1299 D).

era and which will now occupy our attention, the great traditional idea of the relationship of the Eucharist to the totality of the Body of Christ.[44]

---

44 When Guitmond of Aversa later wrote, precisely concerning the fraction into three pieces of the consecrated host: 'nor, however, are the three separate pieces three bodies, but one body', for him it was only a matter of affirming the integrity of the individual body of Christ in each piece: '*Thus the whole host is the Body of Christ, so that the whole Body of Christ might in no particular part and by no one be separated.*' The analogy of the formulations thus does not correspond with an analogy of thought with Amalarius. Nevertheless, about this unity of the individual body in each particular host, Guitmond concludes: '*therefore the communion which we eat of this holy bread and chalice makes us indeed the one body of Christ*', meeting thus the final idea of Amalarius, which was not only that of Amalarius or Guitmond, but the whole Christian tradition. *De corporis veritate*, 1 (PL, 149, 1434 B, C).

We can find many indications of the liturgical allegorism of Amalarius and his successors, its characteristics, its causes and what resulted from it, in the work of R. P. Jungmann, *Missarum solemnia*, 1st part, ch. 8–13. Among the Greek examples of this allegorical genre should be noted Theodore of Mopsuestia's *Catechetical Homily 15* (Tonneau-Devreesse, Rome, 1949).

2

Evolution of the Doctrine

[313–14]

From that time onwards, throughout the Middle Ages, they referred to the *threefold body*. This turn of events is sometimes attributed to one of those errors of attribution that were so frequent at the time. Pseudo-Alcuin's *Liber de divinis officiis*, a compilation that dates from the tenth century or possibly the eleventh century, had reproduced Amalarius's text immediately after indicating that the custom of reciting the *Agnus Dei* at Mass derived from Pope Sergius.[1] Deceived by their proximity, canonists had attributed to Sergius what properly belonged to Amalarius. This is what we find in Ivo of Chartres' *Parnormia*,[2] as well as in the *Sententiae Magistri A*.[3] The same mistake was included in Gratian's *Decrees*.[4] The strange symbolism emanating from the imagination of an author who was, at the very least suspect, thus found itself adorned with the authority that accompanied papal decisions at the same time as it benefited from the hugely popular and rapidly diffused *Decrees*.[5] I might add that this is, alas, how the *threefold body* got as far as insinuating itself among the Princes of the Schools, Albert the Great and Thomas Aquinas!

Indeed from the twelfth century onwards one often finds the introductory words: '*Pope Sergius said*.' Nevertheless such a misunderstanding is not sufficient to explain what an historian calls the 'fascinating prestige of the *threefold body of the Lord*'. Among theologians, liturgists and canonists, this prestige can be found as much before as after Gratian, that is to say as much before as after Amalarius's text was attributed to Sergius. What is more, Amalarius was not in any way

---

1 PL, 101, 1246.

2 Bk. 1 c. 140 (PL, 161, 1076 D).

3 Cf. Fournier-Le Bras, *Histoire des collections canoniques en Occident*, vol. 2, p. 329–30 and G. Le Bras, 'Alger de Liège et Gratien', in *Revue des sciences philosophiques et théologiques*, vol. 20 (1931).

4 *De consecratione*, d. 2, c. 22 (Friedberg, 1321).

5 F. Vernet, *loc. cit.*, col. 1217. M. de la Taille, *Mysterium fidei*, 2nd edn., p. 435, note 1. Cf. J. de Ghellinck, *L'essor de la literature latine au XIIe siècle*, vol. 1, p. 106.

considered a suspect author. The condemnation wrested from the
bishops of Quierzy cannot have fooled many people, who remembered, rather, that another council, called shortly before at Thionville
in 835, had refused, despite an initial offensive from Florus, to pass
any sentence.[6] It may be that for a short time some more prudent
copyists left out the chapter containing the contested theory.[7] The
bitter complaints of Remigius of Lyon bear witness to the rapid and
widespread diffusion of Amalarius's ideas and to the authority that
attached to his name from the moment of his death. Throughout
France, and even beyond, his writings circulated, grave churchmen
consulted him in order to clarify what they believed, and even simple
souls developed a taste for them and became familiar with them
. . .[8] No doubt, here or there, some people had reservations. The
elderly Paschasius Radbertus, who once had probably been visited by
Amalarius in Corbia, had nevertheless not been captivated, and he
sent this warning to his disciple Frudegard: '*Do not pursue folly on the
threefold body . . . , according to the ravings of certain people.*'[9] But if
the accusations from Lyon found an echo, the echo would swiftly fade.
No other trace of any opposition whatever to Amalarius has come
down to us, except for a little anonymous tract from the ninth century,
which would appear to be written by another of Florus's immediate
disciples.[10] On the contrary, most of the liturgists writing after him
depend on him in large measure. The author of the *De divinis officiis*
positively pillaged him. The same is true of the *Expositio divinorum
officiorum*, attributed to John of Avranches.[11] Another liturgist of the
eleventh century, Bernon of Reichenau († 1048), referring to him on
various occasions, never does it without adding praise to his reference:
'*Amalarius, a far from contemptible investigator of the divine offices*',
'*a most diligent researcher*'.[12]

But the most constant and apparently most uniform traditions,
while they remain alive, are never simply repetitions. It even happens,
as has been said, that within the continuity of words, the meaning
becomes notably modified, following the variation or the develop-

---

6 Cf. Héfélé-Leclercq, *Histoire des Conciles*, vol. 4, pp. 91–2.

7 Cf. M. Andrieu, *Immixtio et Consecratio*, p. 33, note 2.

8 *Liber de tribus epistolis*, c. 40 (PL, 121, 1054). Cf. J. de Ghellinck, DTC,
vol. 5, col. 1274.

9 PL, 120, 1365–6.

10 Cf. Dom Morin, *Revue bénédictine*, 1905, p. 166.

11 PL, 101 and 147.

12 *De officio missae*, c. 4, 7 (PL, 142, 1064 C, 1076 B). *Qualiter adventus
Domini celebretur*, c. 2 (1081 C).

ment of ideas connected with them. This certainly happened with the 'threefold body', either with regard to the concrete definition of each of the three bodies, or insofar as they relate symbolically to the three fragments of the host.

The second term – *the body walking on earth* – was designated in too clear a fashion not to remain unchanged. But the third – *the body lying in tombs* – would suffer many vicissitudes, which would have repercussions on the first.

It is remarkable that Amalarius, enumerating the principal parts of the 'body of Christ', makes no mention of the souls of the just who have already reached Heaven. It cannot simply be a matter of his being ignorant of this category among the members of Christ, since he makes clear reference to it elsewhere.[13] But the fact is that such a belief, although far from being unheard of, was nevertheless not widespread.[14] Primarily, perhaps, it is that even among those who, like Amalarius himself, were fully aware of it, it was not a central consideration. The consideration of salvation was still customarily linked to that of the collective destinies of the Church, and eschatological perspectives were still dominated by the dogma of the resurrection of the dead. One of the *Capitula* of Rudolph of Bourges († 866) clearly expresses the fashion that was currently dominant of conceiving the last things:

> . . . *This is done by the universal Church which finds herself on the pilgrimage of mortality, awaiting till the end of the age what was represented in advance by the body of our Lord Jesus Christ, who is the Firstborn from the dead.*[15]

Remigius of Auxerre, commenting on the fifth Psalm, also has the Church saying: '*I, the Catholic Church, will enter into your house, the heavenly Jerusalem, that is the city of the citizens on high.*'[16] If he distinguishes eight ages of the world, it is in order to make of the seventh, before that of eternity, the age of *those who are asleep*.[17] Immortality was generally envisaged as a result of the resurrection, and not

---

13 *De ecclesiasticis officiis*, 4, c. 42 (PL, 105, 1239 C–D).

14 See Julian of Toledo, *Prognosticon future saeculi*, 2, c. 1–11 (PL, 96, 475–80) and 2, c. 55 (522 B). Cf. A. Veiga Valiña, *La doctrina escatológica de San Julián de Toledo* (1940).

15 c. 26 (PL, 119, 716). The Penitential of Rabanus Maurus, c. 33 (PL, 131, 169 A).

16 PL, 131, 169 A.

17 *ibid.*, 634 B. Compare with Gregory Nazianzen, *Praise of Caesarius*, c. 17, n.2 (Boulenger, p. 37).

resurrection as an accidental complement of immortality.[18] Christian hope was *the hope of resurrection*.[19] In order for the living to be consoled in their bereavement, they were most often invited to raise their eyes to the horizon of the final resurrection and the definitive victory of Christ.[20] The office for the dead from both the ancient Mozarabic and Gallican liturgies constantly assumes the same perspectives.[21] Only Christ, by rising from the tomb on Easter morning, had conquered the last enemy.[22] The Head had triumphed and entered into definitive glory, but the members could not follow him there before their own resurrection. Until then, they still only had the hope of salvation.[23] Whatever their present fate and place of rest, they were all therefore in that state of sleep and expectation symbolised by the expression: *lying in the tomb*. The fourth book of the *Liber Officialis* comes back to this point several times, notably in connection with the octave of the feasts of saints. Why such a double feast, at eight days distance? Amalarius replies that it is because on the day of the first feast, we celebrate the 'reception' of the saints who have passed into 'peace', their 'rest', their 'sleep' in their various 'dwellings'. But, on the day of the octave, we already celebrate in anticipation their 'awakening', their 'resurrection', their entry into 'the future world', which is symbolised by the eighth day, the day of the resurrection of the Lord.[24]

However, already in Amalarius we find that the 'saints' who have died in Christ and who make up the third part of his Body were equally designated by the short explanation that followed, as those whose body – the body of flesh – lies in the tomb. The repose of the mortal remains symbolized the sleep of the person himself by a natural transition, rendered almost inevitable by mention of the tomb, the mind passed from one sense of the word 'body' to another, from the mystical and collective sense to the individual and material sense. But this was by way of development, with a subsidiary intention, so to speak, of explaining

---

18 (Neale-Forbes, p. 11).

19 Augustine, *De catechizandis rudibus*, n. 11 (PL, 40, 317). On Augustine, see J. Rivière, *Œuvres de Saint Augustin*, vol. 9, *Exposés généraux de la foi*, pp. 419–20.

20 See Braulio of Saragossa, Ep. 19, 29, 34 (PL, 80, 665 D, 676 B, 680 A).

21 *Liber mozarabicus ordinum* (Férotin, col. 111–49, 422). *Sacramentarium gallicanum vetus* (PL, 72, 539 C, 566–8). Cf. *Gelasianum* (Wilson, p. 295), etc.

22 Cf. the chant of the *Exultet*.

23 Remigius of Auxerre (PL, 131, 170 A). Braulio of Saragossa, *loc. cit.*; Amalarius (PL, 105, 989 B, 1307 A; cf. 1238 D).

24 36 (PL, 105, 1228–9). Cf. c. 9 (1185 D). Durandus of Mende, *Rationale*, 7, c. 1, n. 42.

why the third particle of the host remained on the altar until the end of Mass. Now, it follows that this second sense, instead of simply following on from the first, would reflect back on it. It would initially be with some timidity, thanks to the introduction of an ambiguous formulation: '*the body of the faithful lying in tombs*', as in the *Expositio divinorum officiorum* of Pseudo-John of Avranches:

> The part of the host put in the chalice represents the body of Christ which rose from the dead. The part eaten by the priest or people signifies the body of Christ that still remains on earth. The part left on the altar, which the Church takes as viaticum, signifies the body of the faithful that lies in tombs: this part remains on the altar until the end of the mass, because until the end of the age the bodies of the saints rest in tombs.[25]

But this would soon be followed by a more decisive revision of Amalarius's page, which, in brief, gives greater prominence to the mention of the '*body of the saints*'. This is what we find in the *Panormia*[26] and in Gratian.[27] This is the revised text, attributed to Sergius, that would be quoted by Peter Lombard, Otho of Lucques and Peter Comestor:

> ... What the parts signify is handed down by Pope Sergius, when he says ...: The body of Christ is threefold. The part that is offered and put in the chalice represents the body of Christ which has already risen; the part that is eaten represents him still walking on earth; the part that remains on the altar until the end of mass signifies the body lying in the tomb, because until the end of the age the bodies of the saints will be in tombs.[28]

We have not got so far here as replacing the primitive '*body lying in tombs*' with '*the body lying in the tomb*'. The two do not imply the same thing. But this slight modification was gradually gaining ground. Because a body of flesh, an individual body – a corpse – can clearly not occupy more than one tomb at a time.[29]

This shift in emphasis, which focused attention on the material body of the saints, invited more precise exploration of where the saints

---

25 PL, 147, 203 B, 212 A.
26 Bk. 1, c. 140 (PL, 161, 1076).
27 *De consecratione*, 2.22 (Friedberg, 1321).
28 Peter Lombard, *Sentences*, 4, d. 12, n. 6 (PL, 192, 866). Otho of Lucques, *Summa Senteniarum*, tract. 6, c. 9 (176, 145). Peter Comestor, *Sententiae de sacramentis* (Martin, p. 57).
29 Cf. Peter Lombard, *In I Cor*. (PL, 191, 1645 D).

themselves were, where their souls were, since only their bodies were lying in the tomb. The general response was not long in coming, as we find in Julian of Toledo, who answered that the soul of the saints is in Heaven with Christ. This is the origin of a different sort of note, which would equally entail various nuances. In Bernard of Constance († 1100)[30] and Ivo of Chartres[31] there is a sort of transfer of the image of dormition or rest. The part of the '*Body of Christ*' or the '*Body of the Church*' that has ended its life on earth has not yet reached its Sabbath rest, but nevertheless it is already enjoying rest in Christ: '*it is now resting in Christ*', '*it now, as if on the Sabbath, rests with its head, and already possesses the one robe of immortality*'. This last formulation comes from Ivo of Chartres. It can be observed that the correlation of the saints with Christ their Head is operating here, if it may be so expressed, in both senses, through the exploitation of the symbolism of the Sabbath. To this end – and this is a detail which seems to be particular to Ivo – the first body, or '*substantive body of Christ*', was not defined as risen and glorious, but only as the one '*that rested in the tomb on the Sabbath*'.

Hugh of St. Victor continues to mention the third body in the tomb, and in this he may appear more conservative than Bernard or Ivo. But at the same time he did away with what still looked like certain reservations concerning the happiness of the soul – and by this sign alone he could be recognized as coming after them:

> One part of the body is in the members who have already followed the head and are with the head, where the head itself is . . . Those who have already departed from this life, whose bodies rest in tombs and whose souls are with Christ, are another part of the body.[32]

Among Hugh's disciples, who, like him, mention both the body and the soul, some, such as the author of the *Sermo de excellentia Sanctissimi Sacramenti*,[33] remain faithful to the first nuance that he had set aside: '*as if on the Sabbath rest in the soul*'. Others, on the contrary, such as Lothaire of Segni,[34] apply the '*resting*' to the body alone, while they see the soul '*reigning*' with Christ. The fact is that for some time already, a

---

30 *Micrologus*, 17 (PL, 151, 988).
31 *De convenientia veteris et novi sacrificii* (PL, 162, 559–60).
32 *De sacramentis*, 2, p. 8, c. 10 (PL, 176, 468–9). Peter the Venerable, *Sermo* 2, *In Laudem sepulcri Domini* (PL, 189, 974 A–B).
33 N. 13 (PL, 184, 988–9).
34 *De sacro altaris mysterio*, 6, c. 3 (PL, 217, 907–8).

third group, which was more openly innovative, was only concerning itself with the soul, 'glorified, reigning, triumphant, exultant' . . . This is the case with the *Sententiae Florianenses*, which allied itself with the school of Abelard.[35] Thus also Master Simon,[36] Peter Comestor[37] and Baldwin of Canterbury.[38] And also Richard of Wedinghausen: '*That is the part of the Church that is in glory, and rejoices with Christ in eternal blessedness.*'[39]

In this context, it was becoming something of a paradox to maintain as separate, in any explanation, the two bodies that were being declared united in reality, that is to say the Head and the members who were already equally glorified. Thus they came to be united as one, though only by stages. Already, from Ivo of Chartres onwards, we often see Amalarius's order being changed. The third body was put in second place, or '*the second part*', as Ivo says, while the Church on earth was relegated to the end. A change in symbolism, which I will indicate further on, accompanied this change of order. – Then, from Hugh of St. Victor onwards, whom the *Sermo de excellentia*, Peter Comestor and Lothaire of Segni would imitate, the two parts that have just been brought together here would be united by an accolade: '*Those two parts are virtually together, namely the head, which is Christ, and another part of the body, that is, the virtuous deceased*', says Hugh; and Peter Comestor, more immediately, says: '*The two parts outside the chalice . . . signify Christ and the saints.*' Finally, in a third stage, at about the same period, the decisive step would be taken. The two parts that had been brought together would from then only be one: the whole part of the '*Body of Christ*' would now already be in glory. This first body, once described by Amalarius as the '*body that has already risen*', consisted at that time only of the Head, that is to say the unique person of Christ. The only person it was thinkable to add to him was the Virgin, by consequence of the Assumption, or again, by way of hypothesis, the few holy people who might have been raised from the dead.[40] Now it included all the elect, whose resurrection was no longer taken into account.

The first author in whose work this fusion appears complete was

---

35 N. 74 (Ostlender, p. 33).
36 *Tractatus de sacramentis* (Weisweiler, p. 39).
37 *Sententiae de sacramentis* (Martin, p. 57).
38 *Liber de sacramento altaris* (PL, 204, 771–2).
39 *Liber de canone mystici libaminis*, c. 9 (PL, 177, 467–8).
40 See *infra*, St. Thomas Aquinas.

Hildebert of Lavardin – if indeed the *Versus de mysterio missae* which are commonly attributed to him are indeed his:[41]

> . . . *We too, following the law and Christ not in vain,*
> *Fittingly share the gifts dedicated to God.*
> *For three are the Church's parts, of which one labours*
> *On earth; one already enjoys repose above;*
> *The part remaining is purified by kindly fire,*
> *And, when purified, passes freely to its rest.*
> *Diverse in merit, diverse in allotted place,*
> *The three parts are signified by the broken host.*
> *The part soaked in wine suits the living, while the work*
> *Of flesh and blood is expiated by the Flesh.*
> *For the righteous deceased, of whom the purer part*
> *Needs not this mediation, while the other does,*
> *Reason bids the rest be offered, which is performed,*
> *Yet not for both of them are the same fruits obtained:*
> *For while for the just they pray at sacred altars,*
> *For the (wholly) just the minister offers thanks . . .*[42]

Several verses further on, the same theme reappears. It is worth pointing out the detail that, while placing the elect in the 'first body' with Christ in glory, Hildebert twice takes care only to call them '*semi-blessed*'. In neither of the two passages does he claim glory for them, but only 'rest'.[43] It was a last-remaining scruple that would be found nowhere else after that.

Amid several authors of slightly later date, the fusion between the first two bodies can be found in its fullness. So we find it in the *De sacrificio missae* of Pseudo-Algerius of Liège, who attaches to it an entire doctrine of the fruits of the sacrifice of the Mass.[44] It is found in the same way in the *Speculum Ecclesiae*,[45] in the *Sententiae divinitatis*,[46] and in Stephen of Baugé's *Tractatus*.[47]

This new interpretation, which would rapidly spread and prove triumphant, is the undoubted sign that collective eschatology and the expectation of the final resurrection, which once enjoyed such a high

---

41 Cf. R. P. de Ghellinick (DTC, vol. 5, col. 1255); Hildebert, *Ep.*, 1, 23 (PL, 171, 241 B–C).
42 PL, 171, 1191.
43 1192 C–D and 1193 A–B.
44 PL, 180, 856.
45 7 (PL, 177, 373).
46 Tract. 5 (Geyer, p. 138).
47 *Tractatus de sacramento altaris*, c. 18 (PL, 172, 1303).

profile, were fading out of the picture. In a framework that remained ecclesial, the focus was no longer primarily on the destiny of the Church but on the destiny of each of the faithful. Belief in the 'eschatological vision' was becoming rarer. Theological analysis was making progress, but the progress came with a price. The understanding of the sacrifice and its fruits was losing the grandeur of its simplicity. The profound doctrine of the Body of Christ was in retreat, and a certain spiritualism was being established on the ruins of its ancient forms.

From then on Amalarius's third division therefore seemed to have no object: to be an empty pigeon hole. There was no more *body in tombs*. Was there now going to be a *twofold body*, via an evolution analogous to the one which, in the course of that same twelfth century, was transforming the *threefold body* of Paschasius Radbertus's tradition into a *double body*? – Certainly not. 'That great Church beneath the earth'[48] which, in the original theory, was formed indiscriminately by all those who had died in Christ, had not altogether passed from the tomb to glory. The 'assembly of the Patriarchs' had not been instantly transformed into the *Pleroma* achieved by Christ. Indeed in the ensuing interval, another doctrine had developed considerably, gaining ever-greater practical importance, in strict conjunction with the doctrine of the Mass: that of Purgatory. The souls in Purgatory were the natural heirs of the Just who were formerly represented as still standing on the threshold of bliss. How could the symbolism of sacrifice forget to include those for whom the sacrifice had so often been offered?[49] It was therefore they who would now form the third part of the unique Body of Christ, that third part that Amalarius saw symbolized in the third fragment of the host. Side by side with the living and the saints, here – in an admittedly varied order – were the dead.[50] Next to those still travelling in exile and those already received into bliss, were those who were subject to a final purification.[51] Next to the Church toiling and suffering on earth and the Church at rest in Heaven, was the one whose way to eternal rest was being opened up by a merciful fire.[52] Finally, in terms that were soon to become sacred, next to the Church militant and the Church triumphant was the Church suffering:

---

48 Paul Claudel, *L'épée et le miroir*, p. 157.
49 Cf. Pseudo-Germain (PL, 72, 89 A).
50 *De sacrificio missae* (*supra*, note 44).
51 *Supra*, notes 44, 45, 47.
52 Hildebert, *Versus de mysterio missae*.

> The body of Christ . . . is divided into three parts, because of the three parts of the Church, of which one is triumphant, one is militant, and the third in the pains of purgatory.[53]

According to an opinion reported by Peter Cantor, which led him to propose an embarrassing case of conscience, this is also the origin of the obligation on the celebrant to consume the three fragments himself at the altar, for the good of the three categories of members of the Church; without this the Mass would not be *'full and perfect'*: *'He is obliged to receive the three particles in the sacrament which relate to the state of those who are still alive, of those who are now triumphant, and of those who are now in purgatory.'*[54]

Amalarius's threefold division is thus preserved, and the doctrine developed without overturning the traditional framework. It cannot honestly be said that the change went unnoticed. But it is worth saying that the attribution of the ancient formulation to Pope Sergius in no way intimidated our theologians, who did not in fact have the narrow and entirely static idea of fidelity to Tradition that we occasionally ascribe to them. This attribution no more caused the success of the formulation than it prevented its evolution. Robert Paululus, who was himself no more than a compiler lacking any particular originality, in composing his *De ecclesiasticis officiis* in the last third of the twelfth century, presented and made his own the new way of understanding the *threefold body*. Then he added, without seeing any problem in it: *'Pope Sergius however speaks differently on this; for he wants, etc . . .'*[55] We find the same approach in William of Auxerre's *Summa aurea*.[56] Only later did some people seek to bring about a concordance, such as Albert the Great, whose eclecticism here is somewhat inconsistent:

> . . . *The mystical body . . . is threefold: for one part of it reigns with its head and is triumphant in the heavens; another part still labours militant on earth; and one part is in the pains of purgatory. – Therefore the blessed pope Sergius instituted that one part, etc. He also decreed that the third should remain on the altar at the end after all the mysteries have been consumed, to signify those who*

---

53 Robert of Melun, *Quaestiones de epistolis Pauli, In I Cor.* (Martin, p. 211), etc. Cf. *Statuta synodalia Caducensis, Ruthenensis et Tutelensis ecclesiarum* (1289), c. 16 (Martène and Durandus, *Thesaurus novus anecdotarum*, vol. 4, 711 B).

54 *Summa de sacramentis, de eucharistia*, q. 8 (Dumoutet, in *Archives d'histoire littéraire et doctrinale du moyen âge*, vol. 14, pp. 203–4).

55 39 (PL, 177, 436).

56 Bk. 4 (f° 260 r°).

are in tombs and in purgatory, who will at the end live with Christ through spiritual incorporation.[57]

Robert Paululus and William of Auxerre's *however* was succeeded by an artificial *therefore* that did not succeed in masking the evolution that had taken place.

Nevertheless this evolution had not been as uniform as might have been supposed from what preceded it. I ought now to indicate the existence of a few cases of survival, as well as certain more or less unorthodox intermediate forms, that make the sketch I have just outlined rather more complicated. I am not going to speak of authors like Hildebert of Lavardin,[58] or Pseudo-Damian,[59] who satisfied themselves with quoting a few lines from Amalarius in passing, without commenting on them. Nor am I going to insist on St. Bonaventure, when he wrote: '*Because in the mystical body there is threefold differentiation – for some reign in paradise, some safely wait in the tomb, while others combat meritoriously –, so there are three parts in this sacrament.*'[60] This is certainly nothing more than a survival of language, the 'tomb', in Bonaventure's thought, being purgatory. The case of Honorius of Autun is more interesting. In chapter 89 of his *Sacramentarium*, Honorius transcribes textually, almost in its entirety, the page from the *Liber Officialis*; he even still preserves, on at least one occasion, the '*in tombs*', which by that time had been generally replaced by 'in the tomb'.[61] In the first book of his *Gemma animae*, he reproduces Amalarius's doctrine exactly in his own formulations:

The host is not received as a whole but is divided into three: one is put in the chalice, another is consumed by the priest, while the third is placed in the pyx for the viaticum of the dying, because the body of Christ is threefold: that which was taken from Mary entered heaven by rising from the dead; that which is still in the elect labours on earth; and that which is in the tombs is now resting.

The part put in the chalice is the body of the Lord that has already been assumed in glory. The part eaten by the priest, as if he were an apostle, is the body of Christ, that is, the Church, still labouring on earth. The part left on the altar is the Lord's body resting in tombs,

---

57 *De sacrificio missae*, tract. 3, c. 21, n. 1 (Vivès, vol. 38, p. 157).
58 *Liber de exposition missae* (PL, 171, 1171, note). Otho of Lucques and Lombard (*supra*, n. 25). Cf. de Ghellinck, *loc. cit.*, c. 1251.
59 *Expositio canonis secundum Petrum Damianum* (PL, 145, 891–2).
60 *In IV Sent.*, d. 12, p. 1, a. 3, q. 3 (Quaracchi, vol. 5, p. 286).
61 PL, 172, 795 C–D.

that is, the Church that has died in Christ and will be raised through union with the body of Christ.[62]

Such pure conservatism is rare. We will see further on that Honorius himself did not always take such a firm stand as this. Others kept the original interpretation intact only in order to place the new one immediately next to it. This is what was done by the author of one of the Eucharistic poems that Beaugendre falsely attributed to Hildebert:

The three parts signify the body of Christ;
The first his flesh, the second the buried saints –
Or, the first the purified departed, the second
Those still being purified – the third the living.[63]

We find the same with the author of the *Sententiae divinitatis*.[64] The interpretation that he quotes initially, before also giving what was to become the prevailing version, is identical to that of Pseudo-Hildebert, except that here *'buried'* is replaced by *'received'*: it is a word which was formerly widely understood to refer to the members of Christ who are awaiting the glory of the kingdom of Heaven in their various *'resting places'*,[65] but which, because of its indeterminate nature, could now also just as easily suggest the heavenly dwelling of purified souls.[66] We find the same with Sicard of Cremona, in Book III of his *Mitrale*. At the time when he was writing, the interpretation via the triple Church, militant, suffering and triumphant was no longer a novelty. Like the author of the *Sententiae divinitatis*, he nevertheless still precedes it with the old interpretation, preserved as such under cover of somewhat new words:

the host is divided into three parts ... The first is the mystical body, that is, the Church walking on earth; the second is likewise mystical, sleeping till the day of judgment in the sepulchre; the third consists only of those persons who have been assumed into glory.[67]

We find the same again with St. Albert the Great in his *Commentary on the Sentences*.[68]

---

62 Bk. 1, c. 64 (PL, 172, 363-4).

63 *Quid divisio corporis Chriti in tres partes significet* (PL, 171, 1280 A). Cf. the manuscript Colb. 1367 (reproduced *ibid.*, 1280 B) and *Carmina miscellanea* (1406-7).

64 *loc. cit.*

65 Cf. Amalarius, *Liber officialis*, 4, c. 42 (PL, 105, 1239 C-D).

66 Cf. the *Sententiae* (cited *supra*, note 42).

67 Bk. 3, c. 8; and continuing (PL, 213, 141; c. 6 (138).

68 *In IV Sent.*, d. 13, a. 14.

The former doctrine had equally been presented in two other verses, which became classics, and whose success contributed to its preservation. These verses were still known by the great Schoolmen, and Sts. Bonaventure[69] and Thomas Aquinas[70] made a point of quoting them:

> *The host is divided into parts: the soaked part signifies*
> *The wholly blessed, the dry the living, the reserved the buried.*

St. Thomas would confine himself strictly in his commentary on these words. According to him, the first category only consisted of '*Christ himself and the Blessed Virgin*', and, he added in the *Summa*, '*any other saints, if there are any, who are with their bodies in glory*': they were the ones who possess the '*the full enjoyment of beatitude*', those who are '*fully blest with regard to their soul and their body*'. The return to the primitive theory is as clear as it can be. The second category is not problematic. In the third category – the buried – St. Thomas, again like Amalarius, places all those who, having already died, are living '*in expectation of the fullness of beatitude*': these are what he calls the '*others*'. However, he adds here a specification that bears witness to the more evolved state of the doctrine. These '*others*', he says in the *Summa* and in the *Commentary on the Sentences*, are themselves of two types: '*those who have either only the robe of the soul or none at all*' – '*whose souls are either in purgatory or in heaven*'.[71] – *Things both new and old.*[72]

---

69 *In IV Sent.*, d. 12, p. 1, a. 3, q. 3 (vol. 4, p. 286).

70 IIIa, q. 83, a. 5, ad 8m (Vivès, vol. 5, p. 518).

71 *ibid.*, and *In IV Sent.*, d. 12, q. 1, a. 3 (vol. 10, p. 305).

72 The classic division of the Church into three parts is also expressed in other symbols than those of Amalarius. For example, the symbol of the three parts of the Temple, which is developed in an ancient hymn in the Didache.

King Solomon made the Temple
the likeness and example
of which is Christ and the Church.
But there are three parts in the Temple
Suggesting the figure of the Trinity
The within, the whole, the middle.
The first signifies all the living
The second, then, the dead
The third those brought back to life.

Wycliffe, who quotes this stanza in one of his sermons, himself says: The Catholic Church is divided in three parts, that is to say, the Church militant, the Church sleeping, and the Church triumphant (*Sermonum* p. 4ª, s. 5; Loserth, 1890, p. 42). The doctrinal archaism of 'dormientem' is notable. We find the same turn of phrase in Nicholas of Cusa, *De concordantia catholica*, l. 1, c. 4 and 5: In this Church, seeking a mark of the Trinity, we discover therefore the Church as having a triple order, that is to say, triumphant, sleeping, and militant, etc.

3

Evolution of the Symbolism

[329]

We must not forget that the *threefold body* comes primarily from the exegesis of a rite. The instruction dedicated to it in the *Liber Officialis* arose with reference to the fragment of the consecrated host that remained on the altar, once the fraction, commingling and communion had taken place.

Liturgical usage with regard to this was not the same everywhere. We only need to keep in mind what is useful for understanding Amalarius. While, in the Byzantine Mass, the host was divided into four from the beginning, and in the West itself, the so-called Mozarabic rite had nine parts with a view to signifying the nine principal mysteries of our Saviour, from his '*incorporation*' to his '*reign*', the Roman liturgy as it had been adopted by the Frankish reform never exceeded the number of three. They already had what is now our present usage with, nevertheless, this double difference, that one of the three parts was immediately divided between the priest and the people present at the sacrifice, and another part was reserved in order to be distributed later, according to necessity, among the sick and the dying. Today there still remain a few vestiges of this ancient custom: when the Pope celebrates the pontifical Mass, the third part of the host that he has just consecrated is divided into two for the communion of the deacon and the sub-deacon, and in the Mass for the consecration of a bishop, the consecrated prelate also receives communion from one of the three fragments of the host. As for the commingling, which consists in mixing a particle of the Host with the precious Blood by putting it into the chalice, it was also practised in every liturgy.

The *fraction of the bread* had never been a purely utilitarian operation. St. Paul had already connected it symbolically with his idea of *koinonia*.[1] Linked not only with the memory of the multiplication and the distribution of the loaves, but also with that of the very words of

---

1 Batiffol, *Leçons sur la messe*, p. 184. Cf. Ignatius of Antioch, *Ad Ephesios*, c. 20, n. 2: ἕνα ἄρτον κλῶντες (Lelong, p. 26).

the Last Supper, as well as that of the meal at Emmaus, the gesture of fraction for a long time had a profile that was subsequently lost – at the same time that the rite itself was being displaced within the context of the sacrifice.[2] It would appear that very early on, another symbolic intention accompanied it: was the *breaking apart* during Mass not the living image of the *breaking apart* of Calvary? This is what was already being implied by the way in which certain Eastern liturgies were conveying the words of institution: '*This is my body which is broken for you*',[3] and what is expressed more directly by the profession of faith with which they accompanied the fraction itself: '*At this breaking of the body . . . we believe that we have been redeemed . . . we recall your passion, and that your body was broken for the forgiveness of our sins.*'[4] The *commingling* seems to have had a quite different origin, at least in the Roman liturgy, where it initially served as a conclusion to the rite of the *fermentum* and of the *sancta*: at that time its aim was to signify the continuity of the same sacrifice in the continuity of the one Church.[5] But when the particle destined to be placed in the chalice was simply broken off the consecrated host on the same day, the meaning of the rite changed. Perhaps for a while it was only seen

---

2 In fact, we must distinguish two fractions of different origin: one, a primitive, essential rite, which the Roman missal would surround with solemnity; the other, which emerged when there was a desire to break off a consecrated fragment in order to leave it on the altar. The first came immediately before communion. Then the two rites were merged, but from then on the location was that of the second in date, after the Our Father: 'deeming a double fraction needless, they came to suppress the solemn one at the throne, which was so ancient, so sacred and so expressive, and to retain only the simple one on the altar. No doubt they intended to transfer to this one the magnificent value of the ancient one, but as its position is too distant from the communion rite, and this sense is so little stressed, it goes unnoticed.' (Dom B. Capelle, 'Le rite de la fraction dans la messe romaine', in *Revue bénédictine*, vol. 53 (1941) pp. 38–9; L. Haberstroh, *Der Ritus der Brechung und Mischung, nach dem Missale romanum* (Sankt Gabrieler Studien, 5; Mödling, 1937).

3 Coptic liturgy, Latin of Renaudot. Cf. Le Brun, *Explication des ceremonies de la messe*, vol. 2, new edn, 1860, p. 425. Pseudo-Ambrose, *De sacramentis*, vol. 4, c. 5, n. 21: '*This is my body, which will be broken for many*' (PL, 16, 443 B). Eutychius of Constantinople, *Sermon for Easter*: ἡ κλάσις τοῦ ἄρτον τοῦ σφαγὴν δηλοῖ (PG, 2996 A).

4 Ancient Gallican Mass, Christmas Day, etc. Cf. Le Brun, *op. cit.*, p. 224. It should be noted that *confractio* is the term used by the Roman liturgy to designate this rite. *Ordo romanus I*, n. 19. Cf. *Liber pontificalis*, vol. 1, p. 376.

5 Duchesne, *Origines du culte Chrétien*, 3rd edn, pp. 163, 184. Batiffol, *Leçons sur la messe*, pp. 34–6, 76–7, 88, 90–1, 284–5. Cf. Le Brun, *op. cit.*, vol. 1, pp. 502–4. Amalarius alludes to the *holy things* in his *Eclogae*: '*the bishop approaching the altar first of all adores the holy things*' (PL, 105, 1317 D). The 'reservation' of a part of the host on the altar is possibly connected to the same rite (Batiffol, p. 92).

as a figure of the unity of the sacrament beneath the two species. At any rate, the *commingling* soon appeared as the correlative and necessary complement of the *fraction*: if the former recalled the tearing of Christ's body, that is to say his Passion and death, the latter, through the symbolic reuniting of his body and his blood, called to mind his glorious resurrection. '*The joining together of the body of the Lord*', as the Mozarabic liturgy says.[6]

We might well imagine that Amalarius was not going to let go of this interpretation. His love of allegory, which he attached to the smallest details of every ceremony, became the culminating point of an entire system that read into each of the gestures of the celebrant a recollection of some aspect of Christ's Passion, burial or resurrection. This is how he comments on the Roman text that served him as a guide:

The aforementioned text says: 'When he says, "The peace of the Lord be always with you", he puts part of the host in the chalice'. In my view, this is not in vain. Bodily life is made up of blood and flesh. As long as these two are strong in a human being, the spirit is present. The office (of the Mass) represents that the blood that was shed for our soul and the flesh that died for our body return to their proper substance, and the new man is quickened with life-giving spirit, so that the one who died and rose for us dies no more.[7]

He had said the same thing in his *Eclogues*: '*When the bread is put in the wine, there is a representation of the Lord's soul returning to the body.*'[8]

---

6 At least this is how several commentators interpret this formulation: cf. H. Rabotin, in *Eucharistia*, p. 560; Le Brun, who also quotes several similar formulations in the Eastern liturgies: 'Already in the fifth century, Narsas sees in it (in the rite of commixtion) the affirmation that "the body and the blood are one" and thus a symbol of the resurrection. For the liturgy of St. James it is in the same way "a mark of the unity of the sacred body and of the precious blood" from which results "unity, sanctification and perfection". The same symbolic meaning is found in St. Mark. In Constantinople there is only this brief and obscure formulation: "for the fullness of the Holy Spirit".' If we are to believe Le Brun (*op. cit.*, vol. 1, p. 506), Florus's no less obscure formulation is also to be interpreted as an allusion to the resurrection (Florus, *Expositio missae*, c. 89, n. 1): 'the priest, comixing the the oblation of the Lord, that the chalice of the Lord might contain the fullness of the sacrament . . .' (Duc, p. 155); but I have reservations about this. Florus's formulation is also repeated by Remigius of Auxerre, *De celebratione missae* (Pseudo-Alcuin, *Liber de divinis officiis*; PL, 101, 1270 B).

7 *Liber officialis*, 3, c. 31 (PL, 105, 1152 A). Compare c. 26 (1144 D).

8 PL, 105, 1316 B. Cf. Honorius of Autun, *Gemma animae*, vol. 1, c. 63 (PL, 172, 563 B). Gandulph of Bologna, *Sententiae*, 4, n. 128 (J. de Walter, p. 455), etc.

This, then, is the understanding from which Amalarius takes his starting point. Despite a few formulations that might cast doubt on it,[9] it would seem that he took it from an already established tradition. But, according to the logic of his principle: *'nothing performed in the office is divorced from the mystery'*,[10] he seeks to extend it by giving an account of the fraction in *three* pieces and the precise meaning of each of them. This is when we find – besides the subsidiary interpretation of the *Eclogues* by the three guests at Emmaus[11] – the idea of the *three-fold body*. After the *'part immersed in the chalice'*, which symbolises the risen Christ, comes the *'part that is consumed by the priest or the people'*, in which it is natural to see the *'body walking on the earth'*, since it is received by those who are living on earth. There remains the third part, which will describe the *'body lying'* for two reasons: because it is destined for the viaticum of the dying, and then because it is left on the altar, from after communion to the end of the Mass, just as the *'body lying'* remains waiting for the resurrection until the end of the ages.[12]

No less than its theology, the symbolic nature of the *threefold body* would encounter a number of difficulties. If, following the example of the doctrinal framework, the liturgical framework remained unchanged, within the framework itself the details of interpretation would change: we do not always understand in identical fashion the way that the three 'bodies' are linked respectively to the three fragments of the host. But rites are a far more stable element than theories. Thus the variations that we will now have to note are far less dependent on changes that took place within rites than the variations noted in the previous chapter depended on changes or developments that took place in theology.

The only ritual change concerns the third particle of the host. Little by little, for a variety of reasons,[13] the custom disappeared of 'reserving' it on the altar for viaticum. In the thirteenth century, St. Albert the Great would note that in several religious orders, the Dominicans, the Franciscans, and the Cistercians, and in many secular churches, it was

---

9 *loc. cit*, note 5; and the end of chapter xxxi (PL, 105, 1152 D). Cf. L. Haberstroh, *Der Ritus der Brechung und Mischung nach dem Missale Romanum* (1937); Robilliard, *Revue dessciences philosophiques et théologiques*, 1938, p. 461.

10 PL, 105, 1152 D. Cf. Paschasius Radbertus, *In Matthaeum* (120, 899 C).

11 PL, 105, 1328 C. Cf. Honorius of Autun, *Gemma animae*, 1, c. 63 (72, 563 D).

12 PL, 119, 85 D.

13 (Quaracchi, vol. 4, p. 286). St. Thomas, *Summa theologiæ*, IIIa, q. 83, a. 5, ad 8m. Cf. Batiffol, *Leçons sur la messe*, p. 92, note.

no longer observed.[14] Nearly half a century earlier, Sicard of Cremona was already writing: '*One (part) is* at some time *or other reserved on the altar in a pyx for the viaticum of the sick*',[15] and from the end of the twelfth century, Gandulf of Bologna would explain the note of 'Pope Sergius' on the third body by saying: '*the saying has to be understood according to the varying practice of the Church*'.[16]

This abandonment of an ancient custom, coinciding with the evolution of perspectives concerning the dead, could only precipitate the transformation of the symbolism attached first of all to the '*third part of the sacrifice*'. At the same time losing its basis in ritual and its doctrinal expression, it no longer had any meaning. – But, apart from this case, the variations that can be noted are not due to causes of a liturgical order. In truth, they need no other explanation than the whim of their authors. The fact is that as much as rites are obliged by sacred tradition to be generally stable, nevertheless their symbolic interpretation lends itself to corrections, inventions and amplifications of every type. *Viewed from the outside and in detail*, the tradition is entirely subjective. Within it anyone can exercise a freedom reminiscent of that of the ancient Greeks with regard to their myths. The success of each person's personal inspirations will depend on the ingenuity of which he is capable and on the doctrinal weight with which he has been able to load his symbols. More arbitrarily, it could also depend on the authority that attached to his name in broader terms, or on fortuitous circumstances . . . The stamp of the *threefold body* is fairly firm, the principal idea behind its symbolism was fairly essential and furnished a sufficiently objective illustration of the Eucharistic mystery for it to have the opportunity of providing a long career. But why should this fragment of the host correspond to that part of the body rather than to any other? In this case, unlike what happens in certain others, the symbols were not driven by some sort of necessity. Thus we see as many combinations developing as possibilities could be imagined.

In Amalarius's eyes, the particle in the chalice symbolized the risen body. He was followed in this by many others, either because they were satisfied with the explanation, or simply through routine. This is what we find in liturgists like John of Avranches and Marsilius of Rouen. And we find the same in Thomas Aquinas. But others wondered if they should not rather see in it the symbol of the '*body walking on earth*'. Does not the chalice imply, according to Scripture itself,

---

14 *In IV Sent.*, d. 13, q. 14 (Vivès, vol. 29, p. 358, 359).
15 *Mitrale*, 3, c. 8 (PL, 213, 141).
16 *Sententiae*, 4, n. 127 (J. de Walter, p. 455).

ideas of suffering rather than of glory, and did Christ not speak of the cup of his Passion? Amalarius, who was not that interested in achieving perfect coherence, had been careful to refer to this elsewhere, in a passage from the *Eclogues*.[17] It would therefore appear that the particle put into it by the priest should signify that part of the Body of Christ that is still suffering trials and which, in addition, must imitate here below the Passion of our Saviour in order attain the glory of his resurrection. *To imitate the passion of Christ*: was this not, according to the teaching of the two great Doctors that the Middle Ages never tired of quoting,[18] St. Augustine and St. Gregory, a real participation in the sacrifice and a real communion in the sacred banquet? This was the way many reasoned, the first of whom seems to have been Ivo of Chartres, whose followers soon swelled in number.[19] The '*part placed in the chalice*' would therefore represent the members of Christ '*still living in suffering*', '*in the shipwreck of this age*', '*amid the troubles of this life*'. Or else the chalice was a sort of prison: '*who are detained in this exile*'. A mnemonic verse would lodge the new interpretation in every memory:

> . . . *The third part is the living: this is soaked in the blood.*

St. Thomas who, as we have seen, held to the original tradition, nevertheless made room for this one. Still others came to the same result via a totally different symbolism, in which is reflected the growing attention given to the propitiatory character of the Mass: the living are happily symbolised by the *inserted particle*, because they accomplish the *work of blood and flesh* that the *flesh and blood mingled together* were meant to expiate.[20]

Nevertheless, from the time when the dead in purgatory were seen as represented in one of the three bodies, how could the idea not have emerged of symbolising them through this same *inserted particle*? Did

---

17 PL, 105, 1323 D. Cf. Fulgentius, *Ep.* 14, pp. 41, 42. Cf. Paschasius Radbertus *In Matthaeum*, 9, c. 20 (PL, 120, 690 B). Florus (PL, 119, 74 C, 81 B). Amalarius, *Eclogae* (105, 1326 B).

18 Augustine, Gregory, *Dialogues*, 4, c. 58 (PL, 77, 425). Cf. Origen, *In Matt.* series, c. 92 (Kl., pp. 209-10). Didymus the Blind, *In psalmum 115*, v. 4 (PG, 39, 1556 A).

19 Hugh, Stephen of Baugé, *Speculum Ecclesiae, Sermo de excellentia*, Baldwin of Canterbury, Master Simon, Peter Comestor, Robert Paululus, Pseudo-Hildebert, Innocent III, *Sententiae divinitatis*, Sicard of Cremona, William of Auxerre, etc.

20 Robert Paululus, *De ecclesiasticis officiis*, c. 39 (PL, 177, 436). Similarly, *Versus de mysterio missae* (ch. ii, note 43). Cf. William of Auxerre, *Summa aurea*, 4 (f° 260 r°).

they not make up that part of the body of Christ that is called the Church suffering? And if the chalice is a prison, has purgatory not got a greater claim than earth to represent that chalice?[21] Besides the idea of suffering, does not the chalice also imply the idea of death? As Paschasius Radbertus had explained it, if the Lord cried out: '*let this cup pass from me*', it was doubtless in view of his agonizing Passion, but it was also to show the great terror that accompanies the approach of death.[22] We therefore see the *walking body* threatened with being deposed in its turn from the position that it had won, and forced to seek another symbolic link with which to attach itself to one of the other two fragments . . . This is what happened in Pseudo-Algerius of Liége. There, it would be the part consumed by the priest, that is to say the second in numerical order: does not this *middle portion* work sufficiently well as a description of those who, while still alive in the flesh, are nevertheless '*as if in a midway position*', able to lean to the left or the right according to their free will? This is particularly bogus and feeble symbolism, but it would be admitted that it was proving hard always to find three equally felicitous descriptions for the three bodies.

Not could it be forgotten that if the chalice is a sign of pain, it is equally, and once again, according to Scripture, a symbol of joy: '*My chalice that inebriates, how glorious it is*!' It is '*a cup of sweetness*'.[23] When the souls of the saints were distinguished from the anonymous mass of *those who had fallen asleep* and reunited with Christ in the heavenly dwelling place, there arose a new type of contestant in the candidature for the symbolism for the *immersed part*. It was this that won the day for the author of the *Sententiae florianenses*: '*That part which is seen in the chalice, designates the souls who reign with Christ in the heavens.*'[24] They won the day also, but for another reason, with Richard of Wedinghausen. Before being placed in the chalice, the particle is held in the hand of the priest, who uses it to trace a series of crosses: thus it is as if we hold the saints in our hands, when we imitate them through our faith and our works, and when we associate ourselves with the sufferings of Christ. The author of the *Liber de canone mystici libaminis* has, as we have seen, a taste for recondite symbol-

21 Thus in Peter Cantor (Dumoutet, pp. 203–4; cf. *supra*, p. 324).

22 Cf. Paschasius Radbertus, *In Matthaeum*, 9, c. 20 (PL, 120, 690 C).

23 Paschasius Radbertus, *In Matthaeum* (PL, 120, 895 D). Cf. Ambrose, *De Elia*, c. 10, n. 34 (PL, 14, 708 D).

24 N. 74 (Ostlender, p. 33).

ism.[25] Much more simply, it was normal that the associates of Christ in glory should be described by the same symbol as Christ himself, although they were not raised as he is.[26] Thus the new explanation joined together with the older one. Another didactic poem sought to disseminate it: '*The soaked part signifies the wholly blessed . . .*' St. Bonaventure nevertheless sees a problem in it: the natural significance of the chalice is the Passion, and it is in no way suitable as a description of the blessed. Here is the response that he himself offers:

> *Another of its properties is easy consumption, by which the blessed are signified, who taste without any delay.*[27]

Simply from the symbolic point of view, the response appears feeble. But we must also take into account that '*without any delay . . .*' whose intention is quite clear. St. Bonaventure does not fail to make good use of the opportunity to make a theological point which, in the thirteenth century, was still not superfluous. Besides, whatever it cost, he above all wanted to justify a classification that had been adopted beforehand. It was necessary to use this somewhat arbitrary sleight of hand in order to insert within the *threefold body* this new category of the saints in heaven, without upsetting the entire economy of the formulation.

An examination of the two other parts of the host, the one consumed *dry* by the priest and the one that remains – or that remained – on the altar after communion, would lead us to complete the remarks made about the first fragment. But the reader will no doubt think that this will do. From the thirteenth century onwards, the evolution – if I may use such a word for changes of this sort – had come to an end. Theologians and liturgists, rather than making their personal contribution towards the symbolism of the *threefold body*, or choosing between those of their predecessors, ensured that they did not lose a single one. This, for example, is what Sicard of Cremona is already doing.[28] The eclecticism of a Durandus of Mende,[29] and later still of a Sylvius,[30] would be far more abundant. The principle behind it had

---

25 PL, 177, 467–8.

26 *In IV Sent.*, d. 13, a. 14 (Vivès, vol. 29, pp. 359–60).

27 *In IV Sent.*, d. 12, p. 1, a. 3, q. 3 (Q., vol. 4, p. 286).

28 *Mitrale*, 3, c. 8 (PL, 213, 141).

29 *Rationale divinorum officiorum*, 4, c. 51, n. 21, 22.

30 *In* 3, q. 83, a. 5. Sylvius notes the link between the change in liturgical usage and the difference between the explanations: *according to the usage now customary in the church.*

received the approval of the great schoolmen: '*It is not inappropriate through the same thing to be signifying a diversity.*'[31] St. Thomas had declared following St. Albert,[32] in conformity with the vaster doctrine that found its primary application in the interpretation of Scripture. This did not prevent the catalogue of symbols – Durandus of Mende counts up to six systems – from soon offering nothing but a point of retrospective interest. The *threefold body* no longer played its former role in living theology.[33]

Thanks to the support given to it by the rite, it had nevertheless prolonged its career beyond what might have been supposed. While there had been a risk of its 'dating' very quickly, it had been able to transform itself instead of perishing. Such a fate did not befall its contemporary, Paschasius Radbertus's and Godescalc's *triple mode of the body*. Honorius of Autun had made a spirited attempt, in the twelfth century, to make the most of the opportunity by introducing it, via an ingenious transfer, into the liturgical context prepared by Amalarius. After having enumerated the three bodies of Paschasian tradition: the historical body, the sacramental body and the ecclesial body, and demonstrated their unity in the Holy Spirit, Honorius added:

And because we believe that there is one single body, we make one single offering; but because we believe that it exists in three ways, we divide into three parts the consecrated offering. The part that is put into the chalice signifies that body of the Lord which is received into glory; the part that is consumed by the priest signifies the one that is left as a pledge to the Church; as for the part that is placed in the pyx for Viaticum, it signifies the body whose work is focused on this world as on a prison.[34]

But this attempt gained no followers. No doubt it came too late. The two theories remained independent, and Amalarius's posterity would prove longer than that of Paschasius. Less well received initially than Pseudo-Augustine – because it only later gained the advantage of its pseudonym – Pseudo Sergius, on the other hand, proved more

---

31 *In IV Sent.*, d. 12, q. 1, a. 3, q. 3, ad 4.
32 *In IV Sent.* (Vivès, vol. 24, p. 358).
33 I have only signalled the variations within the Amalarian scheme. The three parts of the host also symbolized other triads: the Trinity, naturally; the three guests at Emmaus; the three orders of Christians: prelates, celibates, married people, themselves designed respectively by Noah, Daniel and Job; the three blessed limbs of Christ: his feet, hands and side . . .
34 *Eucharistion*, c. 1 (PL, 172, 1250).

tenacious. Both nevertheless remain for us the witnesses to the close solidarity of the Church and the Eucharist in the thought of the Middle Ages.

NOTES

Note A

'The Mystery of the Sacrament'

[343]

I am going to give, without any further comment, a double list (which has no pretensions to being exhaustive) of the texts in which I have found the expressions '*mystery of the sacrament*' and '*sacrament of the mystery*'. It may help either to establish a comparison of the two formulations, or to establish the 'scriptural' and 'mysterious' use of both one and the other – to offer a further indication of the intimate way in which both expressions have become fused. (I will also add a list of a few approximate expressions.) The way they alternate is curious. I nevertheless do not believe that it will be necessary, at least in every single case, to seek in the choice of one or the other a conscious and willed setting in opposition. This is how the Council of Frankfurt (794) came to use both one and the other, a few lines distant from each other, with the identical meaning: '*Many and innumerable sacraments of mysteries . . . are found mentioned in the sacred pages . . . Why do you despise the manifest proofs of the most holy apostle Paul, which are full of the mysteries of sacraments?*' (MGH, *Concilia,* vol. II, pp. 127 and 128).

It may perhaps be interesting to note that in St. Hilary, who seems to have been the principal initiator of both formulations, they constitute a sort of particular case of an extremely common habit of language. Hilary, for example, plays on '*flesh of the body*' and '*body of flesh*' (see above, p. 42, note 61). Following Novatian, he passes from the '*body of truth*' to the '*truth of the body*' (above, p. 163, note 151). He has a liking for the Pauline expressions: '*from the body of this death*', '*the body of our humility, the body of his glory*', and in imitation of them: '*taking our sins into his body*' (*De Trinitate*, l. 9, c. 13; PL, 10, 292 A–B). Using a method that is somewhat reminiscent of the one followed in the nineteenth century by the Vicomte de Bonald, he writes: '*in order that it be neither within the meaning of the thing understood, nor beyond the understanding of the thing sensed*', or again: '*which is neither not itself the truth of the name, nor not the name of the truth*' (l. 1, c. 7 and 21; PL, 10, 30 C and 39 B). Instead of '*true divinity*', he says, more solemnly and in more abstract fashion: '*the truth of divinity*' (l. 6, c. 16: PL 10, 144 A), and this expression, as was observed by Fr. Smulders in his *La doctrine trinitaire de saint Hilaire de Poitiers*, p. 149, note 48, 'it is among the personal elements of Hilary's language, from those that most often provoked the greatest obscurity'. Thus, further on, we have '*the eternity of nativity*' (l. 1, c. 34; 47 C) instead of '*the eternal nativity*'; '*a religion of praise*' (l. 11, c. 4; 402 A) instead of '*religious praise*'; or '*eternity of life*' (l. 3, 6.14; 83 C), '*the calumny of inquisition*' (l. 3, c. 18; 86 B), '*the nature of infirmity*' (l. 3, c. 25; 94 A) etc. He also likes to vary his expressions and turn them in on themselves; thus in the same *de Trinitate* book 11, he alternates between: '*the dispensation of the sacrament*' (c. 13, 408 A), '*dispensing the sacraments*' (c. 30, 419 D), '*dispensation and sacrament*' (c. 43, 428 A) '*the sacrament of dispensation*' (c. 49, 432 B; cf. l. 12, c. 45, 462 C, etc.), '*the mystery of dispensation*' (c. 18, 406 A).

I

'*Mystery of the Sacrament*'

Lactance, *Divinae institutions*, l. 7, c. 22: 'Mysterium divini sacramenti nesciebant' (PL, 6, 803 A–B).

Hilary, *De Trinitate*, l. 8, c. 15: 'ille rursum in nobis per sacamentorum inesse mysterium' (PL, 10, 248).

Hilary, *De Trinitate*, l. 9, c. 41 : 'Quod istud, rogo, sacramenti mysterium est ?' (PL, 10, 313 A). (Text cited by Gerhoh de Reichersberg, *In psalmum 18*, PL, 193, 907 C, and *Liber contra dias haereses*, c. 4, PL, 194, 1176 C.)

Optatus, *De schismate donatistarum*, l. 2, c. 12: 'in sacramentorum mysterio' (PL, 11, 965 C).

Ambrose, *Epistula 79*, n. 4: 'Alia sunt sacramentorum perfectiorum mysteria' (PL, 16, 1270 C).

Ambrose, *Sermon pour Pâques* (?): 'Hinc caelestis meriti sanctificatur munere, et sacramenti spiritalis celebri mysterio, saginatur' (Milleloquium ambrosianum, 1789 A).

Ambrosiaster, *In Coloss.*, II, 1–3: 'Omne igitur mysterium sacramenti Dei in Christo est' (PL, 17, 427 A).

Augustine, *Speculum de Scriptura sacra*, praefatio: 'sacramentorum velata mysteriis' (PL, 34, 889).

Augustine, *De opere monachorum*, n. 9: 'Quae sunt spiritualia quae seminavit, nisi verbum et mysterium sacramenti regni caelorum?' (PL, 40, 555).

Gregory of Elvira, *Tractatus 12*: 'ad competentem in secreto animae quasi in pergulam lini mysterium sacramenti absconditur' (Batiffol-Wilmart, *Tractatus Origenis*, p. 135).

Passio sancti Genesii, c. 2: 'cumque sacramentorum mysteria complessent' (Ruinart, p.270).

IVᵉ Concile de Braga (675): 'Ab ipso fonte probabitur, a quo ordinata ipsa sacramentorum mysteria processerunt' (Mansi, II, 155 B).

Isidore of Seville, *Quaestiones in Genesim*, c. 18, n. 3: 'Age nunc, videamus quid sub hujus sacramenti lateat mysterio' (PL, 83, 249 D).

Alcuin, *Epistula 113*: 'Haec omnis doctori in initio fidei et sacramento baptismatis ad salutem accipientis diligenter consideranda sunt, et non desidiose tanti sacramenti mysterium' (MGH, *Epistularum*, IV, p. 165).

Rabanus Maurus, *De clericorum institutione*, l. l, c. 31: 'In sacerdote Melchisedech, hoc dominici sacramenti praefiguratum videmus mysterium' (PL, 107, 321 A).

Ratramnus, *De corpore et sanguine Domini*, c. 50: 'quod ore fidelium per sacramentorum mysterium in Ecclesia quotidie sumitur' (PL, 121, 147 B); c. 101: 'Nec . . . putetur in mysterio sacramenti corpus Domini . . . non a fidelibus sumi' (170 B).

Paschasius Radbertus, *In Matthaeum*, praefatio: 'His ergo septem in Christo reseratis caelestium sacramentorum mysteriis' (PL, 120, 40 D). L. 2: 'qui per eam (columbam) in diluvio juxta mysterium sacramenti fuerat figuratus' (173 A); 'Provida Dei dispensatio . . . quae tam concinna sacramentorum mysteria olim Patribus signanter aperuit' (174 D). L. 6: 'contemplari ineffabilia sacramentorum ejus mysteria' (477 C). L. 8: 'Docuit arcana sacramenti sui mysteria' (555 C).

Hincmar, *Vita Remigii*: 'Et ille rursum in nobis per sacramentorum inesse mysterium creditur' (MGH, *Scriptores rerum merovingiarum*, III, p. 334).

Burchard of Worms, *Decretum*, l. 5, c. 1, ex decretis Julii papae: 'Ab ipso fonte veritatis probabitur, a quo ordinata ipsa *(sic)* sacramentorum mysteria processerunt' (PL, 140, 751 B).

Sacramentaire gélasien: 'jejuniorum magnifici sacramenti digne semper tractare mysteria' (Wilson, p. 20); 'percepti novi sacramenti mysterium' (pp. 68 and 73).

Grimaldus, *Liber sacramentorum*: 'per hujus sacramenti mysterium' (PL, 121, 828 A); 'Sumpta, Domine, caelestis sacramenti mysteria' (832 C).

Peter Damian, *Opusculum 6*, c. 16: 'Sacramenti cujusque mysterium non ex consecrantis est merito' (PL, 145, 122 D).

St. Bruno, *In psalmum 77*: 'Per praedicatores, Scripturas apertas fecit, in quibus hujuscemodi sacramenti mysterium et caetera mysteria continentur' (PL, 152, 1039 D).

Anselm of Laon, *Enarrationes in Matthaeum*, c. 26: 'Caenaculum quod in alto est, altitudinem mysterii sacramentorum Dei significat' (PL, 162, 1468 D).

William of St. Thierry, *Disputatio adversus Abaelardum*, c. 9: 'Ad peragendum sacramenti mysterium' (PL, 180, 280 C).

Vie de saint Bruno de Segni: 'De tanti mysterio sacramenti disputare' (*Acta Sanctorum*, julii, IV, p. 479 D).

Hugh of St. Victor, *De beatae Mariae virginitate*: 'Prius quam divini arcanum sacramenti didicisset' (PL, 176, 867 A).

Raoul of St. Germer, *In Leviticum*, l. 2: 'In agni paschalis immolatione mortem Christi significari, nemini incognitum est. Ibi quoque hujus tanti mysterium sacramenti reperies' (*B. M. P.*, XVII, p. 68 C).

Baldwin of Canterbury, *Liber de sacramento altaris*: 'Caelestium sacramentorum mysteria suo tempore propalanda' (PL, 204, 645 B).

Peter of Poitiers, *Allegoriae super Tabernaculum Moysi*: 'Concavitas mitrae (pontificalis) significat . . . profunditatem mysterii sacramentorum' (Moore-Corbett, p. 45).

St. Thomas Aquinas (?), *Opuscule 57*: 'ad plene cognoscenda hujus mysteria sacramenti.'

Gerson, *Sermo in die corporis Christi*: 'Sublime sancti sacramenti mysterium', 'de sublimi hujus sacramenti mysterio', sancti sacramenti altaris mysterium', 'Dominus noster per digni sui sacramenti mysterium . . .' (*Opera omnia*, Anvers, 1706, pp. 1284, 1287, 1289).

Wycliffe, *De Ecclesia*, c. 4: 'per mysterium sacramentorum Ecclesiae' (Loserth, p. 77).

II

'Sacrament of the Mystery'

Hilary, *Tractatus mysteriorum*, l. 1, c. 5: 'Occulti in Christo et in Ecclesia mysterii sacramentum' (Brisson, p. 82).

Hilary, *De Trinitate*, l. 9, c. 7: 'Haec autem jam ante conditionem sacramenta sunt caelestium mysteriorum constituta, ut unigenitus Deus homo nasci vellet, mansuro in aeternum in Deo homine' (PL, 10, 286 A).

Ambrose, *De virginitate*, c. 10, n. 58: 'Pedes cum semel laveris aeterni fontis irriguo, et mysterii mundaveris sacramento' (PL, 16, 281 A).

Ambrosiaster, *In Ephes.*, V, 31: 'Mysterii sacramentum grande in unitate viri ac feminae esse significat' (PL, 17, 399 B).

Rufinus, traduction d'Origène, *In Jesu Nave*, homilia 1, n. 1: 'Hic ergo ubi primum disco nomen Jesu, ibi continuo etiam mysterii video sacramentum'; homilia 2, n. 1: 'Mysterii tamen hujus figura describitur' (Baehrens, pp. 288 and 297).

Bachiarius Monachus, *Professio fidei*: 'Cum gesta olim evangelici sacramenta mysterii, iterum aetatis nostrae temporibus renovata celebrentur' (PL, 20, 1019 C).

Cassiodorus, *In psalmum 137*: 'Dum corpus et sanguinem ipsius inter summi mysterii sacramenta veneratur' (PL, 70, 980 B).

Xᵉ Concile de Tolède (636): 'Si caret (paschale festum) plenitudinis numero, carere potest et mysterii sacramento' (Mansi, II, 33).

XIIIᵉ Concile de Tolède (683): 'Solita compleant ordinis sui officia vel cetera mysteriorum sibi credita sacramenta' (Mansi, II, 1073).

Claude of Turin, préface au Livre des Juges: 'Historiae haec non parva mysteriorum indicat sacramenta' (MGH, *Epistularum*, IV, p. 610).

Isidore of Seville, *Quaestiones in librum Judicum*, I: 'Historia Judicum non parva mysteriorum vindicat sacramenta' (PL, 83, 379 C; idem dans Pseudo-Bède, PL, 93, 423 A).

Sedulius Scottus, *In I Cor.*, XI: 'Caetera vero; id est, de ipsius mysterii sacramentis' (PL 103, 152 A).

Pseudo-Primasius, *In I Cor.*, XI: 'Ego enim accepi a Domino . . . quoniam Dominus Jesus: Jam hinc quasi oblitus commemorat quam magnum insit hujus mysterii sacramentum' (PL, 68, 533 C–D).

Pseudo-Bede, *Quaestiones in librum IV Regnum*: 'Numerus quindecim annorum quid sacramenti continet in mysterio?' (PL 93, 449 A; cf. 449 B: 'Qui numerus, quid mysterii habeat videamus').

Florus, *Relation du Concile de Kierzy*, c. 6: 'licere nova figurarum genera vel mysteriorum sacramenta sancire' (MGH, *Concilia*, II, p. 780; or PL, 119, 82 D).

Paschasius Radbertus, *Liber de corpore*, c. 14, n. 6: 'Huic sacramento divinitus indulsit, ut sit caro et sanguis ipsius, ut quod caro et sanguis Christi Ecclesiae contulit, hoc totum sacramentum hujus mysterii compleat' (PL, 120, 1321 A–B).

Paschasius Radbertus, *In Matthaeum*, praefatio: 'in aeterno suo consilio hoc mysterii sacramentum semper fuisse absconditum (PL, 120, 40 A). L. 1: 'Sed quia longum est omnia hujus mysterii sacramenta typice explicare . . .' (63 B). L. 2: 'tanti mysterii sacramenta . . . praesignare' (144 B); 'et tum divinis mysteriorum sacramentis in Christi corpore consecretur' (155 A). L. 8: 'donec praeparet eos ad fidem et ad sacramenta mysterii' (567 C).

Gezon of Tortona, *Liber de corpore et sanguine Christi*, c. 41: 'Cum ad missarum fuisset mysteria ventum, sancta sanctorum caepit rursus, sicut in baptismo prius egerat, refugere . . ., atque horrere videbatur acriter ipsius mysterii sacramentum' (PL, 137, 394 D).

Peter Damian, *Sermo 46*: 'Plurima quidem dilectionis vestrae, fratres carissimi, de lectione evangelica, quae multis mysteriorum sacramentis est gravida, possemus exponere' (PL, 144, 751 A).

Peter Damian, *Opusculum 6*, c. 18: 'propter acceptum sacerdotalis mysterii sacramentum' (PL, 145, 124 B).

William of St. Thierry, *Disputatio altera adversus Abaelardum*, 1.2 (PL, 180, 303 B; citation d'Hilaire, *De Trinitate*, cf. *Supra*).

Gerhoh of Reichersberg, *Epistula ad Innocentium papam*: 'Gloriare nunc de sacramentalibus mysteriorum signis, quae apud altare fiunt' (MGH, *Libelli de lite*, III, p. 227).

St. Hildegard, *Scivias*, l. 2, visio 6: 'Sic etiam vinum in consecratione sanguinis Filii Dei non deficiet, sed super altare in sacramento mysterii ejus semper erit' (PL, 197, 526 C).

Peter Comestor, *Sententiae de sacramentis, De baptismo*, n. 5: 'Baptismus dari potest in nomine Patris tantum, etc. Si autem aliquis perverse credens . . . unum de tribus tantum nuncupet, non implevit sacramentum mysterii.' 'Plenum est mysterii Please check this translation – FT, p. 348.sacramentum, si Patrem et Filium et Spiritum sanctum fatearis' (Martin, pp. 15 and 16). (Peter gives these two phrases as if from St. Ambrose. In reality, the first is based on Peter Lombard, *Sentences*, l. 4, d. 3, c. 4, Quaracchi, p. 757; the second on Ambrose, *De Spiritu sancto*, l. 1, c. 3, n. 42, PL, 16, 714 A. But neither Ambrose nor the Lombard would dissent from this passage, '*mysterii sacramentum*'.)

Innocent III, *De sacro altaris mysterio*, l. 1, c. 8: 'Non sine magni mysterii sacramento, cum Christus universos interrogasset apostolos, solus Petrus . . . respondit' (PL, 217, 779 A).

III

Approximate Expressions

Origen, *In Rom.*, l. 5, n. 9: 'Sciebant enim illi quibus mysteriorum secreta commissa sunt divinorum' (Rufin) (PG, 14, 1047 B). *In Num.*, hom. 4, 3: 'vasa sacra, id est mysteriorum sapientiae secreta'; hom.8,1: 'Timeo ergo mysterii hujus secreta discutere' (Bachreus, pp. 23 and 50), etc.

Pseudo-Clement, *Epistolae decretales*, ep.2: 'Tribus enim gradibus commissa sunt sacramenta divinorum secretorum, id est presbytero, diacono et ministro' (PG, 1, 483 C). (Cited by Cardinal Humbert, *Contra Nicetam*, c. 27; PL, 143, 998 A–B).

Hilary, *In psalmum 65*, n. 4: 'Spectet celebres hymnorum sonitus et inter divinorum quoque sacramentorum officia responsionem devotae confessionis accipiat' (Zingerle, p. 251). (LeBrun, *Explication . . . de la messe*, nouv. éd., 1860, vol. I, p. 2, gives also as based on the treatise on Psalm 65, the formula: 'divina mysteriorum sacramenta celebrare'; I have not been able to place it.

Gregory of Elvira, *Tractatus 16*: 'sacrorum mysteriorum arcane'; *Tractatus 17*: 'supercaelestium mysteriorum arcane' (Batiffol-Wilmart, pp. 177 and 186).

Augustine, *Epistula 55*: 'Profundum autem quod terrae infixum est, secretum sacramenti praefigurat' (PL, 33, 216).

Augustine, *De Trinitate*, l. 12, n. 11: 'Quod nisi ad aliquod secretum sacramenti referatur, inane remanebit' (PL, 42, 1004).

Augustine, *Contra Faustum*, l. 12, c. 11: 'ut per Christi passionem reveleretur secreta sacramentorum' (PL, 42, 260).

Fredegisi epistola de nihilo et tenebris: '(Ecclesia) ab ipsis cunabulis secretorum mysteriis instituta' (PL, 105, 753 A).

Paschasius Radbertus, *In Matthaeum*, l. 1: 'Quis hic non videat quanta aenigmata mysteriorum prodantur?' (PL, 120, 59 C). L. 12: 'In mysterio bonum opus fecit, et in sacramento hujus facti devotio multa praefiguravit' (883–884); 'Simillima quidem sunt et divina in hujusmodi rebus sacramenta, quae salute humani generis aguntur, et quotidie mystice in hoc mysterio ut tradita sunt apostolis celebrantur' (892 A).

Vitae Patrum, 16, 2 (de sancto Venantio abbate): 'cui etiam dignatus est arcanorum secreta calestium revelare' (MGH, *A. R. M.*, vol. I, p. 727).

Grimaldus, *Liber sacramentorum*: 'In mysterio aquarum salutis tuae nobis sacramenta sanxisti' (PL, 121, 837 C).

Ex translatione sanguinis Domini, c. 19: 'miraculi sacramentum cognoscens' (Xe siècle; MGH, *Scriptorum*, IV, p. 448).

St. Bernard, *Vie de saint Malachie*, c. 8, n. 17: 'Sacramentorum rite solemnia celebrantur' (PL, 182, 1085 B).

Bonaventure, *In Cena Domini sermo 2*, n. 2: 'sacramentale mysterium', 'ex sacramentali mysterio spiritus roboratur' (Quaracchi, IX, p. 251). *Ibid.*, n. 3: 'Panis quem ego dabo, caro mea est pro mundi vita. Exprimitur in his verbis sacramentale mysterium, quod sanctissima Mater Ecclesia hodie recolit institutum' (p. 253).

Augustine, *Epistula 140*, n. 48: 'Gratias agimus Domino Deo nostro, quod est magnum sacramentum in sacrificio Novi Testamenti' (PL, 33, 558). Cf. *De civitate Dei*, l. 10, c. 20 (41, 298).

Fulgentius, *Epistula 12*: 'in sacrificio sacramentorum' (PL, 65, 391 C).

Bede, *In Leviticum*, c. 7: 'Panes fermentati quos omnino abjecit in sacrificio, nunc jubentur apponi. Sed sciendum est quod hic non ad sacrificium, sed ad sacrificii mysterium opponuntur' (PL, 91, 343 A).

Etherius and Beatus, *Ad Elipandum*, l. 1, c. 75: 'Sacrificium quod a christianis Deo offertur, . . . primus Christus Dominus noster instituit . . . Quod quidem sacramentum Melchisedech rex Salem . . . primus obtulit, primusque mysterium tanti sacrificii imaginarie expressit' (PL, 96, 940 C–D).

Theodulphus of Orleans, *Liber de ordine baptismi*, c. 18: 'Hoc ergo mysterium sacrificii, derelictis a finitis veteribus hostiis, Ecclesia celebrat' (PL, 105, 240 A).

Florus, *Adversus Amalarium I*: 'In mysterio sacrificii . . . vel mutare quidpiam, vel addere aut subtrahere praesumpserunt' (PL, 119, 78 D).

Florus, *Expositio missae*, c. 33, n. 4: 'mysteriorum sacrificia'; n. 5: 'in sacrificiorum ritu' (Duc, p. 115).

Rupert, *De divinis officiis*, l. 2, c. 2: 'Multi namque fidei oculos non habentes, in sancto sacrificio praeter panem et vinum nihil amplius intuentes . . . Latuit enim eos . . . quod illae voces quidquam attineant ad mysterium sacrificii' (PL, 170, 33 C–D).

Algerius of Liége, *De sacramentis corporis*, l. 3, c. 9: 'Quis dubitet sacramentum sacrificii divini, ubicumque fiat, intra Ecclesiam esse?' (PL, 180, 842 B).

Pseudo-Bernard, *Instructio sacerdotis*, p. 1, c. 8, n. 21: 'cum santissimum mysterium caelestis sacrificii celebrare intendis' (PL, 184, 784 C).

Council of Trent, 22ᵉ session, ch. 8: 'Mandat sancta Synodus pastoribus . . . ut frequenter inter missarum celebrationem . . . ex his quae in missa leguntur aliquid exponant, atque inter cetera sanctissima hujus sacrificii mysterium aliquod declarent'.

Note B

On the Eucharist as *'Antitype'*

[351]

It may be that what I said in Chapters 2 and 9 on the relationship between the Eucharist and the sacrifices of the Old Testament and on the relatedness of certain terms in sacramental vocabulary with those concerning Scripture and its interpretation might serve to clarify the somewhat obscure meaning of the word *antitype* (ἀντίτυπος) in the first phase of its Eucharistic use. My only intention here is to show a possible line of enquiry, leaving further research, if there is a call for it, to more skilled labourers.

It is well known that ancient Christian literature in the Greek language has preserved for us several texts in which the Eucharist is given the name of antitypes of the body of Christ. These texts have long constituted an embarrassment: do they not offer testimony against belief in the 'real presence' during the first centuries? Indeed I am suggesting that very early on, in the Greek Church, this troublesome description was abandoned. It was even abandoned as being heretical, or else it was only understood as referring to the species of bread and wine before the moment of the consecration or the *epiclesis*.[1] Would it not be an opportunity to find a satisfactory solution if, by making an effort to break away from the point of view that came more and more to predominate in Eucharistic theology, we came back to a broader and quite concrete point of view, that would appear to have been the original one? Here it would principally be a question of substituting the category of history for the category of essence, at least as a category, so to speak, of primary focus. In this way, the *'antitypes'* of the body of Christ would be like antitypes, not of the body understood in itself, in its essence, its ontological and a-temporal reality, but like antitypes

---

1 *Apophthegmata Patrum* (PG, 65, 157). Sophronius of Jerusalem (87, 3984). Anastasius of Sinai (89, 297). Theophylactus (123, 444 C, 649 D, 1308 C). Cf. Theodore of Mopsuestia (66, 713), Eutychius of Constantinople (86, 2393), etc. Cf. M. Jugie, *L'Epiclèse et le mot antitype de la messe de saint Basile*, in *Echos d'Orient*, 1906, pp. 193–8; and *Messe dans l'Eglise Byzantine* (DTC, vol. 10, col. 1340). J. LEcuyer, *Le sacerdoce chrétien et le sacrifice eucharistique selon Théodore de Mopsueste*, in *Recherches de science religieuse*, 1949 (note 127).

of the body that hung on the cross, the body that was immolated and sacrificed, that is to say of the immolation of the body; in short, like antitypes of the sacrifice of the cross.

Within this perspective, the formulation presupposes another, of which it constitutes the antithesis. Indeed the *antitype* always presupposes, whether implicitly or not, a *type* – in the same way that the *transformation* presupposes a *pre-formation*. We are not lacking in corroboration for such antitheses. They are nevertheless rare enough to need searching for, and the complete formulations need reconstituting by more or less conjectural means. The fact is that at the time when this historical form of thinking about the Eucharist was still predominant, it was entirely spontaneous, and we do not see it emerging from the focused reflection of any of the authors who gave expression to it. It would seem that it never had the opportunity of being expressed in one of those didactic accounts that are the privilege of more advanced periods: accounts where everything is laid out in its proper order, where each element finds its exact place with regard to its corresponding other element, where concepts become clear-cut and where terminology develops in a regular fashion in all its integrated complexity. The historian (or it would be more suitable to say, the pre-historian), thus finds himself obliged to pick now one representative example, now another. He cannot avoid a fairly large element of interpretation, which is not without its risks. Our texts are more allusive than explicit; the essential order that prevails within them does not involve the external symmetry and the polish that we would have the right to expect from any scholastic treatise. At the end of its initial phase, Eucharistic theology did not have its own Colossus, as was the case for the theology of Image and of Resemblance, or like the theology of Mystical Ascents.

Nevertheless, it would appear that the hypothesis that I am proposing is the result of sufficiently numerous indications, it introduces sufficient logic in an impressive number of texts, it is corroborated in a credible fashion by sufficient details taken from enough different authors, and finally it harmonises sufficiently well with what we know from elsewhere of the outlook and language of the Fathers to justify my putting it forward.

* * *

Besides the fairly banal sense of something hard, solid and resistant,[2]

---

2 Plato, *Cratylus*, 420 d. [For an English translation, see C. D. C. Reeve,

antitype also has two principal meanings, which are related in other ways. The first meaning, which we could call exemplarist, or Platonic, although it is not to be found in Plato himself, is: image, imprint, copy, replica. There is a second, more specifically Christian meaning, which is the result of the Christian transposition of this exemplarism: according to this transposition, the relationship being expressed no longer lies between a sensible term and an intelligible or spiritual term, but within history itself it unites, as a sign to those things being signified, the events of the Old Testament and the realities of the New. Each of these two senses is corroborated by one of the two passages where the word is found in the New Testament. The first, in Heb. 9.24: 'It is not as though Jesus had entered a man-made sanctuary which was only modelled on the real one; but it was heaven itself'; the second, in 1 Pet. 3.20–21: 'Now it was long ago, when Noah was still building that ark which saved only a small group of eight people by water – *that water is a type of the baptism which saves you now.*'[3]

Most historians attach the Eucharistic meaning of antitype to the first of these two senses. The Eucharist is presented as the image and as it were the imprint of the body of Christ considered in itself; it is said to be the *antitype of the body*, as it is said in other parallel texts to be the *likeness* or, in Latin, the *figure*, or *sacrament*.[4] In a later period, these different expressions only described the 'species', but initially they certainly described the Eucharist itself.

This is, in fact, the meaning that already seems to be implied in texts like those found in the *Apostolic Constitutions*,[5] the *Didaskalia*,[6] and in the fifth book of mystagogical catechesis attributed to Cyril of Jerusalem.[7] We can compare these texts with Serapion's *Anaphora*, in

---

Cratylus (Indianapolis, 1998). For the English alongside the Greek original, see H. N. Fowler's translation in vol. 167 of the *Loeb Classical Library* series (Cambridge, Mass., 1970).] Justin, *Dialogue*, c. 5, n. 2 (Archambault, p. 28); cf. *I Apol.*, c. 8, n. 2 (Pautigny, p. 14). Origen, *In Jeremiam*, hom. 6, n. 3 (Klostermann, p. 50). Eusebius, *Evangelic Demonstration*, 6, c. 20 (Heikel, p. 286), etc. [English trans. W. J. Ferrar in the original *Early Christian Fathers* collection]; Cf. Origen, *De principiis*, l. 3, c. 1, n. 15 (Koestschau, p. 221); Eusebius, *Theophania*, fragment 5 (Gressmann, p. 16), [English trans. S. Lee, also in the original *Early Christian Fathers* collection]; Proclus, *passim*; etc.

3 Cf. Lundberg, *La typologie baptismale dans l'ancienne Eglise*, pp. 98–116.

4 Thus Tixeront, *Histoire des dogmes*, vol. 2, pp. 177–8.

5 5, 14 (Funk, p. 273); 6, 30, 2 (p. 381). Cf. Batiffol, *L'Eucharistie*, 5th edn, p. 292.

6 6, 22, 2 (Funk, p. 376).

7 c. 20 (PG, 33, 1124; Quersten, pp. 88, 108). Compare 21st catechesis (3rd *Mystagogic*), c. 1 (PG, 33, 1089), and 221, c. 3 (1100 A). Cf. Tixeront, *Histoire des dogmes*, vol. 2, pp. 170–1.

which the priest celebrating the sacrifice offers to God *the likeness of the body, the likeness of the blood.*[8]

The same historians are careful to observe that this language does not exclude a realist interpretation,[9] and no doubt they are right. Does not one of the words attributed to Jesus in primitive times say that the Church 'is the perfect body of Christ and his most clear image'?[10] And when Christ himself is called the 'Image' or the 'Character' of the Father, that in no way excludes his own divinity and his consubstantiality.[11] However, between the Father and the Son there is a personal distinction, which, in any event, is the foundation of this ambiguity in the language. Why should there be such a split in the case of the Eucharist, if within it we have the very body of Christ himself?

We find the response to this question primarily in the second meaning of the antitype. Without denying the connection of its Eucharistic meaning to the first sense, I believe that it is more strongly connected, at least in origin, to the second. This is what is implied by another passage from the *Apostolic Constitutions*, where it says: 'We give you thanks, O Father, for the precious blood of Jesus Christ which was poured out for us and for his precious body, whose likenesses we celebrate, since he himself commanded us to proclaim his death.'[12] In the same way, in Serapion's *anaphora*, the two expressions quoted are the framework for another: '*celebrating the likeness of death*'; and the link made here by Tixeront with '*sacrament*' will itself be significant, if we remember what was said earlier about that word. Even more revealing here is a fragment from St. Irenaeus, which has to be read in its full context:

> ... In the New Covenant the Lord instituted a new offering, according to the words of the prophet Malachi ... these offerings are not in accordance with the Law, which the Lord rejected and dissolved, as 'written by human hands', but according to the Spirit, because God must be worshipped in spirit and in truth. This is why even the offering of the Eucharist is not carnal but spiritual, and therein lies its purity.
>
> Because we offer to God the bread and the cup of blessing, giving him thanks for having ordered the earth to bring forth these

---

8 Brightman, *Journal of Theological Studies*, vol. 1, pp. 105-6.
9 Thus Dom Cabrol, *Messe*, in DTC, vol. 10, col. 1369.
10 Resch, *Agrapha*, 2nd edn, n. 75.
11 Cf. Harvey, edition of the *Adversus Haereses*, vol. 2, p. 504, note.
12 7, 25, 4 (Funk, p. 412).

fruits for our nourishment; then, having completed our offering, we call upon the Holy Spirit, in order that He might bring about this sacrifice, turning the bread into the body of Christ and the cup into the blood of Christ, so that those who receive these antitypes might obtain pardon for their sins and everlasting life.

Therefore those who make these offerings, in memory of our Saviour, are not recalling the institutions of the Jews, but, acting in the Spirit, they will be called children of Wisdom.[13]

The word '*antitypes*' appears here in a context where there is a question of oblation, of sacrifice, of liturgy, where the text of Malachy is being commented on, where the Passion of Christ is being recalled ('in memory of our Saviour'). Besides, the principal intention behind the fragment is not to express the link between the liturgical sacrifice and the sacrifice of the cross: it is principally to consider, in order to contrast them, the carnal sacrifices of the ancient law and the spiritual sacrifice of the Church. It would seem to me that the aim of these two considerations is to make clear the sense of the word '*antitypes*'. No doubt it implies at least one allusion, an explicit or implicit reference to the sacrifice, the liturgy of the present day being placed alongside the cross (since it is a matter of actions, inscribed in time, we have to admit, in both one and the other, a duality in unity); but what justifies its use above all is the reference or the allusion that it contains to the figures – those of the cross or those of the Mass – which foretold the unique Sacrifice in the time of the old Law. An antitype presupposes a type or a proto-type: in conformity with the more generalised use of language in which the relationship between the two Testaments is expressed, this is, in fact, the name that is often given either to the Mosaic sacrifices,[14] or primarily to the sacrifice of Melchizedek.[15] Later on both '*type*' and '*antitype*' would be used interchangeably, and neither word would have anything but the same indeterminate meaning of image or symbol; but in complete contradiction to this, they were originally set against one another by reason of their correlation.[16] This is still apparent in the use that St. Gregory Nazianzen

---

13 Fragment 36 (Harvey, vol. 2, pp. 500–5; in Migne, fr. 38: PG, 7, 1253). We can approach this text of Irenaeus in a passage of the 27th homily, ch. 17, of Macarius of Egypt (PG, 34, 705).

14 Eusebius, *Evangelic Demonstration*, l. 1, c. 10 (Heikel, p. 45).

15 Clement, 4th *Stromata*, c. 25 (Stählin, vol. 2, pp. 319–20). Epiphanius, *Haeresis* 55, c. 6 (PG, 41, 981; Holl, vol 2, p. 331).

16 For example, for Cyril of Jerusalem, the crown of thorns of the Saviour is the antitype of the thorns of Gen. 2.18 (PG, 33, 796 A).

makes of them. When he considers the Eucharist in relation to the past, as a 'memorial', he gives it the name of antitypes;[17] but when he sees in it the pledge and the anticipation of future salvation, then he describes it as a *'type'*,[18] the mystery of the present time, in relation to the consummation, being set in an analogous position to that of the ancient sacrifices in relation to Calvary.

The relationship expressed by *'antitypes'* would thus be neither the relationship of what would later be called 'species' to the reality hidden under those species, nor the relationship of that reality (whatever it might be) to the body of Christ considered as such, in its substance. It would be the relationship of the Eucharist in all its complexity (action and reality, rite and matter, what is perceptible to the senses and its mystical reality) to the body of Christ that was immolated on the cross as much as to the prefigurative sacrifices. Also called now 'bread', now 'mystery', the Eucharist recalls what St. Augustine called *'the sacrifice of the body'*[19] and St. Jerome *'the passion of the Lord'*.[20] It 'represents' and 'refigures' what the ancient sacrifices had 'presented' and 'prefigured'.[21] As 'the bread' is sometimes used to describe the actual action of the sacrifice in its complex unity – by substituting the objective term with the active term – so the description of this bread as an antitype of the body would in reality describe the entirety of the ritual accomplished daily in the Church as an antitype of the sacrifice accomplished on Calvary. It should be said of this term, as it was said of the Latin terms *species, figure* and *likeness*: *'these names designate the Lord's passion'*.[22] In this there would not even be any implicit opposition of appearance with essence, but there would be a mystical relating of a ritual sacrifice to an historical sacrifice and to its figures. The value of this ritual sacrifice, its fulfilment, as it were its interiority (and consequently the reality of the presence of Christ) would not be directly at stake. Nevertheless, the very word antitype, either through its immediate opposition to the word *'type'*, or by all that it evokes

---

17 *Discourse 2*, c. 95 and 8, c. 18 (PG, 35, 497, 809).

18 *Discourse 17*, c. 12 (PG, 35, 980). Similarly, Theodoret, concerning baptism, *In Coloss.*, ii. II (PG, 82, 609 B).

19 *Contra adversaries legis et prophetarum*, l. 1, n. 38 (PL, 42, 626).

20 Ep. 114, n. 2 (PG, 22, 934). Cf. *Adversus Jovinianum*, 2, n. 17 (23, 311 A). And St. Gregory, *In evangelia hom.* 37, c. 2 (PL, 76, 1277).

21 Faustus of Riez, *Homilia de corpore et sanguine Christi*, c. 6 (PL, 30, 274). Hesychius, *In Leviticum* (PG, 93, 891 B). Mozarabic Missal (PL, 85, 477–8). Pseudo Algerius of Liège, *De sacrificio missae* (PL, 180, 853, 856). Cf. Peter Damian, *Opuscule 12*, c. 28 (145, 281 D). Cf. Faustus of Riez, *Sermon 7* (Engelbrecht, p. 251).

22 Ivo of Chartres, *Decretum*, p. 2, c. 9 (PL, 161, 157 D).

of the different situation of the institutions of the New Testament in relation to those of the Old,[23] could be the first positive indication of a realist interpretation of the 'mystery of the Bread'.[24]

---

23 A different situation is again evoked by the opposition of *sacramentum* and *figura* in St. Ambrose, *De sacramentis*, 4, c. 3, n. 10 (PL, 16, 438 B).

24 A text of *Gallicanum vetus* could furnish us with a good term of comparison. It is studied by Martin Rule, '*Transformare*' and '*transformatio*' (*The Journal of Theological Studies*, vol. 12, 1911, pp. 413–27): (PL, 72, 357 B). Cf. Le Brun, *Explication des cérémonies de la messe*, edn. of 1860, vol. 3, p. 506.

Note C

'Mystical body' in Bruno of Wurzburg?

[358]

In St. Bruno of Wurzburg's Commentary on the Psalms (Cochleus ed., printed in the *Bibliotheca magna Patrum*, vol. 18, Lyon, 1677, p. 237 G; H. Denziger ed., in Migne, PL, 142, 353 A) we read, in Psalm 96, this explanation of the title:

> *The land of David is the flesh of Christ, which after the sleep of death according to the common law of death was restored in glory by the unique gift of resurrection. For surely this land is the Church,* that is, the mystical body of Christ.

At this date (the first half of the eleventh century, Bruno having died in 1045) and in this context (where no allusion whatsoever is made to the Eucharist), the expression is doubly surprising. It is not found in the passage of Cassiodorus's commentary from which this one is freely transcribed. Everywhere else, Bruno of Wurzburg himself simply says *'body of Christ'* (*In Psalmos 15 and 117*, col. 87 B and 424 C) or *'flesh of Christ'* (*In Psalmum 15*, 87 A), or *'body of the Church'* (*In Psalmum 132*, 483 C), or *'body of the faithful'* (*In Psalmum 117*, 425 A) . . . , without any adjective, as do all his contemporaries and as would do later writers for more than a century afterwards. We might therefore wonder if we are not dealing here with an addition (as the tone of the text might already lead us to suspect, given that the usual formulation is *'the body of Christ, that is the Church'*, and not *'the Church, that is the body of Christ'*). Unfortunately it is impossible to prove this theory, since the *'codex authenticus'*, which was formerly preserved in Wurzburg cathedral, was hidden under the roof timbers during the troubled years of the sixteenth century, and was almost entirely ruined there. The oldest manuscript, which Denzinger used for his new edition (codex Ebracensis), dates from the fourteenth century. The Cochleus edition is not very trustworthy. I was not able to consult the first edition, that of J. Reyser (1480). Cf. Denzinger, in PL, 142, 28–30. – Presuming that the present text is authentic, we are dealing with an isolated case, which is interesting to note, but which had no influence on the evolution of language that has been under consideration.

Note D

On the Interpretation of Jerome in Eph. 1

[359]

St. Jerome's text on Ephesians 1 has generally been understood by later theologians in the same way as by the authors of the first concordance in the eleventh century. Thus, according to Bellarmine, *De sacramento eucharistiae*, 1.2, c. 23, Jerome distinguishes '*the flesh that is in the Eucharist from that which was crucified, except as regards accidents*'. In his great *Treatise on the Eucharist*, Cardinal du Perron attaches great importance to this text and to its interpretation:

> . . . The difference that he suggests between this spiritual and divine flesh, by which we are nourished in the Eucharist, and that which was crucified, is not a difference of substance, but of quality and of condition . . .
>
> This passage . . . grants us in a single word a solution to all the other passages that our adversaries quote from the Fathers on this subject. For when they allege that St. Ambrose, speaking of the Eucharist, says 'that the body of God is a spiritual body', what better interpreter of this passage could we hope for than St. Jerome, who teaches us that it is not in order to diminish the truth of the presence of the body of Christ in the Eucharist, but in order to exalt the dignity of its condition, that the Fathers call it a spiritual body . . . And when they put forward the objection that St. Augustine said: 'You will not eat this body that you can see, or drink the blood that will be spilt by those who crucify me', what better Oedipus could we hope for to resolve this riddle but St. Jerome, who teaches us that the way in which the flesh of Christ consumed in the Eucharist can be said not to be the same as that which was pierced on the Cross, is not with regard to its essence but with regard to its quality . . .[1]

---

1 1622, pp. 414 and 415–16. Among the more recent authors, A. d'Alès, *De sanctissima Eucharistia*, p. 66, after citation of the text of Jerome; or the authors cited (and approved) by M. S. Weglewicz, *Doctrina sancti Hieronymi de SS. Eucharistia*, pp. 66–7.

Such an interpretation is certainly not entirely wrong. In its negative sense, it triumphs easily over the protestant interpretation that du Perron is dealing with. But the apologetic concerns that are uppermost for him lead him to a minimalism and a banality of meaning, which were not the case with our medieval writers.

Furthermore, in order to gain a proper understanding of passages like the one from St. Jerome, it is not always enough to decide to be objective. It would first and foremost be important to place oneself as closely as possible within the mindset that prevailed at the time of their writing, remembering that their authors' concerns were not, as it were, of a physically ontological order, but of a spiritual and moral order (without any prejudice to the metaphysical implications of what they were saying). The most beautiful Eucharistic texts of Christian antiquity – and the most doctrinally rich – are not objective, abstract and disinterested arguments. They do not separate the internal sacrifice from the external one. 'Never having offered my internal self as a sacrifice', says St. Gregory Nazianzen, 'how could I offer the external sacrifice?'[2] On which du Perron comments: 'With these words he clearly distinguishes the internal, metaphorical sacrifice from the real and external one, which is offered to God in the Eucharist.'[3] Be that as it may. But furthermore, and more directly, Gregory, in this cry full of pathos, was placing both in relation to one another. – This is not simply a question of a literary sort. We are touching on an essential point of ancient theological methodology, or of their way of interpreting Scripture: and this is one and the same thing, particularly as far as the Eucharist is concerned. In the interpretation of Biblical figures, we have the same spiritual sense which, in one of its aspects, is 'mystical' or 'allegorical', that is to say doctrinal, relative to Christ and his Church and, in another aspect, 'moral' or 'tropological', that is to say more precisely spiritual, relative to the life of the inner person. Now, just as the second aspect is entirely rooted in the first, the first is very rarely envisaged without its extensions in the second. 'Dogma' and 'morality', or rather, 'mystery' and 'mysticism' are not two separate domains. Each constantly implies the other, to such an extent that, in many texts, it would be impossible to analyse them separately. This is clearer for St. Augustine than for anyone else. We can see this in two letters of St. Jerome, 120 n. 2[4] and 149.[5] Other examples are:

---

2 *Apologetic Discourse*, c. 95 (PG, 35, 498).
3 *Les diverses œuvres*, 3rd edn, 1633, p. 506.
4 On Matt. 26.29 (Hilberg, vol. 2, pp. 479–81).
5 Hilberg, vol. 3, p. 362.

Origen, *In psalmum*, 19;[6] Eusebius, *On the solemnity of Easter*, n. 7;[7] Remigius of Auxerre, *In psalmum*, 33,[8] etc. Cf. Gregory the Great, *Moralia in Job*, 1.13, n. 26: '*In order that the sacrament of the Lord's passion should not be useless, we ought to imitate what we receive*' (PL, 75, 1029 B). As Amalarius says, after having followed Bede in comparing the four meanings of Scripture with the four feet of the table of the tabernacle: although the moral meaning is only the third foot, it must nevertheless be linked with the second, because it also contains in its own fashion the mysteries of Christ and the Church.[9] The spiritual interpretation of Scripture is at the same time twofold and unique or, as we would say nowadays, dogma and morality are interior to one another, and it is very often in this living unity that the Fathers present them to us.[10]

---

6 PG, 12, 1245–8.

7 PG, 24, 701.

8 PL, 131, 314–15.

9 Amalarius, *Liber officialis*, l. 1, c. 19 (PL, 105, 1036 A–B).

10 I believe that it is a weakness in some recent theories concerning 'typology' not to recognize this fact of tradition or, at least, not to draw sufficient conclusions from it. Cf. '*Typologie*' and '*Allégorisme*', Recherches de science religieuse, vol. 34 (1947), pp. 219–26. *Sur un vieux distique*, Mélanges Cavallera (1948).

Note E

'Bodily' and σωματικῶς

If, in the West, the adverb 'bodily' (*corporaliter*) is a latecomer, σωματικῶς can be found much earlier in the East. We find it repeatedly in Cyril of Alexandria. In several places, the adverb is applied to the Eucharistic presence. Nevertheless, σωματικῶς does not precede *corporaliter*. There is no transition from one to the other. The fact is that, despite the apparent analogy between them, the two adverbs derive a totally different meaning from their context. To that effect, we read in St. Cyril's *In Joannem*: 1.10:

'We are a single body in Christ, because, though many, we form one single loaf and all share in the one Bread.'

Let us be told why, and thereby be taught the strength of this mystical sacrifice of praise. For why does it exist among us? Is it not in order that Christ might dwell in us even *bodily*, through our participation and communion in his sacred flesh? This is said rightly. St. Paul, indeed, writes that the Gentiles have become 'fellow heirs, members of the same body, and sharers in the promise in Christ'. But in what way are they members of the same body? Having received the honour of sharing in the mystical sacrifice of praise, they have become one single body by uniting themselves to Him . . .

Here, it is worth noting that Christ does not say that he will dwell within us only through a disposition of our souls, but through a true physical participation. In the same way, indeed, that by melting together two pieces of wax we make one single piece, so, through this sharing in the body and blood of Christ, he himself comes to dwell in us, and we are united to Him. And it is not possible that the one should be raised to life, who is corruptible by nature, except through *bodily* union with the body of Him who by nature is Life itself . . .

Thus, since we have been shown through this that Christ is the vine and we are the branches, why would we who abide in him through sharing not only spiritually but *bodily* try vainly to separate ourselves again, by alleging that, since it is not in bodily fashion, but rather through faith and charity . . . that we abide in Christ, he himself did not refer to his body as the vine, but only to his divinity? . . . We have demonstrated, on the contrary, that Christ is the vine, and we the branches, both *bodily* and spiritually . . .[1]

We see that Cyril holds firm to that σωματικῶς, which to him seems effective in assuring the realist and 'physical' character of the participation of the faithful in Christ.[2] In his writing the adverb has both a Eucharistic and an ecclesial meaning, according to the synthesis he makes here of the teaching of St. Paul and St. John. It is the same with regard to our own fleshly bodies: the fact is that, according to a tradition that goes back to St. Ignatius of Antioch (not to mention St. John himself) and that Greek thought never lost sight of, the Eucharist is the source of life, it is 'the immortal remedy' of the body as well as of the soul.[3] It is its pledge of future resurrection.[4] Since the faithful should keep in mind the Saviour's resurrection[5] every time that they receive communion, so also ought they to look forward to their own resurrection. The body, said St. Gregory of Nyssa, also calls for eternal nourishment, and it receives it through sharing and becoming one with our Saviour: now, how could an incorporate thing become nourishment for the body?[6] Cyril's thought is near to that of Gregory, it completes and extends it. The bodily presence that Cyril is speaking of here, while being the fruit of the sacrament, lasts well beyond the moment of communion: it is a presence that endures into eternal life.

We therefore find Cyril's σωματικῶς not below, but in some sense beyond his πνευματικῶς: 'even bodily', 'through a participation that is not only bodily, but also corporal'. As is explained by Nicolas

---

1 PG, 74, 3413–44. See again 1.11: '. . . for the Son is among us, on the one hand bodily, as a man, united and fused with us by means of the sacrifice of praise; and also spiritually, as God, through the energy and the grace of his own Spirit, renewing the spirit within us for the renewal of life . . . This receiving in ourselves both bodily and spiritually Him who is truly and by nature the Son . . .' (564–5).

2 The same doctrine, for example, in the fourth mystagogical catechesis of St. Cyril of Jerusalem (?).

3 *Triform Corpus*, ch. 1, nn. 27 and 28. And again the Council of Lestines in 743 (c. 5: Mansi, vol. 12, 378 E).

4 Cf. Athanasius, *Fourth Letter to Serapion*, n. 19 (PG, 26, 668 A).

5 We know that in the majority of oriental liturgies the formula of the first consecration is as much a commemoration of the resurrection as of the death of the Saviour: τόν ἐμὸν θάνατον καταγγέλλετε, τὴν ἐμὴν ἀνάστασιν ὁμολογεῖτε.

6 *Catechetical Discourse*, c. 37 (PG, 45, 93 A); *Life of Moses* (44, 368 C).

Cabasilas, one of the greatest heirs of the Greek tradition represented here by Cyril:

> To those who live in the body, the gift is certainly transmitted by means of the body, but it primarily enters the essence of the soul, and springs up again, from the soul into the body itself. This is shown by the blessed apostle, when he says: 'Whoever abides in the Lord is one single spirit with him'; that is to say that this unity and this coming together take place primarily and principally in the soul ... Everything comes to the body by means of the soul. It is the same with the sanctification that comes from the exercise of virtue and that which comes from the sacraments ...[7]

For Latin writers of the twelfth century, on the contrary, Christ is only said to be *bodily* present in the sacramental species: whether first on the altar, or then within the communicant, as long as the species are not corrupted. It is still an objective presence, previous to any 'spiritual' presence. It is a presence which, in itself, is not yet the presence of grace, but which could just as well become a presence of condemnation, since the unworthy communicant receives the body of Christ *bodily* as much as the saint. Cyril's σωματικῶς therefore has nothing in common with this *bodily*; it is rather more strongly connected to *spiritually*. We might say that σωματικῶς and πνευματικῶς are both equally understood in the 'spirituality' of the Augustinian tradition.

---

7 *Exposition of the Liturgy*, c. 43 (PG. 150, 460-1).

Note F

An Illusion in the History of Theology

[365]

When historians of theology try to define the change that took place in the Middle Ages, and that came to a head with the arrival of Scholasticism, it happens that the outline they give is often deceptive. Too often they argue in the same way as do some historians of philosophy, in whose view Descartes, with the most disputed parts of his system, seems to follow on immediately from St. Thomas, only the strongest of whose ideas are retained, in all their pure and intemporal essence . . . By an inverse process that comes from a symmetrical illusion, these historians of theology seem to believe that rationalizing theology, armed with all the resources of dialectic and metaphysics, and strengthened by all that is in the capacity of intellectual curiosity and the ambitions of scientific ideals, had no ancestry except a theology that, while possibly solid, was devoid of inspiration and thought, a theology of copyists and anthologists . . . As if 'speculative' theology, in the most noble sense of that word, had at long last risen for the first time above the ground on which, up until then, 'positive' theology, understood in its most down-to-earth sense, had been crawling.

In short, philosophers compared Descartes with St. Thomas, without taking into account the interval of time that separates them, or all the undistinguished successors and all the bastard descendants who occupied that interval and defined Descartes's historical context. In the same way, theologians opposed St. Thomas – or Abelard, or St. Anselm – to men like Rabanus Maurus, or like Isidore of Seville, or to still lesser men, to obscure monks of the tenth century and eleventh century, without appearing to suspect that before them had lived Origen, Hilary, Ambrose and Augustine.

Now, it is certainly true that about half-way through the Middle Ages, there was a great renaissance in intellectual life, and theology was transformed by it. We might sum it up symbolically by saying that *questions* succeeded *sentences*, and that *argument* succeeded *anthology*. A new faculty was emerging from its swaddling clothes. This phenomenon has been compared to a thaw. But we should not forget that a thaw is not an absolutely new beginning. It presupposes that something had become frozen, that was once warm and alive. There is, in fact, a cycle of the mind as there is a cycle of nature. Both have their dead periods, their winter. Only, what makes possible the illusion I am trying to combat, is that in the cycle of the mind, contrary to the cycle in nature, each thaw, each 'palingenesis' is a metamorphosis. Springtimes come in succession, but they do not resemble one another. What is reborn is not simply a reproduction of what died at the end of the previous season. It is a flower of a different scent, a fruit with a different flavour. The mind is more inventive than nature.

Let us not be deceived, however. The theology that began with Abelard and the two Anselms and had its apogee in St. Bonaventure and St. Thomas did indeed succeed a theology that consisted above all in making exegetical compilations. The high Middle Ages copied the exegesis of the Fathers, rather as later theologians – say of the fifteenth century, only to mention those who are dead – would copy the dialectic of the great medieval thinkers. But before the theology of those who compiled their texts, there was the theology of the Fathers themselves – and at any rate, there were those who were still following authentically in this line until the dawn of the new era.[1]

When a way of thinking breathes its last, when its period of creativity has long since passed and it only survives in some sense through a phenomenon of memory, then another replaces it. The arrival of the newcomer clearly marks some sort of progress with regard to what came immediately before it. But if one considers the matter with sufficient distance to encompass a broader period, it can be seen this is never anything but progress *secundum quid*. It would be childish to explain everything, for example, by passing from what is confused to what is distinct; no doubt there is always a point of view according to which this could be true, but it is the exclusive choice of this point of view that is arbitrary and mutilating: it presupposes that we only retain from earlier mental efforts what can be considered the prepara-

---

1 Cf. J. H. Card. Newman: 'Patristic and scholastic theology each involved a creative action of the intellect. That this is the case as regards the Schoolmen need not be proved here. Nor is it less true, though in a different way, of the theology of the Fathers. Origen, Tertullian, Athanasius, Chrysostom, Augustine, Jerome and Leo are authors with powerful, original minds, and engaged in the production of original works.' *The Benedictine Schools*, an article published in *Atlantis* in 1859; French translation in J. H. Newman, *Saints d'autrefois*, p. 355. Newman adds this very pertinent comment: 'There is no greater mistake, surely, than to suppose that a revealed truth precludes originality in the treatment of it.'

tion they represent for new systems. The dialectical way of thinking has imposed itself to such an extent in our modern period, that we have ended up by believing that it defines thought itself; that before it appeared on the scene there only ever reigned an era of 'compilation'; that without it, in any case, our understanding could never be truly active and 'creative' . . . In actual fact, the dialectical theology of the Middle Ages at its highest point replaced another way of thinking that, if we take it equally at its highest point, cannot be declared *a priori* to be inferior: that is, the symbolic theology of the Fathers. It was a theology that followed on from another – and that fatally, according to life's laws, showed itself in its own turn unjust and uncomprehending – ; it was not *Theology* that was born, after a long incubation in 'prehistory', as has been written naively.

To put it in other terms that are more traditional, but which have become unfortunately distorted from their original meaning, I might say that, before the *Scholastic* age, a long time before it, there was the *positive* age. This was not the age of what we nowadays call 'positive theology', by means of an elision in the use of the word, of the 'phenomenon of metonymy' that has been brought to light by Fr. Gagnebet,[2] and about which several historians have for some time been correctly expressing some reservations.[3] It was the age of the theology practised by the Fathers themselves.[4] It was a creative age, a constructive age, an age in which doctrine was being built positively (before organizing itself into a body of knowledge in the Schools), through a study that was not content with reading and collating texts, but that sought passionately to understand them. The artisans of this work were those whom St. Ignatius of Loyola called, in accordance with the language that prevailed at that time, the *Positive Doctors*, '*positive and holy doctors*', thus distinguishing them from the '*compilers*', who were the '*Scholastic Doctors*'. He names the most important of them: they were 'Jerome, Augustine, Gregory, etc.'.[5] Most certainly not one of these great artisans, or any of those who succeeded them, dispense us from

---

2 *Le problème actuel de la théologie*, Divus Thomas (Pia cenza), 1943, pp. 263–5.

3 R. Draguet (in *Apologétique*, 1937, p. 1175). F. van Steenberghe (*Siger de Brabant*, p. 387). Fr. Cavallera (*La théologie positive*, in *Bulletin de litt. ecclés.*, 1925, pp. 21–2) and M. Robert Guelluy (*L'Evolution des méthodes théologiques à Louvain d'Erasme à Jansénius*, in *Revue d'hist. ecclés.*, 1941, particularly pp. 123–42).

4 It is again the sense of Du Pin, *Méthode pour étudier la théologie*, ch. 2.

5 *Exercitia spiritualia, Regulae ad sentiendum cum Ecclesia*, reg. 9. See also *Constitutiones Societatis Jesu*, p. IVa, c. 15, 12 and 14. Cf. Bonaventure (Quar., vol. 1, p. lxvi), and the text of J. Major cited by Gagnebet, *loc. cit.*, p. 264.

working in our own turn and facing our own problems, with our own instruments and methods. But, still indispensable though it is, the work that succeeded them should not lead us to ignore theirs, and we can say of Augustine or of Origen, as of Bernard or of Thomas Aquinas, what Péguy wrote one day concerning some pretentious people of our modern era: 'You cannot outstrip Plato.'

We should perhaps be wary of a certain belief, which is more arrogant than enlightened, in one isolated type of understanding, as we would be of one single type of civilization, each one always defined in relation to the one to which we are currently attached. We should perhaps be wary of a certain simplistic philosophy of the history of theology and of dogmatic progress, a philosophy whose presuppositions bear a strange resemblance to the thesis formerly held by M. Brunschvig on the 'ages of understanding': the way in which one differs from the other only consists in the fact that reason gained its certificate of arrival in adulthood several centuries earlier . . .

Note G

An Explanation of Rupert

[368]

Like many other theologians of his time and of later periods, Rupert of Tuy insists on the mortification of the understanding demanded by the *mystery of faith*. He comes back to it repeatedly: one of the reasons why Christ wanted to hide himself under the appearance of bread and wine was to make us believe, despite our senses, in his word. But, in contradiction to what happens with many other writers, this fact is illustrated, in Rupert, by a whole new explanation, which itself constitutes an effort at 'understanding'. It is, furthermore, an explanation that is strongly in conformity with the viewpoint of Christian antiquity, at the same time as with his own ways of thinking, according to which an understanding of mysteries always goes together with that of Scripture. It is a sort of poem around two contrasting pictures, in which the 'pious belief' of those receiving the Bread of Life is opposed to the perverse credulity of those who formerly received the fruits of death: '*Let us believe his word rather than our fleshly* eyes, . . . *and thus we cancel the wicked credulity of our parents by means of a pious credulity in ourselves* . . .'

'Eat, said the devil to our first parents, and you will become like gods' – 'Eat, says Christ to us, this is my body; eat, and you will be the children of God.' '*Against the bread of death, eat the bread of eternal life*.' Our senses no more see the object of the promise in one case than in the other. As our first parents allowed themselves to be tempted by the devil, let us allow ourselves to be tempted by Christ, instead of acting like the Israelites who tempted God in their hearts, saying: 'How will he ever be able to prepare us a table in this desert?' Let us receive from the hand of our Lord the chalice of his bodily death, as the chalice of spiritual death was once accepted from the hand of our ancient enemy. Believe in the Lamb rather than in the serpent. Thus the trick of the first tempter will be outwitted and overcome.

Here is the Bread, the Fruit of the Tree of Life – the Tree of Life himself: he saves us from the death that had come to us through the tree of paradise. The same order which prevailed in our fall should today prevail in our recovery. The Eucharist is the antidote which we needed in order to cure our mortal wound: '*I will bring you an antidote.*' The sacrament of the passion and death of Christ is for us the sacrament of life. It comes to repair the ruin caused by sacrilege: '*all this sacrilege is amended by this sacrament*'. But it is on condition that faith in the Promise of Christ replaces and expiates the faith once placed in the promises of the seducer: '*By a just law, in order to expiate the guilt of wrong belief, faith is required, that you believe what you do not see.*' Today humility alone demands of the believer that he evacuate the pride which caused the first sin.

Cf. *In Exodum* (PL, 167, 662–663 and 666 D); *De Spiritu Sancto*, l. 3, c. 6, 18 and 24 (167, 1646, 1659 and 1665–1666); *In Cantica* (168, 860–861 and 905–907); *In Mathaeum* (168, 1548 and 1551–1552); *Ad Cunonem (169, 204); In Joannem (169, 466–467).*

The contrast between the Eucharist and the fruit of the forbidden tree is a frequent theme; cf. for example, St. Bonaventure, *In cena Domini sermo 3*: '*Adam ate the food forbidden to him and his children with death as the result, but Christ gave the food of life with life as the end*' (Quaracchi, vol. IX, p. 254). What is essential in this could already be found in a sermon of St. Peter Damian.[1] Guitmond of Aversa alluded to it.[2] But Rupert adds many subtle developments to it. They are not usually found in those who came after him. Nevertheless, Gerhoh of Reichersberg (who admired Rupert) still has a long page on it in his commentary on Psalm 22 (PL, 193, 1054 A–D). The same idea is repeated in passing in St. Thomas's opuscule 51, *De sacramento altaris*, c. 7 (Vivès, vol. 28, p. 195):

A cure for infidelity requires that the body of Christ be veiled, so that to the fault of infidelity there should correspond a congruent mode of satisfaction. Consequently, as the unbelief of the first parents began with the hearing of the words of the devil recommending the food that had death concealed within it, and in which their senses took intense delight, so it was fitting that the faith of those to be saved should begin from hearing the word of the Saviour, recommending a food that has true life hidden within it, and in which our senses are piously deceived.

---

1 *Sermo 10* (PL, 144, 553–4).
2 *De corporis veritate*, 1 (PL, 149, 1438–9; cf. 1437 D).